TAKING THEIR PLACE

TAKING THEIR PLACE

A Documentary History of Women and Journalism

Maurine H. Beasley *and* Sheila J. Gibbons

The American University Press
in cooperation with the Women's Institute for Freedom of the Press

Copyright © 1993 by
The American University Press
4400 Massachusetts Avenue, N.W.
Anderson Lower Level
Washington, D.C. 20016

Distributed by arrangement with
National Book Network
4720 Boston Way
Lanham, MD 20706

070.4082
B 379t

Library of Congress Cataloging-in-Publication Data

Beasley, Maurine Hoffman.
Taking their place : a documentary history of women and
journalism / Maurine H. Beasley and Sheila J. Gibbons.
p.   cm.
Includes index.
1. Women in journalism—United States.   2. Women
journalists—United States.   3. Women in the press—United States.
I. Silver, Sheila.   II. Title.
PN4888.W65B45   1993   070.4'082—dc20   92–41011 CIP

ISBN 1–879383–10–1 (pbk. : alk. paper)

The paper used in this publication meets the minimum requirements of
American National Standard for Information Sciences—Permanence
of Paper for Printed Library Materials, ANSI Z39.48–1984.

For our mothers
Maurine Hieronymus Hoffman
and
Georgina Parrish Gibbons Amenta

Acknowledgment is made of the following sources who have given approval for the reprinting and excerpting of material cited: Columns by "Grace Greenwood," *New York Times*, February 1, 1873, and July 9, 1877, copyright by the New York Times Company, reprinted by permission; column by "Fanny Fern" from the Parton Papers in the Sophia Smith Collection, Smith College, Northampton, MA; selection from *On Lynchings: Southern Horrors*, published by Arno Press and the *New York Times*, 1969, as reprinted from copies of the *New York Age* Print in the Howard University Library, permission from the Ayer Company; newspaper article by "Annie Laurie" reprinted in Barbara Belford, *Brilliant Bylines*, published by Columbia University Press, 1986, copyright Barbara Belford, reprinted by permission; material from the Dickey Chapelle papers, State Historical Society of Wisconsin; excerpts from *Ladies of the Press* by Ishbel Ross, copyright 1936 by Ishbel Ross, reprinted by permission of Harper Collins Publishers; excerpts from oral history transcripts reprinted with the permission of the Washington Press Club Foundation, copyright holder, from its Oral History Interviews with Lucile Bluford recorded by Fern Ingersoll, Marvel Cooke recorded by Kathleen Currie, and Ethel Payne recorded by Kathleen Currie as part of its project, "Women in Journalism," in the Oral History Collection of Columbia University and other repositories; unpublished article, "Red-Headed Doll," copyright 1969 Washington Press Club Foundation, from the Records of the Women's National Press Club/Washington Press Club in the Cora Rigby Washington Journalism Archive at the National Press Club, Washington, D.C.; article by Agnes E. Meyer, "Migrant Mexican and Anglo Labor," from the *Washington Post*, April 23, 1946, copyright the *Washington Post*, reprinted by permission of Katharine Graham; excerpts from *The Politics of Women's Liberation* by Jo Freeman, copyright by Jo Freeman, reprinted by permission; *"Ms.: A Personal Report,"* from vol. 1, no. 1 of *Ms.* Magazine, reprinted by permission of *Ms.* Magazine; "Setting It Straight," from *off our backs*, April 25, 1970, reprinted by permission; "My Last Hurrah: Occupying the *Ladies' Home Journal*," by permission of Vivien Leone and William Haddad, *Manhattan Tribune* Syndicate Service; excerpts from "The Heart, the Mind, the Pickled Okra: Women's Magazines in the Sixties," by Nora Magid with permission of the *North*

Contents

Foreword

This work represents a revised and expanded version of the book published in 1977 by Donna Allen and the Women's Institute for Freedom of Press. It was titled *Women in Media: A Documentary Source Book*. That book, intended like this one to be a library resource as well as general text, received favorable attention and was used widely in women and the media classes in journalism schools. Realizing that it had become outdated, we recognized the need for a new edition. In doing research for it, we decided to change the name because we have a quite different book at this point. Yet the salient feature of the first book remains. Readers still have an opportunity to study actual documents that tell the experiences of women in journalism. This time more explanatory material sets the context for the documents within the mass media field. Also, a comprehensive overview provides a summary of women's portrayal and participation within the journalism field. New notes at the end of the chapters, and an "Additional Resources" chapter at the end of the book, offer suggestions for further research.

In editing the documents, we have tried to interject as few comments as possible so as not to impede the reader; brackets indicate our insertions. We also have used the capitalization and spelling in the text of the original documents, except when they might confuse readers. The only style change made within the excerpts has been to italicize the titles of books, magazines, newspapers, and broadcast programs throughout, for the sake of clarity and comprehension. We hope that this book will help tell the absorbing story of women in journalism and inspire others to pursue scholarship in the field.

Introduction
to Original Edition

The Women's Institute for Freedom of the Press has several very good reasons for being pleased to publish this book.

The first reason is, of course, the rapidly growing women's media movement itself, which has created the strong demand for information about women and media. As never before, women are doing a lot of thinking about the structure and influence of mass media on the lives of all of us.

There are new women's media groups and "new (and old) girl" networks springing up in every major city; the media women's professional organizations are discussing new professional concerns; and there is a host of new media businesses, profit and nonprofit: film companies, video, cable, theater groups, artists' collectives, periodicals, recording companies and publishing houses. New organizations of women writers are forming, and conferences and festivals are being held to discuss ways to help each other.

Nor is the phenomenon limited to this country. It is happening with equal vigor all over the world.

Yet almost none of this information is available to the general public—and especially to the female half of the general public who might be most interested in knowing about it—nor is it presently available to the students in journalism and communications schools, or women's studies departments, where it is their function to be studying such phenomena.

Yet, while they may not know the extent, or even the issues, of this new movement, students are aware that something is happening and they want to know more about it. For example, a poll of approximately half of the students in the College of Journalism and Communication at the University of Florida, Gainesville, showed that 139 women and 65 men would either definitely or probably enroll in a course on women and mass communications if one were offered. In raw numbers, this would provide students for many semesters to come and for a great variety of courses. In terms of percentages, 73 percent of the women and 24 percent of the men said they would probably or definitely take such a course.

We are happy to publish material that will be helpful to such students—and their teachers who want to bring their teaching material up to date. Dr. Beasley and Ms. Gibbons, out of their experience in teaching this subject, in both general courses and in their "Women and Mass Communications" course, have discovered the kinds of documents that are most needed by students and that best tell the story of this new development in communications. They have selected and arranged their documents to describe that historical development from 1790 to the present.

We are pleased to publish this volume for what it does contribute as a first-of-its-kind presentation of material that is not available generally. Some of the documents are not available to the public at all. For example, try to find the report of the Equal Employment Opportunity Commission on sex discrimination at the *Washington Post*. Imagine trying to locate copies of the 1972 petition to deny WABC-TV's broadcast license renewal. How many will be able to obtain a copy of the agreement between the Los Angeles Women's Coalition for Better Broadcasting and KNBC-TV? The fact that these are not available in the "public" press means not only that students cannot study them and learn from them, but that others cannot know about these important facets of the women's media movement. They cannot support or join it; they cannot make their special contribution to it.

Therefore, we are pleased to publish this book, finally, because we believe it will be a contribution to that movement as well as to those in the various schools where such developments are the subjects of their study. We believe that these documents will provide stimulating discussions in the movement, in the classroom, and outside of both, and that the result in the years to come will carry us further toward a communication system that includes everyone.

Donna Allen
Women's Institute for Freedom of the Press
July 22, 1977

1
Overview

No institution of American life came under greater criticism during the women's liberation movement of the 1960s and the 1970s than the mass media. Movement leaders recognized the growing importance of the media as a political, economic, and social force. They charged that women as a group were not rightfully represented in it, either in terms of their coverage or participation. Through various means, including legal actions, monitoring projects, license renewal challenges, pressure on advertisers, and group consciousness-raising sessions, the movement demanded that the media be more receptive to women's issues. It viewed the media as central to efforts to liberate women from traditional roles that made them inferior to men.

Not coincidentally, the women's movement arose as an increasing number of women pursued paid employment in all areas of American life, including the media. The movement represented a diverse collection of interest groups, some seeking equal legal rights and others advocating specific goals such as abortion rights. Movement adherents, who ranged from radical separatists to moderate liberals, agreed on one point: The mass media were unfair to women, who made up more than half the population.

Themselves influenced by the women's movement, women working in the mass media helped serve as catalysts for change within their own organizations. They influenced outward media response to the women's movement at the same time as they pressed internally for greater equality.

Consequently the women's movement provides a case study of social change applied to the mass media. Traditionally, news has been seen as the media's most substantial product—the product that sets the agenda for political decision making. Feminists contend that news

1

itself is a form of discourse that has constricted women's opportunity to gain a platform to better themselves.

Tension between the Women's Movement and the Media

From its beginnings the women's movement revolved around the mass media. Two of its leading theoreticians, Betty Friedan and Gloria Steinem, both had extensive experience in journalism. Critics of the movement argued that it thrived on publicity garnered by individuals like Friedan and Steinem who became media luminaries.

Friedan's best-selling book *The Feminine Mystique* launched the movement in 1963 by reaching middle-class women with a message that the mass media had duped them. A writer for women's magazines, Friedan contended that advertisers and editors targeted women for economic exploitation and valued them only as consumers and house-wives. Steinem, also a New York writer, similarly blamed the media for rigid typecasting of women into roles as sex symbols and servers of men.

Like Friedan and Steinem, other advocates of the movement charged that it received biased treatment from male-dominated media deter-mined to ridicule women. They contended that the mass media sensa-tionalized actions such as feminist protests against the annual Miss America pageant and failed to give serious consideration to philosoph-ical and economic questions of inequalities between the sexes. They alleged that media refusal to take the movement seriously gave evi-dence of male determination to keep women suppressed.

Some women in the mainstream media—chiefly the daily press, broadcasting outlets, and national general interest publications—found themselves caught between conflicting interests. On the one hand, the movement spoke to many of their personal concerns. On the other, their emotional involvement ran counter to adherence to accustomed professional values. According to these norms, journalists were sup-posed to be impartial observers of human events who relayed what they have seen or heard to the public. Reporters were routinely cautioned to "keep yourself out of the story." Therefore, how could women cover a story about themselves unless they applied traditional news values developed by men? And if they did that, were they not helping to uphold the male-dominated structure that was a primary target of a movement designed to benefit all women including them-selves?

Confronted by this dilemma, some women turned to alternative feminist media. The women's movement gave birth to some 1,300 feminist publications, which rejected conventional ways of defining and presenting news.[1] Drawing on new technologies that made production relatively easy, the alternative feminist media initially were allied with the "underground" media movement that fought against the Vietnam War and sought to liberalize attitudes toward sex and drugs. When women in the underground press discovered it to be sexist, they developed their own media.

For women in the mainstream media, the women's movement served to make them look at themselves and the roles they played within organizational structures. With their consciousness raised, women did not like what they saw. Widespread dissatisfaction caused groups of women within news organizations to band together to fight sex discrimination. They fought for the hiring and promotion of women and they worked to integrate women into newsrooms on an equal basis with men.

Prior to the women's movement, most newspaperwomen were confined to jobs on women's pages and society sections of newspapers. These positions, which routinely paid less than jobs held by men, kept women out of direct competition with males. Women's pages reinforced the idea of separate spheres for men and women. Men ran the world: The news of their conflict, power, and influence dominated the front pages. Women took care of homes and children: The news of noncontroversial domestic and social pursuits appeared on the women's pages.[2]

Differences in attitudes toward news aimed at men and women carried over into the way the two sexes performed within news organizations. Male editors, reflecting commonly held views of women as a whole in society, saw women as potentially disturbing elements who called for special treatment within office settings. Women, for their part, found news organizations run by a power structure unwilling or unable to recognize their potential for achievement. In 1969, for example, Associated Press (AP) managing editors were cautioned to "provide the reason, the authority and the security to direct a woman in the use of her constant emotional drive," while women were urged to "do your best to do everything the way a male boss wants it done."[3]

In other forms of the media, women experienced equal, if not greater, forms of inequality. Women working for wire services generally were limited to copy for women's pages. At news magazines, women researched articles written and edited exclusively by men. In the general magazine field, women rarely ascended to top editorships even on publications aimed at millions of women. In broadcasting, only an occasional woman appeared as a reporter or correspondent on either network or local news programs. Radio stations confined women to "household hint" programs that paralleled the content of women's pages.

Just as the participation of women was limited in the media, so was their coverage. Depicted in news, advertising, and entertainment as wives, mothers, sex objects, or—even more significantly—not at all, women were not portrayed as individuals capable of independent contributions to the world. It was this treatment, characterized as "symbolic annihilation" that victimized women as a group, according to Gaye Tuchman, a sociologist.[4]

Origins of the Women's Movement

The women's movement grew out of the conflicts that American women experienced in their lives following World War II. During the war the government encouraged them to work at paid jobs to aid the military effort. When peace came, women were told to go home and give their jobs back to returning servicemen. The country wrapped itself in a cloak of suburban domesticity made fashionable by the women's magazines and other media attacked by Friedan. As she put it, "The perpetuation of housewifery, the growth of the feminine mystique, makes sense (and dollars) when one realizes that women are the chief customers of American business."[5] Isolated in their suburban homes, women were manipulated to fulfill themselves by purchasing more and more consumer goods, according to Friedan.

In reality, however, women did not retreat en masse from the labor force even though the popular image of domesticity failed to reflect this fact. As William Chafe, an historian of women, pointed out, "The most striking feature of the 1950s was the degree to which women continued to enter the job market and expand their sphere."[6] When the National Manpower Commission was set up in 1957, it was startled to find that women represented about one-third of the labor force.[7] Women workers increased from 24 percent of the total employed in 1940 to 32 percent in 1960. Surprisingly, the number of employed wives and mothers jumped dramatically, with both husband and wife working in more than 10 million homes by 1960.[8] True, women often worked part-time, but nevertheless paid employment became socially acceptable and economically necessary for both partners in many marriages. Consumerism had turned into a double-edged sword: As it celebrated the joys of household possessions, it drove women outside the home to earn money to buy them.

Few women held positions of authority. Many worked in low-paid clerical jobs considered suitable for women who were "helping out" their families but had no interest in advancing professionally. When the mass media paid attention to the jobs women held, they emphasized the low level of skill involved. A 1956 article in *Life* magazine, for instance, pointed out that women, far better than men, could tolerate repetitious tasks and please others in office settings.[9]

Against this backdrop of increased employment for women but limiting ideology, the concept of women's liberation burst on the scene in the 1960s and 1970s. Even before Friedan published *The Feminine Mystique*, the mass media referred to housewives as "trapped." In 1960 *Newsweek* entitled a cover story: "Young Wives with Brains: Babies, Yes—But What Else?" That same year a CBS television report and articles in the *New York Times, Good Housekeeping, Redbook, Time,* and *Harper's Bazaar* paid at least superficial attention to women's problems of boredom and inability to develop intellectually.[10] These articles drew on ideas advanced by Simone de Beauvoir in *The Second Sex*, published in the United States in 1952. More scholarly than Friedan's work, de Beauvoir's *Second Sex*—which became a best-seller—alleged women were compelled to play a role of "the other" in opposition to men.[11]

In 1961 Esther Peterson, assistant secretary of labor, convinced President John F. Kennedy to appoint a Presidential Commission on the Status of Women, the first government-sponsored group to bring together representatives of a cross-section of American women. Its report, *American Women*, appeared two years later. Given wide attention on women's pages, it paid tribute to women's achievements in the home and applauded their progress in a democratic society. Yet the report also documented widespread discrimination against women in government, education, and employment and made recommendations for change.[12] It led to the establishment of state commissions that gathered more evidence of economic, social, and legal discrimination confronting women.

Although the mass media paid little attention to women's demographics, widespread use of the birth-control pill and other forms of controlling conception altered women's lives after World War II. By the mid-1960s the average American woman bore her last child when she was 28.[13] At the same time, life expectancy was increasing. When Friedan, like de Beauvoir, disputed the Freudian concept that women's lives were controlled by sexual and reproductive functions, her argument addressed changing reality. Women had more than half their lives left after ending their biological role of childbearing.

It was the civil rights movement that directly fueled women's liberation. In 1964 a conservative Virginia congressman, 81-year-old Howard W. Smith, sought to stop passage of major civil rights legislation. He added the word *sex* to Title VII of the pending Civil Rights Act of 1964, which outlawed employment discrimination on the basis of "race, color, religion, or national origin." Women had not been considered by President Kennedy when he sent his civil rights package to Congress the previous year. By including them, Smith hoped to ridicule the proposed legislation, but his joke backfired.

Liberal supporters of civil rights initially opposed Smith's amendment. They argued it would override state laws designed to protect women against dangerous working conditions. Mindful of the fact that women's salaries averaged only about two-thirds those of men, a bipartisan coalition of five congresswomen, however, led a fight for the amendment. They argued that women needed equal rights, not special privileges. "We outlast you, we outlive you, we nag you to death," Katharine St. George, a Republican congresswoman from New York, told her male colleagues during House debate. "But we are entitled to this little crumb of equality."[14]

Capitol Hill insiders soon tagged the measure the "May Craig Amendment," in honor of Craig, a Washington correspondent for Maine newspapers, who was well known for her feminist views. Its passage was assured when Sen. Hubert Humphrey of Minnesota, the Democratic whip, appeared on *Meet the Press*, a televised press conference program that regularly featured Craig. In answer to a question from her, Humphrey said the Democratic leadership had decided to accept the amendment.[15] The importance of adding women to Title VII did not gain immediate attention. The head of the Equal Economic Opportunities Commission (EEOC)—the agency set up to enforce Title VII—called the inclusion of sex "a fluke . . . conceived out of wedlock."[16] Yet, in the decade to follow, women brought more complaints under EEOC than any other group.

Professional women, many of whom had worked together in state commissions on the status of women, mobilized to push the EEOC into action. In 1966 they founded the National Organization for Women (NOW) with Betty Friedan as the first president. The goal: "To bring women into full participation in the mainstream of American society now, exercising all the privileges and responsibilities thereof in truly equal partnership with men."[17] To do so, the group stated, "we will protest and endeavor to change the false image of women now prevalent in the mass media and in the texts, ceremonies, laws and practices of our major social institutions [that] foster in women self-denigration, dependence and evasion of responsibility."[18] One of their first actions was to challenge sex-segregated want ads in newspapers.

The statement marked the rebirth of a feminist movement begun over a century earlier with the woman's rights convention at Seneca Falls, New York, in 1848. That movement peaked when women finally gained the vote, after years of struggle, in 1920. By the mid-twentieth century, feminism as a political philosophy drew only a few adherents committed to the idea of an Equal Rights Amendment. Whether by accident or deliberate omission, NOW's birth received no attention in the *Washington Post*. In the *New York Times*, news of NOW's formation ran beneath recipes for a traditional Thanksgiving dinner. The mass media failed to recognize its potential for revolutionary social change.

By 1970, however, feminist causes occupied the attention of millions drawn into the new women's movement. For some, involvement grew out of firsthand experiences with civil rights and anti–Vietnam War activities in the 1960s. Participation gave women experience in articulating the concepts of freedom and equality. They objected to their treatment by male radicals who orated against injustice but acted as if women existed mainly as sexual objects.[19] From the New Left movement, women borrowed a vocabulary and ideology that they translated into the concept of women's liberation.[20]

At first, women radicals communicated through media of the New Left.[21] In the early 1960s women questioned their personal suppression within the civil rights and antiwar movements in position papers that initially were hand circulated.[22] These attacks on male power made their way into movement newspapers that were themselves blatantly sexist.[23] Eventually the position papers were reprinted in the new genre of feminist periodicals that grew from five modest publications in 1968 to at least 228 newsletters, newspapers, and magazines by 1971.[24] Often these employed the confrontational tone of leftist underground newspapers.

In feminist publications, women continued the kind of emotional self-expression that marked the personal journalism of the New Left. They searched for self-affirmation and identity in a quest for equity in sex roles. They criticized the mass media for mistreatment of women and tried to push the media in a feminist direction. In doing so, they challenged the existing relationship between women and the media—a relationship formed long before the start of the twentieth century.

Women in the Press during the Eighteenth and Nineteenth Centuries

By the 1960s, women had an extensive history of participation in American journalism, although their contributions were omitted from history books.[25] In the colonial period, women assisted male relatives in printing and publishing shops that adjoined homes. During the Revolution, for example, Mary Katherine Goddard ran the *Maryland Journal*, considered one of the best newspapers of its day, and printed the first official copy of the Declaration of Independence with the names of the signers attached. Both Mary Katherine and her mother, Sarah Updike Goddard, managed businesses begun by Mary Katherine's brother, William Goddard, while he traveled throughout the colonies seeking wealth and fame.[26]

Journalistic enterprises represented family endeavors. In the case of the Goddards, William Goddard got the credit; his mother and sister did the work. Widows who followed their husbands as editors and publishers managed enterprises successfully, but they acted to carry out family responsibilities, not to seek independent careers. To a degree, this pattern has continued to the present. Katharine Graham, for example, took over the *Washington Post* after her husband committed suicide and ran it until her son could assume control.

In the nineteenth century, urbanization brought the advent of mass-circulation daily newspapers produced in grimy, noisy downtown offices and printing plants. These were considered off-limits for women, who were expected to conform to the prevailing ideal of "the lady," a genteel creature who remained at home. Writing, however, could be carried on in one's own parlor and was considered suitable for middle-class women, especially if they chose sentimental topics. "Literary ladies," as women writers were called, frequently sold their works—often poetry and human interest material—to newspapers, but they rarely ventured into newspaper offices.

Even Margaret Fuller, whose feminist book *Woman in the Nineteenth Century* helped lay the foundation for the Seneca Falls meeting, did not defy convention when she was employed by Horace Greeley on his *New York Tribune* in 1844.[27] Fuller, believed to be the first woman to serve as a staff member on a major newspaper, lived in the Greeley home and remained apart from the newspaper office. Arriving in Europe in 1846 as a correspondent for the *Tribune*, she sent back reports on the Italian revolution, giving her a claim to being both the first woman foreign correspondent and war correspondent.

For many literary ladies, women's magazines provided socially acceptable havens for creative efforts. Sex-segregated journalism developed before the Civil War, with more than 25 magazines started by 1850 with women as editors or associate editors.[28] Most reinforced the myth of the lady and advised on fashion and proper behavior. These publications advanced the "cult of true womanhood," which called on women to exemplify four virtues: "piety, purity, submissiveness and domesticity."[29] In an oblique way, however, these magazines helped enlarge women's narrow horizons. The most influential, *Godey's Lady's Book*—edited for 40 years by Sarah J. Hale—supported higher education for women and advocated that women be able to support themselves, if widowed or unmarried.[30]

By its emphasis on religious activity, the mythology of nineteenth-century womanhood stimulated interest in moral reform. Resolute women used journalism to support abolition and other causes.[31] Among them stood out Jane Swisshelm, editor of an abolitionist newspaper, the *Pittsburgh Saturday Visiter* [sic]. In 1850, as a correspondent for Greeley's *Tribune*, she became the first woman to demand to sit with men in the Senate press gallery, even though Vice-president Millard Fillmore warned her that "the place would be very unpleasant for a lady."[32] Swisshelm occupied a seat for only one day before returning to Pittsburgh, fearing Greeley's wrath over a story she had written for her own paper on Daniel Webster's alleged family of mulatto children.[33]

The Civil War widened opportunities for women journalists, who traded on the Victorian mystique that women possessed a higher moral sense than men. In Washington a group of women correspondents established careers by writing columns that sympathized with the newly freed black population and lamented the political corruption of the postwar era. A new genre of society reporting developed as writers chronicled the lavish entertainments of the robber barons.

In 1879 a total of 20 women were admitted to the Capitol press galleries before a rules change barred them on grounds that the main representatives of newspapers were the only ones entitled to accreditation. Since the women wrote columns that supplemented dispatches by men, the change effectively excluded them.[34] It came amid increasing competition between male and female journalists. One woman correspondent complained to former President Rutherford B. Hayes, "editors always help the man who is trying to get a woman's work on their paper away from her."[35]

As the newspaper industry expanded in the late nineteenth century, women flocked into journalism. Some—like the famous "Nellie Bly," whose real name was Elizabeth Cochrane—attracted attention by performing stunts. Bly rushed around the world in less than 80 days in 1889 for Joseph Pulitzer's *New York World* to beat the record of a fictional hero. "Stunt girls," as reporters like Cochrane were called, often doubled as "sob sisters," who specialized in gushy, tearful accounts of pathos and romance.

According to U.S. census figures, only 288 women were listed as journalists out of a total of 12,308 persons so classified in 1880, but the numbers soon increased. By 1900 there were 2,193 women in the count, out of a total of 30,098.[36] Many of the women staffed the newly created women's and society pages of metropolitan newspapers, offering advice on fashions, homemaking, manners, and romantic relationships.[37]

Both women's magazines and women's pages reported favorably on the women's club movement, which included organizations of women journalists. Sorosis, the first of the influential women's study clubs, was started in New York in 1868 by Jane Cunningham Croly, a woman's page journalist who wrote as "Jennie June." She founded Sorosis after the New York Press Club, to which she belonged, refused to let her attend a dinner in honor of Charles Dickens.[38] Sorosis grew into a national movement of middle-class women devoted to self-education through literary and cultural, but not political, activities.

Seeking companionship and ways of exchanging information on career prospects, women journalists banded together. Croly started the Woman's Press Club of New York in 1889. In Washington the Woman's National Press Association began in 1882, a year before male journalists formed their first press club.[39] Nine years later a Federation of Women's Press Clubs, bringing together local women's press groups throughout the country, was started in Boston.[40] Taking in women who wrote occasional articles as well as those regularly employed, the clubs somewhat paralleled the growth of male-only press clubs in major cities, but the atmosphere was quite different. Men journalists met to drink and play cards; women met to sip tea and uphold conventional ideas of respectability. Press clubs remained sex-segregated organizations until old barriers began to break down in the late 1960s.

In 1889 the *Journalist*, a weekly trade publication, devoted an entire issue to women journalists, including biographical sketches of 50, ten of whom were black.[41] Restricted in their opportunities because of their race as well as sex, some of the black women nevertheless contributed articles to white as well as black publications, many of which were church sponsored.[42] The *Journalist* praised all 50 women for feminine virtues, even though they sought to earn their own livings, instead of depending on men.

The most notable of the ten black journalists praised—Ida Wells, who became Ida Wells-Barnett following her marriage—subsequently crusaded against lynching.[43] Three years after the *Journalist* article appeared, the office of Wells's newspaper—the Memphis *Free Speech*—was burned. She was threatened with death for editorials condemning the lynching of three black men. Moving to the North, she led antilynching campaigns in the United States and lectured in England on lynching. She later founded self-improvement clubs for black women who were not welcome in white organizations.

In summary, during the nineteenth century, journalism became a way for respectable women to earn a living and to voice social concerns. In doing so, they had to evade barriers erected against their full participation in public life. Consequently a segregated journalism evolved that helped support separate institutions like women's press clubs.

Twentieth-century Women in the Media Prior to Women's Liberation

The suffrage campaign, which culminated in 1920 when women won the right to vote, created new opportunities for women to express themselves journalistically. Women launched their own suffrage newspapers in which they developed a sense of community with other feminists, although they disagreed on political tactics and concepts of ideal women.[44] These editors have been described as "articulate, self-sufficient and committed, occasionally slightly eccentric, but very rarely dull."[45]

Metropolitan newspapers hired a few women journalists to cover the campaign, which reached its zenith during World War I. These women fought to prove their competence. Nine women at the *New York Tribune*, for instance, insisted that they be allowed to write the entire story of the last major suffrage parade in New York, instead of letting men reporters take over as they customarily did when suffrage stories moved to page one.[46]

A bequest from a woman magazine publisher named Miriam Florence Follin, who went by the name of her dead husband Frank Leslie, financed a major publicity campaign for suffrage and trained women in the new field of public relations.[47] Women journalists often, but not always, supported the suffrage cause. (For example, Ida Tarbell, the muckraking journalist who exposed the wrongdoing of the Standard Oil Company, opposed votes for women because she resented feminist ideas that she thought had led her astray from marriage.)[48] Formation of the Women's National Press Club in Washington in 1919 illustrated the rapport between some women journalists and publicists for suffrage. The six founders included members of both groups.[49]

When the first journalism schools opened in the first decades of the twentieth century, women were relegated to subordinate status in terms of assignments, role models, and advising. In line with societal forces that expected women to leave the career world for marriage, journalism schools did not encourage women to compete directly with men. Male students edited school newspapers and wrote "hard news" of politics and public affairs. Women students were expected to excel only at "soft news" feature stories. With rare exceptions, faculties consisted solely of male professors.

Women brought in to counsel female students offered conventional messages on the importance of marriage, if only because of economic need. At the University of Missouri, where the world's first journalism school started in 1908, a woman editor told students that her syndicated women's page was not profitable: "It would probably be difficult, if not impossible, for a woman to make a good living on it alone. It is a good sideline for the wife or daughter of an editor."[50]

Men and women journalism students split into separate social and professional organizations. Male students organized an honorary journalism fraternity, Sigma Delta Chi, in 1909 at DePauw University and refused to allow women to join. In response, seven women at the University of Washington started an honorary sorority, Theta Sigma Phi. Both groups soon became national organizations. Theta Sigma Phi members tried to uphold feminine ideals in the midst of a tough masculine field. "Venturing into the newspaper world, dominated by the rougher sex, would very likely have a coarsening effect upon our manners to say nothing of our morals, so we chose for our flower the violet, 'symbol of womanly modesty,' " Helen Ross Lantz, one of the founders, recalled later.[51] Over the years, the sorority's magazine, the

Matrix, chronicled discrimination against women in journalism and recommended they turn their biggest handicap—their gender—into an asset by specializing in areas like home economics journalism.[52]

A few women moved into newsrooms to replace men during World War I—a phenomenon greatly accelerated during World War II. In 1918 Minna Lewinson was one of 11 women graduated from the Columbia University journalism school along with only eight men, since the others had gone off to war. Lewinson became the first woman to be hired by the *Wall Street Journal*.[53] She left the newspaper in 1923, and it reverted to a male-only hiring policy that stayed in effect for decades. Until the late 1960s Columbia itself held to a sharp quota system for women students, on the grounds that women had only limited job opportunities in journalism.[54]

Nationally, women reporters and editors doubled from 7,105 in 1920 to 14,786 in 1930, but most of them worked in one of three areas: women's pages, magazines, book publishing.[55] Even though women had the right to vote, they rarely covered politics or other forms of standard hard news. Editors told women they were biologically un-suited to reporting. "The general tempo—with the deadline-fighting element always present—is such to bar many women because of nervous temperament," one reporting textbook by a city editor and a journalism professor stated, further asserting, "Most women are inca-pable of covering police and court news."[56]

According to Ishbel Ross, a New York newspaperwoman who wrote the first history of women journalists in 1936, very few women qualified for the coveted nickname "front page girl," accorded those considered capable of front-page assignments.[57] Those who did had to be para-doxes of masculine ruthlessness and feminine gentility. Making sure they acted like comrades, they had to withstand the "noise and pressure and rough language of the city room without showing disap-proval or breaking into tears under the strain of rough criticism," Ross wrote.[58]

The Depression of the 1930s slowed the entry of women in journal-ism. By 1940 the number had risen only to 15,890. When loss of advertising revenues led newspapers to cut back on employees, women were affected more than men. Recognizing this fact, Eleanor Roosevelt held White House press conferences for women only during her years as first lady from 1933 to 1945. She said she hoped to provide women with news that men could not get, as a way of helping women keep newspaper jobs.[59]

The exclusion of men forced some news organizations to hire women to cover her weekly press conferences, to which more than 100 women—all white—were accredited by 1941.[60] Occasionally the conferences produced front-page stories—as when Mrs. Roosevelt announced that alcoholic beverages would again be served in the White House after the end of Prohibition.[61] Often they centered on the first lady as a celebrity, with reporters—many of whom worked for women's pages—asking questions about her clothing, social engagements, family, and personal opinions. In that respect, they illustrated the difficulties of women "making news" in male terms: Their activities did not meet the accepted definition of "hard" news that involved conflict, controversy, power, and changes in the status quo. The most admired and politically active woman of her day, Eleanor Roosevelt was newsworthy mainly because she was married to the president of the United States.

Those few women reporters considered on a par with top male journalists did not bother to attend Eleanor Roosevelt's press conferences. Anne O'Hare McCormick of the *New York Times*, who in 1937 became the first woman to win a Pulitzer prize for reporting, interviewed Franklin D. Roosevelt but paid no attention to Mrs. Roosevelt's conferences, although it was Mrs. Roosevelt who arranged for McCormick to see the president.[62] This illustrated a common tendency: Women who succeeded in journalism often identified with male figures, both in terms of news sources and their own professional mentors.

The prejudice against women in reportorial jobs was highlighted by a group of metropolitan editors who addressed women journalism students at Ohio State University in 1940. As the *Matrix* dryly reported, "There seemed to be a general agreement among the members of the employers' symposium that women don't have any more chance for jobs on newspapers than Jews have of surviving in Germany."[63] Socialized to see themselves as subordinate to men, some women journalists internalized discrimination. A 1938 book on careers for women in journalism reported that 20 percent of a surveyed group of newspaperwomen agreed, "on the whole, newspaperwomen are worth less than newspapermen."[64] Only five percent contended that "if women get poor salaries, it is because they accept them supinely."[65]

Perhaps because of the intense prejudice against women on newspapers, an increasingly large number of women sought careers in allied fields. The 1938 survey showed women's chances of earning good salaries were markedly better in promotional writing and on magazines than in newspaper work.[66] Radio offered additional possibilities. Yet no area afforded women equal opportunities with men. Advertising women reported "invulnerable opposition to admitting women into the upper salary brackets."[67] According to another book offering guidance to those seeking advertising careers, "most executives are men. . . . Many agencies prefer men in this capacity, and some will not consider women under any circumstances."[68] A woman who wished to succeed was warned to "concentrate on her job to the exclusion of everything else . . . home, heart interest, and children."[69]

With the advent of World War II, the employment picture changed dramatically for women in many industries, including journalism. As men were drafted, employers had no choice except to hire women. "Odd, isn't it, how the job picture has changed in war months," Betty Hinckle Dunn, national secretary of Theta Sigma Phi, exclaimed in 1942. "Flippantly I tell my friends, 'The war means more opportunities for women and Negroes.' "[70]

By 1943 women made up 50 percent of the staffs of many newspapers in smaller cities.[71] In Washington there were nearly 100 women accredited to the Capitol press galleries, compared with 30 six years earlier.[72] Women journalists, like their male counterparts, tried to get overseas to the "big story" of the war itself, although both the State Department, which issued passports, and the War Department, which accredited correspondents, discouraged them.[73] A total of 127 women achieved accreditation status, however—although once overseas they met antagonism from some generals and male correspondents.[74]

Even though the war created an ideology that supported women's work outside the home to help the military effort, women journalists did not receive the respect accorded men. Many editors saw them as either too innocent to cover the unsavory elements of hard news or lacking the physical and mental ability of men. The wartime women journalists were ridiculed in a *Saturday Evening Post* article titled "Paper Dolls," which gave the number of replacements nationally as 8,000.[75] Results of a 1944 survey of 66 newspaper publishers showed that fewer than 5 percent hoped to continue to employ all of the women journalists who wished to remain after the war ended.[76]

Some of the women viewed themselves as substitutes and did not fight against discrimination because they thought it contrary to their womanly roles. The Women's National Press Club in Washington, which included some of the nation's most successful women journalists, did not object as an organization to blatant prejudice during World War II, although individual members did. In 1944 Mary Hornaday, a *Christian Science Monitor* correspondent and former club president, protested on her own when women who belonged to the White House

Correspondents' Association and paid its dues were barred from its annual male-only dinner. She also spoke up against the National Press Club ban on permitting women into its premises to cover speeches given by officials to the press.[77]

Similarly, May Craig—the Washington correspondent who became prominent as a *Meet the Press* panelist—objected to the sex-segregated dinners of the White House Correspondents' Association. It was Craig who won a long fight in 1945 for a women's rest room adjoining the congressional press galleries. In her battles Craig, president of the Women's National Press Club in 1943, acted as an individual, as Hornaday did, because the women's press club included those who did not think it "feminine" to demand equal rights.[78]

When peace came in 1945, women of undisputed competence faced demotion from city desks to women's sections. Dorothy Jurney, who had been acting city editor of the *Washington Daily News*, was told she could not be considered for the position permanently because she was a woman. She was asked to train a male successor before moving to the *Miami Herald* as women's editor.[79] Women encountered similar experiences across the country.

By this time, women's pages were changing from their presentation of weddings, society news, and what one early-twentieth-century critic called "glaring drivel"—freckle-removal recipes, fashion "dots and doings," and superficial advice to wives and mothers.[80] Before World War II, some papers instituted "home" pages, which attempted to elevate homemaking into the profession of home economics.[81] During the war, the pages chronicled women's efforts to help the war effort.

One woman publisher, Eleanor "Cissy" Patterson—wealthy granddaughter of the founder of the *Chicago Tribune*—emphasized the women's pages when she ran the *Washington Herald* (which became the *Washington Times-Herald*) from 1930 to 1948. Patterson "put flair and style into the stilted women's pages of the day—a style eventually copied all over the country," according to Carolyn Bell Hughes, one of her staff members.[82] Hughes recalled that Patterson elevated "food into the gourmet category," hired lively writers, ordered that "sex spiced the fashion pictures," and transformed social chitchat into a clue to front-page headlines.[83] The latter feat was performed relatively easily in Washington where diplomacy and high-level political activity occurred on the official party circuit. Yet women's pages were sneered at by male journalists who downgraded achievements by women co-workers.[84]

Coverage of women's organizations on women's pages meant that topics related to women's political role appeared there. In a column on women's clubs, for example, in the *Detroit Free Press* of August 21, 1942, a report of the convention of the National Association of Women Lawyers raised the question of whether an Equal Rights Amendment to the U.S. Constitution would eliminate discrimination or adversely affect women by wiping protective legislation off the books.[85] A women's page columnist in the *Washington Post* in 1946 suggested that males who insisted on sex-segregated social and professional organizations feared women, who dominated the home and church, because of women's "energy, ambition and organizing talents" and were in a "last ditch retreat from 'mother knows best.' "[86]

Political messages aside, in the eyes of many journalists, male and female, women's pages ranked akin to a newspaper Siberia, covering the Four Fs: food, furnishing, fashion, and family.[87] In 1949 *Mademoiselle* magazine discouraged its readers from newspaper work because almost no opportunities existed for women to cover general news following the end of World War II. Surveyed by the magazine, editors of 27 daily newspapers reported women were too unpredictable and emotional for beats outside women's departments. In addition, editors said, women "get married and quit just about the time they're any good to you."[88]

Some women journalists themselves subscribed to the ideal of homemaking as personal fulfillment—the mythology soon to be attacked by Betty Friedan. Advising journalism graduates, Betty Angelo, who resigned a reporting job on the *Detroit News* to get married, urged young women to seek positions on metropolitan newspapers to hunt husbands. "I worked for a big city newspaper five years and met, among numerous other marriageable males, my husband—a newspaper editor on a rival paper," she wrote in the *Matrix*.[89] Women who spoke on college campuses stressed the sublimation of careers to family life. The food editor of the *Deseret News* in Salt Lake City, speaking at Iowa State University in 1956, told how she put her husband and three children ahead of her career: She tested recipes in her kitchen, wrote her stories at home, and had her husband take them to the newspaper office.[90]

Yet women continued to keep employed in media occupations. The number of women employed as editors and reporters in newspaper, magazine, and book publishing rose until by 1960 women represented about 37 percent of the total.[91] The percentage of women employed in public relations jumped a remarkable 258 percent from 1950 to 1960.[92]

In all media areas, however, men held better jobs. Women were subordinated and segregated.

Some women hired during World War II managed to hang onto jobs in the news field because their assignments were so undesirable that men did not want them. Speaking in 1990, Helen Thomas, chief White House correspondent for United Press International (UPI), recalled that she, unlike other women reporters, escaped being fired by the wire service after the war ended because "there weren't too many takers around for the 5:30 a.m. trick."[93] Thomas pointed out that women were denied equal access to news for years in Washington because they were barred from luncheon speeches by heads of state at the National Press Club. It was not until Soviet Premier Nikita Khrushchev spoke in 1959 that, for the first time, the press club allowed newswomen to eat with their male colleagues. The breakthrough came only because women journalists protested "so loud and clear they were heard in Moscow" and Khrushchev threatened not to speak unless they were admitted, Thomas said.[94]

When an exceptional woman gained renown—as in the case of Marguerite Higgins, a *New York Herald-Tribune* reporter who won a Pulitzer prize in 1951 for her coverage of the Korean War—questions were raised as to whether she used sex to get news. According to Richard Kluger, author of an acclaimed history of the *Herald-Tribune*, evidence suggested that Higgins, described as a "windblown blonde," selected "most if not all of her bedmates for intensely practical reasons, to add to her power or promote her career."[95] Contending that few males could "wield their sexuality as strategically," Kluger asked if it was "feminism . . . to use her beauty in such a fashion—or a travesty on the goal of emancipation for her sex?"[96] But Kluger did not ask if a "double standard" confronted her. Did male reporters need to "wield their sexuality" to get stories? And if so, did anyone question their conduct?

As for broadcasting, women fared as poorly, if not more so, as on newspapers. Most women's voices were considered too high and nonauthoritative for news work. Some women gave household hints on the radio and in the early days of television, but most women's programs consisted of soap operas. Prejudices against women on newspapers carried over into the electronic media, although women proved their abilities at broadcasting during World War II when they replaced men. But they did not remain behind the mike when the war ended, except for occasional family programming.[97]

Discrimination encountered by white middle-class women in journalism and broadcasting was magnified in the case of minority women. They were systemically deprived of opportunities for employment in the mainstream press and on broadcasting stations. Limited to jobs on ethnic publications, they earned far less than their white counterparts and experienced resentment from some of their male co-workers. Yet they persevered.

In Missouri, Lucile Bluford—a graduate of the University of Kansas—started work for the Kansas City *Call*, a black weekly, in 1932. In the following decade she was rebuffed 11 times in efforts to gain admission to the University of Missouri School of Journalism to study for a master's degree.[98] To maintain segregation, the State of Missouri established a new school of journalism at Lincoln University, a black institution. It was not until 1989 that Bluford—by this time editor, publisher, and majority owner of the *Call*—received a degree from the University of Missouri. It was an honorary doctorate in humanities, which she accepted "for the thousands of black students who suffered discrimination all those years."[99]

Alice A. Dunnigan, a Kentucky sharecropper's daughter who in 1947 became the first black woman to be accredited to the Capitol press galleries, came to Washington during World War II as a clerk-typist for the federal government. Part-time correspondence for black newspapers eventually resulted in Dunnigan's becoming chief of the Washington Bureau of the Associated Negro Press at the war's end. Her salary barely provided her enough to live on. When she earned extra money writing speeches on the side for a woman government official, a black male colleague unsuccessfully tried to have her accreditation lifted on grounds of conflict of interest.[100] The National Association for the Advancement of Colored People (NAACP) defended her, pointing out that white reporters also supplemented their income with speech writing and related work.[101] "In trying to compare the source of my biggest problem, I concluded that it was based on sex rather than race," Dunnigan said. "It's perhaps jealousy, that's all I know."[102]

Another black woman reporter—Ethel Payne, a correspondent for the *Chicago Defender* and allied black newspapers—encountered hostility when she asked President Dwight D. Eisenhower at a press conference in 1955 if he was planning to issue an executive order ending segregation in interstate travel.[103] Eisenhower's angry answer— "What makes you think I'm going to do anything for any special interest group?"—propelled Payne into the headlines.[104] Although her own newspaper praised her for bringing up the issue, other publications did not. "I was pilloried by the black press as being over-assertive," Payne recalled in 1990.[105] "They wrote columns about it, that I was an embarrassment, that I had gone down and I was showboating, just disturbing the President."[106]

Aside from those on women's pages, women journalists of the pre–women's liberation era found themselves in a cultural bind symbolized by a 1956 painting by Dean Cornwell titled "No Place for a Nice Girl," which is owned by the Chicago Press Veterans Association.[107] It pictures a frightened young woman in a smoke-filled, littered city room dominated by ten disreputable-looking newsmen who appear to resent her presence. The painting posed the question of whether a "nice girl" could be an aggressive "superwoman" capable of competing in journalism.[108]

Within a decade after Cornwell portrayed the plight of the young woman who wanted to be a reporter, shifts in political and social pressures challenged the concept of newsrooms as a male-only preserve. Yet even in the 1960s women were told there was no place for them. "We have a very small bureau, and I'm afraid I can't hire you," the *Newsweek* bureau chief in Chicago in 1966 told Kay Mills, a young reporter who worked on the United Press International radio wire and wanted to advance.[109] "I need someone I can send anywhere, like riots. And besides, what would you do if someone you're covering ducked into the men's room."[110]

The women's liberation movement and its accompanying political developments caught the media unaware. According to David Broder, political columnist for the *Washington Post,* it fell outside the mainstream of political life and did not fit into any one of the areas normally given reporters for their official beats: politics, education, business, labor, police, courts, and so on.[111] "We remain trapped in the assumptions and parochial limitations of our regular beats and the conventional thinking of the institutions and people we regularly cover," Broder wrote in a critique of news coverage of the women's movement.[112] In their criticism of the media, feminists went far beyond examination of news-gathering processes. They demanded equality and struck at the assumption that men and women should occupy separate, and unequal, spheres within journalism.

Feminist Criticism of the Media

Portrayal of Women

When Friedan wrote *The Feminine Mystique,* the book's importance as a media critique was not immediately apparent. Its message—that women had been locked into a constricting wife-mother role by social institutions that preached a spurious doctrine of femininity—ignited the women's movement on a mass basis. Yet three of the nation's major newspapers—the *New York Times*, the *Washington Post*, and the *Washington Star*—did not bother to review the work. The review in the *New York Herald-Tribune* called the book "required reading for . . . those who care about the future development of our society," but it ran under a trivializing headline, "DON'T SWEEP THE LADIES UNDER THE RUG."[113]

A major portion of the book attacked women's magazines for promulgating the myth of the "happy housewife," who lived only to serve others. Friedan, a free-lance writer, wrote the book in 1963 after three women's magazines for which she normally wrote—*McCall's*, the *Ladies' Home Journal*, and *Redbook*—turned down articles she submitted on the dissatisfactions of homemaking.[114] The book encouraged middle-class women to develop themselves intellectually by seeking paid career opportunities outside the home. "What I was writing threatened the very foundations of the women's magazine world—the feminine mystique," Friedan noted.[115]

Yet it was the women's magazines that ran prepublication excerpts—*Mademoiselle*, the *Journal*, and *McCall's*. Their excerpts did not focus on one of Friedan's prime contentions: that American business was manipulating women through the mass media to buy more and more products in an unfulfilling quest for self-realization. According to Friedan, male editors and writers for women's magazines abetted business in denying that women had the intelligence to work in the world of men.[116]

By the start of the next decade, some women had mobilized to attack the way they were portrayed in the media as well as the extent of their representation in decision-making roles. In 1970 the Media Women's Association was formed in New York to challenge the prevailing power of the media to influence women's views about themselves. The group, composed of women working in the media, wrote a series of essays on media sex discrimination that were published in a book, *Rooms with No View*, in 1974. It concluded that a number of diverse magazines were akin in one respect: "They are run by men who have low opinions of the ability of the women who work for them."[117]

The *Ladies' Home Journal* and its male editor, John Mack Carter, received the harshest criticism. The Media Women's Association had been one of four feminist groups that invaded Carter's office on March 19, 1970, for what became an 11-hour sit-in. The demonstrators demanded that the *Journal* change its contents to include material on contemporary women's issues. Numbering about 150, the demonstrators presented Carter with a dummy of an alternative *Journal*, which included articles on abortion, careers versus family, and prostitution.

At the end of the sit-in, Carter promised the feminists an eight-page section, which appeared in the August 1970 issue. Written by a collective of 30 women who critiqued each other's contribution and did not use bylines, the insert expressed feminist opinions on education for women, childbirth, homemaking, marriage, love, and sex. Yet the *Journal* soon returned to its traditional subject matter.

Sometimes feminist journalists themselves ridiculed movement demonstrations to please their male editors. Lindsy Van Gelder, then a reporter for the *New York Post*, said later that she regretted her coverage of the Miss America demonstration because she treated the incident lightly, afraid that "if I reported it straight, it wouldn't get in at all."[118] Similarly the *New York Times*'s women's section—which gained a reputation for being closely tied to the women's movement—did not commit itself wholeheartedly, for fear of violating the ideal of journalistic objectivity. As one reporter put it, the paper went through "periods when the editors say, 'We've had too many women's lib stories lately.' "[119] Charlotte Curtis, women's editor from 1965 to 1974, hesitated to call herself a feminist.[120] This reaction may have stemmed in part from a perceived limited market for feminist news. As illustrated by the failure to ratify the Equal Rights Amendment (which in 1982 fell short of the necessary 38 states' referendum approval), not all women supported feminism.

Nevertheless, in the late 1960s and early 1970s, major newspapers—particularly the *Washington Post*, *Chicago Tribune*, and *New York Times*—began to cover feminist issues such as abortion rights, alimony, and child care in their women's pages. They also changed the names of these sections. To attract male readers as well as to respond to the women's movement, editors transformed women's pages into lifestyle sections. Feminists were not particularly pleased, especially since entertainment material replaced news of women.[121] One 1974 critique emphasized two other points: (1) Slick name changes often did not reflect more than token alteration of food and family copy; and (2) placement of serious subjects there "ghettoized" major contemporary issues affecting women, keeping them off the front page.[122]

Feminist critics argued that the tone of the new women's pages—even more than the substance—reinforced many accustomed ideas about women's roles, although these sections purported to question them. Far from being marginal issues, sexual and reproductive controversies occupied a central role in the women's movement.[123] The bland orientation of lifestyle pages hardly served for serious discussion of these political issues. Lesbian issues, alternatives to conventional marriage, and feminism as it affected women of color fit poorly, if at all, within the confines of lifestyle/women's pages.

Unlike the front pages, which depended for news on official sources (usually white males in powerful positions), lifestyle/women's pages often used press releases from corporations seeking women consumers.[124] For example, in the 1970s General Mills, a food conglomerate that also sells clothing and games, commissioned a series of reports on family life based on survey research. The reports, as well as related public forums, were part of a public relations campaign aimed at identifying General Mills with family life. Run almost verbatim on lifestyle/women's pages, the reports emphasized that Americans continued to endorse values associated with the nuclear family.[125] The findings they cited, however, showed strains in the family and could have been interpreted as evidence of a crumbling family structure.[126] As presented, they pictured families transmitting conservative ideas to their children.[127]

While some feminists started their own publications, other women tried to promote less stereotypical coverage by monitoring media and publicizing the results. Two chapters of the American Association of University Women (AAUW), for example, decided in 1974 to conduct a content analysis of the "Day" (lifestyle) section of the *Portland Oregonian*. In their report they concluded that hard news about women (as opposed to feature news) occupied only 0.3 percent of space, reflecting "the less powerful position of women in all aspects" of life, but still raising the question of how more than half the population could be "such pitiful failures" in news terms.[128]

Activist groups like NOW and other organizations undertook to monitor sex stereotyping in broadcasting, which was considered more detrimental to women than the print media because of the extent of television watching and the power of television imagery. Broadcast monitoring projects carried an implied threat: that women's groups would seek to block renewals of station licenses by the Federal Communications Commission (FCC), which requires that stations operate in the public interest. In raising the specter of license challenges, women's groups followed the example of civil rights coalitions that had complained to the FCC about racist programming.

In 1972 NOW filed a petition against the license renewal of WABC-TV in New York. NOW charged the station with deficiencies in three areas: (1) ascertainment of women's opinions on community issues, (2) news and programming about women's concerns, and (3) employment of women. In support of its petition, NOW cited instances of WABC-TV's failure to carry news items on the congressional passage of the Equal Rights Amendment. It also referred to four prime-time editorials against the women's movement in a six-week period, including one by commentator Howard K. Smith, who declared that discrimination against women was too inconsequential for federal action.

Fear of license challenges spurred some stations to agree to negotiated agreements with women's groups. In 1974 the Los Angeles Women's Coalition for Better Broadcasting, made up of seven women's organizations, signed agreements with two network-owned stations. As a result, stations established women's advisory councils and took other steps to improve their treatment of women.

Women's groups also protested against advertising seen as sexist and demeaning. As never before, women analyzed advertisements and expressed outrage over what they saw and heard. For instance, researchers examined women in magazine advertisements and found that they were shown making independent decisions about purchases for inexpensive items only—chiefly food, cosmetics, and cleaning products—while men were featured in advertisements for expensive articles.[129] Presumably women were not thought capable of major consumer decisions. Feminist groups, determined to demonstrate their influence, applied pressure on advertisers through demonstrations, complaints, and, in some cases, boycotts. To a degree the advertising industry reacted.

In 1975 the National Advertising Review Board, an industry group that receives complaints about advertising, released a study recommending "constructive portrayals" of women in advertising.[130] Advertisers and agency personnel, for example, were urged to depict women as intelligent consumers. But the recommendations were not binding on advertisers or agencies.

Underlying all the complaints regarding the portrayal of women lay a key belief: Women's portrayal would improve if more women themselves worked in professional-level positions in the media. In fighting for the employment and promotion of women, feminists utilized federal law for ensuring social change. They brought legal actions under Title VII of the 1964 Civil Rights Act.

Participation of Women

According to the 1970 U.S. census, women in journalism were outnumbered 2:1 by men and confined to the lower ranks.[131] Similar discrimination appeared in broadcasting. A 1972 survey of 609 commercial television stations reported 75 percent of the women were engaged in office tasks. 18 percent of the stations had no women in upper-level positions, and over 50 percent no women in management.[132]

Are women "going for a discount price?" asked members of Theta Sigma Phi, the journalism sorority. They answered the question affirmatively by means of a national survey of 616 women journalists in 1971.[133] In spite of laws against discrimination, the majority of the women felt or knew that they were not paid as well as their male counterparts for equal work. "Many women feel that they would be in serious trouble with their bosses if they openly insisted on equal pay for equal work," the chair of the committee doing the study concluded, adding, "Quite a few feel they would just be fired and replaced by a man."[134] Even when men were assigned to the traditional domain of women—the women's pages—they were paid more than women. A survey of 335 women's page editors in 1974 showed that the 30 who were male made substantially more than the 305 women: Only 11 of the women were paid more than $17,000 annually, while 15 of the 30 men were in this category.[135]

Because women in the media were accustomed to being discriminated against and feared being replaced, it was not surprising that they did not immediately seek redress under civil rights legislation. Before this occurred, their own consciousness of discrimination had to be raised by the women's movement, which many of them covered.[136] New feminist publications spurred them to examine their own situation. Chief among these, *Ms.*, founded in 1972 by Gloria Steinem and edited by her and other women writers, voiced evidence of discrimination against women in all facets of life, including the mass media. *Ms.* reached a mass audience of 500,000 by 1983, double its initial run.[137] It provided an important new outlet for women to participate more visibly in the media and to question why the media were only superficially interested in social changes affecting women.

Even before *Ms.* appeared, 46 women working at *Newsweek* had led the way for formal protests against discrimination. Long relegated to the role of researchers while men were reporters and writers, the women at *Newsweek* timed their complaint to coincide with the newsmagazine's issue on "Women's Liberation," which featured a cover story written by a woman who was not employed at *Newsweek*. Women at *Time* soon filed similar protests with the Equal Employment Opportunity Commission against their employer's sex-segregated jobs. Following a pattern that became relatively typical in EEOC cases, both these cases were eventually settled when management promised to implement affirmative action plans to make hiring, training, assignments, and promotion opportunities more equitable.[138]

In the following years, numerous other news organizations found themselves the targets of class-action sex discrimination complaints and suits, along with hundreds of other American businesses.[139] Appearing among the news organizations named in these actions were the most respected in the United States: the *New York Times, Washington Post*, Associated Press, *Newsday, Detroit News, Baltimore Evening Sun, Reader's Digest*, NBC, and other broadcasters.[140] Joining with women were labor unions, which belatedly saw the need to fight for equal status for men and women. For years a party to discriminatory contracts that allowed women's page staff members to be paid less than general news or sports section personnel, the Newspaper Guild held a conference in 1970 to set goals for equality.[141]

A ruling by the Federal Communications Commission in 1971 aided the women's cause immeasurably. Previously it had held that minorities should be given equal opportunities in hiring. When it extended that provision to women, it opened the way for their employment on network and local news staffs.[142]

Previously very few women had succeeded in network news. A notable exception was Pauline Frederick, hired in 1948 as the first network correspondent. Carving out a career covering the United Nations, she earned respect, first at ABC and then at NBC until retirement in 1974, by virtue of hard work and intense study of complicated issues.[143] Another pioneer, Nancy Dickerson, worked for CBS and NBC in the 1960s but left NBC in 1970, contending that the women's movement actually hampered her progress by causing men to retaliate against her and downgrade her assignments.[144] A third woman, Marlene Sanders, who joined ABC in 1964 and worked her way up to vice-president, said she was oblivious to sex discrimination: "My models were men around me, and I saw no reason why I shouldn't do what they did, eventually."[145]

Spurred by the women's movement, however, women banded together to push for broadcast opportunities newly available in the 1970s. Catherine Mackin, for example, was one of 27 women who filed a discrimination complaint against WRC-TV, the NBC-owned station in Washington, D.C., in 1971.[146] That same year she became a network correspondent for NBC, remaining there until joining ABC in 1977, where she stayed as a congressional correspondent until her death in 1982.[147] At the time Mackin was hired at NBC, women represented only 4 percent of the 153 reporters at the three broadcast networks.[148]

Preceded by a petition from NOW, the FCC decision helped Mackin gain her network job, just as it advanced the careers of Connie Chung, Lesley Stahl, and others hired in the same period.[149] In Mackin's case, even though she had been a leader in the discrimination complaint against WRC-TV, NBC had nothing to gain by retaliation against her, since CBS was making overtures to her at the time.[150] Not all women involved in sex discrimination complaints, however, found that their situations improved.

In some cases, women who brought complaints discovered themselves subjected to ostracism and the wrath of male bosses. Sometimes, fighting for the rights of others derailed their own careers. For example, reporter Mary Lou Butcher left the *Detroit News* for public relations in 1977 after leading a suit against the newspaper, which finally agreed in 1983 to pay $330,000 to about 90 employees who had been discriminated against.[151] As a result, women moved into areas previously denied to them—sports, photo, state and national bureaus—leading Butcher to say, "It was rewarding to me to see other women just treated as equals."[152]

Widespread salary gaps and other discriminatory practices led women at the *New York Times* to bring suit in 1974. Four years later, a $385,000 out-of-court settlement was reached, specifying affirmative action goals and timetables for hiring and promotion, and giving $223,500 in back pay to women in news and commercial departments.[153] "I credit the lawsuit for my career," commented Linda Greenhouse, who now covers the Supreme Court for the *Times*, explaining that the suit forced editors "to scan the horizon" and promote women.[154]

Like the *New York Times* case, the Associated Press suit was carefully watched by the rest of the industry. Launched in 1973 with a discrimination complaint brought by the Wire Service Guild on behalf of a group of black employees and Shirley Christian, then UN correspondent (who won a Pulitzer prize after leaving the AP to work for the *Miami Herald*), the suit dragged on for a decade.[155] A $2 million out-of-court settlement finally was reached in 1983 that established an affirmative action plan for women and minorities and awarded $850,000 to more than 800 women who had worked at the AP since 1972.[156] At the time, women constituted 22 percent of AP's employees, but by 1988 the percentage had risen to 44.[157]

Fueled by feminist activism, opportunities in general for women in the media increased dramatically in the 1970s and 1980s. Old quotas were abolished—as in the case of the Columbia University Graduate

School of Journalism, which stopped limiting the number of women students admitted after the *Wall Street Journal* started to hire women in 1968.[158] Local press clubs and national journalism organizations were integrated following protests by women.[159] Theta Sigma Phi changed its name to Women in Communications Inc. and voted to admit men in 1972, after the male journalism fraternity, Sigma Delta Chi, added the name Society of Professional Journalists and took in women. Women began to outnumber men in journalism school enrollments, with 53 percent of students being female in 1978, compared to 41-percent female a decade before.[160] Although only two out of 60 recipients of the Nieman fellowships for journalists to study at Harvard University had been female from 1968 to 1973, suddenly more than a third of the winners annually were women.

Clearly women ventured into new domains. By the end of the 1970s, women sportswriters were covering team locker rooms. A woman, Jane Pfeiffer, chaired the NBC board. Six out of 56 publishers of newspapers owned by the Gannett Company were women.[161] In advertising, a few outstanding figures like Mary Wells Lawrence proved that exceptional women could make it to the top.[162] Feminist columnists like Ellen Goodman of the *Boston Globe*, who won a Pulitzer prize in 1980, gave women a voice on commentary pages across the country.

But what effect did women's increasing participation have on the media themselves? Were they different because women had more opportunities to work in them? Did structures, practices, and professional values change? Answers to these questions provide a look at women's present status in the media.

Changes in the Media

With the advent of the Reagan administration, widespread interest in affirmative action cases ceased. Class-action lawsuits, increasingly expensive, became increasingly rare, particularly in the wake of a U.S. Supreme Court decision in 1989 that curtailed affirmative action remedies.[163] Yet the 1970s suits had achieved their aim: Media corporations were hiring and promoting women and minorities. According to some observers, this change could have been expected to occur anyway as the labor market experienced an influx of women. In addition, media companies decided it would be "good business" to diversify staffs in line with an increasingly heterogeneous population. But it seems obvious that the suits played a key role.

The women's movement came at a time of tremendous growth and consolidation of power within media industries. By 1990 diversity of communications ownership had virtually disappeared. In 1987 half or more of U.S. media businesses were controlled by 26 corporations, and projections were made that a half dozen would control most of the media during the 1990s.[164] The Gannett Company owned 82 daily newspapers as well as 26 broadcasting outlets, while Newhouse Newspapers owned 27 newspapers, 70 cable systems, 10 magazines, and 6 book companies. Capital Cities bought the American Broadcasting Company (ABC), giving it ownership of 47 newspapers, 27 broadcasting outlets, and 65 magazines.[165] And so it went. Independent newspapers and broadcasting stations were, increasingly, artifacts of the past. Large media corporations employed increasing numbers of women in line with national labor trends, which saw some 28 million women move into paid employment from 1960 to 1985.[166]

For the first time, media women were allowed to compete professionally with men, but their advance was hard and slow. The old-fashioned women's pages were gone, but news organizations still presented difficult working conditions for women.

Some evidence exists that women on newspapers do not intend to remain there as long as their male counterparts because of the difficulties of combining journalistic jobs with motherhood. A 1988 study by the American Society of Newspaper Editors (ASNE) found that "the news values and professionalism of the women currently in the newsroom are the same as that of their male colleagues," although it discovered differences between men and women in career plans.[167] In 1988 ASNE surveyed a newsroom work force of 55,000 professionals employed at the nation's 1,600 daily newspapers. Women represented 35 percent of the total but 46 percent of the youngest group of hires, having more education and a superior academic record in comparison with men.[168] Minorities made up 6.6 percent of the total force.[169] More women than men were willing to remain as reporters and copy editors rather than aspire to management; they also believed their gender more of an obstacle to advancement than did men.[170] Fewer women than men were married—44 percent of the women, compared with 62 percent of the men—and 28 percent of the women said they planned to leave the field before they were 40, whereas 15 percent of the men planned to.[171]

The finding that both men and women had similar ideas about the nature of news itself countered assertions that women's presence has changed the field. For example, Kay Mills, a *Los Angeles Times* editorial writer, contended in a 1988 book that the presence of women has led to more women being interviewed and more news treatment of sexual harassment and other women's issues, even though most news has remained the same.[172] She cited Associated Press coverage, noting that its news file consists chiefly of event-oriented fact coverage regarding accidents, disasters, and political actions.[173] But—Mills contended—women reporters, more than men, are likely to do an occasional enterprise story on premenstrual syndrome or a similar topic.[174] According to her, the interaction of the women's movement, increasing numbers of women journalists, and coverage of women was "not a conscious act," but one that simply happened.[175]

Why has this interaction not been more direct? First of all, aspiring women gain jobs through the same route as men. Both men and women usually start on campus newspapers and then work their way up to metropolitan dailies. Some large news organizations require that they pass personality tests of motivation, interest, and aptitude.[176] By the time they attain a professional-level position, they have mastered an ideology of news that pretends to be gender free but actually is based on ideas that underpin our male-controlled political-economic system: competition, achievement, independence, rationality, logic.[177] Women subconsciously are expected to "buy into" or "learn" these ideas to compete on a par with men. In doing so, women have to set aside, or overcome, their own history of purveying culture through the private sphere of nurturance and socialization.[178] In competing with men, they have to be "taken seriously," that is, seen as rational malelike individuals, in spite of mass media images that show them mainly in sexual terms.

For these reasons, women professionals have risen in indignation at feminist-inspired notions that the increasing numbers of women in the field will change the ideology of news. When a University of Maryland study suggested in 1985 that women in newsrooms were discriminated against but might, if advanced to decision-making positions, change the nature of news by making it more "attuned to harmony and community," a group of women editors vehemently disagreed.[179] "News is news; it has no sex," declared Linda Cunningham, editor of the *Trenton* (New Jersey) *Times*, at the time.[180]

Professionals nevertheless have been willing to subscribe to the somewhat contradictory theory that the presence of women and minorities contribute to broadening the news, which is seen as a desirable aim. Mills argued that women's increasing presence "has changed some attitudes of their male editors."[181] Yet there is little evidence these attitudes have changed significantly.

In 1989 the Women, Men, and Media Conference, cosponsored by the Gannett Foundation and the University of Southern California, looked at the status of women in the print and broadcast media. Its key findings were as follows:

- Women still were symbolically annihilated by the media, with men determining what is news since women hold only 6 percent of top media jobs and 25 percent of middle-management jobs.
- Women still were confined to lower-paying jobs, with media women earning 64 cents in comparison to media men's $1 (whereas the national average for women in all industries was 65 cents for every $1 paid to a man).
- Women remained underrepresented in major newspapers, with a survey of front pages from ten newspapers in March 1989 showing that 27 percent of the bylines were female, 24 percent of the photographs included women (usually as part of a family group), and 11 percent of the persons quoted were female. (*USA Today*, which emphasizes feature-oriented news, ranked at the top of the list, and the *New York Times* at the bottom.)
- Women fared equally poorly, if not worse, in broadcasting. The percentage of women news correspondents shown on nightly network newscasts increased only six percentage points—from 9.9 percent to 15.8 percent from 1975 to 1989. (A February 1989 study showed the following percentage of stories filed by women: CBS, 22.2 percent; NBC, 14.4 percent; and ABC, 10.5 percent. During that month, women were the focus of interviews on 13.7 percent of the ABC newscasts, 10.2 percent of the CBS newscasts, and 8.9 percent of the NBC newscasts.)[182]

Data that showed women in the media earned substantially less than men came from a 1988 study by Jean Gaddy Wilson of the University of Missouri–Columbia. Based on a survey of 1,599 daily newspapers, 1,219 television stations, and 1,091 radio stations, Wilson's study revealed that "a woman boss earns significantly less than a man in the same job" at the same size media outlet with the same years of experience, costing the woman annually $9,074 in television, $7,793 in newspapers, and $3,323 in radio.[183] The larger discrepancy in television salaries was attributed to higher average salaries there in general.

Wilson found that the entry level was the only place where men and women earned equitable salaries.[184]

The data further showed that women outnumbered men in two areas: as beginning reporters and advertising salespersons (57 percent), and as support and clerical staff (94 percent).[185] Why did women not proceed up the ladder like men? According to the study, "many forces combine to knock them off—evidence of bias in salary and promotion; the historically male-dominated news business; few female role models; the segregation of women into dead-end jobs."[186]

At the top levels, women represented 3 percent of television presidents/vice-presidents, 6 percent of newspaper publishers, and 8 percent of radio presidents/vice-presidents, but their salaries were only 92 percent of what their male counterparts earned.[187] In broadcasting no woman yet had achieved the status of a regular anchor of a nightly network newscast. Minority women fared more poorly than white women in terms of getting on the air. A 1986 study by the NOW Legal Defense and Education Fund Media Project found that stories filed by women of color represented only 0.9 percent of all on-the-air stories on network newscasts.[188]

The newspaper-related findings of the Women, Men, and Media Conference were updated in 1990 with another survey. It was commissioned by the MediaWatch project of Betty Friedan, now a professor at the University of Southern California, and the American Society of Newspaper Editors. The survey showed slight improvements in coverage of and by women in photos, bylines, and story sources on the front pages of 20 U.S. newspapers (the same ten surveyed the previous year plus ten more from smaller markets). The new findings were as follows:

- Females averaged 14 percent as sources in stories, compared with 11 percent in 1989.
- Females represented 28 percent of the bylines, compared with 27 percent the previous year.[189]

Once again the lowest average for use of women as sources was found in the nation's leading newspaper of record, the *New York Times* (6 percent in 1990 compared with 5 percent in 1989). Responding to this finding, Max Frankel, executive editor of the *New York Times*, complained that the survey was "bizarre and unworthy."[190] "As soon as Mr. Gorbachev lets Mrs. Gorbachev do his deciding or even speaking, we will be quoting or photographing more women on page one," he wrote to the ASNE.[191] He told a reporter, "I mean that if you are covering local teas, you've got more women [on the front page] than if you're the *Wall Street Journal.*"[192]

Although the *Washington Post* ranked first in 1990 in the number of women featured in front-page photographs (42 percent compared with 41 percent for *USA Today* in 1989), Ben Bradlee, executive editor, responded scathingly to the survey. "I am damned if I can see what conclusions should be drawn from your findings," he wrote, adding, "The wisdom of the ages appears to cry out for silence."[193] The *Post*'s feminist columnist, Judy Mann, reacted quite differently, saying, "The story those pictures told was of a newspaper that was including in its major stories and features those that involved women. . . . the stories that make newspapers relevant to their entire audience."[194]

Increasingly journalism graduates are specializing in public relations and advertising where starting pay is somewhat better than in newspaper work. In 1987, for example, the annual median starting pay for journalism graduates was $13,900 on daily newspapers, compared to $16,744 in public relations and $15,028 in advertising.[195] In public relations, however, as the number of women has risen from 27 percent of the field in 1970 to 58 percent in 1989, studies have documented increasing salary disparity between men and women practitioners.[196] One study, which referred to public relations as a "velvet ghetto," found that women paid "a million dollar penalty" over the course of their careers because of sex discrimination in salaries.[197] In advertising, women perceive their situation as being far short of equality. The seventh annual survey of advertising women conducted by *Adweek* magazine in 1989 showed that only 44 percent of women who had been in the field for one to five years believed that their pay matched their performance.[198]

With more women majoring in journalism, evidence suggests that entry-level salaries paid to journalism graduates are declining in relation to those paid other graduates. A survey by Michigan State University showed that 1990 journalism graduates could expect starting salaries second from the bottom of those offered graduates in 28 categories—$18,255 annually, just above the $18,157 figure for home economists.[199] The College Placement Council notes that male graduates are offered higher salaries than females. In 1989, for example, in public relations men were offered average salaries of $22,835 compared to $18,532 for women.[200]

In spite of discouraging evidence of women's lack of progress, it would be foolish to discount the impact of the women's movement on the media. It opened the way for many more women to be hired and for some to move into responsible positions. It moved stories about issues of special interest to women onto the front pages, at least to some degree. It led to new magazines with titles like *Working Women, Savvy,* and *Working Mother,* which contain popularized versions of some liberal feminist ideas. As Diane Sawyer, the first woman broadcaster chosen for CBS's *60 Minutes* news program, put it, the presence of women has not changed news coverage, but it means "on the margins you may end up with a very subtle nuance, an inclusion of something that might not have been included otherwise."[201]

Journalists always have the option of including or excluding details, which different reporters do differently. Therefore it stands to reason that women, who are socialized differently than men, may not report exactly the same way as men. Yet the adherence by both sexes to professional values, to which individuals must subscribe if they are to be hired and move ahead in the mainstream media, serves to wipe out most, if not all, of the differences.

As a result, it is not the participation of women in the media, but their power, that becomes the issue. Women operate at a disadvantage because the norms and patterns as well as the language of news—considered the most substantial media offering—reflect male orientations. For years, for example, newspapers insisted on calling women either Miss or Mrs., which made an issue of their marital status, while males either were addressed as Mr. or by their last names.

Feminists who campaigned for the use of Ms. instead of Mrs. or Miss achieved some success by the early 1980s when about half of the nation's newspapers and magazines adopted Ms., according to Richard L. Tobin, a former editor who conducts an annual survey of language usage.[202] Since then the number has dwindled. Very few publications "now use it on the editorial pages although it can be found among weddings, funerals and social events," Tobin reported in 1989, explaining that publications either are sticking with Mr., Miss, and Mrs. or dropping courtesy titles entirely.[203] An exception is the *New York Times,* which adopted Ms. in 1986 after years of resistance to the term. It inaccurately referred to Geraldine Ferraro, who does not use her husband's surname, as Mrs. Ferraro during her 1984 vice-presidential campaign.[204]

In spite of women on copy desks, newspapers still are filled with news articles that incorporate sexist language and assumptions. According to a Minnesota journalism professor, this is a typical lead: "Five blacks broke into the home of a white school teacher, beat him, raped his wife and smashed and looted everything they could find."[205]

The woman is presented as part of the property of the male homeowner who was victimized.[206]

The *Associated Press Stylebook*, known as "The Journalist's Bible" because most newspapers get news from AP and follow its style, calls for women to receive "the same treatment as men in all areas of coverage."[207] The stylebook decrees that "physical descriptions, sexist references, demeaning stereotypes and condescending phrases should not be used."[208] Yet it is full of stereotypical examples, such as "She was as pretty as Marilyn" to illustrate the correct usage of "as."[209] It also calls for use of "man" or "mankind" when "both men and women are involved," warning, "Do not use duplicate phrases such as a man or a woman or mankind and womankind."[210]

In regard to courtesy titles, AP writers are instructed to use Miss, Mrs., Ms., or no title before the last name of a woman, depending on her preference, which must be determined by reporters regardless of the effort involved.[211] The AP thinks it important to label women as married, single, or not willing to specify (thus upholding the old idea that most women gain their identity from males). It does not instruct reporters to determine whether men prefer to be labeled as married, single or unwilling to specify. Women are still pictured as separate and not equal in the *AP Stylebook*.

Conclusion

In short, the media have changed slowly as a result of the women's movement. Significantly, the movement prompted courageous acts on the part of media women who put their own careers on the line to challenge discrimination within their own organizations. These actions—lawsuits and federal complaints of discrimination—unquestionably had an impact in the 1970s. Women served to mediate between the movement and the male-dominated media world, forcing some modifications that would have occurred to an even lesser extent had women not been part of the media itself. One result of more equal hiring and promotion practices has been a double-edged sword: Employers have gained the benefit of a new and relatively cheaper source of labor—women—while women have gained opportunities previously foreclosed.

In their efforts to better themselves, women have been caught in ideological and economic conflicts. One such conflict involves the ideology of the news: that it be unbiased and neutral. The women's movement may have broadened assumptions about the news, but it has not changed mainstream ideas.

Similarly, media techniques and operating procedures have remained the same. Reporters are trained to be detached observers—a role that is difficult for committed feminists to play and still remain within the mainstream media. While women's own media have been essential to networking among feminists, they have not reached a mainstream audience, although ideas initially presented there may work their way into the mainstream. Women who succeed in the mainstream media have to operate according to the same values as those in command, or not move ahead.

Yet some evidence exists that women have added a feminist perspective to some issues. According to David Shaw, media reporter for the *Los Angeles Times*, the "culture" in metropolitan newsrooms "automatically embraces the abortion rights side of the [abortion] argument," largely because of pro-choice women journalists.[212] Some authorities say that the increased presence of women in the press corps has contributed to public scrutiny of the private lives of presidential candidates like Gary Hart.[213] According to Cokie Roberts of National Public Radio, women journalists have brought an end to the "unwritten rule" by which reporters closed their eyes to candidates' marital indiscretions.[214]

Overall, however, the presence of women in the media illustrates an ideological conflict in feminism itself. During the 1970s the women's movement pressed for equality on the idealistic premise that, once given equality, women would prove less selfish, greedy, and socially irresponsible than men. So far, women have not achieved equality; but to achieve what success they have attained, it appears they have had to conform to male standards that undercut feminist objectives. They also have taken on double responsibilities: raising children and taking care of the home as well as participating in paid employment.

This has had a tremendous impact on media audiences. Women have less time to read, with the percentage who were frequent newspaper readers dropping from 61 percent in 1982 to only 45 percent in 1987, according to one study.[215] Yet they increased their readership of magazines and books.[216] Television viewing also markedly declined among working women.

This is not to say that men have remained newspaper readers either. Young people of both sexes are becoming alienated from the news, a 1990 survey by the Times Mirror Corporation, which owns the *Los Angeles Times*, *Baltimore Sun*, and other newspapers, shows. The survey concluded that persons of ages 18 to 29 "know less and care less about news and public affairs than any other generation of Americans in the past 50 years."[217] Newspapers are losing readers of both sexes, but losing women at a faster rate than men. (Male readership dropped from 63 percent in 1982 to 53 percent in 1987.)[218]

In response to social currents in the past decade, feminism has retreated somewhat from the equality position and moved to a cultural feminism mode in which women's traditional qualities of nurturing, emotiveness, and caring are highlighted. To retreat too far in this direction, however, undercuts the political and legal action essential to integrate women fully into public life.

As an ultimate irony, the newspaper industry, in an attempt to regain women readers, is even considering a return to the women's pages. A team headed by Colleen Dishon, associate editor of the *Chicago Tribune*, has developed a prototype, "Womenews," described as a "weekly news report for women on the move," which has been widely circulated to editors and publishers.[219] The entire third page of the full-color 14-page prototype, designed for national circulation, featured a story on Anna Quindlen, who quit writing a feminist column called "Life in the 30s" for the *New York Times* to stay home with her third child and work on a novel.[220] Although the story explains that Quindlen is returning to the *Times* as a weekly columnist on the op-ed page, the focus is on her decision to leave her job.

"I think this is what feminism has always looked like—ordinary women who want the best for themselves, the best for their daughters and the best for their sons," she is quoted as saying.[221] "I gave up this really terrific job to lay the groundwork for future feminists."[222] To many, however, she might be seen as a "superwoman," whose achievements set her far off from the average women that newspapers seek to keep as readers. How many women can afford to stay home with children when dual incomes are needed to maintain most families?

If newspapers lose readers, they are bound to lose advertisers, who provide the financial bases for both print and commercial broadcasting (exclusive of most cable operations). Advertising, however, is often detrimental to efforts to obtain equality, simply because sexism sells. While the civil rights movement made it unacceptable to be an overt racist, to date feminists have not managed to make it unacceptable to be a sexist openly.[223] This can be seen in numerous "gag" gifts, like women's underpants used as automobile trash bags (conveying the "women as garbage" theme).[224] It also comes through in messages from mainstream advertisers who urge women to buy products so they can compete with other women in vying for male attention.[225]

The heavy-handed influence of advertising on media directed to women can be illustrated by the case of *Ms.* magazine, which died as an advertising-supported magazine in early 1990. A few months later it underwent a metamorphosis into an adless publication, designed to pursue environmental causes and to link up with the Third World. In a scathing indictment of advertising written for the new publication, Gloria Steinem, founding editor, detailed the demands that advertisers had made on *Ms.* to push their products.[226] Here is one example: When an article appeared on Soviet women, cosmetics advertisers threatened to cancel their ads because Soviet women photographed for the cover were wearing little or no makeup.[227]

According to a black feminist columnist, the old *Ms.* "snootily" defined feminism "as the property of the upscale white-warrior class."[228] If so, one wonders how much was due to the ideology of advertisers as well as to the ideology of its editors. Unlike the civil rights struggle, feminism was not embraced by all classes of women and men, but mainly by upper-middle-class women able to compete with men professionally.[229]

Within and without the media, these women now face the challenge of making feminism meaningful to younger women who see it as a pejorative term. After the defeat of the Equal Rights Amendment, a feminist columnist who is a college professor wrote in the *New York Times*, "My students told me they objected to feminism because it made women bitter, angry and unattractive to men."[230] Unaware of the discrimination that led their mother's generation into the women's movement, they were ready to embrace the "feminine mystique" that Friedan exposed in 1963.

It appears that feminists now need to find a way to meld values attributed to men with those attributed to females. Otherwise the effects of the women's movement may be eclipsed. As one writer put it, the movement "has lured so many women away from small, nurturing things and into the hard-driving competitive male world, even into such big, un-nurturing things as science, engineering and the military."[231] To these big things, of course, should be added the media.

Some supposedly "male values" speak to excellence within human beings: individualism, reason, the quest for truth, discoveries.[232] These are the values that underlie objective reporting and freedom of the press in a democratic society. But who can argue that these values should not also incorporate social harmony and caring for others, which are supposedly "feminine" concepts. It is impossible to associate either set of values exclusively with either gender without falling into a trap of stereotypical thinking. Most individuals, as well as societies, subscribe to mixtures of the two.

This does not mean that there is no such thing as male domination or injustice to women. The media have not treated women fairly. The conventions of American journalism evolved without input from women in terms of what or who is newsworthy, how reporting is routinized, and what organizational forms are used.[233]

According to Susan Faludi, a *Wall Street Journal* reporter and Pulitzer prizewinner, the press helped create a "backlash" against women's rights in the 1980s. Faludi attributed this to its ability to coin catchy terms that retarded women's progress. These included "the man shortage," "the biological clock," "the mommy track," and "postfeminism."[234]

It is now time to seek new input from women, if the media would continue to attract them as readers and viewers. The women's movement succeeded in presenting at least a minimum of feminist ideas before a mainstream audience, as well as gaining more employment opportunities for women. But any dialogue between advocates for women and the media power structure has been limited to issues raised by a relatively few columnists. To the extent that women, within and without the media, engage in public discussions of feminism (defined as the theory of the political, economic, and social equality of the sexes) as well as debate what makes up women's culture, societal interests are well served. More opportunity for this dialogue to take place is needed.

Notes

1. Martha Leslie Allen, "The Development of Communication Networks among Women, 1963–1983," unpublished Ph.D. dissertation, Howard University, 1988, p . 287.

2. Carl W. Ackerman, "The Inside of a Newspaper Should Be Like the Inside of the Home," text of speech given at the American Press Institute, Columbia University, June 6, 1949, Box 164, Ackerman Papers, Manuscript Division, Library of Congress.

3. "For Men: Ten Commandments for Working with Women," and "For Women: Your Dealings with Men," Associated Press (AP) Managing Editors Association Guidelines, 1969.

4. See Gaye Tuchman, "The Symbolic Annihilation of Women by the

Mass Media," in Tuchman, Arlene Kaplan Daniels, and James Benet, *Hearth & Home: Images of Women in the Mass Media* (New York: Oxford University Press, 1978), pp. 3–38.

5. Betty Friedan, *The Feminine Mystique* (New York: Dell Publishing, 1963), p. 197.

6. William H. Chafe, *The American Woman* (New York: Oxford University Press, 1972), p. 218.

7. Eugenia Kaledin, *Mothers and More: American Women in the 1950s* (Boston: Twayne Publishers, 1984), pp. 61–62.

8. Chafe, *American Woman,* p. 218.

9. "Women Hold Third of Jobs," *Life* (December 24, 1956), pp. 30–35.

10. As noted in Sara Evans, *Personal Politics* (New York: Vintage, 1979), p. 16.

11. See Helen B. Shaffer, "Women's Consciousness Raising," in *The Women's Movement* (Washington, DC: Editorial Research Reports, 1973), p. 11.

12. As discussed by Jane De Hart Mathews, "The New Feminism and the Dynamics of Social Change," in Linda K. Kerber and Jane De Hart Mathews, eds., *Women's America: Refocusing the Past* (New York: Oxford University Press, 1982), p. 407.

13. Carol Hymowitz and Michaele Weissman, *A History of Women in America* (New York: Bantam, 1978), p. 342.

14. Charles W. Whalen, Jr., "Unlikely Hero," *Washington Post*, January 2, 1984, p. A21.

15. Whalen, "Unlikely Hero," p. A21.

16. Judith Hole and Ellen Levine, *Rebirth of Feminism* (New York: Quadrangle, 1971), p. 95.

17. Excerpts from NOW Statement of Purpose, adopted at Organizational Conference, Washington, DC, October 29, 1966.

18. Excerpts from NOW Statement of Purpose.

19. Evans, *Personal Politics*, p. 154.

20. Evans, *Personal Politics*, p. 120.

21. Anne Mather, "A History of Feminist Periodicals, Part II," *Journalism History* 1 (Winter 1974/75): 108–11.

22. Mather, "History of Feminist Periodicals," p. 109.

23. David Armstrong, *A Trumpet to Arms: Alternative Media in America* (Boston: South End Press, 1981), p. 226.

24. Armstrong, *A Trumpet to Arms*, p. 227.

25. To date, only two books on the history of women journalists have been written. See Ishbel Ross, *Ladies of the Press* (New York: Harper & Brothers, 1936) and Marion Marzolf, *Up from the Footnote* (New York: Hastings House, 1977). Neither book is documented.

26. Ellen M. Oldham, "Early Women Printers of America," *Boston Public Library Quarterly* 10 (April–June 1958): 78–82, 150–52.

27. Richard Kluger, *The Paper: The Life and Death of the* New York Herald Tribune (New York: Vintage, 1986), pp. 59–61. For a full discussion of Margaret Fuller as a journalist, see Catherine Mitchell, "The *Tribune*'s Star: Margaret Fuller's New York Journalism," unpublished Ph.D. dissertation, University of Tennessee, 1987.

28. Edith May Marken, "Women in American Journalism before 1900," unpublished master's thesis, University of Missouri, 1932, pp. 51–54.

29. Barbara Welter, "The Cult of True Womanhood: 1820–1860," *American Quarterly* 18 (Summer 1966): 151.

30. Madelon G. Schilpp and Sharon M. Murphy, *Great Women of the Press* (Carbondale: Southern Illinois Press, 1983), pp. 38–39.

31. Bertha-Monica Stearns, "Reform Periodicals and Female Reformers, 1830–1860," *American Historical Review* 37 (July 1932): 686.

32. Jane Grey Swisshelm, *Half a Century* (Chicago: Jansen, McClurg, 1880), p. 130.

33. Swisshelm, *Half a Century*, p. 135.

34. Maurine H. Beasley, *The First Women Washington Correspondents* (Washington, DC: George Washington University, 1976), pp. 19, 24; also see "Women and the Reporters' Gallery," *Journalist* 11 (May 24, 1870): 13.

35. Austine Snead to Rutherford B. Hayes, January 10, 1887, Snead papers, Rutherford B. Hayes Library, Fremont, OH.

36. U.S. Census Bureau figures as quoted in Marken, "Women in American Journalism before 1900," p. 129.

37. Frank Luther Mott, *American Journalism, 1690–1960* (New York: Macmillan, 1962), p. 599.

38. Theodora P. Martin, *The Sound of Our Own Voices* (Boston: Beacon, 1987), p. 48.

39. Mrs. J. C. Croly (Jennie June), *The History of the Woman's Club Movement in America* (New York: Henry G. Allen, 1898), pp. 340–41. See also "The Women's National Press Association," *New Cycle,* organ of the General Federation of Women's Clubs (October 1895): 296–97.

40. Mott, *American Journalism*, p. 599.

41. See *The Journalist* (January 26, 1889).

42. Lucy Wilmot Smith, "Some Female Writers of the Negro Race," *Journalist* (January 26, 1889).

43. Schilpp and Murphy, *Great Women of the Press*, pp. 125–28.

44. Linda Steiner, "Finding Community in 19th Century Suffrage Periodicals," *American Journalism* 1 (Summer 1983): 9–12.

45. Sherilyn Cox Bennion, "Early Western Publications Expose Women's Suffrage Cries," *Matrix* 64 (Summer 1979): 6–9.

46. Ross, *Ladies of the Press*, p. 123.

47. Nancy Baker Jones, "Ida Husted Harper and the Leslie Bureau of Suffrage Education," unpublished paper given at convention of Association for Education in Journalism, Memphis, August 1985, pp. 1–5.

48. Linda Simon, "Introduction to Ida M. Tarbell, *All in the Day's Work* (Boston: G. K. Hall, 1985, reprint of 1939 edition), p. xi.

49. Lonnelle Aikman, draft of first chapter of proposed book on the Women's National Press Club, Box 23, Women's National Press Club files (hereafter referred to as WNPCF), National Press Club Archives (hereafter referred to as NPCA), Washington, DC.

50. Florence R. Boys, woman's page editor of the *Plymouth* (Indiana) *Pilot*, as quoted in "Women and the Newspaper," University of Missouri Bulletin, Journalism Series No. 30, 1924, p. 13.

51. Helen Ross Lantz, "Seven Sisters with Vision," *Matrix* 29 (August 1944): 5.

52. Josephine Caldwell Meyer, "A B C for Jobs," *Matrix* 25 (August 1940): 10–11.

53. Kathleen K. Keeshen, "Journalism's Pulitzer Penwomen," unpublished paper prepared as part of Ph.D. coursework in American studies, University of Maryland, February 1978, p. 12.

54. Carl W. Ackerman, *Report of the Dean of the Graduate School of Journalism for the Academic Year Ending June 30, 1935* (New York: Columbia University, 1935), p. 8.

55. Susan Ware, *Holding Their Own: American Women in the 1930s* (Boston: Twayne, 1982), p. 74.

56. Philip W. Porter and Norval N. Luxon, *The Reporter and the News* (New York: D. Appleton-Century, 1935), p. 8.

57. Ross, *Ladies of the Press*, pp. 3–13.

58. Ross, *Ladies of the Press,* p. 13.

59. Eleanor Roosevelt, *This I Remember* (New York: Harper & Brothers, 1949), p. 102.

60. List of newspaperwomen eligible to attend Mrs. Roosevelt's Press Conferences, Box 6, Eleanor Roosevelt Press Conference Association Papers, Franklin D. Roosevelt Library (hereafter referred to as FDRL), Hyde Park, NY.

61. Ruby A. Black, " 'New Deal' for New Women in Capital," *Editor & Publisher*, February 10, 1932, p. 11.

62. Eleanor Roosevelt to Lorena Hickok, April 3, 1933, Box 1, Lorena Hickok Papers, FDRL.

63. "Employers' Symposium," *Matrix* 26 (October 1940): 7–8.

64. Iona Robertson Logie, *Careers for Women in Journalism: A Composite Picture of 881 Salaried Women Writers at Work in Journalism, Advertising, Publicity and Promotion* (Scranton, PA: International Textbook, 1938), pp. 155–57.

65. Logie, *Careers for Women in Journalism*, p. 155.

66. Logie, *Careers for Women in Journalism*, pp. 69–70.

67. Logie, *Careers for Women in Journlaism*, p. 154.

68. Walter A. Lowen and Lillian E. Watson, *How to Get a Job and Win Success in Advertising* (New York: Prentice-Hall, 1941), p. 284.

69. Lowen and Watson, *How to Get a Job and Win Success in Advertising*, p. 291.

70. Abbie A. Amrine, "This Is Our Day," *Matrix* 27 (October 1941): 15.

71. Marzolf, *Up from the Footnote*, p. 69.

72. Marzolf, *Up from the Footnote*, p. 69.

73. Lilya Wagner, *Women Correspondents of World War II* (Westport, CT: Greenwood Press, 1989), p. 2.

74. See list of accredited women journalists in Wagner, *Women Correspondents of World War II*, app. C, pp. 159–62.

75. Stanley Frank and Paul Sann, "Paper Dolls," *Saturday Evening Post* (May 20, 1944): 95.

76. Rosamond Risser Jones, "The Campus Beat," *Matrix* 31 (February 1946): 30.

77. Helen M. Staunton, "Mary Hornaday Protests Bars to Newswomen," clipping from *Editor & Publisher*, July 15, 1944, Box 23, WNPCF, NPCA.

78. Mrs. Craig 'Hell Fire' on Women's Equality," clipping from *Editor & Publisher*, June 17, 1944, Box 23, WNPCF, NPCA. See also Jennifer L. Tebbe, "Elizabeth May Craig," *Notable American Women: The Modern Period* (Cambridge, MA: Belknap Press, 1980), pp. 171–73.

79. Marzolf, *Up from the Footnote*, p. 75.

80. Marzolf, *Up from the Footnote*, p. 207.

81. Marzolf, *Up from the Footnote*, p. 208.

82. Carolyn Bell Hughes, typescript of memoirs for unpublished book on history of Women's National Press Club, April 1968, Box 23, WNPCF, NPCA, p. 4.

83. Hughes memoirs, p. 5.

84. Meyer Berger, *The Story of the* New York Times, *1851–1951* (New York: Simon & Schuster, 1951), p. 494.

85. Elizabeth Maury, "Women's Clubs" column, *Detroit Free Press*, August 21, 1942, as quoted in Judith Paterson, "Among the Hats and Gloves: The Double Message on the Women's Pages, 1949–1970," unpublished paper delivered at American Journalism Historians Association convention, St. Louis, October 4, 1986, p. 1.

86. Malvina Lindsay, "The Gentler Sex" column, *Washington Post*, February 28, 1946, as quoted in Paterson, "Among the Hats and Gloves," p. 1.

87. Ann Geracimos, "Restyling the Women's Pages," *Avenue* (October 1988): 106.

88. As quoted in Marzolf, *Up from the Footnote*, p. 74.

89. Betty Angelo, "Career: Metropolitan vs. Community Newspaper," *Matrix* 39 (October/November 1953): 14.

90. Millie Willett, "Career vs. the Home and Family," *Matrix* 44 (June/July 1965): 3.

91. Marzolf, *Up from the Footnote*, p. 74.

92. Mary D. Keyserling, "Women Journalists and Today's World," *Matrix* 50 (April 1965): 11.

93. Speech by Helen Thomas at unveiling of plaque honoring Anne Royall, first woman to cover Congress, Hart Senate Office Building, Washington, DC, May 22, 1990.

94. Thomas speech.

95. Kluger, *Paper*, pp. 440–41.

96. Kluger, *Paper*, p. 441.

97. Marzolf, *Up from the Footnote*, pp. 145–46.

98. Loren Ghiglione, *The American Journalist: Paradox of the Press* (Washington, DC: The Library of Congress, 1990), p. 17.

99. Diane E. Loupe, "Storming and Defending the Color Barrier at the University of Missouri School of Journalism: The Lucile Bluford Case," paper presented at annual convention of the Association for Education in Journalism and Mass Communication, Washington, DC, August 1989, p. 20.

100. Oral history interview of Alice Dunnigan by Marcia Greenlee, April 8, 1977, Oral History–31, Schlesinger Library, Radcliffe College, Cambridge, MA, pp. 25–26.

101. Dunnigan interview, p. 26.

102. Dunnigan interview, p. 26.

103. Oral history interview of Ethel L. Payne by Kathleen Currie, September 8, 1987, Washington Press Club Foundation oral history project, Washington, DC, p. 46, NPCA.

104. Payne interview, p. 46.

105. Payne interview, p. 48.

106. Payne interview, p. 48.

107. Ghiglione, *American Journalist*, p. 120.

108. Ghiglione, *American Journalist*, p. 122.

109. Kay Mills, *A Place in the News: From the Women's Pages to the Front Page* (New York: Dodd, Mead, 1988), p. 1.

110. Mills, *Place in the News*, p. 1.

111. David Broder, *Behind the Front Page: A Candid Look at How News Is Made* (New York: Simon & Schuster, 1987), pp. 127–28.

112. Broder, *Behind the Front Page*, p. 128.

113. As quoted in Broder, *Behind the Front Page*, p. 126.

114. Betty Friedan, *The Feminine Mystique: Twentieth Anniversary Edition* (New York: Laurel, 1983), pp. 6–7.

115. Friedan, *Feminine Mystique: Twentieth Anniversary*, p. 7.

116. Friedan, *Feminine Mystique: Twentieth Anniversary*, p. 54.

117. Ethel Strainchamps, ed., *Rooms with No View: A Woman's Guide to the Man's World of the Media* (New York: Harper & Row, 1974), p. 27.

118. Lindsy Van Gelder as quoted in Gaye Tuchman, *Making News: A Study in the Construction of Reality* (New York: Free Press, 1978), p. 138.

119. Tuchman, *Making News*, p. 146.

120. Marilyn Greenwald, "All Brides Are Not Beautiful: The Influence of Charlotte Curtis on Women's News Coverage at the *New York Times*,"

unpublished paper presented at Association for Education in Journalism and Mass Communication, Minneapolis, August 1990.

121. See Zena Beth Guenin (McGlashan), "Women's Pages in American Newspapers: Missing Out on Contemporary Content," *Journalism Quarterly* 52 (Spring 1975): 66–69, 75.

122. Lindsy Van Gelder, "Women's Pages: You Can't Make News Out of a Silk Purse," *Ms.* (November 1974): 12.

123. Ann Snitow, Christine Stansell, and Sharon Thompson, eds., *Powers of Desire: The Politics of Sexuality* (New York: Monthly Review Press, 1983), p. 37.

124. See Nicholas Von Hoffman, "Women's Pages: An Irreverent View," *Columbia Journalism Review* 10 (1971): 52–54.

125. See "Raising Children in a Changing Society," General Mills American Family Report 1976/77, Box 125, Public Relations Society of America Papers, State Historical Society of Wisconsin, Madison (hereafter referred to as PRSA, SHSW).

126. "Raising Children in a Changing Society," Box 125, PRSA, SHSW, p. 20.

127. "Raising Children in a Changing Society," Box 125, PRSA, SHSW, p. 27.

128. See *Media Report to Women* (February 1, 1976): 5.

129. Alice E. Courtney and Sarah Wernick Lockeretz, "A Woman's Place: An Analysis of the Roles Portrayed by Women in Magazine Advertisements," *Journal of Marketing Research* 8 (February 1971): 92–95.

130. See "Advertising Portraying or Directed to Women," release of the National Advertising Review Board, New York, 1975.

131. As cited in Linda Reed, "A Paradox: The Role of Women in Journalism," *Communication: Journalism Education Today* (Winter 1975): 2.

132. See Ralph M. Jennings et al., "Television Station Employment Practices: The Status of Minorities and Women," report prepared for the United Church of Christ, New York, 1972.

133. Doris Quinn, "Are We Going for a Discount Price?" *Matrix* 56 (Summer 1971): 12–15.

134. Quinn, "Are We Going for a Discount Price?" p. 12.

135. See Won Chang et al., "Women's Page Editors: Self-perceived Status," paper presented at the annual meeting of the Association for Education in Journalism, San Diego, August 1974.

136. Marion Marzolf, "The History of Women Journalists," unpublished paper presented in the Distinguished Lecture Series on Women in the Mass Media, University of Maryland, College Park, February 24, 1977, p. 18.

137. Michael Emery and Edwin Emery, *The Press and America: An Interpretive History of the Mass Media*, 6th ed. (Englewood Cliffs, NJ: Prentice-Hall, 1988), pp. 485–86.

138. Marzolf, "History of Women Journalists," p. 18.

139. Peggy Simpson, "The Meek Shall Not Inherit the Newsroom," *Quill* 78 (February 1990): 35.

140. For a discussion of the impact of legal actions on newspapers, see Mills, *Place in the News*, pp. 149–72.

141. Marzolf, "History of Women Journalists," p. 19.

142. Federal Communications Commission, *Report and Order*, Docket No. 19269, RM-1722, released December 28, 1971.

143. David H. Hosley and Gayle K. Yamada, *Hard News: Women in Broadcast Journalism* (New York: Greenwood Press, 1987), pp. 62–66.

144. Nancy Dickerson, *Among Those Present: A Reporter's View of Twenty-five Years in Washington* (New York: Random House, 1976), pp. 207–8.

145. Marlene Sanders and Marcia Rock, *Waiting for Prime Time: The Women of Television News* (Urbana: University of Illinois Press, 1988), p. 23.

146. Hosley and Yamada, *Hard News*, p. 106.

147. Louise Crosby Spieler, "Catherine Mackin: Trailblazer for Women in Broadcast Journalism," unpublished master's degree thesis, University of Maryland, p. 3.

148. Spieler, "Catherine Mackin," pp. 3–4.

149. Hosley and Yamada, *Hard News*, p. 108.

150. Spieler, "Catherine Mackin," p. 59.

151. Mills, *Place in the News*, p. 167.

152. Mills, *Place in the News*, p. 167.

153. Peggy Simpson, "The Shock of Recognition," *Quill* 78 (February 1990): 34.

154. Simpson, "Shock of Recognition," p. 34.

155. Mills, *Place in the News*, pp. 150–51.

156. Simpson, "Meek Shall Not Inherit the Newsroom," p. 34.

157. Mills, *Place in the News*, p. 155.

158. Letter from Melvin Mencher to Maurine Beasley, February 25, 1985.

159. See Maurine Beasley, "The Women's National Press Club: Case Study of Professional Aspirations," *Journalism History* 15 (Winter 1988): 112–20.

160. Paul V. Peterson, "Enrollment Surged Again, Increases 7 Percent to 70,601," *Journalism Educator* 33 (January 1979): 3.

161. Mary E. Utting, "Through the Years, Women Find Niche in Newspapers," *Women in Communications Inc. National Newsletter* (October 1979): 5.

162. Emery and Emery, *Press and America*, p. 664.

163. Peggy Simpson, "And Now, Real Power," *Quill* 78 (February 1990): 35.

164. Emery and Emery, *Press and America*, pp. 657–58.

165. *Presstime* (January 1987), as reprinted in Emery and Emery, *Press and America*, pp. 659–60.

166. Nancy Barnett, "Women and the Economy," in Sara E. Rix, ed., *The*

American Woman 1987–88: A Report in Depth (New York: Norton, 1987), p. 105.

167. Lee Stinnett, ed., *The Changing Face of the Newsroom* (Reston, VA: American Society of Newspaper Editors, 1989), p. 13.

168. Stinnett, *Changing Face of the Newsroom*, p. 19.

169. Stinnett, *Changing Face of the Newsroom*, p. 10.

170. Stinnett, *Changing Face of the Newsroom*, p. 19.

171. Stinnett, *Changing Face of the Newsroom*, p. 19.

172. Mills, *Place in the News*, p. 213.

173. Mills, *Place in the News*, p. 155.

174. Mills, *Place in the News*, p. 155.

175. Mills, *Place in the News*, p. 3.

176. Clark Newsom, "Job Testing," *Presstime* (October 1986): 38.

177. Ramona R. Rush, "A Different Call to Arms: Women in the Core of the Communications Revolution," unpublished paper presented to the Association for Education in Journalism and Mass Communication, Corvallis, OR, August 1983, p. 17.

178. Ramona R. Rush and Sonia Gutiérrez-Villalobos, "From Making of Myths into Hardening of Realities: Media Images and Employment of Women—Case in Point, Latin America," unpublished paper presented to the Association for Education in Journalism and Mass Communication, Minneapolis, August 1990, p. 10.

179. See Susan H. Miller, "Was 'Pink Collar' Ghetto Study Deliberate Sensationalism?" *Editor & Publisher*, November 23, 1985, pp. 31–33, 52.

180. As quoted in Miller, "Was 'Pink Collar' Ghetto Study Deliberate Sensationalism?" p. 52.

181. Mills, *Place in the News*, p. 10.

182. "Where Are Women in the Media? A Summary of Two New Studies," press kit, Women, Men, and Media conference, Washington, DC, April 10, 1989, p. 1.

183. "Where Are Women in the Media?" p. 2.

184. "Where Are Women in the Media?" p. 2.

185. "Where Are Women in the Media?" p. 3.

186. "Where Are Women in the Media?" p. 4.

187. "Where Are Women in the Media?" p. 3.

188. Sally Steenland, "Women in Broadcasting," in Rix, ed., *The American Woman*, 1987–88, p. 217.

189. "About and by Women," report of the Human Resources Committee, American Society of Newspaper Editors, Reston, VA, 1990, p. 2.

190. "About and by Women," p. 11.

191. "About and by Women," pp. 11–12.

192. Eleanor Randolph, "The Newspaper Editors, at a Loss for Words," *Washington Post*, April 4, 1990, pp. B1, 4.

193. "About and by Women," p. 7.

194. Judy Mann, "A Touch of Relevance," *Washington Post*, April 4, 1990, p. D3.

195. Lee B. Becker and Thomas E. Engleman, "1987 Journalism and Mass Communications Graduate Survey," unpublished report, Dow Jones Newspaper Fund/Ohio State University School of Journalism, pp. 14–17.

196. Elizabeth L. Toth, "Feminist Communication Perspectives for Gender Issues in Public Relations," unpublished paper presented at the Association for Education in Journalism and Mass Communication, Minneapolis, August 1990, p. 1.

197. Carolyn Cline, Elizabeth Toth, Judy Van Turk, Lynn Masel Walters, N. Johnson, and H. Smith, *The Velvet Ghetto: The Impact of the Increasing Percentage of Women in Public Relations and Business Communication* (San Francisco: International Association of Business Communicators Foundation, 1986), pp. x–1.

198. Michael Winkleman, "The Seventh Annual Women's Survey," *Adweek* (June 5, 1989): W4.

199. Maurine Beasley, "Journalism Schools Do Not Prepare Their Students for the Realities They Will Face after Graduation," *Chronicle of Higher Education* (May 23, 1990): B1.

200. Beasley, "Journalism Schools Do Not Prepare Their Students for the Realities," p. B1.

201. Jean Gaddy Wilson, "Are Newswomen Changing the News?" *Ms.* (December 1984): 126.

202. Dennis Camire (of the Gannett News Service), "Is 'Ms.' Disappearing from the Lexicon?" *Montgomery* (Maryland) *Journal*, June 23, 1989, p. 2.

203. Camire, "Is 'Ms.' Disappearing from the Lexicon?" p. 2.

204. Betsy Wade, "A Triumph of Reason: The Men at the *Times* Catch Up with the Times," *Ms.* (September 1986): 96.

205. As cited in Jean Ward, "Nondiscriminatory Writing Not High Priority," *Leadtime*, newsletter of Newspaper Division, Association for Education in Journalism and Mass Communication (June/July 1990): 5.

206. Ward, "Nondiscriminatory Writing Not High Priority," p. 5.

207. For a full discussion of the *AP Stylebook*'s references to women, see Carole Eberly, "The Journalist's Bible: Bad News for Women," unpublished paper presented at the Association for Education in Journalism and Mass Communication, Minneapolis, August 1990.

208. Christopher W. French and Norm Goldstein, eds., *The Associated Press Stylebook and Libel Manual* (New York: Associated Press, 1989), p. 231.

209. French and Goldstein, *Associated Press Stylebook and Libel Manual*, p. 74.

210. French and Goldstein, *Associated Press Stylebook and Libel Manual*, p. 127.

211. Eberly, "Journalist's Bible: Bad News for Women," p. 10.

212. David Shaw, "Can Women Reporters Write Objectively on Abortion Issue?" *PressWoman* (April 1991): 12–13.

213. Larry T. Sabato, *Feeding Frenzy: How Attack Journalism Has Transformed American Politics* (New York: Free Press, 1991), pp. 68–69.

214. As quoted in Sabato, *Feeding Frenzy*, p. 68.

215. Susan H. Miller, "Women's Lifestyles: A Special Report," *Scripps-Howard Editors Newsletter* (Spring 1989).

216. Sherry Robinson, "Newspapers Fail Readers, Wilson Says," *Press Woman Agenda* (August 1990): 5.

217. As reported by Eleanor Randolph, "The No-news Generation," *Washington Post*, June 28, 1990, p. D2.

218. Miller, "Women's Lifestyles," p. 12.

219. Womenews prototype developed by the *Chicago Tribune*, distributed to members of the American Society of Newspaper Editors, April 1990.

220. Lisa Anderson, "One Year Later," in "Womenews," p. 3.

221. Anderson, "One Year Later," p. 3.

222. Anderson, "One Year Later," p. 3.

223. Margaret Engel and Molly Peter, "Sexism Still Sells," *Washington Post*, April 5, 1987, p. C1.

224. Engel and Peter, "Sexism Still Sells," p. C2.

225. Comments by Lana F. Rakow, in response to a paper on advertising, "Don't Hate Me Because I'm Beautiful," presented at the Association for Education in Journalism and Mass Communication, Portland, OR, July 1988.

226. "Steinem to Detail *Ms.* Advertiser Pressure in Re-launch Issue in June," *Media Report to Women* (May/June 1990): 1.

227. "Steinem to Detail *Ms.* Advertiser Pressure," p. 1.

228. Barbara Reynolds, "*Ms.* Turns a New Page for Feminists," *USA Today*, March 23, 1990, p. A11.

229. Engel and Peter, "Sexism Still Sells," p. C1.

230. Susan Jacoby, "Hers," *New York Times*, April 14, 1983, p. C2.

231. Cathy Young, "Women in the '90s—Progress, Paradox and Retreat," *Washington Post*, May 20, 1990, p. B5.

232. Young, "Women in the '90s," p. B5.

233. Bernice Buresh, "Center Takes New Look at News," *JAWS Newsletter* (January 1990): 3. JAWS is the acronym for Journalism and Women Symposium, a non-profit educational corporation to advance the interests of women journalists. It has an office at the University of Missouri–Columbia.

234. Susan Faludi, *Backlash: The Undeclared War against American Women* (New York: Crown, 1991), p. 77.

2
Colonial Era
Mary Katherine Goddard: Petition to U.S. Senate

When the Continental Congress arranged for the first official printing of the Declaration of Independence in 1777, it picked a woman—Mary Katherine Goddard of Baltimore—to do the job.[1] Although this seems surprising today, it attracted no attention at the time. Colonial women acted both as printers and newspaper publishers, frequently following their husbands or relatives into these occupations. About 30 colonial women are known to have been printers, publishers, or typesetters, aside from an uncounted number of others who helped male printers in varying degrees. Of the 30 women, six served as official printers for colonial governments and one for a city government, while 16 published newspapers, pamphlets, and tracts.

Among the most outstanding was Mary Katherine Goddard, a member of a prominent printing family. Both her mother, Sarah Updike Goddard, and her brother, William Goddard, were printers and newspaper publishers in Providence, Rhode Island. Working beside them, Mary Katherine Goddard picked up the printing trade in Rhode Island and later managed her brother's printing plant in Philadelphia. She moved to Baltimore when her brother asked her to take over the *Maryland Journal*, Baltimore's first newspaper, which he had founded in 1773. She ran the newspaper while he traveled through the colonies setting up the forerunner of the present postal service.[2]

Mary Katherine Goddard scored impressive achievements during the Revolution. In addition to printing the Declaration of Independence, she made the *Maryland Journal* one of the most vigorous voices of the rebellious colonies, acted as Baltimore's chief printer, and ran bookselling and bookbinding businesses on the side. She also occupied the responsible position of Baltimore postmistress, giving her a claim to being the first woman ever appointed to federal office.

Described as an "expert and correct compositor of types," she functioned both as a craftswoman and a publisher.[3] In the winter of 1777, the Continental Congress, forced by the British to flee from Philadelphia to Baltimore, authorized her to print the first copy of the Declaration of Independence with the names of the signers attached. It was not easy to publish a newspaper during the Revolution, but Mary Katherine Goddard persisted in spite of paper shortages, inflation, and battles over freedom of the press, making the *Maryland Journal* among the best in the colonies.[4] A keen judge of news, she published "extras" or "extraordinaries," as she called them, on significant events including the battle of Bunker Hill and the Continental Congress's call for arms.[5]

Her efforts failed to bring a just reward. William Goddard was not content to let his sister continue operation of the newspaper after it became successful, and he managed to resume control in 1784, leading to a permanent split between the two. In addition, after 14 years as postmistress she was removed in a case of sex discrimination. In 1789 a new postmaster general directed that she be replaced with a man. No reason was given initially, although later it was explained that the Baltimore post office might be given supervision over other offices and "more travelling might be necessary than a woman could undertake."[6]

More than 200 leading citizens petitioned Postmaster General Samuel Osgood to retain her, and she made personal appeals to both President George Washington and the U.S. Senate. They were to no avail and she was forced to resign, even though the plan to expand the functions of her office was never carried out. As postmistress, she had been entitled to 20 percent of the postal receipts, but she had held office during the war when the position had not been profitable. Naturally she resented being stripped of her post when it started to be lucrative, just as she resented losing the newspaper when it began to make money. She continued to support herself as a bookseller and storekeeper until 1816 when, at the age of 78, she died in Baltimore.[7]

Her unsuccessful petition to the U.S. Senate in 1790 to retain her office as postmistress of Baltimore is reprinted below. It was written in the third person.

PETITION

To the Honorable Senate of the United States.

The Representation of Mary Katherine Goddard humbly sheweth, That She kept the Post Office at Baltimore from the Dissolution of the old Government till the Month of November last, a term of fourteen years and upwards—That from the Non-importation Agreement, and various other causes incident to the Revolution, the Income of the Office was inadequate to its disbursements, as will appear by the Schedule hereunto annexed, and in order to accomplish this undertaking, she was obliged to advance hard money to defray the Charges of Post-Riders for several years, when they were not to be procured on any other terms; during which period, the whole of her labour and industry was necessarily unrewarded; therefore, she with great deference hoped, that having thus established and continued the Office when it was worth no Person's acceptance, She would be considered as worthy of being retained whenever it became more valuable.

That She hath been discharged without the smallest imputation of any Fault, and without any previous notice whatever, till an Order arrived from Mr. Burrell whilst at Baltimore, to deliver up the Office to Mr. White, the Bearer of his note, & although he remained several Days in town, yet he did not think proper to indulge her with a personal interview, whereby she might learn (therein) of her removal, or to what motives, it could possibly be ascribed. Such a Procedure contrasted with her conduct in Office, and the approbation of the public, testified by the number and respectability of these, who addressed Messrs. Osgood & Burrell on her behalf, leave no room to question either her inclination or ability to discharge the duties of her appointment.

That sundry public and private applications, prior to the 19th of November last, were made to the above Gentlemen, praying that She might be restored, but no answer was returned, till the latter End of January when a Mr. Osgood wrote to the Merchants of Baltimore, that the Evil was irremediable by him. During this Interval She flattered herself that so long a consideration of the Subject would have infallibly terminated in her favour; but she has since learned that the neglect proceeded more from contempt than a desire of redress.

She also represents that taking her Office, contrary to the Sense & Expectation of the whole Community, and delaying a determination of her Fate so long, whether she should be restored or not, has greatly augmented her anxiety and distress—these are but poor rewards indeed for fourteen Years faithful Services, performed in the worst of times, and acknowledged in the most public manner by all her Co-temporaries & Superiors in Office in these words, "that no change could possibly be for the benefit of the public."

And further, as it has been universally understood that no Person should be removed from Office under the present Government, unless manifest misconduct appeared, and as no such charge could possibly be made against her, with the least colour of Justice, she was happy in the Idea of being secured both in her employ & the protection of all those who wished well to the federal Cause: And if it should so happen that she should be obliged to make room for one of more worth or interest, that she would notwithstanding be allowed a reasonable time to prepare for the Event.

And although Mr. White who has succeeded her might doubtless have been highly meritorious, in the different Offices he has sustained, yet, she humbly conceives, he was not more worthy of public notice & protection in his Station, than She has uniformly been in hers. It must therefore become a matter of serious importance to her, if Government can find no means of rewarding this Gentleman's Services, but by taking her little Office, established by her own Industry in the best years of her life, & whereon depended all her future Prospects of subsistence. In old Countries, People come in & go out, with the Minister of the day & his party; but here She never could suppose that any Minister, Party, or Individual, would deign to cast a wishful Eye upon so small an Object, whilst in the Hands of such a Professor. Various reasons have from time to time been assigned & abandoned, to sanction her removal, but the only one worthy of either notice or belief, is to the following Effect, though equally fallacious with the rest; . . . That the Deputy at Baltimore will hereaforth be obliged to ride & regulate the Offices to the Southward, but that with great deference to the Post Master General will be found altogether impracticable; because the business of that Office will require his constant attendance, as no other than the Principal alone could possibly be relied on, or give satisfaction to the Merchants who frequently make large remittances by post. If therefore the duties of Mr. Burrell's Office are to be performed by any other than himself, it cannot well be attempted by a Deputy, fully occupied with his own; and if two Persons must be employed, according to his new Plan, She apprehends herself, at least, as well qualified to give the necessary Instructions to the Riding Post Master, as Mr. White, or any other person heretofore unexperienced in such business.

That although it has been suggested that the Income of her Office, for a few years last past, has made her amends for her former assiduity care and expence, yet She would beg leave to observe, that from the many failures which have distressed this Community since the Peace, She has met with her Share of losses and misfortunes, a Truth well known to all her Neighbours; And now to deprive her of this Office, to which She has a more meritorious & just claim than any other person, is a circumstance, pregnant with that Species of aggravation, which a Sense of Ingratitude inspires & which is much easier felt than described.

She therefore humbly hopes that the honorable the Senate will take her case into their serious Consideration & grant her such Assistance, as may be in their Power, in restoring her to the public Confidence & the Enjoyment of her former Office, & She will ever pray . . .

Baltimore 29th Jan. 1790.

M.K. Goddard[8]

Notes

1. John H. Hazelton, *The Declaration of Independence: Its History* (New York: Dodd, Mead, 1906), p. 284.

2. See Maurine H. Beasley, "William Goddard," in Perry J. Ashley, ed., *American Newspaper Journalists: 1690–1872*, vol. 43 of the *Dictionary of Literary Biography* (Detroit: Gale Research, 1985), pp. 248–55.

3. Isaiah Thomas, *The History of Printing in America*, vol. 1 (Worcester, MA: Isaiah Thomas Jr., 1810, reprinted New York: Burt Franklin, 1964), p. 26.

4. Joseph T. Wheeler, *The Maryland Press, 1777–1790* (Baltimore: Maryland Historical Society, 1938), p. 11.

5. Margie Luckett, ed., *Maryland Women*, vol. 1 (Baltimore: By the editor, 1931), p. 169.

6. As quoted in Wheeler, *Maryland Press*, p. 14.

7. See "Mary Katherine Goddard," in Madelon Golden Schilpp and Sharon M. Murphy, eds., *Great Women of the Press* (Carbondale: Southern Illinois University Press, 1983), pp. 12–20.

8. From the files of the Maryland Historical Society.

3

Early Political Journalism
Anne Royall

In the early nineteenth century, opportunities dwindled for women in printing and publishing. Yet the colonial tradition of women journalists did not die out entirely. One especially remarkable woman—Anne Royall—published newspapers in the nation's capital from 1831 until 1854.

As a poverty-stricken young woman from the frontier, Anne Royall had made a Cinderella-like marriage to William Royall, a Revolutionary War hero and Virginia aristocrat. Although she inherited his comfortable estate, his relatives managed to break the will, and at the age of 55 she found herself penniless again. Refusing to beg a pittance from the family, she took an amazing step for a woman of her times, traveling by stagecoach over the raw new nation while writing and marketing ten travel books and a novel describing her experiences.[1]

Living partially on the charity of the Masons, her husband's fraternal brothers, she assailed evangelical groups that were stimulating the anti-Masonic fervor of the day. This led to her conviction in 1829 on the charge of being a "common scold."[2] Two newspapermen paid her fine, saying they acted to uphold freedom of the press.[3]

In 1831 at the age of 61, she settled in Washington and started the first of her two newspapers, *Paul Pry*. It lasted five years and was followed immediately by the *Huntress*, which continued until three months before her death in 1854. Both papers showed her commitment to democratic government and to investigative journalism. As an editor, Anne Royall served as a watchdog of public morals, exposing graft and wrongdoing, campaigning for internal improvements, sound money, states' rights, free schools, free thought, and free speech, and against the Bank of the United States.[4]

Judged by some other Washington journalists as a comic figure, she was miserably poor throughout her long career, and died—as she wrote in the last issue of the *Huntress*—with "but thirty-one cents in the world." She received long overdue recognition in May 1990 when the Society of Professional Journalists placed a plaque in her honor in the Senate Press Gallery in the U.S. Capitol. The plaque refers to Royall as "a fearless champion of freedom of the press" and the "first woman to cover the U.S. Congress."[5]

Anne Royall's vigorous personal style and zeal to expose wrong-doing are illustrated in her farewell editorial in the final issue of *Paul Pry* on November 19, 1836. Two of her chief concerns—fear for her country in the face of the coming Civil War, and worry over her poverty—were voiced in the last issue of the *Huntress*, dated July 24, 1854. The *Paul Pry* editorial and excerpts from the final issue of the *Huntress* are reprinted here.

FROM *PAUL PRY*, NOVEMBER 19, 1836

This is the last appearance of *Paul Pry*. Its first appearance was sudden and unexpected—perhaps unwelcome to many. Its exit is likewise sudden, and probably unlamented: like its namesake in the play, it was no doubt an unwelcome visitor by popping in where it was least looked for.[6]

But while the Editress, noways concerned for the frowns and winks of the enemies of poor *Paul*, would draw a veil over its errors, she must say in its defence, it has done more for its friends than they have done for *Paul*; and they will repent their neglect of its admonitions too late. Had they attended to the warnings of *Paul Pry*, their country would not, as it is, be overrun with public swindlers and land gamblers. Nor has *Paul* been paid for its labors. Like its great predecessor, Paul Jones, it has been treated with ingratitude and shameful neglect![7]

Delinquents, we speak to you. If you have hearts, do not suffer this to pass unheeded. Remember the widow, whose husband spent seven years for you, on the fields of your revolutionary battles, and this at his own cost.

Always in the van of the editorial corps, and attacking the enemies of its country in their strong holds, *Paul Pry* dragged them into open day, and pointed them out to the people!

Paul Pry was the first to sound the alarm that traitors were in the camp. It was the first to proclaim the abandonment of reform by Gen. [Andrew] Jackson.[8] It was the first that discovered, and the first to challenge the Post Office loans and the Post Office frauds. It was the first to challenge the organization of the office-holders as a party, at the 4th of July celebration in

Pittsburg and Brownsville in 1833. It was the first that challenged the Indian land frauds of the great land companies, and the perfidy of the Southern Jackson men in selling the country to Mr. [Martin] Van Buren and his political intriguers, to conceal those frauds.[9] *Paul Pry* was the first to put a stop to the enormous swindling of a knot of "God's people," as they impiously call themselves. That is, "good, sound Presbyterian yankees," under the lead of a certain Mr. WM. A. BRADLEY. Millions of dollars were swallowed up by this concern (thank God for removing two of them out of the way), under pretence of drawing money for corporation debts from Congress.[10] *Paul Pry* was the first to trace those pious rogues to their den, and drag them forth. (May a speedy vengeance overtake them.) And it is to *Paul Pry* the citizens of Washington are chiefly indebted for the last act of Congress in behalf of their Holland debt, by putting it out of the power of this pious Bradley and his friends, to finger the cash.

In return, we are proud to acknowledge that the citizens of Washington have ever been the able, willing, and untiring friends of *Paul Pry*. A thousand years of service of ten such papers, rendered to such people, would not, nor could not repay them!!!!

The Editress has only to say, that if the people will do their duty to themselves as faithfully as she has done by them, all will yet be well! But let no man sleep at his post. Remember, the office-holders are desperate, wakeful and vigilant.[11]

FROM THE *HUNTRESS*, JULY 24, 1854

Perhaps we may never publish another paper. Life is uncertain, though we are at the present writing in perfect health.

We return many thanks to our friends in Philadelphia for their kindness in sending us their papers, viz: the *Post*, *American Courier*, and *Saturday Evening Mail*—without any return. This is too much kindness, especially as we can get them at Shillington's for a trifle. Gentlemen, do not kill us with kindness.

CONGRESS—We trust in heaven for three things. First—that members may give us the *means to pay for this paper*, perhaps three or four cents a member—a few of them are behind hand; but the fault was not theirs; it was owing to Sally's sickness.[12] Others again have paid us from two to six dollars. Our printer is a poor man, and we have but thirty-one cents in the world, and for the first time since we have resided in the city (thirty years), we were unable to pay our last month's rent, only six dollars. Had not our landlord been one of the best of men, we should have been stript by this time; but we shall get that from our humble friends.

Second—That Washington may escape that dreadful scourge, the Cholera.

Our third prayer is that the Union of these States may be eternal.[13]

Notes

1. "Anne Newport Royall," in Madelon Golden Schilpp and Sharon M. Murphy, eds., *Great Women of the Press* (Carbondale: Southern Illinois University Press, 1983), pp. 21–36.

2. See Alice S. Maxwell and Marion B. Dunlevy, *Virago! The Story of Anne Newport Royall (1769–1854)* (Jefferson, NC.: McFarland, 1985), pp. 179–96. The authors treat Royall's case as a political prosecution.

3. Bessie Rowland James, *Anne Royall's U.S.A.* (New Brunswick, NJ: Rutgers University Press, 1972), p. 262. As cited in Maxwell and Dunlevy, *Virago!*, p. 195, Royall wrote that she did not know if the fine was ever paid.

4. Maurine Beasley, "The Curious Career of Anne Royall," *Journalism History* 3 (Winter 1976–77): 98–102, 36.

5. Maurine Beasley, "Anne Royall, Huntress with a Quill," *Quill* 78 (May 1990): 32–35.

6. *Paul Pry* was the name of a popular drama from which the newspaper got its title.

7. John Paul Jones was an American naval hero of the Revolution, who died in poverty.

8. Andrew Jackson was elected president in 1828 and served two terms.

9. Martin Van Buren was elected president in 1836.

10. The former mayor of Washington, William A. Bradley, was a political and personal foe whom Royall accused of profiting unjustly from congressional appropriations in order to pay debts of the District of Columbia.

11. From the Rare Book and Special Collections Division, Library of Congress.

12. Sally Stack Poole was Anne Royall's faithful assistant.

13. From the Rare Book and Special Collections Division, Library of Congress.

4

Reform Periodicals
Jane G. Swisshelm
Amelia Bloomer

Desire to reform society brought a group of independent-minded women into journalism before the Civil War. Their causes included temperance, "moral purity" (elimination of prostitution), dress reform, suffrage, and higher education for women, but the abolition movement drew the greatest concern. Although their periodicals were sometimes greeted with alarmed outcries, the reformers refused to give up. Two of the best known were Jane G. Swisshelm and Amelia Bloomer.[1]

Jane G. Swisshelm

Swisshelm began her career in journalism by submitting contributions to Pennsylvania newspapers. These articles attracted so much attention that it was considered unlikely a woman wrote them, and a rumor circulated that the real author was a member of the state legislature.[2] In 1848 she started the Pittsburgh *Saturday Visiter* in sympathy with the Liberty (antislavery) party. This paper made her one of the best-known abolitionists in the nation.

In 1850, she became the first woman Washington correspondent when Horace Greeley engaged her to write for the *New York Tribune*. Although her stay in the capital was brief, she won equal rights to sit in the Senate press gallery with men—despite Vice-president Millard

Fillmore's warning that "the place would be very unpleasant for a lady."[3]

Separating from her husband in 1857, she took her only child, a daughter, and pioneered on the Minnesota frontier, where she founded another abolitionist newspaper, the *St. Cloud Democrat*, and lectured on behalf of abolition. During the Civil War, she returned to Washington, served as Washington correspondent for her St. Cloud paper, and also took employment as one of the first women clerks in the federal government.[4]

Her autobiography, *Half a Century*, was completed in 1880 when she was 68, and she died in 1884.

Chapters 21 and 22 from *Half a Century*, detailing the founding of the *Saturday Visiter*, follow.

CHAPTER XXI
PITTSBURGH *SATURDAY VISITER*

After the war, abolitionists began to gather their scattered forces and wanted a Liberty Party organ. To meet this want, Charles P. Shiras started the *Albatross* in the fall of '47. He was the "Iron City Poet," author of "Dimes and Dollars" and "Owe No Man a Dollar." He was of an old and influential family, had considerable private fortune, was courted and flattered, but laid himself and gifts on the altar of Liberty. His paper was devoted to the cause of the slave and of the free laborer, and started with bright prospects. He and Mr. Fleeson urged me to become a regular contributor, but Mr. Riddle objected, and the *Journal* had five hundred readers for every one the *Albatross* could hope.[5] In the one I reached the ninety and nine unconverted, while in the other I must talk principally to those who were rooted and grounded in the faith. So I continued my connection with the *Journal* until I met James McMasters, a prominent abolitionist, who said sorrowfully: "Well, the last number of the *Albatross* will be issued on Tuesday."

"Is it possible?"

"Possible and true! That is the end of its first quarter, and Shiras gives it up. In fact we all do. No use trying to support an abolition paper here."

While he spoke a thought struck me like a lightning flash, and he had but finished speaking when I replied:

"I have a great notion to start a paper myself."

He was surprised, but caught at the idea, and said:

"I wish you would. You can make it go if anybody can, and we'll do all we can to help you."

I did not wait to reply, but hurried after my husband, who had passed on, soon overtook and told him the fate of the *Albatross*. For this he was sorry, for he always voted a straight abolition ticket. I repeated to him what I had said to Mr. McMasters, when he said:

"Nonsense!" then reflected a little, and added, "Well, I do not know after all but it would be a good idea. Riddle makes lots of money out of your letters."

When we had talked about five minutes, he turned to attend to business and I went to the *Journal* office, found Mr. Riddle in his sanctum, and told him the *Albatross* was dead, the Liberty Party without an organ, and that I was going to start the Pittsburgh *Saturday Visiter*; the first copy must be issued Saturday week, so that abolitionists would not have time to be discouraged, and that I wanted him to print my paper.

He had pushed his chair back from his desk, and sat regarding me in utter amazement while I stated the case, then said:

"What do you mean? Are you insane? What does your husband say?"

I said my husband approved, the matter was all arranged, I would use my own estate, and if I lost it, it was nobody's affair.

He begged me to take time to think, to send my husband to him, to consult my friends. Told me my project was ruinous, that I would lose every dollar I put into it, and begged, entreated me to take time; but all to no purpose, when a bright idea came to him.

"You would have to furnish a desk for yourself, you see there is but one in this room, and there is no other place for you. You could not conduct a paper and stay at home, but must spend a good deal of time here!"

Then I suddenly saw the appalling prospect thus politely presented. I had never heard of any woman save Mary Kingston working in an office. Her father, a prominent lawyer, had employed her as his clerk, when his office was in their dwelling, and the situation was remarkable and very painful; and here was I, looking not more than twenty, proposing to come into the office of the handsome stranger who sat bending over his desk that he might not see me blush for the unwomanly intent.

Mr. Riddle was esteemed one of the most elegant and polished gentlemen in the city, with fine physique and fascinating manners. He was a man of the world, and his prominence had caused his name to become the target for many an evil report in the bitter personal conflicts of political life. I looked the facts squarely in the face and thought:

"I have been publicly asserting the right of woman to earn a living as book-keepers, clerks, sales-women, and now shall I shrink for fear of a danger any one must meet in doing as I advised? This is my Red Sea. It can be no more terrible than the one which confronted Israel. Duty lies on the other side, and I am going over! 'Speak unto the children of Israel that they go forward.' The crimson waves of scandal, the white foam of gossip, shall part before me and heap themselves up as walls on either hand."

So rapidly did this reflection pass through my mind, or so absorbed was I with it, that there had been no awkward pause when I replied:

"I will get a desk, shall be sorry to be in your way, but there is plenty of room and I can be quiet."

He seemed greatly relieved, and said cheerfully:

"Oh yes, there is plenty of room, I can have my desk moved forward and take down the shutters, when there will be plenty of light. Heretofore you have been Jove thundering from a cloud, but if you will come down to dwell with mortals we must make a place for you."

Taking down the shutters meant exposing the whole interior of the room to view, from a very public street; and after he had exhausted every plea for time to get ready, he engaged to have the first copy of the *Visiter* printed on the day I had set. He objected to my way of spelling the word, but finding I had Johnson for authority, would arrange the heading to suit.

I was in a state of exaltation all forenoon, and when I met my husband at dinner, the reaction had set in, and I proposed to countermand the order, when he said emphatically:

"You will do no such thing. The campaign is coming, you have said you will start a paper, and now if you do not, I will."

The coming advent was announced, but I had no arrangements for securing either advertisements or subscribers. Josiah King, now proprietor of the *Pittsburgh Gazette* and James H. McClelland called at the *Journal* office and subscribed, and with these two supporters, the Pittsburgh *Saturday Visiter*, entered life. The mechanical difficulty of getting out the first number proved to be so great that the forms were not on the press at 3 P.M. By five the streets were so blocked by a waiting crowd, that vehicles went around by other ways, and it was six o'clock, Jan. 20th, 1848, when the first copy was sold at the counter. I was in the editorial room all afternoon, correcting proof to the last moment, and when there was nothing more I could do, was detained by the crowd around the doors until it was after eleven.

Editors and reporters were gathered in the sanctum, and Mr. Riddle stood by his desk pointing out errors to some one who should have prevented them, when I had my wraps on ready to start. Mr. Fleeson, then a clerk on the *Journal*, stepped out, hat in hand, and bowing to the proprietor, said:

"Mr. Riddle, it is your privilege to see Mrs. Swisshelm to her lodgings, but as you seem to decline, I hope you will commission me."

Mr. Fleeson was a small man and Mr. Riddle had drawn himself to his full height and stood looking down at him saying:

"I want it distinctly understood that Mrs. Swisshelm's relations in this office are purely those of business. If she requires anything of any man in it, she will command him and her orders shall be obeyed. She has not ordered my attendance, but has kept her servant here all the evening to see her to her friend's house, and this should be sufficient notice to any gentleman that she does not want him."

During the ten years we used the same editorial-room, Mr. Riddle was often absent on the days I must be there, and always secured plenty of light by setting away the shutters when I entered. He generally made it necessary for me to go to his house and settle accounts, and never found it convenient to offer his escort to any place unless accompanied by his wife.

The *Visiter* was three years old when he turned one day, examined me critically, and exclaimed:

"Why do you wear those hideous caps? You seem to have good hair. Mrs. Riddle says she knows you have, and she and some ladies were wondering only yesterday why you do make yourself such a fright."

The offending cap was a net scarf tied under the chin, and I said, "You know I am subject to quinsy, and this cap protects my tonsils."

He turned away with a sigh, and did not suspect that my tonsils had no such protection outside the office, where I must meet a great many gentlemen and make it apparent that what I wanted of them was votes! votes!! Votes for the women sold on the auction block, scourged for chastity, robbed of their children, and that admiration was no part of my object.

Any attempt to aid business by any feminine attraction was to my mind revolting in the extreme, and certain to bring final defeat. In nothing has the church of Rome shown more wisdom than in the costume of her female missionaries. When a woman starts out in the world on a mission, secular or religious, she should leave her feminine charms at home. Had I made capital of my prettiness, I should have closed the doors of public employment to women for many a year, by the very means which now makes them weak, underpaid competitors in the great workshop of the world.

One day Mr. Riddle said:

"I wish you had been here yesterday. Robert Watson called. He wanted to congratulate us on the relations we have for so long maintained. We have never spoken of it, but you must have known the risk of coming here. He has seen it, says he has watched you closely, and you are an exception to all known law, or the harbinger of a new era in human progress."

Robert Watson was a retired lawyer of large wealth, who watched the world from his study, and philosophized about its doings; and when Mr. Riddle had given me this conclusion, the subject was never again referred to in our years of bargaining, buying and selling, paying and receipting.

CHAPTER XXII.
RECEPTION OF THE *VISITER*

While preparing matter for the first number of the *Visiter*, I had time to think that so far as any organization was concerned, I stood alone. I could not work with Garrison on the ground that the Constitution was pro-slavery, for I had abandoned that in 1832, when our church split on it and I went with the New School, who held that it was then anti-slavery. The Covenantors, before it was adopted, denounced it as a "Covenant with death and an agreement with hell." I had long ago become familiar with the arguments on that side, and I concluded they were fallacious, and could not go back to them even for a welcome into the abolition ranks.

The political action wing of the anti-slavery party had given formal notice that no woman need apply for a place among them. True, there was a large minority who dissented from this action, but there was division enough, without my furnishing a cause for contention. So I took pains to make it understood that I belonged to no party. I was fighting slavery on the frontier plan of Indian warfare, where every man is Captain-lieutenants, all the corporals and privates of his company. I was like the Israelites in the days when there was no king, and "every man did that which was right in his own eyes."

It seemed good unto me to support James G. Birney, for President, and to promulgate the principles of the platform on which he stood in the last election. This I would do, and no man had the right or power to stop me. My paper was a six column weekly, with a small Roman letter head, my motto, "Speak unto the children of Israel that they go forward," the names of my candidates at the head of the editorial column and the platform inserted as standing matter.

It was quite an insignificant looking sheet, but no sooner did the American eagle catch sight of it, than he swooned and fell off his perch. Democratic roosters straightened out their necks and ran screaming with terror. Whig coons scampered up trees and barked furiously. The world was falling and every one had "heard it, saw it, and felt it."

It appeared that on some inauspicious morning each one of three-fourths of the secular editors from Maine to Georgia had gone to his office suspecting nothing, when from some corner of his exchange list there sprang upon him such a horror as he had little thought to see.

A woman had started a political paper! A woman! Could he believe his eyes? A woman! Instantly he sprang to his feet and clutched his pantaloons, shouted to the assistant editor, when he, too, read and grasped frantically at his cassimeres, called to the reporters and pressmen and typos and devils, who all rushed in, heard the news, seized their nether garments and joined the general chorus, "My breeches! oh, my breeches!" Here was a woman resolved to steal their pantaloons, their trousers, and when these were gone they might cry, "Ye have taken away my gods, and what have I more?" The imminence of the peril called for prompt action, and with one accord they shouted, "On to the breach, in defense of our breeches! Repel the invader or fill the trenches with our noble dead."

"That woman shall not have *my* pantaloons," cried the editor of the big city daily; "nor my pantaloons," said the editor of the dignified weekly; "nor my pantaloons," said he who issued manifestos but once a month; "nor mine," "nor mine," "nor mine," chimed in the small fry of the country towns.

Even the religious press could not get past the tailor shop, and "pantaloons" was the watchword all along the line. George D. Prentiss took up the cry, and gave the world a two-third column leader on it, stating explicitly, "She is a man all but the pantaloons." I wrote to him asking a copy of the article, but received no answer, when I replied in rhyme to suit his case:

> Perhaps you have been busy
> Horsewhipping Sal or Lizzie,
> Stealing some poor man's baby,

Selling its mother, may-be.
You say—and you are witty—
That I—and, tis a pity—
Of manhood lack but dress;
But you lack manliness,
A body clean and new,
A soul within it, too.
Nature must change her plan
Ere you can be a man.

This turned the tide of battle. One editor said, "Brother George, beware of sister Jane." Another, "Prentiss has found his match." He made no reply, and it was not long until I thought the pantaloon argument was dropped forever.

There was, however, a bright side to the reception of the *Visiter*. Horace Greeley gave it respectful recognition, so did N. P. Willis and Gen. Morris in the *Home Journal*. Henry Peterson's *Saturday Evening Post, Godey's Lady's Book*, Graham's and Sargent's magazines, and the anti-slavery papers, one and all, gave it pleasant greeting, while there were other editors who did not, in view of this innovation, forget that they were American gentlemen.

There were some saucy notices from "John Smith," editor of *The Great West*, a large literary sheet published in Cincinnati. After John and I had pelted each other with paragraphs, a private letter told me that she, who had won a large reputation as John Smith, was Celia, who afterwards became my very dear friend until the end of her lovely life, and who died the widow of another dear friend, William H. Burleigh.

In the second number of the *Visiter*, James H. McClelland, a secretary of the county convention, published its report and contributed an able article, thus recognizing it as the much needed county organ of the Liberty Party.[6]

Amelia Bloomer

Amelia Bloomer—a governess before her marriage at the age of 21 to Dexter C. Bloomer, a lawyer, editor, and reformer—turned to journalism to promote temperance. Having written articles for her husband's newspaper in Seneca Falls, New York (scene of the first woman's rights convention in 1848), Bloomer started her own temperance newspaper there in January 1849.

The paper, named the *Lily*, attracted notoriety the next year when Bloomer defended the right of women to appear in full pantaloons under short skirts as an alternative to the heavy constricting costumes fashionable in the mid-nineteenth century. Soon she adopted the controversial garb herself, which she wore for six to eight years, and found herself deluged with inquiries about the "bloomer costume." It drew rage from clergy and editors who accused women of wanting to violate established order by wearing "the pants in the family."[7] Like other feminists, Bloomer gave up the attire because of ridicule that deflected attention from other feminist issues.[8]

A friend of Elizabeth Cady Stanton—to whom she introduced Susan B. Anthony, Stanton's partner in the suffrage campaign—Bloomer attended the initial Seneca Falls woman's rights convention and slowly converted to suffrage.[9] Her chief interest, however, remained temperance. She continued to edit the *Lily* when she moved with her husband to Ohio in 1853, but she sold the newspaper when the couple moved two years later to Council Bluffs, Iowa.[10] Happily married to a prosperous man—her husband became mayor of Council Bluffs—Bloomer, like Stanton and Anthony, championed easier divorce laws to improve women's status in marriage.[11] She died in 1894 in Council Bluffs at the age of 76. Her husband then published her writing. Reproduced here are two editorials from the *Lily*. The first explained the rationale for the newspaper. The second advocated giving women legal control over their own property.

FROM THE *LILY*, JANUARY 1849

It is woman that speaks through *The Lily*. It is upon an important subject, too, that she comes before the public to be heard. Intemperance is the great foe to her peace and happiness. It is that above all which has made her home desolate and beggared her offspring. It is that above all which has filled to its brim her cup of sorrow and sent her moaning to the grave. Surely she has a right to wield the pen for its suppression. Surely she may, without throwing aside the modest retirement which so much becomes her sex, use her influence to lead her fellow-mortals away from the destroyer's path. It is this which she proposes to do in the columns of this paper. Like the beautiful flower from which it derives its name, we shall strive to make the *Lily* the emblem of "sweetness and purity"; and may heaven smile upon our attempt to advocate the great cause of Temperance reform![12]

FROM THE *LILY*, MARCH 1850

The legislature of Tennessee have in their wisdom decided after gravely discussing the question that women have no souls, and no right to hold property. Wise men these, and worthy to be honored with seats in the halls of legislation in a Christian land. Women no souls! Then, of course, we are not accountable beings: and if not accountable to our Maker, then surely not to man. Man represents us, legislates for us, and now holds himself accountable for us! How kind in him, and what a weight is lifted from us! We shall no longer be answerable to the laws of God or man, no longer be subject to punishment for breaking them, no longer be responsible for any of our doings. Man in whom iniquity is perfected has assumed the whole charge of us and left us helpless, soulless, defenseless creatures dependent on him for leave to speak or act.

We suppose the wise legislators consider the question settled beyond dispute, but we fear they will have some trouble with it yet. Although it may be an easy matter for them to arrive at such a conclusion, it will be quite another thing to make women believe it. We are not so blind to the weakness or imperfections of man as to set his word above that of our Maker, or so ready to yield obedience to his laws as to place them before the laws of God. However blindly we may be led by him, however much we may yield to his acquired power over us, we cannot yet fall down and worship him as our superior. Some men even act as though women had no souls, but it remained for the legislature of Tennessee to speak it to the world.

We have not designed *ourself* saying much on the subject of "Woman's Rights"; but we see and hear so much that is calculated to keep our sex down and impress us with a conviction of our inferiority and helplessness, that we feel compelled to act on the defensive and stand for what we consider our just rights. If things are coming to such a pass as that indicated by the above decision, we think it high time that women should open their eyes and look where they stand. It is quite time that their rights *should be discussed*, and that woman herself should enter the contest.

We have ever felt that in regard to property, and also as to many other things, the laws were unjust to women. Men make laws without consulting us, and of course they will make them all in their own favor, especially as we are powerless and cannot contend for our rights. We believe that most women are capable of taking care of their own property, and that they have the right to hold it, and to dispose of it as they please, man's decision to the contrary notwithstanding. As for ourselves, we have no fears but we could take care of a fortune if we had one, without any assistance from legislators or lawyers, and we should think them meddling with what did not concern them should they undertake to control it for us.

The legislature of our own state has taken a step in advance on this subject and granted to women the right to their own property. We trust this is but a forecast of the enlightened sentiment of the people of New York, and that it will pave the way to greater privileges, and the final elevation of woman to that position in society which shall entitle her opinions to respect and consideration.[13]

Notes

1. See Bertha Monica Sterns, "Reform Periodicals and Female Reformers: 1830–1860," *American Historical Review* 37 (1931/32): 678–99.

2. Margaret Farrand Thorp, *Female Persuasion: Six Strong-minded Women* (New Haven, CT: Yale University Press, 1949), p. 59.

3. Jane Grey Swisshelm, *Half a Century* (Chicago: Jansen, McClurg, 1880), p. 130.

4. Maurine H. Beasley, *The First Women Washington Correspondents* (Washington, DC: George Washington University, 1976), pp. 6–9.

5. Robert M. Riddle was editor of the *Pittsburgh Commercial Journal*, which printed occasional letters by Swisshelm against the Mexican War and slavery.

6. Swisshelm, *Half a Century*, chs. 21 and 22.

7. Susan J. Kleinberg, "Introduction to the Paperback Edition," in Dexter C. Bloomer, *Life and Writings of Amelia Bloomer* (Boston: Arena Publishing, 1895, reprinted New York: Schocken Books, 1975), p. xii.

8. Bloomer, *Life and Writings of Amelia Bloomer*, pp. 70–71.

9. Kathleen Barry, *Susan B. Anthony: A Biography of a Singular Feminist* (New York: New York University Press, 1988), p. 63.

10. Sterns, "Reform Periodicals and Female Reformers," p. 694.

11. Carl N. Degler, *At Odds: Women and the Family in America from the Revolution to the Present* (New York: Oxford, 1980), p. 175.

12. Reprinted from Bloomer, *Life and Writings of Amelia Bloomer* (1895).

13. Reprinted from Bloomer, *Life and Writings of Amelia Bloomer* (1895).

5

Foreign Correspondence
Margaret Fuller

Horace Greeley described Margaret Fuller as "the most remarkable and in some respects the greatest woman whom America has yet known."[1] An intimate of Ralph Waldo Emerson and Henry Thoreau, she won literary fame as an author, critic, feminist, and transcendentalist philosopher. Her journalistic career is less well known, but she deserves the title of the first woman foreign correspondent.

Traveling to Europe in 1846 as a writer for Greeley's *New York Tribune*, Fuller reported on social conditions in the British Isles, France, and Italy, and interviewed leading literary and political figures. In Italy, she covered an unsuccessful revolution led by Giuseppe Garibaldi, who fought to defend a newly formed republican government against French and Austrian troops. At the time, Italy was divided into sections governed by different rulers including the pope. Garibaldi's efforts were thwarted by a French siege of Rome staged to restore papal authority. Italy did not become a unified nation until 1870. Fuller provided first-person accounts of the French bombardment.

A precocious child who read Virgil in the original Latin at the age of seven, Fuller played a major role in New England intellectual life as a teacher, writer, and conversationalist with notables of the transcendentalist movement. She became a coeditor of the *Dial*, a quarterly literary journal of the transcendentalists, in 1840. Four years later Greeley hired her as his first woman staff member, naming her literary critic for the *Tribune*. She also wrote exposés on public institutions and promoted a home for freed women convicts.

Before she went abroad, she published *Woman in the Nineteenth*

Century, a classic book on American feminism that helped lay the foundation for the Seneca Falls convention on women's rights in 1848. In her book she pointed out that those who considered women too delicate for politics had overlooked their exploitation in the labor force: "Those who think the physical circumstances of Woman would make a part in the affairs of national government unsuitable, are by no means those who think it is impossible for negresses to endure field-work, even during pregnancy, or for sempstresses to go through their killing labors."[2]

Fuller's Roman experiences brought her both personal happiness and tragedy. A love affair with a Roman nobleman—Giovanni Angelo, Marchese d'Ossoli—absorbed her in revolutionary activities, including direction of an emergency hospital. They apparently were married in the summer of 1849, almost a year after the birth of a son who was left with a nurse in the mountains during the revolution.[3]

After Rome fell, the couple was reunited with the child and lived in Florence until 1850 when, returning to the United States, all three lost their lives in a shipwreck outside of New York Harbor, a few weeks after Fuller's fortieth birthday.

Margaret Fuller's European dispatches in the *New York Tribune* were collected by her brother, Arthur B. Fuller, after her death and published in *At Home and Abroad, or Things and Thoughts in America and Europe*. An excerpt of her account of the siege of Rome—dated July 6, 1849, and sent to the *Tribune*—is reprinted here.

LETTER XXXIII

Rome, July 6, 1849

If I mistake not, I closed my last letter just as the news arrived here that the attempt of the democratic party in France to resist the infamous proceedings of the government had failed, and thus Rome, as far as human calculation went, had not a hope for her liberties left. An inland city cannot long sustain a siege when there is no hope of aid. Then followed the news of the surrender of Ancona, and Rome found herself alone; for, though Venice continued to hold out, all communication was cut off.

The Republican troops, almost to a man, left Ancona, but a long march separated them from Rome.

The extreme heat of these days was far more fatal to the Romans than to their assailants, for as fast as the French troops sickened, their place was taken by fresh arrivals. Ours also not only sustained the exhausting service by day, but were harassed at night by attacks, feigned or real. These commonly began about eleven or twelve o'clock at night, just when all who meant to rest were fairly asleep. I can imagine the harassing effect upon the troops, from what I feel in my sheltered pavilion, in consequence of not knowing a quiet night's sleep for a month.

The bombardment became constantly more serious. The house where I lived was filled as early as the 20th with persons obliged to fly from the Piazza di Gesu, where the fiery rain fell thickest. The night of the 21st–22nd, we were all alarmed about two o'clock A.M. by a tremendous cannonade. It was the moment when the breach was finally made by which the French entered. They rushed in, and I grieve to say that, by the only instance of defection known in the course of the siege, those companies of the regiment Union which had in charge a position on that point yielded to panic and abandoned it. The French immediately entered and intrenched themselves. That was the fatal hour for the city. Every day afterward, though obstinately resisted, the enemy gained, till at last, their cannon being well placed, the city was entirely commanded from the Janiculum, and all thought of further resistance was idle.

It was true policy to avoid a street-fight, in which the Italian, an unpractised soldier, but full of feeling and sustained from the houses, would have been a match even for their disciplined troops. After the 22nd of June, the slaughter of the Romans became every day more fearful. Their defences were knocked down by the heavy cannon of the French, and, entirely exposed in their valorous onsets, great numbers perished on the spot. Those who were brought into the hospitals were generally grievously wounded, very commonly subjects for amputation. My heart bled daily more and more at these sights, and I could not feel much for myself, though now the balls and bombs began to fall round me also. The night of the 28th the effect was truly fearful, as they whizzed and burst near me. As many as thirty fell upon or near the Hotel de Russie, where Mr. Cass has his temporary abode.[4] The roof of the studio in the pavilion, tenanted by Mr. Stermer, well known to the visitors of Rome for his highly-finished cabinet pictures, was torn to pieces. I sat alone in my much exposed apartment, thinking, "If one strikes me, I only hope it will kill me at once, and that God will transport my soul to some sphere where virtue and love are not tyrannized over by egotism and brute force, as in this." However, that night passed; the next, we had reason to expect a still more fiery salute toward the Pincian, as here alone remained three or four pieces of cannon which could be used. But on the morning of the 30th, in a contest at the foot of the Janiculum, the line, old Papal troops, naturally not in earnest like the free corps, refused to fight against odds so terrible. The heroic Marina fell, with hundreds of his devoted Lombards. Garibaldi saw his best officers perish, and himself went in the afternoon to say to the Assembly that further resistance was unavailing.

The Assembly sent to Oudinot, but he refused any conditions—refusing even to guarantee a safe departure to Garibaldi, his brave foe.[5] Notwithstanding, a great number of men left the other regiments to follow the leader whose courage had captivated them, and whose superiority over difficulties commanded their entire confidence. Toward the evening of Monday, the 2d of July, it was known that the French were preparing to cross the river and take possession of all the city. I went into the Corso with some friends; it was filled with citizens and military. The carriage was stopped by the crowd near the Doria palace; the lancers of Garibaldi galloped along in full career. I longed for Sir Walter Scott to be on earth again, and see them; all are light, athletic, resolute figures, many of the forms of the finest manly beauty of the South, all sparkling with its genius and ennobled by the resolute spirit, ready to dare, to do, to die. We followed them to the piazza of St. John Lateran. Never have I seen a sight so beautiful, so romantic, and so sad. Whoever knows Rome knows the peculiar solemn grandeur of that piazza, scene of the first triumph of Rienzi, and whence may be seen the magnificence of the "mother of all churches," the baptistery with its porphyry columns, the Santa Scala with its glittering mosaics of the early ages, the obelisk standing fairest of any of those most imposing monuments of Rome, the view through the gates of the Campagna, on that side so richly strewn with ruins. The sun was setting, the crescent moon rising, the flower of the Italian youth were marshalling in that solemn place. They had been driven from every other spot where they had offered their hearts as bulwarks of Italian independence; in this last stronghold they had sacrificed hecatombs of their best and bravest to that cause; they must now go or remain prisoners and slaves. *Where* go, they knew not; for except distant Hungary there is not now a spot which could receive them, or where they can act as honor commands. They had all put on the beautiful dress of the Garibaldi legion, the tunic of bright red cloth, the Greek cap, or else round hat with Puritan Plume. Their long hair was blown back from resolute faces; all looked full of courage. They had counted the cost before they entered on this perilous struggle; they had weighed life and all its material advantages against liberty, and made their election; they turned not back, nor flinched, at this bitter crisis. I saw the wounded, all that could go, laden upon their baggage cars; some were already pale and fainting, still they wished to go. I saw many youths, born to rich inheritance, carrying in a handkerchief all their worldly goods. The women were ready; their eyes too were resolved, if sad. The wife of Garibaldi followed him on horseback. He himself was distinguished by the white tunic; his look was entirely that of a hero of the Middle Ages—his face still young, for the excitements of his life, though so many, have all been youthful, and there is no fatigue upon his brow or cheek. Fall or stand, one sees him a man engaged in the career for which he is adapted by nature. He went upon the parapet, and looked upon the road with a spyglass, and, no obstruction being in sight, he turned his face for a moment back upon Rome, then led the way through the gate. Hard was the heart, stony and seared the eye, that had no tear for that moment. Go, fated gallant band! and if God care not indeed for men as for the sparrows, most of ye go forth to perish. And Rome, anew the Niobe! Must she lose also these beautiful and brave, that promised her regeneration, and would have given it, but for the perfidy, the overpowering force, of the foreign intervention?

I know that many "respectable" gentlemen would be surprised to hear me speak in this way. Gentlemen who perform their "duties to society" by buying for themselves handsome clothes and furniture with the interest of their money, speak of Garibaldi and his men as "brigands" and "vagabonds." Such as they, doubtless, in the same sense as Jesus, Moses, and Aeneas were. To me, men who can throw so lightly aside the ease of wealth, the joys of affection, for the sake of what they deem honor, in whatsoever form, are the "respectable." No doubt there are in these bands a number of men of lawless minds, and who follow this banner only because there is for them no other path. But the greater part are the noble youths who have fled from the Austrian conscription, or fly now from the renewal of the Papal suffocation, darkened by French protection.

As for the protectors, they entirely threw aside the mask, as it was always supposed they would, the moment they had possession of Rome. I do not know whether they were really so bewildered by their priestly counselors as to imagine they would be well received in a city which they had bombarded, and where twelve hundred men were lying wounded by their assault. To say nothing of the justice or injustice of the matter, it could not be supposed that the Roman people, if it had any sense of dignity, would welcome them. I did not appear in the street, as I would not give any countenance to such a wrong; but an English lady, my friend, told me they seemed to look expectingly for the strong party of friends they had always pretended to have within the walls. The French officers looked up to the windows for ladies, and, she being the only one they saw, saluted her. She made no reply. They then passed into the Corso. Many were assembled, the softer Romans being unable to control a curiosity the Milanese would have disclaimed, but preserving an icy silence. In an evil hour, a foolish priest dared to break it by the cry of *Viva Pio Nono!*[6] The populace, roused to fury, rushed on him with their knives. He was much wounded; one or two others were killed in the rush. The people howled then, and hissed at the French, who, advancing their bayonets, and clearing the way before them, fortified themselves in the piazzas. Next day the French troops were marched to and fro through Rome, to inspire awe in the people; but it has only created a disgust amounting to loathing, to see that, with such an imposing force, and in great part fresh, the French were not ashamed to use bombs also, and kill women and children in their beds.[7]

Notes

1. William H. Hale, *Horace Greeley: Voice of the People* (New York: Harper & Brothers, 1950), p. 115.

2. Barbara Belford, *Brilliant Bylines* (New York: Columbia University Press, 1986), p. 14.

3. Margaret Fuller, *Woman in the Nineteenth Century* (Boston: Jewitt, 1855), pp. 34–35.

4. Lewis Cass, Jr., was the U.S. chargé d'affaires in Rome.

5. Nicholas Charles Oudinot was a French general and marshal of France.

6. "Long Live the Pope!" (Pius IX).

7. From Margaret Fuller, *At Home and Abroad, or Things and Thoughts in America and Europe*, edited by Arthur B. Fuller (Boston: Crosby, Nichols, 1856).

6

Ladies' Periodicals
Sarah J. Hale: Godey's Lady's Book

Aside from resolute individuals like Anne Royall and Jane Swisshelm, most middle-class women in pre–Civil War America led lives restricted to the home and family. Although millions of women—both slaves and immigrant whites—labored unceasingly, the eyes of society saw only one image of womanhood: the "lady," a wan, modest creature who reflected her husband's glory and encased her mind in a sentimentality as stifling as the corset in which she laced her body.

This myth of the lady and its attendant cult of domesticity, endorsed by clerical opinion, was disseminated in a new kind of sex-segregated journalism that developed during the period. More than 25 publications aimed at women were founded between 1806 and 1849 with women as editors or associate editors.[1] Some 60 intended for (if not edited by) women made their appearance between 1830 and 1850, but often did not last.[2] Most, like the tearful novels aimed at women readers, reinforced the social proprieties limiting women to the home.

The most famous—*Godey's Lady's Book*—was founded in Philadelphia in 1830 by Louis A. Godey and edited for 40 years by Sarah Josepha Hale, the foremost woman journalist of her day.[3] A New England widow who turned to journalism to support her five children, Mrs. Hale carefully stayed within the bounds of convention. Although she composed sermons on wifely duties, she labored valiantly to advance the position of women, believing them to be finer and purer than men. She also published stories and articles by a large number of women writers.[4]

Sarah Hale supported higher education for women, campaigned to improve their nutrition and health in an era that romanticized female weakness, fought for retention of property rights by married women, pioneered for day nurseries, and advocated that young women prepare to support themselves if, due to the death or incapability of male relatives, it became necessary. She argued that public school teaching, missionary work, and medicine were particularly appropriate fields for women because of their superior sensibilities. However, she did not support woman suffrage.[5]

Serving as editor until the age of 90, she retired in 1877 and died the following year.

In the "Editors' Table" each month in *Godey's Lady's Book*, Sarah J. Hale expressed her own opinion on issues affecting women. The following editorial appeared in January 1853.

EDITORS' TABLE

There is an old legend that the nineteenth century is to be the "Century of Woman."

A late English writer, commenting on this, says: "Whatever the wisdom or the foolishness of our forefathers may have meant by this, English women know but too well that, up to this time (1851), the middle of the century, it has not been theirs. Those who deny are perhaps even better aware of it than those who allow."

Now, we differ in opinion with this English writer. The century, thus far, has been marked as woman's above any or all preceding ages. Even in the times of chivalry, when men worshipped her charms, they had little respect for her intellect or her intelligence. The mass of men were ignorant; physical force, diplomatic cunning, and religious superstitions ruled the world. There was no organ of public opinion, by which woman as woman could be heard, or through which she could make her powers of mind apparent. And the writer we have quoted above acknowledges this, as he goes on to say—

"In no century, perhaps, has so much freedom, nay, opportunity, been given to woman to cultivate her powers, as best might seem to herself. Man leaves her room and space enough. She is no longer called pedantic, if her powers appear in conversation. The authoress is courted, not shunned. Accordingly, the intellectual development of English women has made extraordinary progress. But, as the human being does not move both feet at once, except he jumps, so, while the intellectual foot has made a step in advance, the practical foot has remained behind. Woman stands askew. Her education for action has not kept pace with her education for acquirement. The woman of the eighteenth century was, perhaps, happier, when practice and theory were on a par, than her more cultivated sister of the nineteenth. The latter wishes, but does not know how to do many things; the former, what she wished, at least that she could do.

"What then? Shall we have less theory? God forbid! We shall not work better for ignorance. Every increase of knowledge is a benefit, by showing us more of the ways of God. But it was for the increase of 'wisdom,' even more than of knowledge, that David prayed—for wisdom is the practical application of knowledge.

" 'Not what we know, but what we do, is our kingdom,' and woman, perhaps, feels that she has not found her kingdom."

No, woman has not yet attained her kingdom; but she is preparing for it. This intellectual education was a necessary preliminary; she could not do the work of an educator properly till she was herself educated. And this has been accomplished since the present century began. Woman is now prepared for a sphere of activity, and, in our country, this sphere is already opened. Within the last twenty-five years, the teacher's office in schools, as well as at home, has been passing into her hands. There are, probably, at this time, from sixty to one hundred thousand female teachers of public and private schools in the United States. Women are editors, authors, and artists, and a few have entered the arena—where their greatest honors as public benefactors are yet to be won—of medical science.

Now, let no reader imagine we are about setting up for "Woman's Rights." God has given her the care of humanity in its helplessness of infancy—in its sorrows and sicknesses. She should be educated as the Conservator of health, physical as well as morally—as the Preserver, Teacher, Inspirer.

The need of her aid is now felt and acknowledged by the wise and good men of our land. They call her to the Mission field. Since this century commenced, about twelve hundred American women have gone as missionaries to the heathen. Is not this a wonderful advance in her sphere? Since the days of the Apostles and the early fathers of the church, never has the helping power of woman in the church been thus permitted. Her office of Deaconess—instituted by the Apostles—had been nearly suppressed, till within this present century it is again revived, or reviving. Let us hope every Christian church will soon have its Deaconesses, to take care of the poor and sick of their own sex.

But the idea that seems to have met the most pressing need of the missionary and progressive spirit of the century is that of "FEMALE MEDICAL MIS-SIONARIES." This was first advanced in the *Lady's Book* of March last, and steadily advocated through the year.

But it is said, "Woman cannot go abroad to attend the sick—their domestic employment precludes them from practice. What shall they do, when they are called for and cannot go?" Just what the male doctor does when he is called for, and cannot go—stay at home. Just what everybody else does, when he is asked to do a thing and cannot—let it alone. "But the people will not employ them if you make them doctors." Very well, then, let them employ others. We don't expect people employ those whom they do not choose to employ; and we are willing to say that, if woman never practices medicine, she would be amply repaid for studying it. Another says, "You will break up the medical profession, you will drive all the men out of it, and even those who are now in it will starve." They may as well starve as the women. They have as much physical strength, and as many hands and feet, to earn their daily bread, as women have, and, if they cannot cope with women in the medical profession, let them take an humble occupation, in which they can.

We admit that woman has her own sphere in which to act, as much as man. She is better calculated for some duties than for others, and we maintain that there are none, within the whole range of these duties, for which she could have been better designed, or more in her sphere of usefulness, than in this of medicine. Tell about this being the appropriate sphere of man, and his alone! With tenfold more plausibility and reason might we say, it is the appropriate sphere of woman, and hers alone. The order of nature—the constitution of families—the nature of human society—the earthy origin of the race—the commission of the child first to the care of woman—the delicacy of females— all these proclaim her fitness to be the good physician.[6]

Notes

1. Edith May Marken, "Women in American Journalism before 1900," unpublished master's thesis, University of Missouri, 1932, pp. 51–54.

2. Helen W. Papashvily, *All the Happy Endings* (New York: Harper & Brothers, 1956), p. 40.

3. Frank Luther Mott, *A History of American Magazines*, vol. 1 (Cambridge, MA: Harvard University Press, 1957), p. 537.

4. Ruth E. Finley, *The Lady of Godey's: Sarah Josepha Hale* (Philadelphia: J. B. Lippincott, 1931), p. 25.

5. See Edward H. Sewell, Jr., "Sarah Josepha Hale," in Sam G. Riley, ed., *American Magazine Journalists: 1741–1850*, vol. 73 of the *Dictionary of Literary Biography* (Detroit: Gale Research, 1988), pp. 159–67.

6. In *Godey's Lady's Book* (January 1853), at the Library of Congress.

7

Suffrage Newspapers
The *Revolution*
and
The *Woman's Journal*

It was not woman's subordinate status itself that turned a few outspoken women into the first feminists in the United States. When women abolitionists found their crusades against slavery hampered by sex discrimination, they revolted and demanded equality with men, including the right to vote. The delegates at the Seneca Falls convention of 1848 disagreed with the view that women ought to be kept legally inferior because they were thought to be mentally inferior to men. One of the prime organizers was Elizabeth Cady Stanton who soon teamed up with Susan B. Anthony in a half-century collaboration to improve women's status.[1]

After the Civil War, Stanton and Anthony insisted that suffrage be extended to women as well as Negro men, and succeeded in securing the introduction of a woman's suffrage amendment. It did not pass; but while the two were campaigning for it in Kansas, they met a wealthy supporter, George Francis Train, who offered to back them in a weekly newspaper.[2]

The Revolution was that paper. Published in New York, it began in January 1868 and lasted two and a half years. Anthony was the publisher and Stanton was a coeditor. The 16-page paper espoused easy divorce, condemned prostitution, and, among other positions, opposed the Fifteenth Amendment, contending that it should not pass because it would give the vote to Negro men without women also being included. Supporting the equal rights efforts of women on all fronts—in unions, professions, education, and organized religion—it made a spirited contribution to women's cause. Most of its editorials were written by Stanton and signed ECS.[3]

The *Revolution* did not suit conservative supporters of the women's vote, including Lucy Stone, abolitionist and wife of another abolitionist, Henry Blackwell, both of whom felt strongly that suffrage campaigns for women and Negro men should be entirely separate. When in 1869 Stanton and Anthony organized the National Woman Suffrage Association limited to women, the Stone group established the American Woman Suffrage Association—open to men and representatives from "recognized" (or "respectable," i.e., more moderate) suffrage organizations—and launched its own newspaper, the *Woman's Journal*, financed by a joint stock company and published in Boston.[4]

The Stone Association garnered a majority of the nation's suffragists with a moderate platform giving priority to votes for Negro men and calling for women to work for the vote on the state and local levels, assuming that national suffrage eventually would result. Milder in tone than the *Revolution*, the *Woman's Journal* reported on local enfranchisement activities and served as the voice of middle-class professional and club women. Its success marked the demise of the *Revolution*.

The *Revolution* and *Woman's Journal* did not limit the field of suffrage newspapers. Blocked from getting a fair hearing in the mainstream press, women started scores of their own publications. In exhaustive research, Sherilyn Cox Bennion identified at least 12 suffrage newspapers in the American West, all edited by women from 1869 until 1914.[5] She concluded that they "provided a forum for a cause which had time—and justice—on its side."[6] Another scholar, Linda Steiner, concluded that in the suffrage press "women evolved intellectually and emotionally satisfying communal models for acting, thinking, judging and feeling."[7]

In existence until 1914, the *Woman's Journal* was edited for most of its long life by Lucy Stone, Henry Blackwell, and their daughter Alice Stone Blackwell. Other distinguished writers contributed to it, including Julia Ward Howe, author of the "Battle Hymn of the Republic," who wrote the newspaper's first editorial on its appearance, January 8, 1870.

An editorial by Elizabeth Cady Stanton from the *Revolution*, dated February 5, 1868, follows. It is paired with the "Salutatory" by Julia Ward Howe from the first issue of the *Woman's Journal*.

INFANTICIDE AND PROSTITUTION

Scarce a day passes but some of our daily journals take note of the fearful ravages on the race, made through the crimes of Infanticide and Prostitution.

For a quarter of a century, sober, thinking women have warned this nation of these thick coming dangers and pointed to the only remedy, the education and enfranchisement of woman; but men have laughed them to scorn. Let those who have made the "strong-minded" women of this generation the target for the gibes and jeers of a heedless world repent now in sackcloth and ashes, for already they suffer the retribution of their folly at their own firesides, in their sad domestic relations. Wives sick, peevish, perverse, children deformed, blind, deaf, dumb and insane; daughters silly and wayward; sons waylaid at every corner of the streets and dragged down to the gates of death, by those whom God meant to be their saviors and support. Look at these things no longer as necessary afflictions, sent to wean us from earth as visitations from Providence; but as the direct results of the violation of immutable laws, which it was our duty to study and obey. In the midst of all these miseries, let us regard ourselves as guilty sinners and not helpless saints. God does not wink, even at the sins of ignorance.

We ask our editors who pen these startling statistics to give us their views of the remedy. We believe the cause of all these abuses lies in the degradation of women.

Strike the chains from your women; for as long as they are slaves to man's lust, man will be the slave of his own passion.

Wonder not that American women do everything in their power to avoid maternity; for, from false habits of life, dress, food and generations of disease and abominations, it is to them a period of sickness, lassitude, disgust, agony and death.

What man would walk up to the gallows if he could avoid it? And the most helpless aspect of this condition of things is that our Doctors of Divinity and medicine teach and believe that maternity and suffering are inseparable.

So long as the Bible, through the ignorance of its expounders, makes maternity a curse, and women, through ignorance of the science of life and health find it so, we need not wonder at the multiplication of these fearful statistics. Let us no longer weep, and whine, and pray over these abominations; but with an enlightened conscientiousness and religious earnestness, bring ourselves into line with God's just, merciful and wise laws. Let every thinking man make himself today a missionary in his own house. Regulate the diet, dress, exercise, health of your wives and daughters. Send them to Mrs. Plumb's gymnasium, Dr. Lewis's school, or Dr. Taylor's Swedish movement cure, to develop their muscular system, and to Kuczkowski to have the rhubarb, the sulphur, the mercury and "the sins of their fathers" (Exodus XX:5) soaked out of their brains.

ECS[8]

SALUTATORY

The New Year had just stepped across its threshold, and after it, clinging closely to its skirts, comes our new enterprise. We begin the year's work with the year, hoping that both may prosper. We have begun many new years with this same vision of work and of usefulness, never quite realized. But the progress of time makes our tasks clearer to us, and we may say that never was work more joyous to us than that which at present stands ready to our hand.

The cultivation of wide and tender relations with the beings nearest to us in nature and sympathy, the removal of a thousand barriers of passion and prejudice, the leaping out of the whole heart of womanhood towards a new future, a future of freedom and of fullness—our prospectus shows us such things as these. To see them even in a dream is blessed, but these are of the prophetic dreams that enjoin their own fulfillment.

We who stand beside the cradle of this enterprise are not young in years. Our children are speedily preparing to take our place in the ranks of society. Some of us have been looking thoughtfully toward the final summons, not because of ill health or infirmity, but because, after the establishment of our families, no great object intervened between ourselves and that last consummation. But these young undertakings detain us in life. While they need so much of care and of counsel, we cannot consent to death. And this first year, at least, of our journal, we are determined to live through.

The classic "*plaudite omnes*" was looked for at the end of the drama. Our "*adjurate omnes*" comes more properly at the beginning. "Call no man happy till he is dead," said Solon, very wisely. But beginnings of life and works are greeted with congratulation because they open up new hopes and new chances. So we say to you, friends, that you may not indeed dare to call us entirely fortunate until our work shall have done its work. But fortunate we are in being able to make a beginning, and in this good fortune we ask you to rejoice with us. Be friendly to our babe. Inquire for it often, and when you have good things to share, send us some of them. A newspaper, you know, is not clever for nothing. It eats up silver, and gold, and brains. It is tended by tutelary devils, who also must eat. Be mindful of this. The need and the hands willing to supply it being met and announced, do not suffer the want of material support to hinder the two from a helpful yoking together. So, help us, friends of men and women! Help us, you who from your larger or lesser means reserve always a certain proportion for the needs of humankind.

We must not promise too much, but we may promise that the trust confided to us in the *Woman's Journal* shall be administered by us in the interests of humanity, according to our best understanding of them. As we claim admission to life in its largeness and universality, it will not become us to raise side issues and personal griefs. Too much labor lies before us to allow us time for complaints and criminations, were such utterances congenial to us. Our endeavor, which is to bring the feminine mind to bear upon all that concerns the welfare of mankind, commands us to let the dead past bury its dead. The wail of impotence becomes us no longer. We must work as those who have power, for we have faith, and faith is power. We implore our sisters, of whatever kind or degree, to make common cause with us, to lay down all partisan warfare and organize a peaceful Grand Army of the Republic of Women. But we do not ask them to organize as against men, but as against all that is pernicious to men and to women. Against superstition, whether social or priestly, against idleness, whether aesthetic or vicious, against oppression, whether or manly will or feminine caprice. Ours is but a new manoeuvre, a fresh phalanx in the good fight of faith. In this contest, the armor of Paul will become us, the shield and breastplate of strong and shining virtue. And with one Scripture precept we will close our salutation. With sisterly zeal and motherly vigilance, "Let brotherly love continue."

J.W.H.[9]

Notes

1. The relationship between Stanton and Anthony is explored in an excellent biography, Kathleen Barry, *Susan B. Anthony: A Biography of a Singular Feminist* (New York: New York University Press, 1988).

2. Eleanor Flexner, *Century of Struggle: The Woman's Rights Movement in the United States* (New York: Atheneum, 1973), pp. 150–51.

3. Lynne Masel-Walters, "Their Rights and Nothing More: A History of *The Revolution*, 1868–70," *Journalism Quarterly* 53 (1976):243–51.

4. Lynne Masel-Walters, "A Burning Cloud by Day: The History and Content of the *Woman's Journal*," *Journalism History* 3 (1977):103–10.

5. Sherilyn Cox Bennion, *Equal to the Occasion: Women Editors of the Nineteenth-century West* (Reno: University of Nevada Press, 1990), p. 57.

6. Sherilyn Cox Bennion, "Woman Suffrage Papers of the West, 1869–1914," *American Journalism* 3 (1986):140.

7. Linda Steiner, "Finding Community in Nineteenth Century Suffrage Periodicals," *American Journalism* 1 (1983):12.

8. In the *Revolution*, February 5, 1868, available at the Library of Congress.

9. In the *Woman's Journal*, January 8, 1870, available at the Library of Congress.

8

Newspaper Correspondence
Sara Willis Parton
Mary Clemmer Ames
Sara Clarke Lippincott

Before and after the Civil War women began to establish careers as newspaper columnists. Writing, along with teaching, constituted a respectable pursuit for middle-class women, although they often shielded their identity from the public by use of flowery pen names. While indulging in the sentiment of the day, their chatty columns, often touching on domestic situations, enlivened the pages of newspapers and helped enlarge women's role in society.

Sara Willis Parton

Sara Willis Parton, who wrote as "Fanny Fern," stood out as the most popular columnist. Born in 1811, she was the daughter of Nathaniel Willis, founder of an early magazine for juveniles, *The Youth's Companion*, to which she contributed before her marriage to a banker, Charles Eldredge. When she was left a widow in 1846 and lacked funds to support herself and her children, her father—although himself well off—forced her into a marriage of convenience with a jealous widower, as the best means of maintaining herself and her children.[1]

Desperately unhappy, she took the then-shocking step of leaving her husband, who later obtained a divorce. Unable to support herself by teaching and sewing, she became Fanny Fern and wrote short satirical pieces for magazines and newspapers. Her columns drew so much attention that some people speculated Fanny was a man because she wrote "indelicately" on relations between the sexes. It was four years before her identity became commonly known.[2]

After her collected writings, *Fern Leaves from Fanny's Port-folio*, became a best-seller in 1853, she was hired for $100 a week (considered a huge sum) to write a weekly column for the *New York Ledger*, with which she remained for the rest of her life, never missing an issue. She also published four more collections of her works, two books for young people, and two novels, including one—*Ruth Hall*, a scathing portrayal of her relatives—that caused a literary uproar. The novel is read today as an expression of nineteenth-century thinking on social issues.

In 1856 she became the wife of James Parton, a biographer 11 years younger. Her own experiences provided lifelong sympathy with other women; she advocated equal pay with men, greater opportunities, and eventually, in 1858, came out for woman suffrage. She died in New York in 1872.

Reprinted below is a typical Fanny Fern column, in which she pokes fun at social constraints on men and women.

SUMMER TRAVEL

July 12, [1856]

Take a journey at this elevation of the thermometer! Not I! Think of the breakfastless start before daybreak—think of the twelve hours' ride on the sunny side of the [railroad] cars, in the neighborhood of some persistent talker, rattling untranslatable jargon into your aching ears; think of a hurried repast in some barbarous half-way house; amid a heterogeneous assortment of men, women and children, beef, port and mutton; minus forks, minus spoons, minus castor [condiments], minus come-a-table waiters and four shillings and indigestion to pay. Think of a "collision"—disemboweled trunks and a wooden leg; think of an arrival at the crowded hotel; jammed, jaded, dusty and dolorous; think of your closetless sentry box of a room, infested by mosquitoes and Red Rovers [insects]; bed too narrow, window too small, candle too short, all the world and his wife a-bed, and the geography of the house an unexplained riddle. Think of your unrefreshing vapor-bath sleep; think of the next morning, as seated on a dusty trunk, with your hair drooping about your ears, through which the whistle of the cars and the jiggle-joggle of the brakeman are still resounding, you try to remember with your hand on your bewildered forehead, whether your breakfast robe is in the yellow trunk or the black trunk and if in either, whether it is at the top, bottom or in the middle of the same, where your muslins and laces were deposited, what on earth you did with your dressing comb, and where, amid your luggage, your toilet slippers may possibly be located. Think of a summons to breakfast at this interesting moment, the sun meanwhile streaming in through the blind chinks with volcanic power. Think of all that, I say.

Now if I could travel incog. in masculine attire, no dresses to look after, no muslins to rumple, no bonnet to soil, no tresses to keep smooth, with only a hat and things, a neck-tie or two, a change of—of shirts—nothing but a moustache to twist into a horn when the dinner bell rings; just a dip into a washbasin, a clean dicky, a jump into a pair of—trowsers [*sic*] and above all liberty to go where I liked, without being stared at or questioned; a seat in a chair on its hind-legs, on a breezy doorstep, a seat on the stairs in a wide hall, "taking notes"; a peep everywhere I choose, by lordly right of my pantaloons; nobody nudging somebody, to inquire why Miss Spinks the authoress wore her hair in curls instead of plaits; or making the astounding discovery that it was hips, not hoops, that made her dress stand out—that, now, would be worth talking about; I'll do it. But stop—I should have to cut my hair short—I should have to shave every morning, or at any rate go through the motions; men would jostle rudely past me, just as if they had never said such pretty things to me in flunces [*sic*]; I should be obliged, just as I had secured a nice seat in the cars, to get up and give it to some imperious woman who would not even say "thank you"; I should have to look on with hungry eyes till "the ladies" were all served at table; I should have to pick up their fans, and reticules and handkerchiefs whenever they chose to drop them; I should have to give up the rocking-chairs, arm-chairs and sofas for their use and be called a "brute" at that; I should have to rush out of the cars with five minutes grace at some stopping place, to get a glass of milk for some "crying baby" with a contracted swallowing apparatus and pursued for life by the curses of its owner, because the whistle sounded while his two shilling tumbler was yet in the voracious baby's tight grip. No, no. I'll stay a woman, and what's more, I'll stay at home.[3]

The Civil War enlarged opportunities for women in many areas, including journalism. Women left the confines of their homes to serve as nurses, to organize relief activities, and to teach the newly freed slaves. When the war ended, they continued their activities in teaching, welfare work, and education.

In the field of journalism, one group of women established national reputations as Washington correspondents, often using pen names (as was common in those days) to sign their contributions to leading publications. Coming from abolitionist backgrounds, they defended the black population and civil rights. They also held up to ridicule the excesses of Gilded Age politics—particularly the Credit Mobilier scandal, which exposed members of Congress who benefited financially from gifts of railroad stock.

As soon as there was a sizable number of women Washington correspondents, however, they were barred from the Capitol press galleries.[4] In 1879 the Congressional Directory listed 20 women correspondents entitled to gallery privileges—about 12 percent of the total of 166 correspondents. Within two years, after the rules were changed in 1879 to exclude women and others not considered "bona fide" journalists from the galleries, women correspondents began increasingly to be relegated to covering society gossip instead of politics.[5]

Two of the most outstanding of the early women correspondents were Mary Clemmer Ames, who wrote for the *Independent* in New York, an influential weekly, and Sara Clarke Lippincott, who wrote as "Grace Greenwood" for the *New York Times* in the 1870s. Others were Emily Edson Briggs, the "Olivia" of the *Philadelphia Press*, and Mary Abigail Dodge, whose pen name was "Gail Hamilton," of the *New York Tribune*.[6]

Mary Clemmer Ames

The life of Mary Clemmer Ames, said to be the highest paid newspaperwoman of her day, illustrated the cultural conflicts besetting a woman living in the Victorian age and trying to maintain her image as a "respectable home-loving lady" at the same time as she climbed to the top of a competitive masculine occupation. A nurse in Union hospitals during the war, Mary Ames turned to a literary career when the war ended and her marriage to a Methodist minister failed.

Launching her first "Woman's Letter from Washington" in the *Independent* in 1866, she continued this highly acclaimed column until her death in 1884 at the age of 53. Yet, shortly after she began it, she told her readers that fame held no appeal to her as a refined woman who modestly shrank from public notice and preferred the domestic scene to the political arena. She justified her journalistic career, however, by holding that women writers had a moral duty to purify politics even if their efforts brought them unwelcome attention.

From 1869 to 1872, she wrote for the *Brooklyn Daily Union* as well as the *Independent*—so impressing Henry C. Bowen, publisher of both, that he paid her a record $5,000 a year. A foe of the scandal-ridden Grant administration, she defended the press against attacks from those exposed as corrupt. Following her divorce, she wrote under her maiden name, Clemmer, which she continued to use after her marriage to Washington journalist Edmund Hudson.

Following is an excerpt from Mary Clemmer's "A Woman's Letter from Washington" in the *Independent* on March 7, 1878. The reference to the "sober" Blaine is to James G. Blaine of Maine.

A WOMAN'S LETTER FROM WASHINGTON
By Mary Clemmer

I do not presume to say that all-night sessions are never necessary. 'Tis a pity that, if ever necessary, they are equally demoralizing. It is a hard strain, even on a man's nerves (and, wonderful to tell, some men have nerves), to sit for seventeen consecutive hours in the dulling, deadening atmosphere of the Senate. Instead of doing the sensible thing, as we may be sure nine out of ten common-sense women would do—proceed to get a comfortable dinner, at a reasonable hour—through all the hours they fill their unfortunate stomachs with odds and ends of tobacco, hard apples, etc., washed down by brandy, whisky, and wine, till they find themselves in a sufficiently unhappy and perverted condition of body and soul to enable them to draw up a code of laws for the lower Pandemonium. They have only to visit the cloak-room a sufficient number of times to be, in common parlance, "ready for anything." They pull off their boots, take off their coats, stretch themselves at full length in their stocking-feet on the sofas; or they strut, swagger, and reel about the floor, lean over their desks, and repeat the dubious stories of the cloak-room to their comrades, or, filled with "fight," they mumble, blubber, and bluster in vain attempt to utter one coherent sentence. The majority of the senators do none of these things. I would gladly give the names of many who would not, were it not for the shame of their comrades. Whatever the strain, there are men who meet it patiently, faithfully, honorably, like the gentlemen that they are. But, if twelve senators are drunk, and act accordingly, the number is quite sufficient to cast disrepute upon the entire Senate. When the story is told in the public journals, the heading is not "Twelve Senators Drunk." It is "The Senate on a Drunk." This is a heading that I have read in one of the leading journals of the land. I am so utterly imbued with the futility of attempting to make the crooked straight that my impulse was not to mention the matter. The Capital teems with tales of "the glorious past," of Daniel Webster's "drunks," of the toddies and tantrums of many other illustrious men. Why take up the burden of the old sullied strain and proclaim to the land? Still the Senate gets drunk. Though women struggle to the van, shutting up grog-shops, striving, with voices full of tears, with these very senators; still they get drunk, and the world is no better than it used to be. This was the instinctive feeling. I was ashamed for these men, who had such reason to be ashamed of themselves, and, for the sake of the women who loved them, did not want to mention their names. Nor do I now. I refer to the fact already disgracefully public, because, in spite of it, after all, on the whole, I do believe the world to be better than it used to be. In Daniel Webster's day, if the entire Senate had lain drunk under its desks, it would not have sent the thrill of disapprobation, disgust, and shame through the land which moves it now it knows that twelve or fifteen senators were drunk enough in public convocation to make asses of themselves. To-day not only the many senators who did not drink at all, but the drunkards themselves, are ashamed as they recall that night. One generation ago it was quite the common thing. To-day no one is more certain than the participants that such a scene cannot be repeated with impunity; that, if it comes, it will be followed not more surely by disgrace than by defeat.

The opposite was true once. But now people in power are no longer afraid to set the seal of their disapprobation upon promiscuous liquor-drinking. This is true at the White House. It is true also of Speaker Randall, who does not even offer it to his guests. There are Cabinet ministers, also, who do not provide liquors at their public entertainments. These facts mark a new and higher era in official example. It is but the feeling of the masses reaching a climax. The spirit of the people is turned against the sum of horrors entailed by liquor-drinking. The Senate has yet to set the seal of its power on this damning traffic; the seal of its example on tippling and drunkenness. Think of the inspired tones, the tender eloquence of Frances Willard poured in vain on these drunken legislators, as it was, not two weeks ago! Think of the thousands of temperance petitions fluttering through the length of the land into this Senate Chamber, only to drop unheeded from senatorial hands! How could it be otherwise? one asked in that night session, as he counted thirty-five brandy-bottles with empty tumblers in one cloakroom, as he gazed upon the "spreads" set out in the Sergeant-at-Arms's room, as he gazed at a senator vomiting over the costly furniture of the Secretary's room, and at other senators who seemed to be mounting the air, or pawing the ground, or lying back in their seats telling ribald stories to shouting men who were perfectly sober. There was one senator, of long experience and national repute, so drunk he could not stand unsupported at his desk. Even his faithful handkerchief, which almost never fails him, dropped from his hand. Two men, one on either side, held him up, prompting him to utter his "amendment," which he slowly mumbled out, amid shrieks of laughter. At last he sank down in a drunken stupor. His amendment was voted down; when he awoke, [he] arose, and repeated it, amid the wildest mirth of the Senate, who gathered around him almost crazy with merriment. In the middle aisle stood Blaine, perfectly sober, shaking his finger and shouting at a third senator, who bears an honored name in a great state, who a moment later staggered to the cloak-room, helped on by beneficent chairs, that saved him from the floor, and who only reached a sofa to sink at once into a drunken sleep, where he slept, while two feet away another senator thundered at him simple and easy questions, which he was too drunk even to hear. When he awoke, at last, another senator, as drunk as he was, staggered up in front of him, clapping both uncertain hands upon his shoulder; and the two stood thus wavering together like two swinging pendulums, gazing and muttering at each other in the most maudlin manner. The ludicrous picture was too much for the most serious, and both gallery and Senate leaned back and shouted aloud with amusement. There was another senator, who has a reputation for refinement of dress and manner. His personal friends assure me that he "is as sensitive as a woman"; which is unfortunate as he insists on the masculine prerogative of getting "tight." The night he perambulated the Senate Chamber as if "his feet were caught in a skein of sewing silk," and he, in the effort to disentangle them, was disjointing at the knees, with a terrific bump threatening to annihilate the back of his curly head. His affections were of such a lively character that he insisted on hugging and kissing every senator whom he fell against. He was also burdened with a wild desire to speak. His best friend could not keep him still. He broke in, with unintelligible sentences, upon every speaker, and when he attempted to vote fell over his desk.

All this, and a thousand deal more, went on in the Senate Chamber, with the Senate of the United States in full session. With all these senatorial bacchanals afloat, not even sixty sober senators could redeem the aspect of the legislative chamber or make it look other than a convocation of men engaged in the wildest spree.

There was not a senator from New York nor from New England who was intoxicated. There were many senators from the West and from the South who were perfectly sober. Yet the liquor lunatics were all from the South and the West. The masculinity in public life needs a thorough purging of some kind. Making utter exception of perfectly honorable men, whom I know and honor, I am still profoundly impressed with the low tone of public morality and by the utter necessity of its purifying and uplifting. A coarseness which amounts to filthiness always and to brutality often is everywhere apparent in public places. You see it even in the huge spittoons, which should be hung around the neck, as they set at the feet of every doorkeeper, even of the Ladies' Gallery. A lady speaks to one of these men, and until he disburdens his jaws and empties his mouth of a nasty squid, which he does before her face, he cannot even answer her! As masculine muscle still prevents my casting my vote on this subject, I demand (with not a tear in my voice) that no man who makes a public use of tobacco shall ever be appointed to wait upon American ladies in the Capitol. If senators choose to get drunk and to disport upon the Senate floor as buffoons, let not the door of the upper gallery, through which ladies pass to behold them, be defiled even by tobacco. Let the drunkenness and the nastiness be all shut below, while it is given up to men. Do you wonder that the senators shrank so utterly from the invasion of the Senate Chamber by women? The best senators think that politics are not high enough for women. They show such a very decided fondness for them themselves that they continue to monopolize them entirely; but they are not good enough for "my wife." "Do you think I could bear to see my wife in such a place as the Senate Chamber was on Friday night?" said a senator, who has been besieged by suffrage women for the past month, in pathetic tones. "No! no!" with a mournful shake of the head. "Politics are not high enough for women." My friend is utterly sincere. There are many other senators, who never get drunk, who are equally so. Nevertheless, I pass through the "thinness" of their argument as if it had not fell upon me. It is too light for me even to feel its touch. You are honorable, fine-minded men. I admire you considerably; but I don't mind you, not I! You are no freer from nonsense than your brethren are from cant. You know a thing or two—here and there a language, and considerable about law. You are perfectly certain what you want, and what you don't want; but, bless me, you don't know half as much as you think you do. Some of the subtle forces forcing the human race up the path of progression are beyond your ken. Remember, brother, you abide on the plane of tobacco-juice, brandy-bottles, and doubtful stories. They are not yours, you may not tell them; but you live where they are, so you must not take on airs to me. You can't awe me, simply because you are a man. You can arouse my reverence only through exalted qualities. Greatness never assumes. Greatness never says: "I am great; thou art small." Greatness says: "Mine is the human nature; so, too, is thine. Inspire me. I will not hinder thee. Freer by nature than thou, I will not add the smallest weight to thy lifting hands. Use as I use the great gift of human life, according to thine impulse and thy power. What am I, to assume to dictate to thee?" The other sort of senator, who turns his back on woman in politics—save as she appears there in the lobby, or in worse places—is the senator who gets drunk, who wants the brandy-bottles, the "spreads" in the Sergeant-at-Arms's room, the sprees, the dirty stories, all to himself. In such flights an elegant lady might be in the way, you know. When you falteringly say "It would be degrading to the lady herself," I am constrained to answer: "That is all bosh!" A thousand doorkeepers more than I already encounter, with spittoons around their necks, or ten thousand drunken senators, making gyrations to the invisible, could not degrade me an atom, nor any lady. I should immediately proceed to help make a law that would keep the senators sober or keep them at home, and the tobacco-imbibing doorkeepers would suddenly grow invisible. They should certainly provide for their numerous small children and serve their country outside of its Capitol. A humiliating sight, and so humiliating that I shall not witness it again, is that of women pleading, begging of such men for that political equality, which no company of men will ever grant; which, when it comes, as come it will, must come through that greater development and education of men, which can come only by women. When women as a sex are great enough to make men more humble as men, great enough to fill any position to which they aspire, a few women will not have to plead. Let petitions to Congress from tens of thousands of women continue to come in to Congress. In spite of Father Christiancy, who don't want them to come, yet says "he will vote for woman suffrage when the majority want it," let them continue to come, that he may not be left in ignorance of that "majority"; and, at dignified intervals, let a great woman make a great speech, to back the petitions. But don't use the weapons of weakness. For mercy's sake, don't "gad-fly" the men. The Lord never made a man that will not run from that sort of operation; and who can blame him?

The masculine creature has an instinctive aversion to being nagged. And I, who have an equal compassion for the weaknesses of both sides of humanity, for one, don't want him nagged. His lovely neighbor, who may wear to his delight the rose of womanhood for him, or be a jabbing thorn stuck in his side, will never make out much in her own behalf, while his muscles unfortunately continue tougher than hers, if she persists in irritating him in any way. Even his tremendous "judgment" will go under if you make him "mad." And as for you and your "cause," it is lost the moment you make yourself ridiculous. That moment he ensconces himself on the throne of his masculine prerogative, into which the ridiculous finds it not impossible to enter. But never mind. If through your weakness he is on that throne, your beating against it will only be the wave breaking on the rock. So don't appoint "female prayer-meetings" in the Senate lobby; and, when you have said one brave, broad, honest say, *say no more*, but go home and stay there. It weakens your influence, it harms your cause to pursue senators and representatives, as they have been pursued for the last month. Thoughtful men will not forget the heroic utterances of Elizabeth Cady Stanton; Dr. Thompson, of Oregon; Mrs. Lawrence, of Massachusetts; and other ladies who addressed the Senate Committee of Privileges and Elections, in January.

*   *   *

As, for the first time this winter, I have written slightly of woman suffrage, letters are coming in to me addressing me concerning "My Cause." Let me assure my friends that I have no "cause" but the cause of human nature. I simply believe in the equality of humanity; that every creature God has made has an equal right to make the most and the best of itself, of all its powers; and that in the struggles of growth it should not be hindered in the slightest by law, by so-called religion, nor by human selfishness.

I do not care more for the rights of women than for the rights of men. If I speak more tenderly of women, it is because ages of physical servitude have put them at such great disadvantage. We lean toward the worsted side—the side weakened by suffering. But a woman should be femininely strong, as a man should be masculinely brave. "Superior to her sex" is a phrase that should be blotted from English speech. Because I believe in the future of the human race, I believe in the growth, the perfect development, the emancipation of woman, for the sake of the whole.

Washington, D.C., Feb. 27, 1878[7]

Sara Clarke Lippincott

Sara Clarke Lippincott first came to Washington as a young woman before the Civil War and worked as an assistant editor on an abolition newspaper, the *National Era*. As Grace Greenwood, she was one of a number of women writers in the 1850s who gained success under a floral pseudonym to suit the era of sentimental literature.

Returning to the capital following a successful career as a writer of children's books and lecturer on patriotic themes, she wrote a series of columns for the *New York Times* from 1873 until 1878. In her columns, Grace Greenwood attacked corruption, supported the cause of women government workers, and was appalled by the willingness of the Hayes administration to permit the return of white supremacy in the South.

A supporter of woman suffrage, she opposed divorce even though her own marriage proved tragic. Her husband, Leander Lippincott, was indicted in a conspiracy to file false land claims and disappeared in 1878, while she was traveling abroad to provide her only child, a daughter, with a musical education. A prolific author of newspaper and magazine articles, she continued to write almost up to the day of her death in New Rochelle, New York, at the age of 80.

Excerpts from two of Sara Clarke Lippincott's Grace Greenwood columns from Washington for the *New York Times* are reprinted here. One dates from 1873 and the other, 1877.

WASHINGTON NOTES
By Grace Greenwood

Tuesday, Jan. 20, 1873

A newspaper paragraph tells me that the late earthquake in Idaho lifted one man "two feet into the air." The feelings of that poor man can be readily realized by every member of Congress implicated in this unfortunate dis-Credit Mobilier. The disclosure seems to come to them as a sudden shock—to surprise and bewilder them—a fact which to my mind is a proof that they were, none of them, in the first place, consciously and perversely dishonest in the transaction. But the absolute ignorance, in some cases, of the fact of owning stock of this sort at all is a singular feature of the case. What poor heads for business these patriots and statesmen have! How forgetful and inaccurate are they in pecuniary matters. Why, women could scarcely do any worse. I am not going to preach a lay-sermon to our unfortunate brothers who have so suddenly passed from the warm sunshine of worldly favor into the cold shadow of suspicion and obloquy. In the discredited word of some of them, I have a faith as tenacious as that of the little boy who in a dispute with his sister exclaimed, "It's true, for ma said so; and if ma says it's so, it's so, if it ain' so." I am sorry for them all, but I can only say "the pity of it," and hope for a good deliverance. One thing, however, has forcibly struck me, as it doubtless has many others: it is that those have fared best in this business who have been the most daring and outspoken. Next to blamelessness is fearlessness. Next to absolute moral purity is moral courage. We know there can be courage without purity, but it is difficult to believe there can be purity without courage. I like to see a man face the music, even if it play the "Death March," or worse, the "Rogue's March." As politic as plucky were the honorable gentlemen who simply said, "Yes, I took some of the stock, and am only sorry I had not the means to take more."

For them the storm has blown over. The world may set them down as defiant and morally obtuse, but it can neither pity nor laugh at them. Open confession is good for the soul, but it must be of the prompt, unhesitating sort. Neither gracious nor efficacious is a late, reluctant avowal, like that of the Yankee deacon under church discipline, who obstinately fought the charge, prevaricated and doubled on his tracks till the close of his trial, then rose, in the last ditch of his pew, and said, "Brethren, if you will have it so, I plead guilty. I own up, for I don't think it is the part of a good Christian to hold out when a thing is fairly proved agin him."

But if a tithe of what is charged is true, surely something is out of joint; there must be serious deficiencies in pay and privileges, if any of our faithful servants in Congress "needs must play such pranks as these." Let the country look to it that they be no more so sorely tempted. The proposition to increase their salaries is most timely. Do that, and double their mileage, conserve the franking privilege, and make their railroad passes transferable, so that they can turn a penny now and then by disposing of them. Let us, the people, make any sacrifice to secure moral immunity to these representative men, who dwell in "a city set on a hill, which cannot be hid"—who are lights set in the great brazen candlesticks of the nation. To be able to meet their needs, let a deaf ear be once more turned to the demand of the poor clerks of the departments for an increase of salary; refuse yet again the humble petition of the women for equal pay for equal services. *They* are used to refusal, to waiting, to disappointments—as well used as is the *anquilla* to being skinned or the *astacus* to being boiled. Let us economize in every way, whatever it may cost us; let us do without statues to our dead heroes, the only heroes we are sure of—though no grist goes to the Mills, *pere et fils*, and more than one lady sculptor models in vain, and sits herself like Patience on a monument smiling at the Library Committee; let us sell the marble of the Washington Monument; let us dismiss the Board of Public Works. Only make Congress thoroughly comfortable, and all these good things shall be added. While this beloved body is in its present impecunious and unprotected state, exposed to the seductive wiles of shrewd men of the world and heartless adventurers, there can be no peace or security, political or moral, for any of us.

A stern Democratic statesman said to me the other day, "The disgrace of this transaction, Madam, will cling to the descendants of these men for generations." I shuddered, but disposed, as I always am, to look on the bright side of things, replied, "Ah, no; let us hope that in those times there will be so much bigger jobs of the sort, more undeniable and disreputable bargains and sales, that this will sink into insignificance and be forgotten." Progress is the law of the universe. I doubt not that they had their modest little Credit Mobilier affairs in the time of Jefferson and the elder Adams. Talleyrand, that Solomon of profane history, says: "The present age has produced a great many new things, but not a new mankind."

I, as a woman, am disposed to be especially charitable. If I had been born to regard the world as "mine oyster," to believe money and power my right, as one of the irresponsible lords of creation—if I had been a poor struggling politician, an underpaid patriot voting and office-seeking, and going to Congress for a century or so, I might thus have been tempted, might thus have succumbed—in a sort of a way—been subsidized and Mobilier-ized without knowing it. Let us women not "think of ourselves more highly than we ought to think," but be humble and thankful. The pious Mohammedan father says to his son, while pointing to the profane Frank, "But for the mercy of God, thou mightest have been as one of these."[8]

THE NEW ORDER OF THINGS
From Our Special Correspondent
Washington, Tuesday, July 3, 1877

Many times during the past six months I have been called to account in various quarters for my political utterances, denominated "heresies" and "vagaries." Sometimes I have been strangely misunderstood, but often too well understood for the pleasure of my critics, especially of the reformed Republican school. I have been sharply rebuked by my brothers, as an indiscreet sister—"speaking out in meeting," and revealing the secrets of the vestry, the deacons, the elders, and holy men generally. I have been roughly reminded that I was a woman, and told that I ought to be sternly remanded by public opinion to woman's proper sphere, where the eternal unbaked pudding and the immemorial unattached shirt-button await my attention. That same sphere is a good one to fall back upon. I can "rastle" with cooking and sewing as well as any of my gentler sisters, but just at present I confess I prefer serving up a spicy hash of Southern Democratic sentiment to concocting a pudding, and pricking with my pen "the bubble reputation" of political charlatans to puncturing innocent muslin with my needle. I hear I am accused of "making war on the civil service reform." I deny the charge. I attack only the poor pretense, the idle parade, the misleading semblance of reform. Of the great system of moral and political reform in Government service, which is the text of so many eloquent leaders, which is to so many political enthusiasts "the substance of things hoped for, and the evidence of things not seen," we really know little here, where it is popularly supposed to be making such magnificent headway—and perhaps is. It works out of sight in the deeps of Cabinet councils and departmental negotiations and diplomacies—"caverns measureless to men."[9]

Notes

1. Joyce C. Warren, "Introduction," to Fanny Fern (Sara Willis Parton), *Ruth Hall and Other Writings* (New Brunswick, NJ: Rutgers University Press, 1986), p. xiii.

2. Warren, "Introduction," p. xi.

3. From Fern, *Ruth Hall and Other Writings*.

4. Donald A. Ritchie, *Press Gallery: Congress and the Washington Correspondents* (Cambridge, MA: Harvard University Press, 1991).

5. Maurine H. Beasley, *The First Women Washington Correspondents* (Washington, DC: George Washington University, 1976), p. 24.

6. For a comprehensive discussion of Briggs and other women correspondents, see Ritchie, *Press Gallery*, pp. 145–62.

7. From the *New York Independent*, March 7, 1878, and available in the collection of Ames clippings at the Rutherford B. Hayes Memorial Library, Fremont, Ohio.

8. From the *New York Times*, January 20, 1873.

9. From the *New York Times*, July 3, 1877.

9

Pioneer
African-American Journalists
Ida Wells-Barnett

In 1886 the *Journalist*, a trade publication, estimated that 500 women worked regularly on the editorial side of American newspapers, while two years later it estimated there were 200 women on New York newspapers alone. In 1889 the weekly publication devoted an entire issue to women journalists, including biographical sketches of 50 individuals, ten of whom were black, representing all geographical areas of the country. In praising their achievements, the editor noted that all women journalists were still "true women" even though they supported themselves by wielding a pencil instead of a needle to sew on buttons for the "lords of creation." Many of the black women mentioned sold articles to both black and white publications.

Of the black group, Ida Wells (later Ida Wells-Barnett) achieved the most distinguished career.[1] Born to slave parents, she called for equal rights for her race. She brought a test case in Memphis that challenged segregated railroad cars, and she criticized the inadequate Memphis schools for Negroes. When this latter act caused the loss of her job as a teacher in Memphis, she became an owner of the *Memphis Free Speech* and devoted herself to her journalistic career.[2]

After three of her friends were lynched in 1892, she wrote eloquent editorials against the crime of lynching. Her newspaper office was destroyed as a result, and she moved to New York to work for the *New York Age* and continued to crusade against lynching.[3] She founded both Negro women's clubs and antilynching societies and lectured widely in the United States and England. Following her marriage in 1895 to Ferdinand L. Barnett, lawyer and editor, she lived in Chicago and wrote for several newspapers up to her death in 1931. She also tried to aid southern blacks moving to Chicago.

Reprinted here is the section titled "Some Female Writers of the Negro Race," written by Lucy Wilmot Smith in the *Journalist* on January 26, 1889. It is followed by a chapter from *Southern Horrors: Lynch Law in All Its Phases*, a book written by Ida Wells-Barnett and published by the *New York Age* in 1892, giving the background for the destruction of her newspaper.

SOME FEMALE WRITERS OF THE NEGRO RACE

The Negro woman's history is marvelously strange and pathetic. Unlike that of other races, her mental, moral, and physical status has not found a place in the archives of public libraries. From the womb of the future must come that poet or author to glorify her womanhood by idealizing the various phases of her character, by digging from the past, examples of faithfulness and sympathy, endurance and self-sacrifice and displaying the achievements which were brightened by friction. Born and bred under both the hindrances of slavery and limitations of her sex, the mothers of the race have kept pace with the fathers. They stand at the head of cultured, educated families whose daughters clasp arms with the sons. The educated Negro woman occupies vantage ground over the Caucasian woman of America, in that the former has had to contest with her brother every inch of the ground for recognition; the Negro man, having had his sister by his side on plantations and in rice swamps, keeps her there, now that he moves in other spheres. As she wins laurels he accords her the royal crown. This is especially true in journalism. Doors opened before we knock, and as well equipped young women emerge from the class-room the brotherhood of the race, men whose own energies have been repressed and distorted by the interposition of circumstances, give them opportunities to prove themselves; and right well are they doing this by voice and pen. On matters pertaining to women and the race, there is no better author among our female writers than MRS. N.F. MOSSELL—Her style is clear, compact and convincing. Seven years teaching in Camden, N.J., and Philadelphia, her present home, and the solid reading matter, viz.: The Bible, "Paradise Lost," *The Atlantic Monthly* and *The Public Ledger*, which was her daily food while under her father's roof, gave her a deep insight into human nature, and the clear mode of expression which makes her articles so valuable to the press. Her career began many years ago, when Bishop Tanner—then editor of *The Christian Recorder*—was attracted by an essay on "Influence" which he requested for publication. Short stories followed, and from then to the present, she has been engaged constantly on race journals. "The Woman's Department" of the *New York Freeman* was edited by her with much tact and *The Philadelphia Echo* is always more readable when containing something from her pen. For three years she has been employed on the *Philadelphia Times*,

Independent and *Philadelphia Press Republican,* following the particular lines of race literature and the "Woman's Question." Mrs. Mossell's experience in journalism is that editors are among the most patient of men; that the rejection of an article by no means proves that it is a failure; that sex is no bar to any line of literary work; that by speaking for themselves women can give the truth about themselves and thereby inspire the confidence of the people. Besides newspaper work her home life is a busy one, assisting her husband, a prominent physician of Philadelphia, whose own literary life has been an incentive to her. Spare moments are given to the completion of a book, on a race question, which will soon be launched on the current of thought and society.

MRS. LUCRETIA NEWMAN-COLEMAN is a writer of rare ability. Discriminating and scholarly, she possesses to a high degree the poetic temperament and has acquired great facility in verse. Her last poem, "Lucile of Montana," ran through several numbers of the magazine *Our Women and Children,* and is full of ardor, eloquence and noble thought. Mrs. Coleman has contributed special scientific articles to the *A.M.E. Review* and other journals, which were rich in minute comparisons, philosophic terms and scientific principles. She is a writer more for scholars than for the people. A novel entitled *Poor Ben,* which is the epitome of the life of a prominent A.M.E. Bishop, is pronounced an excellent production. Mrs. Coleman is an accomplished woman and well prepared for a literary life. She was born in Dresden, Ontario, went with her missionary father to the West Indies where he labored a number of years, thence to Cincinnati, O., where he was pastor of a church, and after his death she went with her mother to Appleton, Wisconsin, to take advantage of educational facilities. After graduating from the scientific course of Lawrence University, she devoted her time to literary pursuits, and now ranks with the most painstaking writers.

MISS IDA B. WELLS, (IOLA), has been called the "Princess of the Press," and she has earned the title. No writer, the male fraternity not excepted, has been more extensively quoted; none have struck harder blows at the wrongs and weakness of the race. T. T. Fortune (probably the "Prince" of the Negro press) wrote after meeting her at the Democratic Conference in Indianapolis: "She has become famous as one of the few of our women who handle a goose-quill with diamond point as easily as any man in the newspaper work. If Iola was a man, she would be a humming independent in politics. She has plenty of nerve and is as sharp as a steel trap."

Miss Wells' readers are equally divided between the sexes. She reaches the men by dealing with the political aspect of the race question, and the women, she meets around the fireside. She is an inspiration to the young writers and her success has lent an impetus to their ambition. When the National Press Convention, of which she was Assistant Secretary, met in Louisville she read a splendidly written paper on "Women in Journalism; or How I Would Edit." By the way, it is her ambition to edit a paper. She believes that there is no agency so potent as the press in reaching and elevating a people. Her contributions are distributed among the leading race journals. She made her debut with the *Living Way*, Memphis, Tenn., and has since written for *The New York Age, Detroit Plaindealer, Indianapolis World, Gate City Press*, Mo., *Little Rock Sun, American Baptist*, Ky., *Memphis Watchman, Chattanooga Justice, Christian Index* and *Fisk University Herald*, Tenn., *Our Women and Children* magazine, Ky., and the Memphis papers, weeklies and dailies. Miss Wells has attained much success as teacher in the public schools of the last named place.

MRS. W. E. MATHEWS (VICTORIA EARLE)—Ten years ago "Victoria Earle" began taking advantage of opportunities offered for acting as "sub" for reporters employed by many of the great dailies. She has reported for the *New York Times, Herald, Mail* and *Express, Sunday Mercury, The Earth, The Phonographic* [*sic*] *World*, and is now New York correspondent to the *National Leader*, D.C., *The Detroit Plaindealer*, and the *Southern Christian Recorder*. Under various *noms de plume* she has written for the *Boston Advocate, Washington Bee, Richmond Planet, Catholic Tribune, Cleveland Gazette, New York Age, New York Globe*, and the *New York Enterprise*, besides editing three special departments. Reportorial work is her forte, yet her success in story writing has been great. She contributes to the story department of *Waverley Magazine, The New York Weekly* and *Family Story Paper*. "Victoria Earle" has written much; her dialect tid-bits for the Associated Press are much in demand. She has ready several stories which will appear in one volume, and is also preparing a series of historical textbooks which will aim to develop a race pride in our youth. She is a member of the Women's National Press Association and no writer of the race is kept busier.

MISS MARY V. COOK (GRACE ERMINE)—Whatever honors have come to Miss Cook are the results of persevering industry. She has edited the Woman's Department of the *American Baptist*, Ky., and the Educational Department of *Our Women and Children* in such a manner as to attract much attention to them. Her writings are lucid and logical and of such a character as will stand the test of time. Aside from journalistic work her life is a busy one. She has appeared on the platform of several national gatherings and her papers for research, elegance of diction and sound reasoning were superior. She holds the professorship of Latin at the State University, her Alma Mater, yet, however great her mental ability, it is overmatched by her character. Her life is the chrystalization [*sic*] of womanly qualities. She moves her associates by a mighty power of sympathy which permeates her writings. She is a good news gatherer and is much quoted, is a native of Bowling Green, Ky., where her mother, a generous hearted woman who sympathizes with her aspirations, still lives. Miss Cook is interested in all questions which affect the race.

In the mild countenance of MRS. AMEILIA [*sic*] E. JOHNSON can be read the love and tenderness for children which was demonstrated last year by the publication of *The Ivy*, an eight-page journal devoted especially to the interests of our youth. It was a good paper filled with original stories and poems and information concerning the doings of the race. Mrs. Johnson is keen, imaginative and critical; story writing is her forte. It is a part of her nature to weave her thoughts into pleasing imagery. Even when a child she would follow the scratches on her desk with a pencil and tell wonderful stories of them to her seatmate. She has written many of them at different times and is now engaged in writing a story book to be used in Sunday-school libraries. Many short poems from her pen find snug resting places in corners of weeklies. There is a vein of wit and humor in her sayings—a pith and transparency which makes her articles extremely readable. Of all the writers before the public none possesses in a higher degree the elements of a skillful critic. She has contributed to the *Baptist Messenger*, Md., *The American Baptist*, Ky., and *Our Women and Children* magazine. Mrs. Johnson was educated in Canada— taking a thorough French course—and has taught both French and English branches in Baltimore, her present home.

LILLIAN ALBERTA LEWIS (BERT ISLEW).—Those who know much about the newspapers of the race, know something of Bert Islew's Budget of Gossip in the spicy "They Say Column" of the *Boston Advocate*. Bright, witty, sparkling, one would not think Bert Islew's career antedates only three years and that she was barely twenty when she caught the public ear. The early atmosphere she breathed may have developed a public spiritedness. Was born in the home of Hon. Lewis Hayden, that good man whose name is closely associated with the Crispus Attucks monument. When but thirteen years old and in the graduating class of the Bowdoin Grammar School she entered a prize essay contest and carried off the third prize, although the other contestants were older High School pupils and graduates. This fired her ambition, and soon after graduation she wrote a novel entitled, "Idalene Van Therese," which, for lack of means is unpublished. Then came her successful career with the *Advocate*. In addition to her newspaper work, she has for several years been the private stenographer and secretary to the widely known Max Eliot, of the *Boston Herald*. This position calls for proficiency; and Bert Islew's record for taking down copy verbatim is among the highest in New England. Then, too, her position in the *Herald* office calls for special articles and reportorial work which she does creditably. She is recognized in all circles for her ability, and works side by side with editors and reporters without an iota of distinction being made.

To the ready pen of MISS MARY E. BRITTON (MEB) is due many of the reformatory measures which have given the race equal facilities on railroads in Kentucky. The energy and resolute vim of her character is traced in her writings, especially when advocating woman's suffrage and the same moral standard for both sexes. She has studied language from the standard English and American authors and her diction is remarkably chaste. Miss Britton was editor of the "Woman's Column" of the *Lexington Herald*, contributes special articles to the *Courant*—the Kentucky educational journal—the *Cleveland Gazette*, *The American Catholic Tribune*, the *Indianapolis World* and *Our Women and Children* magazine. Her own ambition to excel prompts her to inspire others and nearly all her articles have this [message] and [this] was exhibited in those written for *The Ivy*, the children's paper. The local papers of Lexington, Ky., her home, and the *Cincinnati Commercial* have published and commented on her articles.

MISS IONE E. WOOD—There is a dash of freshness, a breezyness in Miss Wood's writings, a clear, decided ring which will yet be heard in louder tones. She has very pronounced views on total abstinence and is an enthusiastic member of the Woman's National Suffrage Association. She contributed several stories to *The Ivy* and now edits the Temperance Department of *Our Women and Children* magazine. Miss Wood will make a clever reporter. She is now tutor in Greek in the Kentucky State University.

MISS KATIE D. CHAPMAN sends from her far away Dakota home, spritely poems and other contributions to racial journals. She is only eighteen, but the public is becoming familiar with her bright thoughts and unique expressions. She has read much and will write much. Her contributions have appeared principally in *The Christian Recorder* and *Our Women and Children*. Her ambition was stirred when but five years old by receiving a book as reward for [memorizing] a poem. She will devote her talent to juvenile literature.

OCCASIONAL CONTRIBUTORS.—Among those who do special work and contribute valuable articles to weeklies and monthlies are Mesdames Francis E. W. Harper and L. F. Grimke, Philadelphia; Cora C. Calhoun, former editor of the Woman's Department in the *Chattanooga Justice*; Olive B. Clanton, New Orleans; Lavinia E. Sneed, Ky.; Josephine Turpin Washington, Selma; Misses Georgia M. DeBaptiste, Ill.; Julia K. Mason, D.C.; Alice Henderson, Ark.; and Meta Pelham, one of the essentials on the *Plaindealer* staff.

EDITORS.—*The Western Herald* was edited by Mrs. Amos Johnson, Keokuk, Ia.: *The Lancet*, by Miss Carrie Bragg, Petersburg, Va.; *The Musical Messenger*, by Miss Amelia L. Tighlman, Montgomery, Ala.; *The St. Matthew's Lyceum*, by Mrs. M. E. Lambert, Detroit, Mich.; *The Ivy*, by Mrs. A. E. Johnson, Baltimore, Md., and Miss A. E. McEwen is Assistant Editor of the *Herald*, Montgomery, Ala.

This article includes only a few of our writers. When we remember the very difficult circumstances of the past, the trials and discomforts of the present, we are indeed cheered with the prospects. In the busy hum of life it is difficult to make one's way to the front, and this is true of all races, hence, we are not at all discouraged since our sisters have had such ready access to the great journals of the land. When the edge of prejudice shall have become rusted and worn out, the Negro woman shall be heard most potently in the realm of thought; till then we shall strive.

Lucy Wilmot Smith
1889[4]

THE OFFENSE
[By Ida Wells]

Wednesday evening, May 24th, 1892, the city of Memphis was filled with excitement. Editorials in the daily papers of that date caused a meeting to be held in the Cotton Exchange Building; a committee was sent for the editors of the *Free Speech*, an Afro-American journal published in that city, and the only reason the open threats of lynching that were made were not carried out was because they could not be found. The cause of all this commotion was the following editorial published in the *Free Speech*, May 21st, 1892, the Saturday previous.

"Eight negroes lynched since the last issue of the *Free Speech*, one at Little Rock, Ark., last Saturday morning where the citizens broke (?) into the penitentiary and got their man; three near Anniston, Ala., one near New Orleans; and three at Clarksville, Ga., the last three for killing a white man, and five on the same old racket—the new alarm about raping white women. The same programme of hanging, then shooting bullets into the lifeless bodies was carried out to the letter.

"Nobody in this section of the country believes the old thread bare lie that negro men rape white women. If Southern white men are not careful, they will over-reach themselves and public sentiment will have a reaction; a conclusion will then be reached which will be very damaging to the moral reputation of their women."

The Daily Commercial of Wednesday following, May 25th, contained the following leader:

"Those negroes who are attempting to make the lynching of individuals of their race a means for arousing the worst passions of their kind are playing with a dangerous sentiment. The negroes may as well understand that there is no mercy for the negro rapist and little patience with his defenders. A negro organ printed in this city, in a recent issue publishes the following atrocious paragraph: 'Nobody in this section of the country believes the old thread-bare lie that negro men rape white women. If Southern white men are not careful they will over-reach themselves, and public sentiment will have a reaction; and a conclusion will be reached which will be very damaging to the moral reputation of their women.'

"The fact that a black scoundrel is allowed to live and utter such loathsome and repulsive calumnies is a volume of evidence as to the wonderful patience of Southern whites. But we have had enough of it.

"There are some things that the Southern white man will not tolerate, and the obscene intimations of the foregoing have brought the writer to the very outermost limit of public patience. We hope we have said enough."

The *Evening Scimitar* of same date, copied the *Commercial*'s editorial with these words of comment: "Patience under such circumstances is not a virtue. If the negroes themselves do not apply the remedy without delay it will be the duty of those whom he has attacked to tie the wretch who utters these calumnies to a stake at the intersection of Main and Madison Streets, brand him in the forehead with a hot iron and perform upon him a surgical operation with a pair of tailor's shears.''

Acting upon this advice, the leading citizens met in the Cotton Exchange Building the same evening, and threats of lynching were freely indulged, not by the lawless element upon which the deviltry of the South is usually saddled—but by the leading business men, in their leading business centre. Mr. [J. L.] Fleming, the business manager and owning a half interest [in] the *Free Speech*, had to leave town to escape the mob, and was afterwards ordered not to return; letters and telegrams sent me in New York where I was spending my vacation advised me that bodily harm awaited my return. Creditors took possession of the office and sold the outfit, and the *Free Speech* was as if it had never been.

The editorial in question was prompted by the many inhuman and fiendish lynchings of Afro-Americans which have recently taken place and was meant as a warning. Eight lynched in one week and five of them charged with rape! The thinking public will not easily believe freedom and education more brutalizing than slavery, and the world knows that the crime of rape was unknown during four years of civil war, when the white women of the South were at the mercy of the race which is all at once charged with being a bestial one.

Since my business has been destroyed and I am an exile from home because of that editorial, the issue has been forced, and as the writer of it I felt that the race and the public generally should have a statement of the facts as they exist. They will serve at the same time as a defense for the Afro-American Sampsons who suffer themselves to be betrayed by white Delilahs.

The whites of Montgomery, Ala., knew J. C. Duke sounded the keynote of the situation—which they would gladly hide from the world, when he said, in his paper, *The Herald*, five years ago: "Why is it that white women attract negro men now more than in former days? There was a time when such a thing was unheard of. There is a secret to this thing, and we greatly suspect it is the growing appreciation of white Juliets for colored Romeos." Mr. Duke, like the *Free Speech* proprietors, was forced to leave the city for reflecting on the "honah" of white women and his paper suppressed; but the truth remains that Afro-American men do not always rape (?) white women without their consent.

Mr. Duke, before leaving Montgomery, signed a card disclaiming any intention of slandering Southern white women. The editor of the *Free Speech* has no disclaimer to enter, but asserts instead that there are many white women in the South who would marry colored men if such an act would not place them at once beyond the pale of society and within the clutches of the law. The miscegenation laws of the South only operate against the legitimate union of the races; they leave the white man free to seduce all the colored girls he can, but it is death to the colored man who yields to the force and advances of a similar attraction in white women. White men lynch the offending Afro-American, not because he is a despoiler of virtue, but because he succumbs to the smiles of white women.[5]

Notes

1. See "Ida B. Wells-Barnett Crusader," in Madelon Golden Schilpp and Sharon M. Murphy, *Great Women of the Press* (Carbondale: Southern Illinois University Press, 1983), pp. 121–32.

2. Barbara Belford, *Brilliant Bylines* (New York: Columbia University Press, 1986), pp. 88–89.

3. August Meier, "Preface," to Ida B. Wells-Barnett, *On Lynchings: Southern Horrors, A Red Record, Mob Rule in New Orleans* (New York: Arno Press and the New York Times Company, 1969).

4. From the *Journalist*, January 26, 1889, available at the Library of Congress.

5. From *Southern Horrors: Lynch Law in All Its Phases* (1892), reprinted in Wells-Barnett, *On Lynchings*.

10

Stunt Reporters and Sob Sisters
Elizabeth Cochrane
Winifred Black Bonfils

With Joseph Pulitzer's *New York World* leading the way, new formulas for metropolitan newspapers emerged in the late nineteenth century, combining colorful and sensational news, crusades, illustrations, and extravagant promotion. Casting off its preoccupation with politics, the press turned to human interest reporting, employing an increasing number of women reporters. Although most were restricted to the new women's and society pages, designed to capitalize on department store advertising aimed at housewives, a few women reporters were allowed to work in city rooms beside men reporters. Sally Joy White, believed to be the first woman regularly employed as a staff writer on a metropolitan paper, started on the *Boston Post* in 1870.[1]

Editors frequently exploited the sex of capable women reporters by assigning them stunts deemed especially daring for women or making them "sob sisters," specializing in tear-jerking accounts of flamboyant events. Women reporters ascended in balloons, descended in diving bells, dressed up like beggars and waifs, feigned madness, and posed as servants in the homes of society figures to pursue exciting and scandalous tidbits for their readers.[2]

Elizabeth Cochrane

The most famous stunt reporter byline of all, "Nellie Bly," belonged to a determined young woman from Pittsburgh named Elizabeth Cochrane. As a teenager she started reporting to support herself after her father's death, receiving her pseudonym from a Pittsburgh editor who took it from a Stephen C. Foster song. Following crusades against factory conditions in Pittsburgh, she tackled the New York journalistic scene in 1887, and resolved to reach the top. It did not take her long.

She landed a job on the *New York World* by exposing the mistreatment of patients at the Blackwell's Island insane asylum, after pretending to go berserk and being committed there. When her sensational revelations led to a grand jury investigation, Nellie Bly's career soared. More first-person accounts enthralled readers as she had herself arrested for theft to expose women's prisons, masqueraded as an invalid to investigate free medical care, toiled in department stores and factories to picture the plight of underpaid employees, posed as an unemployed servant to reveal employment agency practices, and foiled the schemes of Central Park mashers who seduced young women.[3]

But her greatest triumph came in 1889 at the age of 24 when she raced around the world to beat the record of Phineas Fogg, the hero of Jules Verne's romance *Around the World in Eighty Days*. As she made the journey in 72 days, 6 hours, and 11 minutes, Pulitzer promoted her as a front-page heroine, personifying the independent American girl, the fascination of travel, and the excitement of journalism. One of the greatest publicity stunts of all time, the trip was rooted in theatrical—not journalistic—goals, making Nellie Bly a national celebrity with clothes, games and toys named for her. Most of the stories about her trip were written by other reporters, apparently because she was too busy traveling to file dispatches by the then-primitive cable, although on her final dash from California to New York by train she dictated notes of her adventures for publication.

Nellie Bly's first complete account of her trip around the world in 73 days appeared in the *New York World* on January 26, 1890, one day after she returned from her record-breaking journey. Headed "From Jersey Back to Jersey," it was prefaced with two paragraphs by the *World* noting that she had dictated the article on the train while "speeding from Chicago to New York at nearly fifty miles per hour," in the midst of being feted by well-wishers. Excerpts are reprinted here.

FROM JERSEY BACK TO JERSEY

M. Jules Verne said it could not be done. I have done it. He told me when he met me at Amiens that if the tour was made of the world in seventy-nine days he would applaud with both hands. It has been made in seventy-two days, and M. Verne may now applaud and two hands will not do; he must use four. It was only sixty-eight days from the time I left American soil until I touched it again. During that time I was in many different climes. But only here, in God's own country, have I passed amid fruit and flowers in valley, and over mountain-tops amid snow and frost, all within the space of sixteen hours. In no country save America is the passage from orange groves to snow-crest mountains possible in the same space of time.

I have roasted and I have frozen since leaving home. I have dined on India curry, on Chinese chow and Japanese eel and rice. I have travelled on French and English trains, on English boats, on burros, in jinrickshas, in bullock carts, in catamarans, sampans, gherrys and a half a dozen other conveyances peculiar to Eastern countries in my trip around the world.

Everybody knows that the idea was to make a tour of the world in seventy-five days. At many junctures since my departure have I been compelled to face what looked like failure. Did I ever give up hope of success? No, not exactly. Never having failed, I could not picture what failure meant, but I did tell the officers of the *Oceanic*, when success seemed very, very hazy, owing to the unexpectedly stormy weather, that I would rather go into New York successful and dead than alive and behind time.

When the whistle blew and the steamer *Victoria* moved off from the dock, then for the first time I regretted that I was leaving America. . . .

Miss Jusson, a niece of Carl Schurz, was the only lady besides myself travelling alone. She was going to Germany to her father. There were many bets made on the boat as to whether I would arrive in Southampton in time to catch the India Mail. I took all that were offered. When we failed to arrive at Southampton at the time the steamer was due I felt a little nervous, but still trusted to my never-failing luck.

LANDING IN ENGLAND

At 2:30 Friday morning, Nov. 22, we anchored off Southampton, but shortly afterwards the tug which lands passengers came alongside. A few people came on board, and I waited, with the rest of the passengers, trying to pick from the crowd *The World*'s London correspondent, who was to meet me. To show the interest passengers took in my welfare, one gentleman whom I had never met before leaving New York, said that if *The World*'s correspondent failed to meet me that he would leave the boat at Southampton and see me safely to London. This gentleman had his ticket purchased to Germany, and would have sacrificed all this to assure himself of my safety.

When the tug landed at the pier we had to face the Custom-house officials. *The World* correspondent marched boldly in with my little solitary bag in his hand: "Will you swear that you have no tobacco or tea?" "It is not his, it is mine," I said, at which he smiled and put a crossmark on the bag and allowed us to go free. There was some little delay about the train, the last regular one having left before our arrival, but arrangements were made, owing to the heavy mail, to run a special mail train to London that morning. This was not by any special arrangement of *The World*, but was my own usual good luck.

UP TO LONDON

I was hurried from the Custom-House out to where a dark train stood. A guard, as they call them there, came along, and with a key large enough for a policeman's club, opened a door and I stepped into an English coach. I must say that they leave much to be desired. First, I stumbled over something. Then I was bothered with the odor of the oil lamp. When I sat down I began to investigate the obstacle which had almost put me into the car headforemost. I found what looked to be a long piece of iron, but which I learned was a foot-warmer. They think this is comfortable travelling in England. My feet burned through the thin soles of my shoes while I froze about my shoulders.

In the morning they told me it was daylight or I would not have known it. I have a recollection of dim lights and a gray, dusty shade overhanging the city, and some fine buildings and people beginning to hurry when I reached London. As we glided over the beautifully paved streets I thought with shame of the streets of New York. *The World* correspondent asked, "What do you think of the streets compared with those of New York?" "They are not bad," I replied, patronizingly, determined in true American style not to hear one word against home. After getting my ticket and passport we went to the Victoria Street Station. We gave ourselves time for a light breakfast and started again on an English train. This was more uncomfortable, if anything, than the other, for here the footwarmer was cold. I was on my way now to Amiens to see M. Jules Verne, the author of *Around the World in Eighty Days*. The boat on which we crossed the English Channel was a wretched thing. The people lounged about as if fearing seasickness, but at the same time drank and ate. I sat on deck and enjoyed the beautiful sky and water.

IN LA BELLE FRANCE

We landed at Bologne. Here, I think, my baggage was examined, but I did not see it done as one of the men in the boat with me took charge of it and also found us places in the train bound for Amiens. In the mean time we went into the restaurant on the edge of the pier and had something to eat. I found the waiters able to speak English and willing enough to take American money. The trip to Amiens was slow and tiresome, but I was fully repaid for the journey by meeting M. Jules Verne and his wife, who were waiting for me at the station in company with *The World*'s Paris correspondent. . . .

THE ARRIVAL AT BRINDISI, ITALY

We were due at Brindisi at 12 o'clock, but when it came midnight and we were not yet there I began to get nervous. The train stopped at last and there was a great rush and a good deal of yelling on the part of the men outside, mainly in broken English. The guard took charge of the fair girl and her invalid father and myself. One omnibus was hired for the lot, with an English-speaking driver. There was a little oil-lamp in the front which gave out a weak glimmer and a strong odor. The glimmer at last went out, but the odor remained. Two fat women had so many boxes that when they got them all into the omnibus we had to sit as much on the seats as we could. We drove first to the steamer bound for Bombay, where we bade farewell to the Englishman and his sweet daughter. Then we drove back to the ship that was to carry me to victory or to failure.

ON BOARD THE P. AND O. STEAMER

The two fat women and their numerous bundles and boxes were landed and carefully led up the gang-plank to the ship. Here we found a crowd of men waiting to see the new arrivals. Some one pointed out the purser's room and he looked at my ticket and told me where my cabin was. The picture presented by the cabin interior was unique. Two bushy heads were thrust out of two lower berths and two faces, with wide, inquiring eyes, wore expressions of dismay when they saw that they were threatened with another cabin-mate. Two mouths uttered shrieks of impatience. The upper berth was filled with boxes and loose clothes and boots and such things were scattered over the floor of the cabin. I returned to the purser and handed him a letter from Mr. —, asking him to give me every attention. Then the purser looked at his papers and told me to take cabin 104. There was but one girl to peep out here to see who was entering the room. She proved afterwards to be the prettiest girl on board the ship.

SENDING A CABLE

I put down my hand-bag and went out to the guard who was waiting to take me to the telegraph office, where a cable might be sent to *The World*. The purser said I had not much time, but it could be done. The telegraph office was in a building down a dark street. The little room was bare, and there was only a desk, one sheet of telegraph paper, a bottle without any ink in it and one pen. It had one small window, like a stamp-window in a post-office. But the office was closed, and there was nothing to do except to wait and send a cable from Ismalia.

"The agent is taking a nap, but we'll get him up," said the guard hopefully as he rang a bell near the closed window. He rang it several times, and then the window opened with a creak, as if long unused to business. A dark, sleepy looking face appeared. The guard spoke in Italian and I finished it up in English, to which the man responded quite well. I wrote my cable, after answering his inquiries as to what country New York was in and paying the bill.

NEARLY MISSED THE BOAT TO INDIA

Then we thought of the ship. "The man said we had but a moment," I cried breathlessly to the guard. I might possibly have missed my ship.

"Come," was all he said as his face paled and we started out of the door and down the narrow, dark street.

"Can you run?" he asked, quietly, and I, feeling the anxiety in his tones, felt myself tremble. "Come, I would not have you lose this boat for £50," he cried, and taking my hand without further words we tore madly through the dark streets and along the water's edge.

A whistle blew!

All power seemed to leave me. We stopped in the middle of the street and looked blankly and hopelessly into each other's faces.

"My boat!" I gasped, while my heart ceased beating. And again we started in a mad race which brought us by a sudden curve breathless at the foot of the plank. I uttered a prayer of thanks when I saw the *Victoria* still there. The boat bound for Bombay was gone, but I was saved.

SAFE ON BOARD

I hurried up the gang-plank, leaving the guard to bargain with the venders of chairs on shore, but I would not stay on land another second. I got my chair, testified my thanks to the guard, and went to bed tired but happy. . . .

NOW FOR CHINA . . .

We arrived at the picturesque city of Singapore on the 18th of December, and having a few hours to spare there visited the gardens, the museums, the temples and other points of interest. Some people even here could speak English. I saw the first Chinaman and a Chinese funeral, which was very interesting. During the voyage from Singapore to Hong Kong we had the monsoon against us, but the *Oriental*, which was making its first trip to China and was trying to make a record, fought it bravely and reached Hong Kong two days ahead of my itinerary, Dec. 23. Here was another five days' wait before I could leave for Yokohama. European citizens were very good to me and the newspapers were most kind in mentioning my trip. Christmas Day I spent in Canton, China, eating my lunch in the Temple of the Dead, where there are hundreds of bodies, some of which have been lying in caskets for seventy-five years. While eating my dinner in company with two gentlemen and a Chinese guide, the priests were chanting masses in a room opposite for the repose of recently departed souls.

SIGHT-SEEING IN CHINA

I visited the leper city, saw the shops, the ivory carvers and many other things of interest. On the execution ground eleven people had been beheaded the day before. I returned to Hong Kong after nightfall, because there is no accommodation in Canton for English people. Even the foreign representatives are given a tract of land outside the city walls, which is guarded by soldiers and no Chinese are allowed to enter there, nor can foreigners come near the Chinese city after night has fallen. On Dec. 28 I started for Yokohama on the Occidental and Oriental steamship *Oceanic*. New Year's Eve was celebrated on the boat. A quiet little crowd of Anglo-Americans sat up and welcomed in the New Year, those who could, and those who could not trying to sing "Auld Lang Syne."

YOKOHAMA AT LAST

We had a stormy trip across to Yokohama, bad winds and rough seas, and reached that interesting Japanese town on the morning of Jan. 3. There was a delay here and I went to Tokio, where the Mikado lives, saw the famous Shiba Temple and everything else of interest. I also visited Kama Kura where the great god Diabutsu lives. When our vessel got into port I was waited upon by a representative of a Japanese paper. He presented me with copies of the paper containing a translation of *The World*'s story of my visit to Jules Verne, and also an account of my trip around the world. He interviewed me in a very amusing way, having all the questions written down on paper beforehand in English, which he read over and filled in as I replied. He was a Japanese but spoke English very well. He presented me with copies of the paper containing the interview, which I have brought home with me as a treasured souvenir.

JAPANESE DANCING-GIRLS

The most interesting sight to me in Yokohama were the dancing-girls. I became so infatuated with their beauty and performance that I spent all of my evenings there enjoying and admiring their graceful dancing. The Consul-General's son being absent, his mother, Mrs. Greathouse, called upon me at the hotel. I also met Mrs. Seidmore, who is there with her son, the Assistant Consul. The United States Navy boat *Omaha* gave me a luncheon, and the day I started from Yokohama, Jan. 7, the band on the *Omaha* played for me "Home, Sweet Home," "Hail Columbia" and "The Girl I Left behind Me." Everybody I met in Yokohama did their utmost to make my stay enjoyable.

ACROSS THE PACIFIC

The trip across the Pacific was very tempestuous. In the first three days we were 110 miles ahead of the *Oceanic*'s last record when she broke the record; but all this and more were lost when we struck the headwinds, which stayed with us the greater part of five days. I cannot say more of the crew than that they were perfect, from the captain down. They did everything for the comfort of the passengers, and, strange to say, with all the rough weather, only one or two suffered from seasickness. I could not have felt more grieved over getting into San Francisco one day later than they had expected than did the officers in charge of the *Oceanic*. How I landed in San Francisco and took *The World*'s special train at 9 A.M. Jan. 2, and was whirled across the continent, greeted with kindness and hearty welcomes at every point, has already been told in *The World*.

Nellie Bly.[4]

Elizabeth Cochrane continued her career for five years, then married a wealthy industrialist, Robert L. Seaman, who was 50 years her senior. After his death in 1910, she lost her fortune through several business failures and returned to work as an obscure columnist writing on orphans for William Randolph Hearst's *New York Journal.* She died in 1922.[5]

Winifred Black Bonfils

The champion sob sister, Winifred Black Bonfils, wrote as "Annie Laurie," churning out tearful copy that drew millions of readers. Associated mainly with newspapers owned by Hearst during her 50-year career, she specialized in covering celebrated trials and conducting exposés that revealed social injustices. Through masquerades and other ingenious methods of getting news, she proved a valuable asset to Hearst, who practiced "yellow journalism," that is, sensationalism based on sex and crime news with a veneer of civic responsibility.[6]

Born Martha Winifred Sweet in 1863, she was left an orphan at the age of 15. Initially she pursued a career as an actress but soon left the stage to work for Hearst's *San Francisco Examiner* where she became a West Coast counterpart to Nellie Bly. Later she worked for Hearst's *New York Journal.* Her first exposés involved posing as a poor woman to investigate conditions in a public hospital and taking undercover jobs in factories that exploited woman workers. On one occasion she obtained an interview with President Benjamin Harrison by hiding under a dining car table and popping out with notebook in hand when Harrison sat down for dinner.[7]

Twice married, she brought up three children while holding all types of journalistic positions for Hearst, ranging from reporting to acting as managing editor. But her specialty remained stories with headlines of this type: "Why Young Girls Kill Themselves" and "Strange Things Women Do for Love."[8] Working as a journalist until her death, she died in San Francisco in 1936, a beloved figure whose body lay in state at the city hall.

Reprinted below is one of her most famous stories: a firsthand account of conditions in Galveston, Texas, following a hurricane in 1900 that killed about 6,000 people—making it one of the nation's worst disasters. To get to Galveston, Annie Laurie disguised herself as a boy.

Corpse-laden Waters Lit by Funeral Pyres
Winifred Black Crosses the Dismal Bay of Death
to the Desolate City of Disaster
By Winifred Black (Annie Laurie)

GALVESTON (Texas), Sept. 14—I begged, cajoled and cried my way through the lines of soldiers with drawn swords who guard the wharf at Texas City and sailed across the bay on a little boat which is making irregular trips to meet the relief trains from Houston.

The engineer who brought our train down from Houston spent the night before groping around in the wrecks on the beach looking for his wife and three children. He found them, dug a rude grave in the sand and set up a little board marked with his name. Then he went to the railroad company and begged them to let him go to work.

The man in front of me on the car had floated all Monday night with his wife and mother on a part of the roof of his little home. He told me that he kissed his wife good-bye at midnight and told her that he could not hold on any longer; but he did hold on, dazed and half conscious, until the day broke and showed him that he was alone on his piece of dried wood. He did not even know when the women that he loved had died.

Every man on the train—there were no women there—had lost some one that he loved in the terrible disaster, and was going across the bay to try and find some trace of his family—all except the four men in my party. They were from outside cities—St. Louis, New Orleans and Kansas City. They had lost a large amount of property and were coming down to see if anything could be saved from the wreck.

They had been sworn in as deputy sheriffs in order to get into Galveston. The city is under martial law, and no human being who cannot account for himself to the complete satisfaction of the officers in charge can hope to get through.

We sat on the deck of the little steamer. The four men from out-of-town cities and I listened to the little boat's wheel ploughing its way through the calm waters of the day. The stars shone down like a benediction, but along the line of the shore there rose a great leaping column of blood-red flame.

"What a terrible fire!" I said. "Some of the large buildings must be burning." A man who was passing the deck behind my chair heard me. He stopped, put his hand on the bulwark and turned down and looked into my face, his face like the face of a dead man, but he laughed.

"Buildings?" he said. "Don't you know what is burning over there? It is my wife and children, such little children; why, the tallest was not as high as this"—he laid his hand on the bulwark—"and the little one was just learning to talk.

"She called my name the other day, and now they are burning over there, they and the mother who bore them. She was such a little, tender, delicate thing, always so easily frightened, and now she's out there all alone with the two babies, and they're burning them. If you're looking for sensations, there's plenty of them to be found over there where that smoke is drifting."

The man laughed again and began again to walk up and down the deck.

"That's right," said the U.S. Marshal of Southern Texas, taking off his broad hat and letting the starlight shine on his strong face, "that's right. We've had to do it. We've burned over 1,000 people to-day, and to-morrow we shall burn as many more.

"Yesterday we stopped burying the bodies at sea; we had to give the men on the barges whiskey to give them courage to do their work. They carried out hundreds of the dead at one time, men and women, negroes and white people, all piled up as high as the barge could stand it, and the men did not go out far enough to sea, and the bodies have begun drifting back again."

"Look!" said the man who was walking the deck, touching my shoulder with his shaking hand. "Look there!"

Before I had time to think I did look, and I saw floating in the water the body of an old, old woman, whose hair was shining in the starlight. A little further on we saw a group of strange driftwood. We looked closer and found it to be a mass of wooden slabs with names and dates cut upon them, and floating on top of them were marble stones, two of them.

The graveyard, which has held the sleeping citizens of Galveston for many, many years, was giving up its dead. We pulled up at a little wharf in the hush of the starlight; there were no lights anywhere in the city except a few scattered lamps shining from a few desolate, half-destroyed houses. We picked our way up the street. The ground was slimy with the debris of the sea. Great pools of water stood in the middle of the street.

We climbed over wreckage and picked our way through heaps of rubbish. The terrible, sickening odor almost overcame us, and it was all that I could do to shut my teeth and get through the streets somehow.

The soldiers were camping on the wharf front, lying stretched out on the wet sand, the hideous, hideous sand, stained and streaked in the starlight with dark and cruel blotches. They challenged us, but the marshal took us through under his protection. At every street corner there was a guard, and every guard wore a six-shooter strapped around his waist.

"The best men!" said the marshal. "They've all left their own misery and came down here to do police duty. We needed them. They had to shoot twenty-five men yesterday for looting the dead. Not Americans, not one of them. I saw them all—negroes and the poor whites from Southern Europe. They cut off the hands of their victims. Every citizen has orders to shoot without notice any one found at such work."

We got to the hotel after some terrible nightmare-fashioned plodding through dim streets like a line of forlorn ghosts in a half-forgotten dream. At the hotel, a big, typical Southern hotel, with a dome and marble rotunda, the marble stained and patched with the sea slime, the clerk told us that he had no rooms. We tried to impress him in some way, but he would not look up from his book, and all he said was "No room" over and over again like a man talking in his sleep.

We hunted the housekeeper and found there was room, and plenty of it, only the clerk was so dazed that he did not know what he was doing. There was room, but no bedding, and no water, and no linen of any sort.

General McKibben, commander in charge of the Texas division, was down stairs in the parlor reading dispatches, with an aide and an orderly or two at his elbow. He was horrified to see me.

"How in the world did you get here?" he said. "I would not let any women belonging to me come into this place of horror for all the money in America. I am an old soldier, madam. I have seen many battlefields, but let me tell you that since I rowed across the bay the other night and helped the man at the boat steer to keep away from the floating bodies of dead women and little children, I have not slept one single instant.

"I have been out on inspection all day, and I find that our first estimate of the number of the dead was very much under the real. Five thousand would never cover the number of people who died here in that terrible storm.

"I saw my men pulling away some rubbish this very morning right at the corner of the principal street. They thought there might be some one dead person there. They took out fourteen women and three little children. We have only just begun to get a faint idea of the hideous extent of this calamity. The little towns along the coast had been almost completely washed out. We hear from them every now and then as some poor, dazed wretch creeps somehow into shelter and tries to tell his pitiful story. We have only just begun our work.

"The people all over America are responding generously to our appeals for help, and I would like to impress it upon them that what we need now is money, money, money and disinfectants. Tell your people to send all the quicklime they can get through. I wish I could see a dozen trainloads of disinfectants landed in this city to-morrow morning. What we must fight now is infection, and we must fight it quick and with determination or it will conquer us."

The men of my party came over and took me from the great damp tomb of a room, where I was trying to write, to the Aziola Club across the street.

There were eighteen or twenty men there, most representative of the city of Galveston, rich, influential citizens. They had all been on police duty or rescue work of some sort. The millionaire at the table next to me wore a pair of workmen's brogans, some kind of patched old trousers and a colored shirt much the worse for wear. He had been directing a gang of workmen who were extricating the dead from the fallen houses all day long.

The man on my right had lain for four hours under a mass of rubbish on Monday and had heard his friends pass by and recognized their voices, but could not groan loud enough for them to hear him. He told us what he was thinking about as he lay there with a man pinned across his chest and two dead men under him. He tried to make his story amusing and we all tried to laugh.

Every man in that room had lost nearly every dollar he had in the world, and two or three of them had lost the nearest and dearest friends they had on earth, but there were no sighs, and there was not one man who spoke in anything but tones of courageous endurance. In the short time I have been here I have met and talked with women who saw every one they loved on earth swept away from them out into the storm.

I have held in my arms a little lisping boy not eight years old, whose chubby face was set and hard when he told me how he watched his mother die. But I have not seen a single tear. The people of Galveston are stunned with the merciful bewilderment which nature always sends at such a time of sorrow.[9]

Notes

1. Marion Marzolf, *Up from the Footnote* (New York: Hastings House, 1977), pp. 19–20.

2. Marzolf, *Up from the Footnote*, pp. 33–34.

3. Barbara Belford, *Brilliant Bylines*, New York: Columbia University Press, 1986), pp. 114–120.

4. From the *New York World*, January 26, 1890, available on microfilm at many libraries.

5. See "Elizabeth Cochrane Seaman," in Madelon Golden Schilpp and Sharon M. Murphy, *Great Women of the Press* (Carbondale: Southern Illinois University Press, 1983), pp. 133–47.

6. See "Winifred Black Bonfils," in Schilpp and Murphy, *Great Women of the Press*, pp. 148–57.

7. Belford, *Brilliant Bylines*, pp. 99–105.

8. Edith May Marken, "Women in American Journalism before 1900," unpublished master's thesis, University of Missouri, 1932, p. 94.

9. From the *San Francisco Examiner*, September 15, 1900.

11

Investigative Reporting
Ida M. Tarbell

As the twentieth century dawned, mass circulation magazines began to change the shape of American journalism. Technological innovations, including the reproduction of photographs and the use of cheap glazed paper, made magazines attractive and available to millions of readers for the first time.[1] Some of these publications specialized in exposing political and financial corruption in American life. Theodore Roosevelt, who was not totally in sympathy with this movement, dubbed it "muckraking," drawing an analogy to the "Man with the Muckrake" in *Pilgrim's Progress*, who refused to look up from the floor even though a heavenly crown awaited him. The movement, which took place chiefly from 1902 to 1912, was led by *McClure's Magazine*, whose staff included three of the most able muckrakers: Lincoln Steffens, Ray Stannard Baker, and Ida M. Tarbell.[2]

In 1902 *McClure's* published a serialized version of Tarbell's *History of the Standard Oil Company*, a factual and well-documented account of the manipulations that had created the giant trust. At the time she received the assignment, Tarbell already had established a reputation for careful research in connection with two successful series on the lives of Napoleon and Lincoln.

She brought personal knowledge of the subject to her task of reporting on Standard Oil. Born in 1857, she had grown up in the booming oil town of Titusville, Pennsylvania, where she had witnessed the sharp practices of the company under John D. Rockefeller. She saw Rockefeller's ruthlessness ruin her own father's business. With a dedication to objectivity buttressed by a two-year study of voluminous records and interviews with key oil-industry figures, Tarbell wrote a sober account of the company's unfair methods far more damaging than an emotional outburst. Her articles, published in a book in 1904, caused a sensation and brought her fame.

Her passion for accuracy stemmed in part from her education at Allegheny College in Meadville, Pennsylvania, where she studied science. Turning to journalism, she spent eight years on the staff of the *Chautauquan* magazine before traveling to Paris to study women's participation in the French Revolution. There she met S. S. McClure, who urged her to return to New York and work on his popular publication.

After the success of the *History of the Standard Oil Company*, Tarbell, along with Steffens and Baker, left *McClure's* and, with others, purchased the *American Magazine*, which they ran cooperatively until its sale in 1915. Subsequently Tarbell lectured on the Chautauqua circuit on such subjects as the social responsibility of business, disarmament, and the League of Nations, which she favored.

Although her mother had been a feminist, Tarbell did not favor woman suffrage, feeling that public life was incompatible with motherhood.[3] At 82, she published her autobiography, *All in the Day's Work*, five years before her death in 1944. In chapter 12 of the book, Tarbell described her impressions upon first seeing Rockefeller, as well as her distress at the muckraker label. Excerpts are reprinted here.

ALL IN THE DAY'S WORK
MUCKRAKER OR HISTORIAN?
By Ida Tarbell

Not a few of the personal experiences in gathering my materials left me with unhappy impressions, more unhappy in retrospect perhaps than they were at the moment. They were part of the day's work, sometimes very exciting parts. There was the two hours I spent in studying Mr. John D. Rockefeller. As the work had gone on, it became more and more clear to me that the Standard Oil Company was his creation. "An institution is the lengthened shadow of one man," says Emerson. I found it so.

Everybody in the office interested in the work began to say, "After the book is done you must do a character sketch of Mr. Rockefeller." I was not keen for it. It would have to be done like the books, from documents; that is, I had no inclination to use the extraordinary gossip which came to me from many sources. If I were to do it I wanted only that of which I felt I had sure proof, only those things which seemed to me to help explain the public life of this powerful, patient, secretive, calculating man of so peculiar and special a genius.

"You must at least look at Mr. Rockefeller," my associates insisted. "But how?'' Mr. Rogers himself had suggested that I see him. I had consented. I had returned to the suggestion several times, but at last was made to understand that it could not be done. I had dropped his name from my list. It was John Siddall who then took the matter in hand.[4]

"You must see him," was Siddall's judgment.

To arrange it became almost an obsession. And then what seemed to him like a providential opening came. It was announced that on a certain Sunday of October 1903 Mr. Rockefeller before leaving Cleveland, where he had spent his summer, for his home in New York would say good-bye in a little talk to the Sunday school of his church—a rally, it was called. As soon as Siddall learned of this he begged me to come on. "We can go to Sunday School; we can stay to church. I will see that we have seats where we will have a full view of the man. You will get him in action."

Of course I went, feeling a little mean about it too. He had not wanted to be seen apparently. It was taking him unaware.

Siddall's plan worked to perfection, worked so well from the start that again and again he seemed ready to burst from excitement in the two hours we spent in the church.

We had gone early to the Sunday-school room where the rally was to open— a dismal room with a barbaric dark green paper with big gold designs, cheap stained-glass windows, awkward gas fixtures. Comfortable, of course, but so stupidly ugly. We were sitting meekly at one side when I was suddenly aware of a striking figure standing in the doorway. There was an awful age in his face—the oldest man I had ever seen, I thought, but what power! At the moment Siddall poked me violently in the ribs and hissed, "There he is."

The impression of power deepened when Mr. Rockefeller took off his coat and hat, put on a skullcap, and took a seat commanding the entire room, his back to the wall. It was the head which riveted attention. It was big, great breadth from back to front, high broad forehead, big bumps behind the ears, not a shiny head but with a wet look. The skin was as fresh as that of any healthy man about us. The thin sharp nose was like a thorn. There were no lips; the mouth looked as if the teeth were all shut hard. Deep furrows ran down each side of the mouth from the nose. There were puffs under the little colorless eyes with creases running from them.

Wonder over the head was almost at once diverted to wonder over the man's uneasiness. His eyes were never quiet but darted from face to face, even peering around the jog at the audience close to the wall.

When he rose to speak, the impression of power that the first look at him had given increased, and the impression of age passed. I expected a quavering voice, but the voice was not even old, if a little fatigued, a little thin. It was clear and utterly sincere. He meant what he was saying. He was on his own ground talking about dividends, dividends of righteousness. "If you would take something out," he said, clenching the hand of his outstretched right arm, "you must put something in"—emphasizing "put something in" with a long outstretched forefinger.

The talk over, we slipped out to get a good seat in the gallery, a seat where we could look full on what we knew to be the Rockefeller pew.

Mr. Rockefeller came into the auditorium of the church as soon as Sunday school was out. He sat a little bent in his pew, pitifully uneasy, his head constantly turning the farthest right or left, his eyes searching the faces almost invariably turned towards him. It was plain that he, and not the minister, was the pivot on which that audience swung. Probably he knew practically everybody in the congregation; but now and then he lingered on a face, peering at it intently as if he were seeking what was in the mind behind it. He looked frequently at the gallery. Was it at Siddall and me?

The services over, he became the friendly patron saint of the flock. Coming down the aisle where people were passing out, he shook hands with everyone who stopped, saying, "A good sermon." "The Doctor gave us a good sermon." "It was a very good sermon, wasn't it?"

My two hours' study of Mr. Rockefeller aroused a feeling I had not expected, which time has intensified. I was sorry for him. I know no companion so terrible as fear. Mr. Rockefeller, for all the conscious power written in face and voice and figure, was afraid, I told myself, afraid of his own kind. My friend Lewis Emery, Jr., priding himself on being a victim, was free and happy. Not gold enough in the world to tempt him to exchange love of defiance for a power which carried with it a head as uneasy as that on Mr. Rockefeller's shoulders.

My unhappiness was increased as the months went by with the multiplying of tales of grievances coming from every direction. I made a practice of looking into them all, as far as I could; and while frequently I found solid reasons for the complaints, frequently I found the basic motives behind them—suspicion, hunger for notoriety, blackmail, revenge.

The most unhappy and most unnatural of these grievances came to me from literally the last person in the world to whom I should have looked for information—Frank Rockefeller—brother of John D. Rockefeller.

Frank Rockefeller sent word to me by a circuitous route that he had documents in a case which he thought ought to be made public, and that if I would secretly come to him in his office in Cleveland he would give them to me. I knew that there had been a quarrel over property between the two men. It made much noise at the time—1893—had gone to the courts, had caused bitterness inside the family itself; but because it was a family affair I had not felt that I wanted to touch it. But here it was laid on my desk.

So I went to Cleveland, where John Siddall had a grand opportunity to play the role of sleuth which he so enjoyed, his problem being to get me into Mr. Rockefeller's office without anybody suspecting my identity. He succeeded.

I found Mr. Rockefeller excited and vindictive. He accused his brother of robbing (his word) him and his partner James Corrigan of all their considerable holdings of stock in the Standard Oil Company. The bare facts were that Frank Rockefeller and James Corrigan had been interested in the early Standard Oil operations in Cleveland and had each acquired then a substantial block of stock. Later they had developed a shipping business on the Lakes, iron and steel furnaces in Cleveland. In the eighties they had borrowed money from John D. Rockefeller, putting up their Standard Oil stock as collateral. Then came the panic of '93, and they could not meet their obligations. In the middle of their distress John Rockefeller had foreclosed, taking over their stocks, leaving them, so they charged, no time in which to turn around although they felt certain that they would be able a little later, out of the substantial business they claimed they had built up, to pay their debt to him. Their future success proved they could have done so.

I could see John Rockefeller's point as I talked with his brother Frank. Frank Rockefeller was an open-handed, generous trader—more interested in the game than in the money to be made. He loved good horses—raised them, I believe on a farm out in Kansas; he liked gaiety, free spending. From his brother John's point of view he was not a safe man to handle money. He did not reverence it; he used it in frivolous ways of which his brother did not approve. So it was as a kind of obligation to the sacredness of money that John Rockefeller had foreclosed on his own brother and his early friend James Corrigan. He was strictly within his legal rights and within what I suppose he called his moral right.

But the transaction left a bitterness in Frank Rockefeller's heart and mind which was one of the ugliest things I have ever seen. "I have taken up my children from the Rockefeller family lot. (Or "shall take up"—I do not know now which it was.) They shall not lie in the same enclosure with John D. Rockefeller."

The documents in this case, which I later analyzed for the character sketch on which we had decided, present a fair example of what were popularly called "Standard Oil methods" as well as what they could do to the minds and hearts of victims.

The more intimately I went into my subject, the more hateful it became to me. No achievement on earth could justify those methods, I felt. I had a great desire to end my task, hear no more of it. No doubt part of my revulsion was due to a fagged brain. The work had turned out to be much longer and more laborious than I had had reason to expect. . . .

The book was published in the fall of 1904—two fat volumes with generous appendices of what I considered essential documents. I was curious about the reception it would have from the Standard Oil Company. I had been told repeatedly they were preparing an answer to flatten me out; but if this was under way it was not with Mr. Rockefeller's consent, I imagined. To a mutual friend who had told him the articles should be answered Mr. Rockefeller was said to have replied: "Not a word. Not a word about that misguided woman." To another who asked him about my charges he was reported as answering: "All without foundation. The idea of the Standard forcing anyone to sell his refinery is absurd. The refineries wanted to sell to us, and nobody that has sold or worked with us but has made money, is glad he did so.

"I thought once of having an answer made to the *McClure* articles but you know it has always been the policy of the Standard to keep silent under attack and let their acts speak for themselves."

In the case of the Lloyd book they had kept silent, but only because Mr. Rockefeller had been unable to carry out his plans for answering.[5] What he had proposed was a jury of the most distinguished clergymen of the day to consider Mr. Lloyd's argument and charges. Certain clergymen invited refused unless there should be a respectable number of economists added to the jury. That, apparently, Mr. Rockefeller did not see his way to do, and the plan was abandoned. So far as I know Mr. Lloyd's book was never answered by the Standard Oil Company.

But I wanted an answer from Mr. Rockefeller. What I got was neither direct nor, from my point of view, serious. It consisted of wide and what must have been a rather expensive anonymous distribution of various critical comments. The first of these was a review of the book which appeared in the *Nation* soon after its publication. The writer—one of the *Nation*'s staff reviewers, I later learned—sneered at the idea that there was anything unusual in the competitive practices which I called illegal and immoral. "They are a necessary part of competition," he said. "The practices are odious it is true, competition is necessarily odious." Was it necessarily odious?

I did not think so. The practices I believed I had proved, I continued to consider much more dangerous to economic stability than airing them, even if I aired them in the excited and irrational fashion the review charged. As I saw it, the struggle was between Commercial Machiavellism and the Christian Code.

The most important of the indirect answers was an able book by Gilbert Holland Montague.[6] It separated business and ethics in a way that must have been a comfort to 26 Broadway.

As soon as published, Mr. Montague's book became not exactly a best seller but certainly a best circulator—libraries, ministers, teachers, prominent citizens all over the land receiving copies with the compliments of the publisher. Numbers of them came back to me with irritated letters. "We have been buying books for years from this house," wrote one distinguished librarian, "and never before was one sent with their compliments. I understand that libraries all over the country are receiving them. Can it be that this is intended as an advertisement, or is it not more probable that the Standard Oil Company itself is paying for this widespread distribution?"

The general verdict seemed to be that the latter was the explanation.

Some time later there came from the entertaining Elbert Hubbard of the Roycroft Shop of East Aurora, New York, an essay on the Standard extolling the grand results from the centralization of the industry in their hands.

I have it from various interested sources that five million copies were ordered printed in pamphlet form by the Standard Oil Company and were distributed by Mr. Hubbard. They went to schoolteachers and journalists, preachers and "leaders" from the Atlantic to the Pacific. Hardly were they received in many cases before they were sent to me with angry or approving comments. For a couple of years my birthday and Christmas offerings were sure to include copies of one or the other of these documents with the compliments of some waggish member of the *McClure* group.

I had hoped that the book might be received as a legitimate historical study, but to my chagrin I found myself included in a new school, that of the muckrakers. Theodore Roosevelt, then President of the United States, had become uneasy at the effect on the public of the periodical press's increasing criticisms and investigations of business and political abuses. He was afraid that they were adding to the not inconsiderable revolutionary fever abroad, driving people into socialism. Something must be done, and in a typically violent speech he accused the school of being concerned only with the "vile and debasing." Its members were like the man in John Bunyan's *Pilgrim's Progress* who with eyes on the ground raked incessantly "the straws, the small sticks, and dust of the floor." They were muckrakers. The conservative public joyfully seized the name.

Roosevelt had of course misread his Bunyan. The man to whom the Interpreter called the attention of the Pilgrim was raking riches which the Interpreter contemptuously called "straws" and "sticks" and "dust." The President would have been nearer Bunyan's meaning if he had named the rich sinners of the times who in his effort to keep his political balance he called "malefactors of great wealth"—if he had called them "muckrakers of great wealth" and applied the word "malefactors" to the noisy and persistent writers who so disturbed him.

I once argued with Mr. Roosevelt that we on *McClure*'s were concerned only with facts, not with stirring up revolt. "I don't object to the facts," he cried, "but you and Baker"—Baker [Ray Stannard Baker, another muckraker] at that time was carrying on an able series of articles on the manipulations of the railroads—"but you and Baker are not *practical*."

I felt at the time Mr. Roosevelt had a good deal of the usual conviction of the powerful man in public life that correction should be left to him, a little resentment that a profession outside his own should be stealing his thunder.

This classification of muckraker, which I did not like, helped fix my resolution to have done for good and all with the subject which had brought it on me. But events were stronger than I. All the radical reforming element, and I numbered many friends among them, were begging me to join their movements. I soon found that most of them wanted attacks. They had little interest in balanced findings. Now I was convinced that in the long run the public they were trying to stir would weary of vituperation, that if you were to secure permanent results the mind must be convinced.

One of the most heated movements at the moment was the effort to persuade the public to refuse all gifts which came from fortunes into the making of which it was known illegal and unfair practices had gone. "Do not touch tainted money," men thundered from pulpit and platform, among them so able a man as Dr. Washington Gladden. The Rockefeller fortune was singled out because about this time Mr. Rockefeller made some unusually large contributions to colleges and churches and general philanthropy. "It is done," cried the critics, "in order to silence criticism." Frequently some one said to me, "You have opened the Rockefeller purse." But I knew, and said in print rather to the disgust of my friends in the movement, that there was an unfairness to Mr. Rockefeller in this outcry. It did not take public criticism to open his purse. From boyhood he had been a steady giver in proportion to his income— 10 percent went to the Lord—and through all the harrowing early years in which he was trying to establish himself as a money-maker he never neglected to give the Lord the established proportion. As his fortune grew his gifts grew larger. He not only gave but saw the money given was wisely spent; and he trained his children, particularly the son who was to administer his estate, to as wise practice in public giving as we have ever had. That is, it did not take a public outcry such as came in the early years of this century against the methods of the Standard Oil Company to force Mr. Rockefeller to share his wealth. He was already sharing it. Indeed, in the fifteen years before 1904 he had given to one or another cause some thirty-five million dollars.

If his gifts were larger at this time than they had ever been before, his money-making was greater. If they were more spectacular than ever before, it may have been because he thought it was time to call the public's attention to what they were getting out of the Standard Oil fortune. At all events it seemed to me only fair that the point should be emphasized that it had not taken a public revolt against his methods to force him to share his profits.[7]

Notes

1. Kathleen Brady, *Ida Tarbell: Portrait of a Muckraker* (New York: Seaview/Putnam, 1984), p. 92.

2. Jean Folkerts and Dwight L. Teeter, Jr., *Voices of a Nation: A History of Media in the United States* (New York: Macmillan, 1989), pp. 322–29.

3. Robert Stinson, "Ida M. Tarbell and the Ambiguities of Feminism," *Pennsylvania Magazine of History and Biography* 101 (1977):217–39.

4. Henry H. Rogers was an old friend of the Tarbell family and a vice-president of Standard Oil who met with Tarbell during preparation of her series.

5. Henry D. Lloyd was the author of a book hostile to the Standard Oil Company: *Wealth against Commonwealth* (New York: Harper, 1894).

6. See Gilbert H. Montague, *The Rise and Progress of the Standard Oil Co.* (New York: Harper, 1904).

7. Ida M. Tarbell, *All in the Day's Work* (New York: Macmillan, 1939).

12

Metropolitan Journalists
Ishbel Ross: Front-page Reporters

After World War I the number of women entering journalism continued to increase although male editors rarely gave them the opportunity to handle the same kind of story as men reporters. In 1910 the U.S. census showed 4,000 women employed full-time as journalists, but by the end of the 1920s that number had tripled to about 12,000, representing one out of every four journalists in the country. Many of these women, however, were still confined to the women's pages or to feature writing and stunt and sob-sister reporting.[1]

But occasionally a few managed to break into the masculine preserve of "hard" news—crime, politics, courts, government, general assignment—or gain a seat at the copy or city desks where decisions were made on news content. One who proved that she could hold her own with any man was Ishbel Ross, a talented woman from Scotland, who came to New York in 1919 as a reporter for the *Tribune* after working briefly in Canada.

During more than a decade with the *New York Tribune*, Ross "seemed to come closer than any of the others [i.e., newspaperwomen] to the man's idea of what a newspaperwoman should be," according to her city editor, Stanley Walker. Although Walker claimed many newspaperwomen were "slovenly, incompetent vixens," he gave her credit for "unflustered competence." He stated his views in *Ladies of the Press*, the first history of women reporters, written by Ross in 1936.[2]

Ross researched the book shortly after she left reporting in 1933, following her successful coverage of some of the biggest stories of the day, including the kidnapping of the Lindbergh baby. While assigned to the celebrated Hall-Mills murder trial, she met Bruce Rae, a rival reporter for the *New York Times*, whom she later married. Her decision to give up journalism to write books came after the birth of a daughter.

For *Ladies of the Press*, she interviewed scores of newspaperwomen in different parts of the United States, making the book a valuable source today. It was among the first of her 16 published books, many of them biographies of famous women, including Elizabeth Blackwell, Clara Barton, and the wives of presidents. She died in New York in 1975 at the age of 79.[3]

Ladies of the Press sketched the careers of women in all phases of journalism from society pages to foreign correspondence. In the opening chapter, Ross told the exciting story of those few women who, weathering what she called "storms of prejudice," had been able to advance to covering top news stories. She titled the chapter "Front-page Girl." Excerpts follow.

FRONT-PAGE GIRL

Five years after the Civil War an eighteen-year-old girl named Sally Joy left the plush security of her home in Vermont and talked herself into a job on the Boston *Post*. It was only a matter of weeks until the men in the office were lining the floor with papers to keep her white satin ball gown from picking up the dust.

Sally did not need this newsprint carpet laid for her ambitious feet. It merely set the key for the befuddled dismay with which the normal newspaper man regards the unwelcome sight of a woman in the city room. Things have changed in the newspaper world since Sally's time. The typewriter has taken the place of the pen; the linotype has supplanted hand composition; there is little dust on the floor of the metropolitan city room; and the girl reporter rarely shows up during working hours in a white satin gown.

She must be free to leap nimbly through fire lines, dodge missiles at a strike, board a liner from a swaying ladder, write copy calmly in the heat of a Senate debate, or count the dead in a catastrophe. She never takes time to wonder why someone does not find her a chair, change the ribbon of her typewriter or hold smelling salts to her nose as she views a scene of horror.

"I want to be treated like a man," said Sally, who was a little ahead of her time. But she could not persuade her colleagues that she was anything but a helpless female. At first there was indignation about having "a woman on the sheet" and the youth assigned to escort her to all functions beginning after seven o'clock was the butt of the staff.

But the girl reporter hung on and got her reward. She was sent without masculine aid to cover a suffrage convention in Vermont, traveling with Lucy Stone and Julia Ward Howe. As the only woman at the press table, an admiring colleague chronicled her presence:

"Miss Sally Joy of Boston has a portfolio at the Reporters' table in the Convention for the *Post* of her native city. She is pretty, piquante, and dresses charmingly. She has a high regard for Mrs. Bloomer, although she diverges from that good lady on the science of clothes. Miss Joy has made a reputation as a newspaper correspondent and reporter of which any man might be proud. And this is saying a good deal for a woman. Miss Joy is as independent as she is self-supporting and she votes for Woman's Suffrage."

Sally was neither the first nor the best of the early women reporters. She was merely the symbol of a point of view that has changed surprisingly little in the last half century. She went from the Boston *Post* to the *Herald* to do a society column. She called herself Penelope Penfeather and sometimes wrote about fashions and the home. In due time she married and faded into the mists, but not until she had helped to found the General Federation of Women's Clubs and had served as the first president of the New England Women's Press Association.

Her demand to be treated as a man has echoed innumerable times in city rooms throughout the country. And all that she stood for is still regarded as a threat to the peace, honor and coziness of that sound haunt of masculinity— the city room, practically as sacred to men as a stag club or the pre-Volstead saloon.

To-day there are nearly twelve thousand women editors, feature writers and reporters in the country. They have found their way into all of the large newspaper offices and most of the small ones. They have invaded every branch of the business, but have not made much impression in the front-page field.

This does not mean that they have failed to make themselves felt in newspaper work; on the contrary, their success has been substantial. They hold executive posts. Two have dominant voices in important papers on the Eastern seaboard. Many of them edit small papers of their own. They run Sunday magazines and book supplements, write editorials, do politics, foreign correspondence, features, straight news, criticism, copy reading and sports writing, as well as the old standbys—the woman's page, clubs and social news.

They excel in the feature field and dominate the syndicates. They stop only at the political cartoon. They function in the advertising, business, art, promotion and mechanical departments, as well as in the editorial rooms. They have arrived, in a convincing way. But the fact remains that they have made surprisingly little progress on the front page, which is still the critical test. Not even a score of women take orders direct from the city desks in New York. The proportion is even less in other cities. They come singly or in pairs on a paper, rarely more. There are just as few on the general staff as there were at the turn of the century.

Whenever possible, they are steered into the quieter by-waters of the newspaper plant, away from the main current of life, news, excitement, curses and ticker machines. They are segregated where their voices will not be heard too audibly in the clatter. They get tucked away on the upper floors where the departments flourish. They lurk in the library, diligent girls wedded to the files.

Most of them would rather be where they are. The specialists increase in number and usefulness each year. They have better hours, fair pay, a more leisured existence. They get their own following. They don't have to beat the drums every day they live. They can make dinner engagements and keep them. They have time to buy their hats.

But out in the city room—where high-powered lights blaze on rows of desks, where copy readers bend like restless caterpillars over the reporter's work, where the city editor usually resembles a sedate professor rather than the Mad Hatter of the films, where phones jangle and tickers click—only two or three women can be found, working quietly at their typewriters in a fog of abstraction.

They are the front-page girls who somehow have weathered storms of prejudice—the odd creatures who have been pictured as doing things only slightly more impossible than they all have attempted at one time or another. They are on the inner newspaper track. They are there because they have felt the bewitchment of a compelling profession. There is little else they can do once they have tasted its elixir. Strange music sings in their ears. Visions haunt them as they walk the streets. They fall asleep with the sound of rumbling presses in their heads. They have seen too much and it hasn't been good for their health.

For the woman reporter goes beyond the news into the raw material from which it springs. She catches the rapt look of the genius and the furtive glance of the criminal. She detects the lies, the debauchery and the nobility of her fellow men. She watches the meek grow proud and the proud turn humble. She marvels only when people who have feared publicity get drunk with it, and strain for a place on the front page.

She walks unscathed through street riots, strikes, fires, catastrophes and revolution, her press card opening the way for her. She watches government in the making, sees Presidents inaugurated, Kings crowned, heroes acclaimed, champions launched on the world. She has a banquet seat with the mighty. She travels far and wide in search of news, and uses every vehicle known to man. She sees a murderer condemned to death and watches the raw agony of his wife while he dies.

Nine times out of ten her day's work takes her to the fringes of tragedy. News visits a home most often to annihilate it. The shadow of a reporter falling across the doorstep may presage the collapse of a lifetime of work. The woman reporter must face harsh facts without any qualms about her business. She must be ready for such hazards as may befall her. She must be calm and full of stamina. For she will savor strange bitters as well as alluring sweets; endure fatigue and disappointment beyond reason; withstand rebuffs that wither or exhilarate in turn; meet abuse with the equanimity born of self-control; and function with complete belief in what she is doing and loyalty to her paper.

She must have a sound sense of the values of life and great capacity to withstand the shocks of human emotion. She must see with clairvoyance, judgment or experience the salient points of any situation; be resourceful and good-natured; have initiative and enough perception to avoid being taken in. She must know how to get her facts, to weigh them with sagacity and, above all, how to write.

Where is this paragon to be found? No editor believes that she exists. She probably doesn't. And if she did, she would not have much chance to prove it, for although women have hit the sky in feature writing, they still have a long way to go to establish themselves as first-string news reporters. . . .

Lorena Hickok repeatedly wrote the news leads on stories of national importance for the Associated Press, which has gone in heavily for women after years of indifference to their merits. Genevieve Forbes Herrick brought distinction to her craft by her work for the Chicago *Tribune*. She outmatched her competitors time and again, doing the major stories of the day with grace, speed and accuracy. Marjorie Driscoll, of the Los Angeles *Examiner*, is another example of the finest type of news writer.

Grace Robinson has starred so often in the role of front-page girl that she has no competitor in the number of big stories she has covered within a given period of time. She did the Hall-Mills and the Snyder-Gray trials for the New York *Daily News*, and scores of other assignments that any man might envy. Elenore Kellogg, who died in the summer of 1935, led the *World* repeatedly with brilliantly handled news stories, and had the satisfaction of seeing her work under banner heads. Ruth Finney, a Scripps-Howard star, tops the field for Washington. She has achieved spectacular success in the political field and ranks with the best men in the Press Gallery. . . .

The most sensible usually make the best reporters. The women who have gone the farthest in journalism are not those who have yipped the most loudly about their rights. Unless aggressiveness is backed by real ability, as in Rheta Childe Dorr's case, it is only a boomerang. Nothing has done more to keep women reporters in the shade. Peace at any price is the city room philosophy.

It is absurd to maintain that a woman can do everything a man can do on a paper. She can't get into the Lotus Club in New York, or cross the Harvard Club threshold. She is denied the chummy Senator's room in Washington when he has no time to answer her questions except as he changes for dinner.

The rule does not work so conclusively the other way. The only obstacle the gentlemen of the press have encountered is Mrs. Roosevelt's Monday morning conferences. The youths who are picked for the pink tea assignments are welcomed with joy at the woman's meeting. It is a sad reflection for the woman reporter who swears by her sex that the most pampered scribe at feminine gatherings is usually the man—and a man who would rather not be there.

But admitting that there are a few places from which women reporters are debarred, this is scarcely an important argument against their usefulness. It has no more significance than the inability of a man to write a good fashion story without expert aid. The functions of the city staff are always interchangeable. A woman may cover a subway wreck and a man do a fashion show on the same afternoon, with excellent results in both cases. A good reporter can do telling work with almost any set of facts, short of relativity. He need not be a specialist. He need not even be initiated.

But the feeling is there and the seasoned newspaper woman has to recognize it. If she is wise she will go on her way, taking things in her stride. She will not fuss over periods of quiet. She will mind her own business, take the assignments handed out to her and never grouse unduly. She cannot always live in the new writer's seventh heaven. There are dull days with nothing but obits to write. But be sure as she lives, news will stir again. She will watch it rustle through the office. The city editor will come over to her, hand her a bulletin, and from this cryptic note may spring the story of the decade. . . .

The doubts raised by editors about her are legion. Can she write? Usually. Can she spell? At least as well as her masculine colleagues, often better. Is she lacking in a sense of humor? Rarely. Reporting now is largely realistic, except for the occasional word orgies at a sensational trial, and then it is an assumed frenzy, done with the tongue in the cheek. News writers have too much sense to beat their breasts in public now. Their editors no longer expect it. The public would laugh.

But the most serious charge brought against the newspaper woman is inaccuracy. This is the one real chink in her armor. Precision of thought is the first requisite of good reporting. As far back as 1898 Arnold Bennett seized on this weakness in the woman reporter. His criticism is much the same as the city editor's to-day. No amount of careful work has served to uproot it. Even the most unprejudiced editor shudders a little when a new woman walks through the city room. Will her sentences parse? Will she get the paper in a libel suit? Will she verify every fact? Will she know how to round up a story? Will she cause trouble in the office? He values the women who happen to have succeeded in his own organization, but he thinks of them always as the exceptions. He has not yet been able to accept the species without reservation.

Therefore, the newspaper woman has to be twice as careful as the newspaper man in order to make headway at all. The tradition of sloppy work dies hard. She has every reason to worry when the copy boy brings the wet paper fresh from the presses and lays it on her desk. There is something particularly appalling about the error in print. Her eye rushes to the head the copy reader has given her story. It isn't vanity that makes her read every line with care. She is desperately anxious to know if everything is right.

The layman who cherishes the foolish belief that only half of what he reads in a newspaper is true, never dreams of the conscientious work that lies behind the columns he hastily scans. No human being but a well-trained reporter would hunt through five books of reference to get a middle initial correct. No one else would find so many ways of checking a circumstance that the average person accepts at face value.

The reporter scourges himself to perfection. Yet the public still believes that he is slipshod, inaccurate, a deliberate falsifier. In actual fact, the conscientious news writer on a responsible paper is the most slavishly exact person in the world. He splits hairs and swears by books of reference. He has a passion for verification, an honest love for facts. The good woman reporter has the same exacting code. The crispness of her style, the keen viewpoint, the explicit phrase, the potent paragraph, are all nullified if she does not have the essential newspaper virtue of absolute accuracy.

Often her early training has a bearing on the exactitude of her mental processes. The newspaper women have arrived at their various goals by odd routes. They have taught and nursed and been stenographers. They have scrubbed floors and sold in shops and danced in the chorus. The present tendency is for them to break in fresh from college. Some have wandered into the profession by accident; others have battered their way in; a few have simply walked in the front door without knocking. But the same spirit of enterprise has propelled most of them into the exciting newspaper game. . . .

On the whole, newspaper women make few demands on their city editors. They would gladly work for nothing, rather than be denied the city room. They scarcely ever fuss about their salaries, which range from $35 to $150 per week in the large cities, and from $7 to $50 in the smaller ones. They rarely ask for increases, or complain about their fare. They work hard and have a somewhat touching faith in what they are doing. They are seldom lazy. But the highest compliment to which the deluded creatures respond is the city editor's acknowledgment that their work is just like a man's. This automatically gives them a complacent glow, for they are all aware that no right-minded editor wants the so-called woman's touch in the news.

The fact remains that they never were thoroughly welcome in the city room and they are not quite welcome now. They are there on sufferance, although the departments could scarcely get along without them. But if the front-page girls were all to disappear tomorrow no searching party would go out looking for more, since it is the fixed conviction of nearly every newspaper executive that a man in the same spot would be exactly twice as good.

They may listen to smooth words and chivalrous sentiments, but what every city editor thinks in his black but honest heart is: "Girls, we like you well enough but we don't altogether trust you."[4]

Notes

1. Marion Marzolf, "The Woman Journalist: Colonial Printer to City Desk," *Journalism History* 1 (Winter 1974/75): 105–6.

2. Stanley Walker, "Foreword," to Ishbel Ross, *Ladies of the Press: The Story of Women in Journalism by an Insider* (New York: Harper & Brothers, 1936), xi, xii.

3. For biographical information on Ross, see Beverly G. Merrick, "An Exemplary Lady of the Press: Ishbel Ross Engenders a Bill of Rights for Newspaperwomen on the Male-dominated City Desk of the 1920s," unpublished paper presented at the Association for Education in Journalism and Mass Communication convention, Boston, August, 1991.

4. Ross, *Ladies of the Press*, ch. 1.

13

War Correspondents
Rheta Childe Dorr

In spite of overwhelming odds against them, resolute women journalists have insisted on their right to cover wars. During the Spanish-American War, both Joseph Pulitzer of the *New York World* and his archrival, William Randolph Hearst of the *New York Journal*, carried stories written by women about the hostilities. These tended to focus on a "woman's angle" featuring care of the wounded and accounts of Cuban refugees in Florida. But Anna N. Benjamin, a reporter for *Leslie's Illustrated Newspaper*, refused to limit herself to behind-the-lines activity and resolved to follow American troops to Cuba in 1898.

"I know what you think," the 23-year-old woman was quoted as telling a British correspondent. "You think it ridiculous my being here, you are laughing at me wanting to go, that's the worst of being a woman. But just let me tell you, I'm going through to Cuba and not all the old generals in the army are going to stop me."[1]

She won her goal and soon was scooping her competitors with news of American victories. The next year she covered the Philippine insurrection and, in pursuit of news, journeyed on to Japan, China, and Russia. She died in Paris at the age of 27.

During both World War I and World War II, experienced women journalists insisted on the right to be war correspondents. In World War I, Peggy Hull—a *Cleveland Plain Dealer* reporter—was determined to go to France to cover U.S. forces there, but editors would not send her. She finally persuaded Newspaper Enterprise Association, a news-feature syndicate, to hire her as a correspondent. Reporting on troop camps and accompanying the American expeditionary force to

Siberia, she became the first woman correspondent officially accredited by the War Department.[2]

The best-known World War I correspondent, Rheta Childe Dorr, won distinction both as a journalist and as a feminist. In 1917 Dorr announced to her editors at the *New York Mail* that she was going to Russia to cover the Revolution there. They were not surprised. Then 50 years old and at the height of her career, she already had proven her ability to succeed at undertakings requiring exceptional courage.

Dorr, who had been a feminist from the age of 12, decided in 1898 to leave an unsympathetic husband in Seattle, and, with her two-year-old son, moved to New York with a determination to have a journalistic career. After a long struggle, she found a job on the *Evening Post*, where she wrote about industrial conditions affecting women workers.

During a 1906 trip to Europe, Dorr developed close ties with the suffrage movement in England and later became the first editor of the *Suffragist*, a militant publication in the United States. She also continued her reform efforts for women workers by laboring, herself, in laundries and factories to gain firsthand material for magazine articles on sweatshop conditions.[3] She returned to newspaper work in 1915 when she joined the staff of the *New York Mail*.

Although a socialist at one point, Dorr became disillusioned with the communist program after she arrived in Russia. She believed that the Bolshevik forces were infiltrated by German spies eager to bring down the new republican government that had overturned the czar. As a supporter of the republic, she accompanied the woman's Battalion of Death, a regiment commanded by Botchkareva, a formidable peasant woman, on its trip to the front lines. Its mission, which ultimately proved unsuccessful, was to rally demoralized government troops by demonstrating the dedication of Russian women. Her articles ran on the front page of the *New York Mail* for weeks and were later collected in a book, *Inside the Russian Revolution*.[4] (See the excerpt below.)

Dorr made several subsequent trips to Europe as a war correspondent but was refused permission to go to the front lines because she was a woman. Although injured in a motorcycle accident in Washington in 1919, she continued to write books, including her autobiography, *A Woman of Fifty*. Dorr died in 1948.[5]

World War II opened doors to women journalists. With men reporters in the armed forces, women moved into new jobs in the male-dominated city rooms and proved that they were able to cover stories written under deadline pressure as well as feature assignments.[6]

Women also moved into radio jobs in programming, production, and on-the-air spots.

About 125 women attained accreditation as World War II war correspondents in spite of discouragement from U.S. officials reluctant to provide credentials.[7] Among those reporting for the wire services were Inez Robb of International News Service and Ruth Cowan of the Associated Press. Another World War II correspondent, Marguerite Higgins of the *New York Herald Tribune*, later received a Pulitzer prize for her coverage of the Korean War. Higgins became the first woman war correspondent to win a Pulitzer.

Women correspondents encountered varying degrees of prejudice. Higgins was once commanded to leave Korea because the army claimed "there are no facilities for ladies at the front." She protested to Gen. Douglas MacArthur, who rescinded the order.[8]

Perhaps more than anyone else it was Margaret Bourke-White, a photojournalist for *Life* magazine, who proved that competence as a war correspondent had no relationship to sex. Born in 1904, Bourke-White started her photographic career with a $20 secondhand camera that had a cracked lens.[9] She went on to earn a national reputation as a photographer in Cleveland who captured the dynamism of industry.[10] The perfection of her compositions, which transformed factories into "Gothic cathedrals," caught the attention of Henry Luce, who hired her as a photographer for *Fortune* magazine. During the 1930s she and novelist Erskine Caldwell, who later became her husband, collaborated on a documentary of misery among southern sharecroppers.[11]

When *Life* magazine was launched in 1936, she starred as one of its original staff members, creating memorable pictures in the United States and Europe, including scenes of the Nazi attack on Moscow in 1941. During World War II, she became the first woman correspondent accredited to the U.S. Army Air Force, and covered the fighting in North Africa and Italy. The army used her as a model for its first set of uniforms for women correspondents, which included a pink dress for special occasions.[12]

In spite of her fame, she met opposition from authorities when she sought permission to cover the war on the same basis as a man. To get to North Africa for the Allied invasion, she was forced to go by sea, instead of air, because flying was considered too dangerous for a woman. Her ship was torpedoed, but she escaped in a lifeboat, continuing to shoot pictures. She had to plead for months before receiving permission to fly on bombing raids.[13]

Later she covered riots in India between Moslems and Hindus and journeyed to South Africa, where she descended 2,000 feet in a basket to photograph the interior of a gold mine. On her way back to the United States from covering the Korean conflict in 1952, she suffered the first symptoms of Parkinson's disease, a nerve disorder against which she waged a courageous but losing struggle for nearly two decades. Margaret Bourke-White died in 1971 at the age of 67.

As an example of the style of early women war correspondents, an excerpt from Dorr follows. The selection reprinted here is from *Inside the Russian Revolution*, describing her trip to the front lines with the woman's battalion.

TO THE FRONT WITH BOTCHKAREVA

Women of all ranks rushed to enlist in the Botchkareva battalion. There were many peasant women, factory workers, servants and also a number of women of education and social prominence. Six Red Cross nurses were among the number, one doctor, a lawyer, several clerks and stenographers and a few like Marie Skridlova who had never done any except war work. If the working women predominated, I believe it was because they were the stronger physically. Botchkareva would accept only the sturdiest, and her soldiers, even when they were slight of figure, were all fine physical specimens. The women were outfitted and equipped exactly like the men soldiers. They wore the same kind of khaki trousers, loose-belted blouse and high peaked cap. They wore the same high boots, carried the same arms and the same camp equipment, including gas masks, trench spades and other paraphernalia. In spite of their tightly shaved heads they presented a very attractive appearance, like nice, clean, upstanding boys. They were very strictly drilled and disciplined and there was no omission of saluting officers in that regiment.

The battalion left Petrograd for an unknown destination on July 6 in our calendar. In the afternoon the women marched to the Kazan Cathedral, where a touching ceremony of farewell and blessing took place. A cold, fine rain was falling, but the great half circle before the cathedral, as well as the long curved colonnades, were filled with people. Thousands of women were there carrying flowers, and nurses moved through the crowds collecting money for the regiment.

I passed a very uneasy day that July 6. I was afraid of what might happen to some of the women through the malignancy of the Bolsheviki, and I was mortally afraid that I was not going to be allowed to get on their troop train. I had made the usual application to the War Ministry to be allowed to visit the front, but I did not follow up the application with a personal visit, and therefore when I dropped in for a morning call I was dismayed to find the barrack in a turmoil, and to hear the exultant announcement, ''We're going this evening at eight.''

It was an unseasonal day of rain, and I spent reckless sums in droshky hire, rushing hither and yon in a fruitless effort to wring emergency permits from elusive officials who never in their lives had been called upon to do anything in a hurry, or even to keep conventional office hours. Needless to say, I found nobody at all on duty where he should have been that day. Even at the American Embassy, where, empty-handed and discouraged, I wound up late in the afternoon, I found the entire staff absent in attendance on a visiting commission from home. The one helpful person who happened to be at the Embassy was Arno Dosch-Fleurot of the New York *World*. "If I were you," he said, "I wouldn't worry about a permit. I'd just get on the train—if I could *get* on—and I'd stay until they put me off, or until I got where I wanted to go. Of course they may arrest you for a spy. In any other country they'd be pretty sure to. But in Russia you never can tell. Shepherd, of the United Press, once went all over the front with nothing to show but some worthless mining stock. Why not try it?"

I said I would, and before eight that evening I was at the Warsaw Station, unwillingly, participating in what might be called the regiment's first hostile engagement. For at least two thirds of the mob that filled the station were members of the Lenine faction of Bolsheviki, sent there to break up the orderly march of the women, and even if possible to prevent them from entraining at all. From the first these spy-led emissaries of the German Kaiser had sworn enmity to Botchkareva's battalion. Well knowing the moral effect of women taking the places of deserting soldiers in the trenches, the Lenineites had exhausted every effort to breed dissension in the ranks, and at the last moment they had stormed the station in the hope of creating an intolerable situation. In the absence of anything like a police force they did succeed in making things painful and even a little dangerous for the soldiers and for the tearful mothers and sisters who had gathered to bid them good-by. But the women kept perfect discipline through it all, and slowly fought their way through the mob to the train platform.

As for me, a mixture of indignation, healthy muscle and a rare good luck carried me through and landed me in a somewhat battered condition next to Adjutant Skridlova. "You got your permit," she exclaimed on seeing me. "I am so pleased. Stay close to me and I'll see you safely on."

Mendaciously perhaps, I answered nothing at all, but stayed, and every time a perspiring train official grabbed me by the arm and told me to stand back Skridlova rescued me and informed the man that I had permission to go. At the very last I had a bad moment, for one especially inquisitive official asked to see the permission. This time it was the Nachalnik, Botchkareva herself, who came to the rescue. Characteristically she wasted no words, but merely pushed the man aside, thrust me into her own compartment and ordered me to lock the door. Within a few minutes she joined me, the train began to move and we were off. That was the end of my troubles, for no one afterwards questioned my right to be there. At the Adjutant's suggestion I parted with my New York hat and early in the journey substituted the white linen coif of a Red

Cross nurse. Thus attired, I was accepted by all concerned as a part of the camp equipment.

The troop train consisted of one second class and five fourth class carriages, the first one, except for one compartment reserved for officers, being practically filled with camp and hospital supplies. In the other carriages, primitive affairs furnished with three tiers of wooden bunks, the rank and file of the regiment traveled. I had a place in the second class compartment with the Nachalnik, the Adjutant and the standard bearer, a big, silent peasant girl called Orlova. Our luxury consisted of cushioned shelves without bedding or blankets, which served as seats by day and beds by night. We had, of course, a little more privacy than the others, but that was all. As for food, we all fared alike, and we fared well, friends of the regiment having loaded the train with bread, butter, fruit, canned things, cakes, chocolate and other delicacies. Tea-making materials we had also, and plenty of sugar. So filled was our compartment with food, flowers, banners, guns, tea kettles and miscellaneous stuff that we moved about with difficulty and were forever apologizing for walking on each other's feet.

For two nights and the better part of two days we traveled southward through fields of wheat, barley and potatoes, where women in bright red and blue smocks toiled among the ripening harvests. News of the train had gone down through the line, and the first stage of our journey, through the white night, was one continued ovation. At every station crowds had gathered to cheer the women and to demand a sight of Botchkareva. It was largely a masculine crowd, soldiers mostly, goodnatured and laughing, but many women were there too, nurses, working girls, peasants. Occasionally one saw ladies in dinner gowns escorted by officer friends.

The farther we traveled from Petrograd, the point of contact in Russia with western civilization, the more apparent it grew that things were terribly wrong with the empire. More and more the changed character of the station crowds reminded us of the widespread disruption of the army. The men who met the train wore soldiers' uniforms but they had lost all of their upright, soldierly bearing. They slouched like convicts, they were dirty and unkempt, and their eyes were full of vacuous insolence. Absence of discipline and all restraint had robbed them of whatever manhood they had once possessed. The news of the women's battalion had drawn these men like a swarm of bees. They thrust their unshaven faces into the car windows, bawling the parrot phrases taught them by their German spy leaders. "Who fights for the damned capitalists? Who fights for English blood suckers? We don't fight."

And the women, scorn flashing from their eyes, flung back: "That is the reason why we do. Go home, you cowards, and let women fight for Russia."

Their last, flimsy thread of "peace" propaganda exhausted, the men usually fell back on personal insults, but to these the women, following strict orders, made no reply. When the language became too coarse the women simply closed the windows. No actual violence was ever offered them. When they left the train for hot water or for tea, for more food or to buy newspapers, they walked so fearlessly into the crowds that the men withdrew, sneering and growling, but standing aside.

There was something indescribably strange about going on a journey to a destination absolutely unknown, except to the one in command of the expedition. Above all it was strange to feel that you were seeing women voluntarily giving up the last shred of protection and security supposed to be due them. They were going to meet death, death in battle against a foreign foe, the first women in the world to volunteer for such an end. Yet every one was happy, and the only fear expressed was lest the battalion should not be sent at once to the trenches.[14]

Notes

1. Charles B. Brown, "A Woman's Odyssey: The War Correspondence of Anna Benjamin," *Journalism Quarterly* 46 (Autumn 1969): 523–30.

2. Marion Marzolf, *Up from the Footnote* (New York: Hastings House), pp. 42–43.

3. Zena Beth McGlashan, "Club 'Ladies' and Working 'Girls': Rheta Childe Dorr and the *New York Evening Post*," *Journalism History* 8 (1981): 7–13.

4. See Zena Beth McGlashan, "Women Witness the Russian Revolution: Analyzing Ways of Seeing," *Journalism History* 12 (1985): 54–61.

5. See Susan G. Motes, "Rheta Childe Dorr," in Perry J. Ashley, ed., *American Newspaper Journalists: 1901–1925*, vol. 25 of the *Dictionary of Literary Biography* (Detroit: Gale Research, 1984), pp. 77–83.

6. For a biased male look at women replacing men on newspapers, see Stanley Frank and Paul Sann, "Paper Dolls," in John E. Drewry, ed., *More Post Biographies* (Athens: University of Georgia Press, 1947), pp. 206–17.

7. Lilya Wagner, *Women War Correspondents of World War II* (New York: Greenwood, 1989), pp. 152–62.

8. See "Marguerite Higgins," in Madelon Golden Schilpp and Sharon M. Murphy, *Great Women of the Press* (Carbondale: Southern Illinois University Press, 1983), pp. 191–99.

9. Vicki Goldberg, *Margaret Bourke-White: A Biography* (New York: Harper & Row, 1986), p. 26.

10. Goldberg, *Margaret Bourke-White*, pp. 88–89.

11. For a critical evaluation, see William Stott, *Documentary Expression and Thirties America* (New York: Oxford, 1973), pp. 216–23.

12. Julia Edwards, *Women of the World: The Great Foreign Correspondents* (New York: Ivy Books, 1988), pp. 128–41.

13. "*Life*'s Bourke-White Goes Bombing," *Life* (March 1, 1943): 17–23.

See also "Margaret Bourke-White" in Schilpp and Murphy, *Great Women of the Press*, pp. 179–90.

14. From Rheta Childe Dorr, *Inside the Russian Revolution* (New York: Macmillan, 1917).

14

Racial Discrimination
Lucile Bluford
Marvel Cooke

Black women journalists have had to contend with twin barriers: discrimination based on race as well as gender. Their achievements, often overlooked in the general field of journalism history, are now being chronicled by African-American scholars and others interested in the ways a group of unusually strong women have used their journalistic skills to fight for social change. The excerpts below tell part of the story.

Lucile Bluford

In a 1989 interview, Lucile Bluford—editor and publisher of the *Kansas City Call*, an African-American newspaper where she has worked since graduation from the University of Kansas in 1932—described her efforts to break down the segregation barrier that prevented her enrollment for a master's degree at the University of Missouri–Columbia in 1939. Today she holds a doctorate in humanities from the University of Missouri, awarded in 1989 in recognition of her outstanding political writing. Five years earlier the university had presented her with a Missouri Honor Medal for distinguished service to journalism.

Interview with Lucile H. Bluford by Fern Ingersoll,
Kansas City, Missouri, May 15, 1989

INGERSOLL: Today I think we'll talk mostly about your attempt to enter the University of Missouri. But, first, I wanted to ask you about being managing editor of the [Kansas City] *Call* at about that same time. Was it about 1937 that you were made managing editor, the year before you tried to enter the University of Missouri?

BLUFORD: No, that wouldn't have been the year before that. I tried to enter the university back in, oh, that was '39.

INGERSOLL: Then it wasn't very long after that, I guess, after you became managing editor that you decided to apply to the University of Missouri. Tell me whatever you can remember about that whole story.

BLUFORD: Well, that's kind of a long story. I hope you're familiar with the Gaines case.[1] . . . Gaines came here to speak. . . . I believe it was the spring of 1939.—He spoke up here at Centennial Methodist Church, two blocks [from] here at Nineteenth and Woodland. . . .

And I remember I took him to the station, to the Union Station, and he was going to Chicago. I put him on a train. And he later disappeared from up in Chicago, but that was afterwards.[2] But, anyway, he wasn't going to apply [to law school at the University of Missouri] until September. . . .

So I said, "Well, I believe I'll apply for graduate work in journalism and I can find out what the University of Missouri would say." So that was really the basic reason that I did it, because I was just kind of curious about what the university would do, see.

INGERSOLL: Yes.

BLUFORD: So I wrote out to Lawrence [Kansas] and got the University of Kansas to send my credentials down to the University of Missouri [at Columbia] and applied to go down there. And the University of Missouri answered [that I had] accepted credits and said that I could come down and enroll such and such a time in a certain building. And I saw that building, too, when I was down there the other day.

INGERSOLL: Did you? When you went there to get your honorary degree?

BLUFORD: Uh-huh. I said, "That looks like that same hall where I was standing."

INGERSOLL: My goodness.

BLUFORD: That was Jesse Hall. . . . S. W. [Woodson] Canada, the registrar, gave me a date to come down and I wired or I wrote the NAACP, I think, and told them I had applied. I don't know whether I wrote then or later, after I went down there. But anyway, I went down and a couple of lawyers from here went with me. I think it was Carl Johnson, I believe, who later became a judge. He's president of [the Kansas City chapter of] NAACP. And James Herbert, I think. They drove me down there or just rode down with me. I don't remember whether I drove or they drove. But they didn't go in with me or anything like that.

So we got there and I went in the building. I saw a line of students standing in line. I guess, I don't know whether I asked anybody if this was the registration line or not. I just knew what it was, so I just stood in line. And I guess I'd been standing in line about, oh, I don't know, twenty minutes or something like that. And somebody came up and tapped me on the shoulder and said, "Miss Bluford?" I said, "Yeah." "Mr. Canada would like to see you in his office."

So I went on with this young man to Mr. Canada's office. And he told me that he couldn't admit me to the university. And I said, "Why?" I said, "The Supreme Court decision said that you should admit me." "Yeah." But he said, "The Supreme Court decision in the *Gaines* case is not final yet." He said, "The order has got to come down from the Supreme Court to the Missouri Supreme Court, to the District Court, and then to the university." And it hadn't come down to the university. [Chuckles.] That was his reason for not admitting me. See, they didn't know I was black until I was standing in line.

But the funny part about it was, there were other people of color there from all parts of the world. Not American Negroes, but Indians and Chinese, all kinds of folks, you know. And nobody paid any more attention to me than they did to them or anybody else. . . . Didn't pay a bit of attention. So when I left there I did go to the journalism department and looked around and met some of the folks over there. And, again, there wasn't anything unusual about it, you know. So then I think is when I wired the NAACP and told them that they had turned me down. Then a correspondence developed and they decided to sue. . . .

And so they filed a *mandamus* suit asking the court to order the University of Missouri to admit me. See, the state had a choice. They had a choice. All the Supreme Court told them to do was provide the same educational courses, professional courses, and all for blacks that they did for whites within the borders of the state of Missouri.

Prior to that, see, Lincoln University was the school for the blacks. But Lincoln didn't have any professional schools. No law, no medicine, no journalism, no engineering, no anything. Just a liberal arts college . . . .

So anyway, they filed a suit and we had a trial. Let's see now. We had a trial down at Columbia, Boone County [Missouri]. But in the meantime, the state preferred to take the building option. First they built a law school in St. Louis. They did it in a real big hurry. Oh, incidentally, this reminds me of something. They built it in an old building that had been used for the Poro Beauty College. . . . But that had closed so they built this law school in that old Poro Building. Got lawyers from various parts of the country and had a staff. I think they did it during the summer so they were ready to open just about in September. See, September is when Gaines was supposed to be going.

INGERSOLL: Yeah.

BLUFORD: So they built that in St. Louis. . . . They conducted a law school for a while. Then they appropriated money to build a journalism school for me at Lincoln rather than just going on and let me in. One person, one student in there. Instead of doing that, they built a whole school down there.

So in the meantime, we had the trial. Well, I don't know exactly when the trial—you know, I can't say how long it was when we had the trial.

INGERSOLL: January 1940 was the time you were on the stand for about four hours or so.

BLUFORD: Yeah, I was on the stand a long time.

INGERSOLL: A long time?

BLUFORD: Yeah. I don't know what kind of witness I made. But anyway, we had that trial and we lost. We lost. And I remember one of the lawyers for the state said, "She doesn't really want to go to the University of Missouri. She's got a job. She's working for the *Call*. Blah, blah, blah," you know. "She doesn't need to go and the only thing she's trying to do is break down the pattern of segregation."

Well, that was true, but we couldn't admit it, see. We couldn't admit that. But years later now, what he said was exactly right. We were trying to break down that barrier of discrimination. That's exactly what we were trying to do.[3]

Marvel Cooke

The Cooke excerpt deals with Cooke's experiences as the only African-American and woman reporter on the staff of the *Compass*, a liberal New York daily where she worked from 1950 to 1952. A graduate of the University of Minnesota, Cooke worked for the *Amsterdam News*, a black newspaper in New York, in the 1930s and participated in a strike there to organize a unit of the Newspaper Guild (a union for reporters and other employees). Through her guild activity she was recommended for a job on the *Compass*.

Interview with Marvel Cooke by Kathleen Currie, New York City, November 1, 1989

COOKE: Jack McManus [the *Compass* editor-in-chief] gave me a very, very hard time, and rightfully so in the beginning, because in the black press— and it still is true, I imagine—we had at least three or four days to develop a story. I was accustomed to taking my time to go into the background, you know. I wasn't accustomed to that kind of pace.

CURRIE: What did they do?

COOKE: Well, they said, "You know, you're on a daily now. We don't have time to go into backgrounds in the way you have been accustomed to. Maybe tomorrow you can bring another facet to the story. It has to be done at a different pace than you've been accustomed to." I understood that, and I think I was young enough then to have made the adjustment. It wasn't that hard.

But I still seemed to have trouble with Jack McManus. Everything I wrote, he criticized. Finally, Richard Carter—I call him Dick—and the other members of the union [American Newspaper Guild] felt that I was being unfairly criticized. "Let's make a complaint about this." I'll never forget the day we faced Jack McManus. I didn't want to go in with the committee, but I had to. Dick said, "We on the desk can't understand why you complain so much about Marvel's copy. It certainly is superior to some others on staff." And he mentioned a few names. "You don't have any complaints about their copy, but every time something by Marvel Cooke is brought into your office, you have a complaint about it."

And I must say, to his credit, Jack McManus said, "Well, I'll tell you what happens to me. I'm not accustomed to women on the desk and when I walk out there and see her, I feel I can't use my four-letter words. I just can't express myself the way I want to."

I remember my answer to him. I said, "I don't use those words myself. Actually, they never have been in my vocabulary, but I know them. I couldn't have walked the streets of Harlem and written stories and not be familiar with them. I can write them and they don't disturb me. It just disturbs me that people are unable to express themselves except in these kinds of words." After that, we started getting along. But I found myself still trying to please Jack McManus. I worked so hard to please Jack McManus, I was sort of like in a straitjacket, you know. . . .

CURRIE: Did you propose stories?

COOKE: As a matter of fact, I did propose the slave-market series. . . .

CURRIE: Essentially, just for the record, the slave market is [i.e., was] made up of day workers?

COOKE: Day workers, yes. People who needed to augment their very small income in order to live. They did it this way. They'd go up and stand and be assessed as to their brawn, and hired by the women of the community to do day work.

CURRIE: And there was a place in the Bronx where they would go?

COOKE: There may have been more than this one place, but I did know about Westchester Avenue, about 176th Street. . . .

CURRIE: So you decided you'd pose as one of these women?

COOKE: Yes, pose. I had never done anything like that before.

CURRIE: Whose idea was it that you were going to pose?

COOKE: It was mine. It would take a black woman to do it. I had my proper paper bag with my work clothes in it. I went up and stood with several women at that corner, hoping to get hired. The women were suspicious of me because, I guess, no matter how hard I tried, I didn't look quite like they looked.

CURRIE: How did they look?

COOKE: Well, their nails weren't done, you know. I mean, their lifestyle was so different from mine that I guess I just didn't look the way they looked. They were suspicious of me. They didn't know what I was doing up there. They had never seen me before. I remember my husband used to drive me up there and drop me two blocks away, and he'd say, "I wouldn't speak to you for anything in the world. You just look awful." But I obviously didn't look "right." So I remember there was a bet on at the paper that I would not get a job.

CURRIE: Why is that?

COOKE: Because they didn't think I could look like these women, you know. I didn't look like I could do a day's work, anyway, and nobody was going to hire me. And the bet was, I remember, a quart of Scotch. If I didn't get a job, I would give them a quart of Scotch so they could have a party, and if I did get one, I'd get a quart of Scotch.

So I went up there several days, I think at least four days, and stood there hours. I had five days to get this experiment going. I stood there hours with my little bag, looking downcast and harassed, and I couldn't get hired. Nobody would hire me.

CURRIE: Did someone talk to you?

COOKE: Nobody! They'd just look at me and pass me by. So the last day—this was the last day of the experiment, I said, "I'm just going to owe my co-workers a quart of Scotch. I'll never get hired." A man came up to me. We were standing at a corner where there was a men's store—featured shirts and things like that. And a man came up to me and he said, "Are you looking for a job?"

I said, "Yes, sir."

And he said, "Do you clean?"

I said, "Yes, sir." I thought to myself, "I know what you're supposed to do."

CURRIE: You know what you're supposed to do, but you don't really clean.

COOKE: That's right! [Laughter] So there came a rap on the window of this store, and a man beckoned to me: "Come here." He said, "I've noticed you out there. No woman should go off with a man, because you don't know, really, what he wants. If I were you, I would not take that job."

So I went back. I said, "The man in the store has hired me." And I thought, "This is the end." I went back to the corner and stood there for a few minutes. Then I was very hungry, and there was a ten-cent store, Woolworth's, up the street. I thought, "Well, I'll go up there and get a cup of coffee or something." Walking up the street, a woman, I guess, noticed my bag and my downcast look. She said, "Are you looking for work?"

I said, "Yes, ma'am."

CURRIE: She was on the street, too?

COOKE: She had obviously come from that corner, and there was nobody on it, because I had just left. I was the last one. So she said, "Do you do day's work?"

I said, "Yes, ma'am." This is the first time in my life I had ever said "ma'am" to anybody. I said, "Yes, ma'am."

And she said, "Well, I came to the corner too late to get someone. Would you work for me?"

I said, "Yes, ma'am!" I didn't say it like that, but that's the way I felt. "I got my quart of Scotch now!"

Anyway, I will never forget that experience as long as I live. I had a woman who used to come in once a week to help me, and that very day, Rebecca was at my house, but I never asked her to do things I was asked to do.

CURRIE: Did you get in her car with her?

COOKE: She didn't have a car. We walked to her apartment, which was close by. She had exactly the number of rooms as I have here, not as well arranged or anything. Of course, it would be better if I had linoleum on my living-room floor now, because it couldn't be as dirty as this carpet is. But she had linoleum all the way through her apartment. Her bedroom had linoleum on the floor, the living room, kitchen area. She didn't have a real kitchen. She said, "I want you to clean the bedroom first." And she gave me a pail of water, not a mop, but a washcloth. I had to do it on my knees, wash up this woman's floor on my knees. I had never—my mother had had people working for her in Minnesota. Nobody had had to do anything like that! But I did it. I was very happy to do it, because you know, it was part of the story.

She was cooking, and I noticed she was very clean and I wouldn't mind eating anything that she cooked. I remember it was lamb stew and it smelled very good, and I was getting hungry. I had to do the bathroom on my hands and knees. Just before I was to do the living room also on my hands and knees, she had asked me what my name was, and I said, "Marjorie." She said, "Marjorie, would you have something to eat?" I thought, "Thank God!" And she sat down and gave me some crackers and a glass of tea. I wasn't used to drinking hot things out of a glass, but a glass of tea and some marmalade or something like that, and she sat there and ate her lamb stew. You know, I couldn't imagine doing Rebecca, who was here at my house, that way. That's what she gave me to eat, and she ate her lamb stew—with relish.

When we got through, I finished up the living room on my hands and knees, and she asked me would I do windows. I said, "That's one thing I don't do."

Well, I'm a little ahead of the story, because the girls on the corner had decided I wasn't a plant, and they had become friendly with me. They said, "You've never had a job. You've never done this before. If you get a job, be careful to see what time it is that you go in, because they have a way of setting back the clock on you. If you've put in five hours, they'll say it's four. But you set your clock with whatever time you see in that house," and gave me a few other pointers like that. I had set my watch. She had a clock on the wall, the kitchen wall, and I'd set it with that.

So anyway, I did her floors, all of them, and then she asked me to iron. I am the world's worst ironer. I don't believe anyone irons as poorly as I do. What she had was some men's shirts and some curtains, the kind of curtains that have the flounces around them, you know. I ironed those shirts, and I told my husband afterwards I didn't put a wrinkle in them. I didn't know that I was capable of ironing that well. But I ironed well, and I ironed those curtains with the flounces around them. I was so tired, I was about to drop dead.

So she said, "Well, I have some windows I would like you to wash."

I said, "Well, I don't do windows." I thought, "I've had enough experience here with this woman now."

CURRIE: You had enough for the story.

COOKE: Yes. I said, "I don't do windows." I said, "By the way, I have some children. I always am home when they come home from school, so I have to leave."

So she said, "Oh, I'm so sorry, Marjorie, because I really like you."

I said, "Thank you."

She said, "Would you come next week?"

I thought, "You've seen the last of me!" I said, "Yes, ma'am. I'll be up on the corner." [Laughter]

The pay was seventy-five cents an hour. That was sort of standard. So I had set my watch and it was now three o'clock. I had gone in there at ten o'clock. So I was owed five times seventy-five cents, whatever that is.

CURRIE: You were owed five hours.

COOKE: Five hours. She had set her clock back to two o'clock. I said, "There's something wrong with your clock. It must have stopped, because I set my watch with it, and my watch says three o'clock."

She said, "Oh, yes, I guess it must have stopped." But she was going to fleece me out of that seventy-five cents.

CURRIE: She was trying to fleece you out of the seventy-five cents.

COOKE: That's right.

CURRIE: Did you get the seventy-five cents:

COOKE: Yes, I did. She said, "Oh, my clock must have stopped."

I said, "Yes, it had to, because my watch is accurate."

So she said, "Margie, I'm looking forward to seeing you next week. You can come straight here."

I said, "You can meet me on the corner."

So I went to the ten-cent store, I called up the *Compass* office, and I said, "I worked today. You owe me a quart of Scotch."[4]

Notes

1. Note by Ingersoll: "Lloyd Gaines, a black man, was refused admittance by the University of Missouri Law School. The NAACP, National Association for the Advancement of Colored People, filed a suit but was defeated in the Missouri Supreme Court. In 1938 the U.S. Supreme Court ruled in *Missouri ex rel. Gaines v. Canada* that a state must provide equal educational facilities for blacks.—Fern Ingersoll."

2. Gaines was never found and is thought to have been murdered.

3. From the Women in Journalism Oral History Project of the Washington Press Club Foundation, Washington, DC, and available in the Oral History Collection of Columbia University and other repositories.

4. From the Women in Journalism Oral History Project.

15

Newspaper Families
Eleanor "Cissy" Patterson
Agnes E. Meyer

From the colonial period to the present, women have contributed to journalism through their family relationships. Susan Henry, editor of *Journalism History*, has pointed out that three generations of women have played an important role in establishing the Otis-Chandler media dynasty of the *Los Angeles Times*.[1] On the East Coast, Helen Rogers Reid—as vice-president of the New York *Herald Tribune* during the 1930s and 1940s—proved far more capable at management than her husband, Ogden, the newspaper's president. A genteel but poor young woman who had worked her way through Barnard College in New York, she was employed as a secretary for the Reid family before her marriage.[2]

In Washington, two extraordinary women dramatized the influence of women family members on newspaper publishing during the 1940s. One was Eleanor Medill "Cissy" Patterson, a granddaughter of Joseph Medill, who had acquired a fortune from ownership of the *Chicago Tribune*. The other was Agnes E. Meyer, wife of Eugene Meyer, the owner of the *Washington Post*.

Eleanor "Cissy" Patterson

After two unhappy marriages—one to a Polish count who mistreated her, and the second to a lawyer with whom she moved in high society—Patterson convinced William Randolph Hearst to let her take over the operation of his *Washington Herald*. Although she had no experience in running a newspaper, the business ran in her blood. Her brother, Joseph Medill Patterson, founded the *New York Daily News*. His daughter, Alicia Patterson, followed suit by founding *Newsday* on Long Island. In the 1920s, Eleanor Patterson wrote features for Hearst as well as two thinly disguised novels about her own life. She was also a director of both the *New York Daily News* and *Chicago Tribune* companies.[3]

As a publisher she managed the *Herald* capriciously but well, hiring talented women writers and building circulation while engaging in publicized feuds with competitors including Meyer. In 1937 she leased the evening *Times* from Hearst along with the morning *Herald*. Two years later she bought both newspapers, combined them into an all-day publication, and by 1943 was making a profit on the largest-circulation newspaper in Washington.[4]

Patterson's instability, which led her to impulsive firings, increased as she aged. She quarreled with her cousin, Col. Robert McCormick, head of the *Tribune*, and carried a gun, suspicious of her associates. She was found dead of an apparent heart attack at her estate in Maryland in 1948 at the age of 66. The employees to whom she had left the newspaper sold it back to Colonel McCormick, who found it unprofitable and, in 1954, sold it to Meyer. He consolidated it with the *Washington Post*.

The selection that follows provides a look at her complicated personality, which fluctuated from warm and generous to cold and calculating. It was written in 1968 by a former *Times-Herald* reporter for a book planned, but never published, on the history of the Women's National Press Club, an organization of Washington women journalists.

RED-HEADED DOLL
By Vade Ward Marcantonio

Christmas CAN be grim for any one of us at some time or another, but it evidently always was for the late Eleanor Patterson, owner of the extinct but once flamboyant *Times-Herald*.

I can tell you of a very special Christmas in her life, 1944, when there were two presents which did make her sombre eyes smile—even if only fleetingly.

We had a column called the "Enquiring Photographer," later written by Jacqueline Bouvier (Kennedy). During the Christmas season of 1944 the Enquiring Photographer (I do not recall his name) visited St. Ann's Orphanage and asked all the children there what they wanted most from Santa Claus. One little girl said "a red-headed doll" and this is what caught "Sissy's" [sic] eye when she read the evening edition—for Cissy, Mrs. Patterson, had famous dark, dark red long, very long, hair. Beautiful it was too.

I shall never forget her proud, cat-like entrances into the city room, and that great head of hair. I always made a point of pretending not to notice her, for I did not wish to attract her fear-inspiring attention.

Well, when she saw that bit about the little orphan wanting a doll with red hair, the unpredictable Sissy determined that every child in that orphanage should have exactly what he or she wanted from Santa—with her being Santa, of course. Not just *any* present, but exactly what was wanted—but most especially that child was to get the doll with red hair—yes, with red hair just exactly the color of hers! That was the catch!

The advertising department got the assignment of finding the presents. William Shelton and his men struggled through the fairly simple requirements of visiting [i.e., locating] clowns, elephants "as big as Sister Mary" and just ordinary boy/girl big-eyed wonders. But nowhere could a doll be found which had the long copper-chestnut hair of the "boss."

Now on a grim deadline, Shelton passed on the assignment of the red-haired doll to the city room—and that's where I came into the picture. I made a suggestion. Those who had been struggling with the assignment considered the suggestion a bolt of lightning. Me—, well, it seemed the simplest thing on earth. Money no object. Right? Right! Well, why not get a wig from the beauty parlor Sissy frequented, have it dyed the exact color of red, and affix it to the one lucky doll?

Idea conceived, executed, presto—doll. A happy advertising room, city room, and an unhappy me. As author of the "plan" I was to take the doll over for Mrs. Patterson to see. This boss-lady of ours was a creature of moods, and I felt this was not so much "the desirable" assignment, as it was finding a patsy to take the blame if the, yes, rather vain Mrs. Patterson didn't approve of the color of "her" hair.

It was 1944—war time everywhere, and now it was my time for the front lines. On the way over to Dupont Circle I hailed a cab (remember sharing?) which already had a Marine corporal in it. I wasn't too tall myself, and the box I was wielding with its special prize was literally almost as long as I was tall. The corporal helped me get it in the car—and the softly falling snow caught on his long eyelashes. Yes, I remember those eyelashes. When he found out what was in the box he had to look. He fell in love with Mrs. Patterson then and there. I wish I had told her. What trickled down his cheeks might have been melting snow, but I think it wasn't.

Miss Margaret Barney, Cissy's private secretary, came down to collect me at the front door and we waded our way through toilet paper—all along the route up the elevator to Mrs. Patterson's third floor bedroom. Why toilet paper? Because her several poodles like to unroll it, that's why. I could see it was a little hard on Miss Barney.

Meeting Mrs. Patterson—especially under such circumstances—was a bit undoing. She was on the phone with someone who shall remain nameless. She extended the phone some distance from her ear, fixed me with her minx-stare and drawled, "God damn fool. He's a big bore." Then back on the phone she purred. "Yes, dahling?" I felt sorry for him. The man she was talking to was one who would inherit a million dollars as his part of her *Times-Herald*.

However, my real dread was strictly reserved for myself. How would the red-headed doll strike this miserably rich woman?

I did not panic. After all, retreat is ignominious, especially through toilet paper. And anyway when she beckoned me to come forward—I just did—automatically. I opened the box. She loved "little Eleanor" and I breathed silent prayers of thanks to some nameless beauty parlor operator.

The rest of what happened that evening is not part of this story—except just one more thing. The doll was her main Christmas present, she said, and it had made her very happy. There was one other.

Her hand was resting on something round and made of glass. She turned it upside down, twisted it around and around and then stood it upright for me to see. It was one of those paperweight winter scenes. "It's from Evalyn Walsh McLean," she explained, "one of the few people in the world with as much money as I have. I can trust her. She doesn't want anything from me."

The snow in the paperweight fell softly but none touched the eyelashes of Mrs. Eleanor Patterson nor came melting down her cheeks.[5]

Agnes E. Meyer

The next selection is reprinted from the *Washington Post* as an example of the journalistic work of Agnes Meyer, mother of Katharine Graham, current chair of the board of the *Post* company. Known for her intellectual prowess, Agnes Meyer helped establish the *Post* as the leading newspaper in the nation's capital.

Following graduation from Barnard College, she was one of the first women to work as a reporter for the *New York Sun* before traveling to Paris where she moved in literary and artistic circles. Her marriage in 1910 to Eugene Meyer, a wealthy international financier, brought her the opportunity to continue intellectual pursuits, including her studies of Chinese language and art.[6]

After Eugene Meyer purchased the *Post* in 1933, she wrote frequently for the newspaper on social and literary subjects. A close friend of the German writer Thomas Mann, she translated and reviewed his works. She also traveled throughout the United States to report to *Post* readers on homefront conditions during World War II. She campaigned against overcrowded schools, lack of community facilities for health and welfare, and racial discrimination. Her efforts to seek establishment of a Department of Health, Education, and Welfare prompted President Harry Truman to complain, "There's hardly a day I don't get a letter from that woman or from Eleanor Roosevelt telling me how to run this job."[7]

A philanthropist who received 14 honorary degrees, Meyer died in 1970 at the age of 83. Reprinted here is one of a series of articles she wrote on migrant workers in Texas in 1946. Note that the immensely wealthy Meyer reported she "scrambled" along a dirt bank to inspect personally the "burrows" occupied by "wetbacks" (illegal immigrants from Mexico).

RIO GRANDE PROBLEM
MIGRANT MEXICAN AND ANGLO LABOR
By Agnes E. Meyer

HARLINGEN, Tex., April 22—From Robstown we drove almost 135 miles due south to Raymondville, first through tilled land then through great stretches of prairie, much of it belonging to the famous King Ranch. The temperature was over 100 degrees but the dry, clear air is not oppressive. As the onion crop is being harvested in this area, the enormous flat stretches are filled here and there with big crews. In one field so many children were at work that I jumped from the car to photograph them. As I was focusing on an ambitious 5-year-old boy with a full red-netted onion bag on his back, the others flocked toward me. Although these children from 5 to 15 had already worked four hours, they were full of spontaneous gaiety. They immediately took charge of me. It was all I could do to keep them from lining up in military formation so that the lady could get a really nice picture. The soft warmth of these children of Mexican origin or descent, their reticence and gentle kindliness, to say nothing of their beauty, are irresistible.

The children often look sad in repose. When they sing their voices are plaintive. Their smile is not the bright sunny smile of our children. It is more like the moon coming from behind clouds. We talk to each other in sign language. Many of the children definitely enjoy the migratory trek. I asked one little lad what he wanted to be when he grew up and he replied stoutly: "I'd like to be an onion clipper like my father and travel around."

But the effects upon their lives are disastrous. Some of them have never been to school, and most of them are retarded. They get discouraged sitting around in the first or second grades until they are 12 or 14 years old because of irregular attendance, lack of suitable clothing, or inability to understand English. Yet special classes for these children, child labor laws, and other well-meant plans seem to be utterly hopeless as long as the agricultural work of these children is essential to the bare subsistence of the family. One of the best things the labor camps are doing is to encourage all the children to go to school regularly as long as they are in residence. A bus comes every day to take them to the nearest public school. At the Harlingen Labor Center, which has one of the steadiest, skilled populations, the youngsters who had gone to school regularly for several years were making normal progress.

In the midst of the big onion field where I was photographing, there stands a huge celanese factory occupying several acres. Its many aluminum-colored, slender shafts of different altitudes make it look like some wondrous mirage. It was set down in this onion tract because of the proximity of an oil and cotton supply. My heart warms to its strange beauty. If only enough industry would move into this area of abundant raw materials and over-abundant labor supply, the lives of these wretched people could be transformed.

We then lunched in a crowded little cafe in Raymondville. A curious bit of Americana in one of the shop windows caught my eye. In the center were two pictures of Christ, one a head, the other a crucifixion, completely surrounded by photographs of [movie stars] Joan Crawford, Clark Gable, Robert Taylor, Lana Turner, Van Johnson, etc., at least 30 or more. The sign: "Your choice 50 cents."

At the Raymondville Labor Supply Center the onion crop had attracted a sudden influx of over 400 people in the last few days. The camp was jammed to capacity, a population of 1200.

Here I saw families of wet-backs, those who have come across the border illegally, for the first time. They can be readily distinguished from our citizens of Mexican descent. By their more neglected appearance, their facial stolidity and in some cases, by an inferior way of living, they prove that on the whole our economy, however unjust to the Mexican immigrant, has done something for them. The wet-back families bring few, if any, possessions, sleep on the bare bedsprings, and cook on open fires in front of their shelters as they cannot manage the oilstoves provided by the camp. The adults are mostly in the fields and many of the children. When we found a girl of 8 or 10 at home, she was looking after four or five younger brothers and sisters. . . .

Nobody knows how many wet-backs are in the Valley, because they live here, there and everywhere. With some members of the state Extension Service, I scrambled along the bank of a mesquite-shaded irrigation ditch near the town of Bishop, where numbers of them had hidden their makeshift dwellings. Some had improvised tents of dried cornstalks. Others had burrowed into the ground and covered the cave with old pieces of timber, pasteboard or dried grass. As the occupants were all at work, I could examine these hide-outs to heart's content. Most of them were obviously occupied by single men. But they had their holy pictures tacked on the wall, and the neatness of these burrows was astonishing. The dirt floors were swept clean, their few pots and pans were orderly and freshly washed; clothes were carefully strung on a line.[8]

Notes

1. Susan Henry, "Dear Companion, Ever-ready Co-worker: A Woman's Role in a Media Dynasty," *Journalism Quarterly* 64 (1987):301–12. See also

Henry, "Changing Media History through Women's History," in Pamela J. Creedon, ed., *Women in Mass Communication: Challenging Gender Values* (Newbury Park, CA: Sage, 1989), pp. 34–57.

2. Richard Kluger, *The Paper: The Life and Death of the New York* Herald-Tribune (New York: Vintage, 1989), pp. 285–88.

3. Frank Luther Mott, *American Journalism: A History, 1690–1960* (New York: Macmillan, 1962), p. 661.

4. David Denker, "Eleanor Medill Patterson," in Edward T. James, *Notable American Women: 1607–1950*, vol. 3 (Cambridge, MA: Harvard University Press, 1974), pp. 26–28.

5. In the Records of the Women's National Press Club/Washington Press Club in the Cora Rigby Washington Journalism Archive at the National Press Club, Washington, DC.

6. Susan M. Hartmann, "Agnes Elizabeth Ernst Meyer," in James, *Notable American Women*, vol. 3, pp. 471–73.

7. As quoted in Chalmers M. Roberts, *The* Washington Post: *The First 100 Years* (Boston: Houghton Mifflin, 1977), p. 265.

8. From the *Washington Post*, April 23 (Tuesday), 1946.

16
Early Days in Broadcasting
Ruth Crane

With the advent of commercial radio in the 1920s, women found their opportunities severely limited. Newscasting was reserved for men because station managers and advertisers held that men's voices alone carried authority and believability. Still, some women managed to find a place behind the microphone, although they were largely restricted to traditional women's fare—housekeeping hints and recipes interspersed with interview shows and public service programs.

When Mary Margaret McBride, a well-established magazine and newspaper reporter, began her radio career in 1934 in New York, she was told to pretend to be a wise old grandmother and dispense homey philosophy. In the midst of a sentence she finally burst out into the microphone, "Oh, what's the use? I can't do it! I'm not a grandmother! I'm not a mother. I'm not even married. Nothing about all this I'm saying sounds real to me and that's because it isn't. The truth is I'm a reporter and I would like to come here every day and tell you about places I go and people I meet. Write me if you'd like that. But I can't be a grandmother any more!"[1]

Her listeners responded and she was launched on one of the most successful careers in radio history, earning the accolade "Lady Number One of the Air" for her daily interview program that continued on network radio until her retirement in 1960.[2]

One woman radio pioneer was the actual first lady, Eleanor Roosevelt. While in the White House, she signed contracts with commercial sponsors to give radio commentaries that told about her activities and promoted the programs of her husband's administration. She used most of the proceeds for charities.[3]

Other women entered off-the-air aspects of broadcasting. Judith Cary Waller was the first manager of WMAQ, a Chicago station that began broadcasting in 1922. She remained in broadcasting after the station was sold to NBC in 1931, although she was moved from station manager to public service director for the network's central division. She held the job until retirement from NBC in 1957.[4]

In the tense days before World War II broke out in Europe, Edward R. Murrow hired an old friend, photojournalist Mary Marvin Breckinridge, to broadcast over his CBS *World News Roundup.* Breckinridge made about 50 broadcasts from seven countries including Nazi Germany in 1939 and 1940 before her marriage to a diplomat, Jefferson Patterson. Fluent in several languages, she possessed a strong, low voice and was an excellent prospect for a successful career in broadcasting if marriage had not forced her resignation. The U.S. State Department would not allow her to continue broadcasting because of her husband's post at the U.S. Embassy in Berlin.[5]

During World War II, women were used on the airwaves to promote the war effort. But newscasting remained a field "for men only" well into the era of television that caught hold in the 1950s.

Yet, by virtue of hard work, women began to be taken seriously as newscasters. In 1946 Pauline Frederick was hired by ABC even though she received regular news assignments only if men were not available.

"I had to make my own opportunity to cover real news," she recalled in a 1974 interview with a journalism student, Gioia Diliberto. "I was told by my editor that there was great objection to a woman being on the air for serious issues, and he had orders not to use me. But he said if by chance, I got an exclusive, he'd have to use me, adding 'though I'll slit your throat if you tell anyone I gave you this advice.' "[6]

Frederick kept quiet but worked very hard to get exclusive stories at the United Nations. After covering a foreign ministers' conference, she asked her chief for regular news assignments. He turned her down—she told Diliberto—answering, "It isn't that you haven't proved yourself, but when listeners hear a woman's voice, they'll turn off their radios, because a woman's voice just doesn't carry authority."[7]

Continuing to persevere in spite of prejudice, Frederick began television broadcasting in 1948 and became TV's first successful newswoman, covering the United Nations for NBC from 1953 until her retirement in 1972.

Difficulties encountered by women in early-day radio and television were discussed by Ruth Crane Schaefer—who spent 27 years in broadcasting in Detroit and Washington, D.C.—in an interview conducted in 1975 as part of an oral history project of the American Women in Radio and Television. A somewhat shortened version is reprinted here.

Mower Interview
[with Ruth Crane Schaefer]

MOWER: My name is Pat Mower. I'm a member of the Washington, D.C., chapter of American Women in Radio and Television. The date is November 18, 1975, and I am in the home of Mrs. Ruth Crane Schaefer to interview her about her early days in radio and television—as a part of the AWRT Oral History Project on women pioneers in the broadcasting industry. Interviews will be placed on permanent record in the Library of The Broadcast Pioneers in Washington, D.C.

Mrs. Schaefer was born Ruth Franklin in Springfield, Missouri. She received her early schooling in Missouri. Then, special courses at Drury College, the University of Missouri—and later at Northwestern University and The Chicago Art Institute gave her a background in journalism, theatricals, salesmanship and literature which prepared her for a successful career in both radio and television.

Ruth, I know your broadcasting career began in the very early days of radio but just when, how and where did you get that first radio job?

CRANE: Well, it was in 1929 and you remember that things were pretty bad then, or were getting bad—I mean financially. I was in Detroit and had to look for a job. I applied at two places—the J. L. Hudson Company as a fashion writer and WJR, the radio station—not knowing what I might be required or even able to do there. Oddly, I was accepted at both places and I guess I took the WJR job because it was within walking distance of where I lived. Of course, it turned out to be a lucky choice because the broadcasting business came through the depression better than many other businesses.

MOWER: That's right. I remember those depression days and how difficult it was to get any kind of a job. What about your qualifications for a radio job, Ruth? I know your background. Was it helpful at all in fitting you for what you went into in radio?

CRANE: I guess I was as much qualified, or maybe more so, than most people but I hadn't anything that exactly fitted the broadcasting business. No one else had either in those days.

MOWER: There really weren't any college or university courses for radio, were there?

CRANE: Not at that time. Of course, some came along later at the University of Michigan and I helped teach some classes there—but that was perhaps 10 years later. I had some dramatic experience and had written copy for some store magazines in Chicago—advertising copy—and had taught shorthand at night while attending Northwestern University. In Detroit I had done market research for an advertising agency and, of course, I could type and that was important.

MOWER: That is an asset, isn't it?

CRANE: I've tried to get so many younger people to understand that, but they don't always want to. Anyway, Leo Fitzpatrick, head of WJR, and later President of the National Association of Broadcasters, said, "Well, there isn't any job open, but we do need people and if you can make a job for yourself, O.K.—$30 a week to start."

MOWER: Big money, too!

CRANE: Well, in those days it was sufficient.

MOWER: Right—it really was big money then.

CRANE: So, I went to work—9 to 5 or 6 or something of the sort—and I just helped out wherever I was needed. I soon observed that the time salesmen were coming into the studio with some commercial material scribbled on the back of an envelope and handing it to the announcer who, if he could read it at all, made little effort to put it together—and there was no record kept of what was actually said. We weren't making recordings in those days anyway. So, I decided that that procedure needed organizing and I did it—to everyone's relief. So, I became Commercial Editor, a job that I kept on with even during my tenure as Women's Editor.

MOWER: Then did that develop into a permanent job or something else?

CRANE: Yes, they had a woman on the air conducting a Foods Program but her family responsibilities and her health made it necessary for someone else to fill in for her frequently and so they called on me for that. This was a daily program called Mrs. Page's Household Economy and eventually I became the regular six days a week Mrs. Page.

MOWER: You were on as Mrs. Page—not as Mrs. Crane?

CRANE: Oh yes. You know in those days we always took a name other than our own on the air.

MOWER: I know and I always wondered why.

CRANE: Well, you know, I think possibly the station management felt that our ability to do a job might be questioned, if people knew exactly who we were, so we were given a pseudonym so we wouldn't be recognized. Oh, I was Alice Franklin—I think you mentioned that my maiden name was Franklin— and then Mrs. Page and I had several other names, I think. Eventually I became Ruth Schaefer after marriage but I continued on with the name Ruth Crane on radio and TV.

MOWER: Really your—may I say your most "famous" name in the broadcasting business was Ruth Crane?

CRANE: Well, yes. You see, I had established that in Detroit and when I came to WMAL in Washington it was necessary for me to carry on with it. Also Crane was a better radio name than Schaefer which has so many spellings.

MOWER: At that time there weren't specific requirements made, were there, as to—oh, you know, ability to broadcast or type of voice or background. It was more being in the right place at the right time, wasn't it?

CRANE: That's right. Mr. Fitzpatrick had said, "I want a regular Michigan mid-western type voice. I don't want anything southern. I don't want any broad A's. I want it down-to-earth." Well, I had enough dramatic experience to cover up what remained of my early Missouri twang—I guess I did—anyway, that was it. So, I started out giving cooking information on the air.

MOWER: Oh, really! You mean cooking lessons?

CRANE: Not exactly that, but it was a program directed to women covering all aspects of homemaking. We gave recipes, certainly, household hints and general news of interest to women. Remember radio was fairly new then—in 1929—the depression was on and many women were more or less house-bound and they welcomed a friendly voice with knowledge of their daily problems and what appeared to be an effort to help them.

Everyone was fascinated with radio anyway, and the women's program was the only—with the possible exception of the Farm Program—the only radio vehicle that gave listeners an actual feeling of participating—of knowing the person on the air. What I mean is radio news, music and plays, you know, they didn't have the "you and me" relationship with the same problems—reading the letters, giving identity to the listeners, giving names, making the listener a part of it. A woman's program did that so listener mail was tremendous in those days, particularly on a 50,000 watt station covering three states and a large part of Canada.

MOWER: Ruth, I was just thinking the other day—you know, now you hear credits given on radio and you see the credits given on television for all types of programs—so many writers, so many producers, so many assistant production people, and so forth—I know the answer myself, but I just want to ask you this—when you were doing all this programming, how much help did you have?

CRANE: I didn't have any, of course—that's very simple. I was holding down two other jobs. I was on the sales staff, I was Commercial Editor and I was Women's Editor or Mrs. Page. Oh, I got a raise to $35 a week, too.

MOWER: That was good.

CRANE: Yes—well, you know, women broadcasters weren't very well paid in those days. I don't know how well they are paid now, but in 1944 when I left WJR in Detroit after 15 years there I think I was making $85 a week—that was all—and this covered all the jobs I had—the Women's Program Director, the Commercial Editor and the sales work that I did. Men on the air with far less responsibilities were paid much better, of course.

MOWER: Ruth, were women broadcasters—that is women on the air in those days—did they all do just food and household hints?

CRANE: Practically all, at that time. Each station usually had one woman personality on the air and at that time few of us had invaded the news or sports or other fields. You know, a man's voice was supposed to denote authority and knowledge and not very many of the women did interviews even. This, too, was a man's field. But, remember this, our sponsors were almost entirely foods and household items sold to women. Our bosses and sponsors wanted program material that fitted in with their products. We did our own commercials, of course, as you know. There weren't any transcribed commercials until later. And so, the transition was a very natural one from giving information about how to do something and the product to do it with. The familiar voice selling the product became more believable. I'm speaking of the early days, of course, perhaps up to the mid-forties. But early in the forties opportunities were expanded and women did take on the chores previously assumed to be a man's field. Just don't deprecate, though, the kind of job that the women did in the earlier years. It was listened to eagerly by housewives who felt their interests shared. It was helpful information that they could use in money saving ideas and they wanted a friend on the air.

MOWER: And, Ruth, didn't you get a great deal of what was called fan mail from those very women?

CRANE: Oh, yes, and very personal letters, commenting, asking questions and that sort of thing.

MOWER: Questions about your own personal life and that sort of thing in addition to asking questions about the type of thing you'd had on the air?

CRANE: Oh, yes, the fan mail was tremendous, especially on a 50,000 watt station covering three or four states.

I remember, speaking of the sort of broadcasting that we did during those early years, I remember later on I was irate when one of our own AWB[s] members who had gone on to news reporting, mentioned disdainfully women on the air telling how to revive a wilted lettuce leaf and such things. Believe me, I would gladly have passed on such information and I think it would have been happily received. I didn't think then, and still don't, that the only really proud function of women on the air is to deliver what the newcomers at that time and perhaps still do call hard news. There is a lot of other information, as is well known and practiced, that women find interesting and beneficial when expounded by an expert. Of course, the whole situation is expanding now.

MOWER: Well, Ruth, as I recall, the woman broadcaster didn't just do a fifteen-minute or thirty-minute program on the air as sometimes they do today. She usually had many other duties around the station in addition to the time she was on the air. In most cases they were also designated as a Director of Women's Programs or Director of Women's Activities—

CRANE: Yes, that was giving us a nice high-flown title. Actually, it covered almost anything. I had to go out and make talks to women's groups and—well, for awhile I did auditions, too—I remember that—that is, audition appointments—I didn't always listen to the auditions. And there were just countless duties that one was called on to do. I mean there was no time requirement. You worked from 9 o'clock or 8:30 in the morning until 5, 6, or midnight—whenever you were through.

MOWER: You were a combination public relations and promotional director in a way, too, because many of the stations didn't have much personnel at that time, did they?

CRANE: Yes, that was a job that I assumed on my own, more or less, a sort of PR job and publicity job. Oh, one of the newscasters was supposed to be the publicity man but did very little about it, and I did that. Of course, there was no objection on the part of the station management as to how many jobs I held or what I did as long as I didn't ask to be paid for it.

MOWER: Doing all of these things probably set the woman up as a very important personality around the station. Was she attributed a great deal of respect by other members of the staff?

CRANE: That's the funniest question I've heard yet. No—and I've checked this with many other women who were in radio and TV too. I think a phenomenon of the early days of both radio and TV—and, for all I know, it still exists—is that the Women's Director who had her own shows was inescapably considered a character by her station associates. Oh, of course, some were—I've known some who really were, and I'm sure you have, too. But, oddly, the lowest branch on the organization tree was usually that of the woman who did foods, children's programs, women's activities and so on, no matter how well sponsored and notwithstanding this woman in almost all cases was also her own complete staff—writer, program director, producer, public relations, innovator, outside speaker, often saleswoman for her own sponsors, radio or TV and sometimes both. But a character nevertheless she was expected to be and they all made jokes about it and all that. You were really not supposed to know anything about food or household or any of the subjects you were broadcasting on. Our efforts were not taken very seriously by our associates even though the announcers and technicians were often the veritable beginners on the staff. And the jokes directed at her were not always innocent. Later on in TV it became almost the practice, according to several of the early women broadcasters who told me about it—and it was in my case as well—for the floorman, the cameraman and others to make away ahead of time with the food she had prepared in advance for use on her show. You know—she opens the oven door or the refrigerator door and ha-ha nothing is inside.

MOWER: Great big joke, hunh?

CRANE: Oh, yes, of course. We tried putting locks on the refrigerator and all, but they'd break it open. And the management didn't do anything about it. Or, in the case of a complicated commercial requiring what was called an "idiot sheet" it was considered uproariously funny to turn it backwards or turn it so fast that it couldn't be read correctly. Strangely, as I say, the management of the station did nothing or at least too little to correct these occurrences. And, I've heard this from other broadcasters as well. I don't understand it.

MOWER: Ruth, television must have been quite a departure from the type of programs you had been doing on radio. When did you actually start your television program?

CRANE: That was in '46.

MOWER: That was here?

CRANE: Yes, that was in addition to the radio I was doing here. By then, by the way, I had acquired a secretary.

MOWER: Oh, good for you! How did you get into TV? I know WMAL had a TV station but did you go to the boss and have a completed script and that kind of thing and say, "I'd like to be on television"?

CRANE: I got into TV simply by being there—that's all. And, naturally, they wanted to use the same people as long as they could. They didn't want to put on another staff to operate TV—we all doubled up. And so, there I was. I had been warned some time previously that I would be expected to go on TV eventually, and I, at that time, was President of the National Association of Women Broadcasters and was pretty busy with that and my radio job and making speeches and heaven knows what all. And one day Ben Baylor, who was the sales manager, called me into his office and said, "Now, look, you're to start your TV program a week from Tuesday." It was to be an evening program because they were not on during the daylight hours then. I said, "Well, all right, I guess so, what do you plan to have me do?" He said, "What do I plan to have you do? That's your job. You put on a program— that's all I'm requiring—you put on a program." So, I had a week to plan it. Well, Christmas was approaching and I decided to do a sort of burlesque on Christmas shoppers. I borrowed the materials from a department store and it was real good, actually, for a first program. As a matter of fact, I look back on it now when I come across the script and think, that wasn't bad.

MOWER: But you had it all to yourself as far as the preparation and getting the people and the whole thing set up—writing the script?

CRANE: Oh, yes, of course. All through my TV career I had that all to do with the help I had, which was sometimes one and sometimes one and a half persons to help me, but theirs were strictly clerical duties. There was the planning, the writing, the preparation, the rehearsing—but we rarely re- hearsed on TV—we didn't have time. We just went on. I think that's almost as well, really. I didn't regret that particularly.

MOWER: You had a program called "The Modern Woman" program, I remem- ber, that ran for several years.

CRANE: Yes, it was "The Modern Woman" on radio and "The Modern Woman" on TV, and that ran for, oh goodness, I'd have to—well, we started in '46 and that ran for about 9 years, I believe. In addition to that, I did other TV programs.

MOWER: I remember you had a shopping program of some kind.

CRANE: It was a very interesting development in TV. It had national publicity— national recognition. Many people attempted to copy the program, but for various reasons none of the others happened to be as successful as our own. "Shop by Television" was sponsored by the Hecht Company on TV. It was on in the evening. We took orders directly over the telephone. That is, we had telephones installed on the set and we had operators there. We frequently did about $6000 worth of sales directly on the phone. We demonstrated—Jackson Weaver and I demonstrated the materials, and sometimes very funny things happened on the program. It was a very popular listening, looking or viewing program even by people who didn't care to order anything because most anything could happen—such as the time I was displaying plastic dinnerware and said, "Now this is unbreakable and you can put it in your dishwasher," and so on and threw it on the floor to display its unbreakability. Well, you know what happened.

MOWER: It broke, I suppose.

CRANE: Naturally. A lot of things happened like that, but we always made a joke about it. We didn't take it seriously, and I think people enjoyed that.

MOWER: So you really combined a little entertainment with the shopping service.

CRANE: That's what we tried to do, and I think we succeeded, really. As I say, that program was a departure from the usual thing. Actually, the National Association of Broadcasters put out a brochure on it for the benefit of other stations.

Well, there were a lot of things in those days because TV was new, and no one knew what to do any more than I did programwise. We were allowed to do whatever we wanted to do. There was no set format, and it gave us the opportunity for innovations and experiment.

Let's see—on my daily afternoon show in order to encourage interest in TV and bolster TV set sales, I devoted one hour a week to demonstrate the activities and personalities of important women's clubs, selecting only the larger organizations. One hundred fifty members of each one, including the officers and members were invited to the studio to take part. Now, that doesn't sound unusual, of course, but it was in those days. It wouldn't sound unusual now. However, members who could not be invited by the space limitation in the studio were required to hold TV teas for 20 members or more in each home. The program consisted of introducing the officers and members and demonstrating and telling about the work of the organization. This required a stage and many props, of course, and then when the program ended samples of all my sponsors' products—mostly foods, of course, and other products, too—were handed out, and we then served tea in the studio to the company—and foods prepared from the sponsors' products. Fortunately, I had an angel food cake mix, potato chips and coffee among my sponsors. And, fortunately, too, as I said, by that time I had an assistant. Thus, in order to see the work and the personnel of the organization on TV—that was excitingly new, if you can imagine that. Many of the members, you see, had to buy TV sets for their own families to see them on TV, as, of course, did the members who were asked to give the teas for the members in their homes. Well, of course, that was just one thing.

MOWER: I suppose you always had some funny or peculiar things happen on this type of a TV program which was put on—I guess we could say "informally." That's what it amounted to in comparison to the way they do television today?

CRANE: Oh, heavens yes, not rehearsed. For example, the man who came to demonstrate the proper way to open a bottle of champagne couldn't open the bottle of champagne. Things were always happening like that. I think that's one of the reasons why people watched the program.[9]

Notes

1. Morleen G. Rouse, "Daytime Radio Programming for the Homemaker, 1926–1956," *Journal of Popular Culture* 12 (Fall 1978): 315–19.

2. David H. Hosley and Gayle K. Yamada, *Hard News: Women in Broadcast Journalism* (Westport, CT: Greenwood Press, 1987), pp. 3–4.

3. Maurine H. Beasley and Paul Belgrade, "Eleanor Roosevelt: First Lady as Radio Pioneer," *Journalism History* 11 (Autumn/Winter 1984): 42–48.

4. Mary E. Williamson, "Judith Cary Walter: Chicago Broadcasting Pioneer," *Journalism History* 3 (Winter 1976/77): 111–15.

5. Hosley and Yamada, *Hard News*, pp. 7–11.

6. As quoted in Gioia Diliberto, "Ladies in the Mensroom: Three Profiles of Female Journalists," unpublished master's thesis, University of Maryland, 1975, p. 11.

7. As quoted in Diliberto, "Ladies in the Mensroom," p. 13.

8. Mower's note: AWB is the Association of Women Broadcasters.

9. "Mower Interview" with Ruth Crane Schaefer, 1975, from the oral history project of American Women in Radio and Television, Broadcast Pioneers Library, Washington, DC.

17

Women's Pages

In. Out. In.

As this book went to press, the women's pages of daily newspapers were making a comeback. Converted into "lifestyle" pages and sections in the early 1970s, traditional women's pages disappeared as anchors for news about women. They were replaced by sections heavy on entertainment coverage and personality profiles. But by 1990, as newspaper readership by women continued to slide, editors began to debate whether the demise of a newspaper section dedicated to women readers might not have had something to do with the loss of those readers.

First, some history.

Women's pages in U.S. newspapers trace their origins to the late nineteenth century, when publishers launched them in an effort to target a new market for advertisers. Joseph Pulitzer generally is credited, with his *New York World*, with launching pages devoted to women's fashions and society news and articles about women of achievement.[1]

For the next 50 years, women's page articles illustrated methods of self-improvement, urged community involvement, and offered tips on successful homemaking. World War II brought a more serious tone to women's pages with features on the surge of women into the work force, but the women's page editors did not abandon the basics of the "home page" formula.[2] The image of an idyllic home and hearth as a woman's main priority—with career achievements as admirable but secondary pursuits—continued in newspaper women's pages through the 1960s.

During the first half of the twentieth century, women journalism students and reporters continued to be steered into women's page work. This was a double-edged sword; on the one hand, the section was considered special, above the rough-and-tumble newsgathering techniques of the mostly male newsroom; on the other hand, it was considered light, frivolous, with editorial content inextricably entwined with the agenda of advertisers and product publicists. Women's sections were coldly dismissed by Janet Stewart, assistant managing editor of the *Philadelphia North American*, in a 1924 profile in *Editor & Publisher* magazine.

From *EDITOR & PUBLISHER*, OCTOBER 18, 1924

The ordinary human-interest writing which goes under the name of sob-stuff, Miss Stewart would have none of.

She does not care for the usual run of woman reporting. She is not a feminist, however. She is too intelligent to take this title to herself.

Yet she would ban the woman's page from every newspaper in the country, even though she admits it must be a circulation builder. To her, the "women's angle" is a senseless phrase.

"There are far too many 'women's pages' in this country," Miss Stewart believes. "Women will never have any intellect as long as they are herded off, as it were, on to the women's pages. They will be forever kept at the same grade of intelligence.

"There is no more reason for this feature than there is for a men's page. News belongs to the people, not to a sex."[3]

While feminism was not invisible on the women's pages, it was dressed up in the latest fashions and accessories. Agnes Hooper Gottlieb analyzed dozens of articles in the *Washington Post*'s women's pages from 1940 to 1970, and discovered many that could be said to contain feminist ideas.

In 1940, the *Post*'s women's pages for the first week of April featured two articles of feminist content: the profile of a novelist, and the preview of a speech on job hunting which was to be given to the American Association of University Women. These articles were written in the standard formula of the women's page, a tradition-bound style that, when examined now, appears to be extremely sexist in its approach. Novelist Ethel Hueston, the author of 28 books when the article was written, is referred to in the story as Mrs. Randolph Blinn. The section also featured articles that reek of sexism—the photo of a woman in a business suit under the headline, "LADY EXECUTIVE OR LADY OF LEISURE," with the caption, "Mrs. Marjorie Austin plays the part of career woman here, although she herself is a successful young wife and mother." The implications are obvious.[4]

During World War II, women journalists moved into slots at newspapers vacated by male colleagues called to active duty. At the war's end, many were forced to relinquish their jobs to the returning men and accept lesser positions in the newsroom or a return to the women's section. The contributions of women during the 1940s were well understood, but were widely regarded as necessary performance during a national emergency rather than appropriate, logical assignments for journalists who just happened to be women. Women with hard-news reporting assignments were few.

Consider the remarks of Carl W. Ackerman, dean of the Columbia University School of Journalism, to members of the Seminar on Women's Pages of the American Press Institute (API), on June 6, 1949:

THE INSIDE OF A NEWSPAPER SHOULD BE
LIKE THE INSIDE OF A HOME

I wish at the outset to pay tribute to you and to the women you represent, not because you are women but because you are women journalists.

In the early days of this School there was opposition to the admission of women students and there was a great deal more skepticism than there is today.

Looking back over the years to the advancement of women as journalists, I am reminded of the strong prejudices of college professors. Several decades ago when Dean Van Amridge was asked for his advice in regard to admitting women and men on an equal basis in the classroom, his classic reply was that no teacher could teach mathematics to a boy if there was a girl in the room and that if a boy could learn mathematics with a girl in the room he would never grow up to be a man.

So times have changed in Universities and in newspaper offices and the accomplishments of women reporters, editors and columnists are recognized today as on a par with any similar contributions by men journalists.

In addition, women journalists, as journalists, have exerted a tremendous, unpublicized influence because their work on the whole has been concerned with positive living.

The front pages of newspapers are filled each day with stories of crises, disaster, tragedies—all of the destructive developments which accumulate second by second during the day. But the inside of a newspaper is like the inside of a home. There are tragedies, unhappiness and strife in many homes, but in the overwhelming majority of homes there is a wholesome quest for improvement; there is more happiness than sorrow; more love than hate. The spiritual strength of a nation is safeguarded in the home. In writing about health, schools, the church, food, child care, home living and other similar subjects women as journalists contribute to the uplifting of our national life. There is as much wholesomeness in the inside of a newspaper as there is in the inside of a home. The newspapers are indebted to women as journalists for this development.

As we look back this evening on your achievements, we are challenged also by the future responsibility of women as journalists.

Newspapers need both men and women. One of the challenges confronting us is how to advance and improve the cooperation of men and women journalists on our daily newspapers. The lead in the future development must be taken by women as journalists, because as every wife knows, men are set in their ways. They resist new ideas too frequently. Only the patience and understanding of a woman journalist can improve cooperation.

Women as journalists are challenged also by the always prevalent defeatism. Women as journalists must endeavor to keep idealism alive, to inspire hope and faith even when they are confronted by cynical, disillusioned or sophisticated states of mind.

There are also unexplored fields for women as journalists. Very little progress has been made in the reporting of labor news by women journalists. There are millions of women who are employed or who are wives of men who are employed and the impact of labor problems, interpretation of these problems from a woman's point of view open up to all of us new vistas of the position which women as journalists may occupy in the future on our daily newspapers.

While you are here at the American Press Institute you will be concerned with a wide range of immediate problems confronting you, but I hope also while you are here that you will have an opportunity of reflecting upon the philosophy and the future of your profession. Women as journalists have been conspicuous contributors to the development of the modern daily newspaper. But the opportunities and challenges of the future are even greater than your achievements. As you improve the inside of the daily newspaper you also contribute to the improvement of the inside of the home which is more important to the progress of civilization than any other social institution.

Strive, therefore, always to make the inside of the newspaper resemble the inside of our homes.[5]

The sea change in newspaper women's pages came nearly 20 years after Ackerman's speech, but the groundwork for it was being laid at that time and in the decade that followed. The practice of relegating stories about women to the women's pages brought to those sections news and information about national, international, and important cultural events simply because the source of the news was a woman. Hooper Gottlieb attributes this to "a conscious realization by women editors of the section that if these women were not covered on the women's page, they would not be covered at all."[6] A 1977 study of women's page/lifestyle editors supported this finding: Women editors (65 percent) were more likely than their male counterparts (45 percent) to have devoted more than 10 percent of their section to coverage of the women's movement.[7]

"Thus," Hooper Gottlieb writes,

Clare Boothe Luce spoke on the dangers of communism and received coverage on the women's page; Rep. Katharine St. George's discussion of the presidential campaign was delegated to the women's pages; a new statue in the U.S. Capitol made the women's page because the statue was that of a woman . . . a speech by the (woman) secretary of the Republican National Committee that noted that women would have equal representation at the convention for the first time appeared on the women's page.[8]

But in spite of broadened content, the women's pages "remained dominated by weddings and engagements, women's club activities and high-society fashion," wrote scholar Jennifer A. Hamlin. "News reporters continued to regard women's pages staffs as a coffee party of non-journalists owned by their advertisers. A women's section assignment was dreaded as a dead-end beat for any talented writer."[9] It was a low-paying one, too: In 1970, at least 27 newspapers with contracts with the Newspaper Guild were paying women's page reporters as much as $60 a week less than other reporters.[10]

The newsroom debate over what a woman's section should be, or even if it should be published at all, reached a crescendo in the newsrooms of the late 1960s. By then, the women's movement and the civil rights movement were developing broad bases of support, and the content of many women's pages looked anachronistic in light of the public debate for equal rights, pay equity, reproductive choice, and career advancement.

Newspapers began experimenting. Major metropolitan dailies led the way, with papers such as the *Los Angeles Times* and the *Washington Post* being the first to move the hearth/home focus out of the sections, renaming them, respectively, "View" and "Style."

As Shelby Coffey, editor of the *Los Angeles Times* who for six years had edited the *Washington Post*'s Style section, recalled in a 1983 interview,

There was an outcry at first from people who were confused or who missed the old section. After all, on the first day of Style, we featured a hard-hitting profile of one of the Weathermen (an underground radical group) and that was quite a shock to people used to Mrs. Dean Rusk pouring tea. . . .

The former section, "For and About Women," simply covered social Washington in the Old School way. We went to a full lifestyle section—with big profiles, arts reporting and coverage. Humor. We still do a lot of parties but in a much more sophisticated way, not simply recording who showed up.[11]

Ruth D'Arcy, former women's editor of the *Detroit News*, described the change there:

We moved out of the women's page concept in the early 1970s simply because the old approach wasn't working anymore—not even with women. We had studies that showed that less than 30 percent of women readers were reading the material being put out exclusively for them. Watching the success of the *Washington Post*'s Style section and others, we felt it was time for a wider, richer approach.[12]

In 1971, Seymour Topping, then assistant managing editor of the *New York Times*, wrote to Charlotte Curtis, then editor of the *Times*'s women's page:

We have been studying for some time now the question of a more suitable description for what now is designated in the front-page News Index as Women's News. The present description has become progressively more unsatisfactory. . . . What has been known as the Women's Page is read by readers of both sexes and covers a variety of subjects broader than the present description suggests. . . . Secondly, an increasing number of our women readers are becoming alienated by the use of the term Women's News.[13]

Less than six months later, the "Food, Fashion, Family and Furnishings" section became indexed as "Family/Style."

Reducing the amount of traditional women's service features in women's sections did not necessarily mean that more progressive coverage for and about women increased in that section or anywhere else in the newspaper. Said Zena Beth Guenin McGlashan in her study comparing traditional sections with these new lifestyle pages, "Entertainment . . . appears to have gobbled up space that, some critics contend, should be used for other stories."[14]

Opinions differ on whether women were shortchanged with these modifications of the women's pages. In *A Place in the News: From the Women's Pages to the Front Page*, Kay Mills makes a case for the change: "The evolution of the women's pages into today's feature sections marked a belated recognition that all parts of a newspaper should be prepared for all people, not just for female people or male people."[15] Bob Shaw, features editor of the *Des Moines Register*, feels that the conversion of women's sections into lifestyle sections in the early 1970s is directly connected to women's declining interest in reading a daily newspaper.[16]

In an effort to bring them back, women's pages are making a comeback. Metropolitan newspapers are experimenting with standing features, sections, and pages targeting women. In 1990, the American Society of Newspaper Editors released a prototype women's section called "Womenews" at its annual conference. The prototype had a dynamic graphic look and was packed with quick reads on life management issues, including career, health, family, networking, and how-to information, such as auto maintenance.

"A product such as Womenews could stem the proliferation of women's magazines that now try to give women what Womenews can do in a more timely fashion," said Colleen Dishon, associate editor of the *Chicago Tribune*, who was a member of the team that developed the prototype. "The women's magazines have been able to do it because newspapers haven't." In 1991, Dishon led the development of "Womanews," a meatier Sunday section replacing "TempoWoman," a women-oriented Sunday companion to the *Tribune*'s lifestyle section, "Tempo."

Also in 1991, ASNE released the findings of a reaction survey to yet another prototype women's section, test-published in the *Lexington (Kentucky) Herald-Leader*. Readers reacted favorably to "You: News for Today's Women," a 12-page pullout of "news-you-can-use" types of items. "A clear majority liked the fact that the section states explicitly it is for women," said *Herald-Leader* editor Tim Kelly.[17]

"When women tell newspaper editors they do not see themselves in the newspaper, they suggest that the newspaper does not see life complete and whole, the way they see it, live it," Dishon maintains. "Newspapers, to save themselves from becoming irrelevant to women readers, must reflect what's going on in women's lives. Women must see themselves reflected in the newspaper in general and in specific places."[18]

Notes

1. Marion Marzolf, *Up from the Footnote: A History of Women Journalists* (New York: Hastings House Publishers, 1977), pp. 205–6.
2. Marzolf, *Up from the Footnote*, pp. 208–9.
3. Philip Schuyler, "Woman Executive Discusses Ideal Daily—Miss Janet H. Stewart, Assistant Managing Editor of the *Philadelphia North American*, Is a 'Regular Newspaper Man,' according to Her Chief—Hates the 'Woman's Angle,' Sob Stories and Women's Pages," *Editor & Publisher*, October 18, 1924.
4. Agnes Hooper Gottlieb, "Feminism and Femininity: An Analysis of *The Washington Post*'s Women's Page, 1940–1970," paper presented to the History Division, Association for Education in Journalism and Mass Communication, Minneapolis, August 1990, p. 9.
5. Carl W. Ackerman, "The Inside of a Newspaper Should Be Like the Inside of a Home," informal remarks at a dinner in honor of the members of the Seminar on Women's Pages of the American Press Institute at Columbia University, New York, Monday, June 6, 1949, Carl W. Ackerman Papers, Box 164, Manuscript Division, Library of Congress.
6. Hooper Gottlieb, "Feminism and Femininity," pp. 24–25.
7. Sharyne Merritt and Harriett Gross, "Women's Page/Lifestyle Editors: Does Sex Make a Difference?" unpublished paper, Governors State University, June 1977, table 7.
8. Hooper Gottlieb, "Feminism and Femininity," pp. 24–25.
9. Jennifer A. Hamlin, "Women's Pages in American Newspapers: Growth and Change," Moeller Award paper presented at the Association for Education in Journalism, August 1977.
10. Ellen Hoffman, "Woman in the Newsroom," *Columbia Journalism Review* (Winter 1970/71): 53–55, cited in Hamlin, "Women's Pages in American Newspapers," p. 7.
11. Denis Horgan, "Liberating the Women's Page," *Washington Journalism Review* (May 1983): 20.
12. Horgan, "Liberating the Women's Page," p. 19.
13. Memorandum, Seymour Topping to Charlotte Curtis, January 27, 1971, cited in Marilyn S. Greenwald, "All Brides Are Not Beautiful: The Influence of Charlotte Curtis on Women's Pages at *The New York Times*," paper presented to the Committee on the Status of Women, Association for Education in Journalism and Mass Communication, Minneapolis, August 1990, p. 13.
14. Zena Beth Guenin McGlashan, "Women's Pages in American Newspa-

pers: Missing Out on Contemporary Content?" *Journalism Quarterly* 52, no. 1 (Spring 1975): 68.

15. Kay Mills, *A Place in the News: From the Women's Pages to the Front Page* (New York: Dodd, Mead, 1988), p. 110.

16. Maria Braden, "Women: Special Again," *Washington Journalism Review* (June 1991): 31.

17. Braden, "Women: Special Again," p. 31.

18. Douglas E. Kneeland, "Years of Research Led to *Tribune*'s 'Mininewspaper' for Women," *Chicago Tribune*, June 17, 1991, p. 13.

18

Development of
Alternative Media

Women in North America asserted themselves in significant new ways during the 1960s and 1970s, as did members of minority groups. In the United States, the civil rights movement forced people to confront racism. Sweeping national legislation was enacted to change policy, if not attitudes. As minority groups and women knew, attitudes change very slowly, regardless of the laws on the books.

The women's suffrage movement of the nineteenth century had given birth to its own communications: newspapers, magazines, journals. Women of the era whose agenda went beyond getting the vote also were prolific writers and editors. For both groups of feminists, there was a constant struggle to keep their periodicals afloat. Few women had sufficient personal finances to sponsor publications, or male relatives sympathetic to more personal, professional, or civic autonomy for women. By the 1920s, after women in the United States had secured the right to vote, the momentum of the women's movement faded.

Women's rights were pushed back onto the nation's agenda in the 1960s by women looking for many of the same things that had been sought by their nineteenth-century sisters: personal growth; intellectual freedom; financial security; equal opportunity in education, career, and politics. And, like their counterparts a century earlier, the media played an important role in the process.

The women's movement that surfaced in the 1960s had trouble getting its message across from the beginning. Many people, knowing only what the mass media told them about it, were without sufficient information to judge the movement's significance. What they thought of the movement was generally a reflection of what they had read or heard or were shown about it.

The feminists—both radicals and moderates—were eager to tell their story. But many were hesitant to share it with the mass media. Some of the movement organizers were veterans of "New Left" politics or civil rights campaigns, which they felt had been hampered by the mass media's faulty analysis and coverage of events in which they participated. Yet they understood the potential of the mass media for education—good as well as bad—because of the vast numbers of the public these media reached.

A number of feminists simply would not cooperate with establishment media at all, regardless of the sex of the reporter on the story. They felt that the media's need to condense inevitably resulted in oversimplification and distortion of feminist news, particularly in television and radio. They also did not believe that the media's majority of male editors would permit accurate reporting of women's issues or the women's movement, or that they and these "gatekeepers" would even agree on what women's issues were.

The underground newspapers that had amplified the influence of the peace and student movements of the same decade provided little comfort to the feminists. Women on their staffs complained that male reporters' and editors' liberal politics did not extend to female–male relationships, either in the newsroom or in the newspaper's columns. As in the nineteenth century when the women who had fought hard for the abolition of slavery found that they could expect no help from abolitionists in advancing rights for women, the women of the 1960s discovered that many of the male student activists who demanded more freedoms on college campuses or who worked tirelessly for racial desegregation showed considerably less enthusiasm when women staked their claims for equality.

The chauvinism within underground publications—and the exploitative sexual content of some them—helped propel women into a separate movement of their own (and ultimately to form their own publications). The recognition that sharing of information is the lifeblood of any social movement led feminists to create their own instruments of communication.

"Through its power to give women control over their own ideas and words, a separatist dimension is inherently a part of the women's media movement," says Marilyn Crafton Smith, associate professor at Appalachian State University.[1]

Anne Mather, in her exhaustive study of feminist periodicals in the United States, observed,

The women's liberation press showed phenomenal growth in the late 1960s and early 1970s. In the five-year period beginning in March 1968, the feminist press grew from one national newsletter with an estimated circulation of 1,000 readers (*the Voice of the women's liberation movement*) to include more than 560 periodicals, one of which alone had a print order of 550,000 (*Ms.*). . . . Although the first periodicals appeared in large cities or on the coasts, the movement spread to communities of every size in every region of the country.[2]

In 1967 a number of women's groups were formed around the country. For the most part, women's liberation comprised disparate groups with various agendas. By 1968 they were becoming aware of sister groups or activities by women in other cities that paralleled their own.

One major concern all of them faced was how to put women in touch with one another and how to provide an amplifier for their opinions, concerns, and theories so that they could draw on one another's strategies and resources.

The Westside Group in Chicago started a newsletter in March 1968 under the editorship of Joreen, a radical feminist who instituted a revolving editorship for the publication. The *Voice of the women's liberation movement* carried articles on movement activities, political theory, and women in the Third World and parodied advice columns and advertisements. It featured a feminist comic strip. In spring 1969, after seven issues, the collective that published *Vwlm* announced that they were giving up their journalistic efforts in order to concentrate on building up the women's movement in the Chicago area. By fall 1969, other feminists around the country began publishing for the movement.

Joreen is Jo Freeman. Her recollections of the founding of the *Voice of the women's liberation movement* and the reactions of feminists to media coverage of the movement—excerpted from her book, *The Politics of Women's Liberation*—follow.

FROM *THE POLITICS OF WOMEN'S LIBERATION*

The advocates of "women's liberation" liked the term not so much because of its implied identification with Third World and black liberation movements but because they wanted to define the terms of debate in what they saw as a potentially significant movement. They had been educated by the misunderstandings created by the referent "the Negro problem" which inevitably structured people's thinking in terms of "the problem with Negroes" rather than racism and what to do about it. They were also aware of the historical "women question" and "Jewish question" which led to the same mistake. The problem, they felt, was not one of women, but of women's liberation and the best way to get people to think of the problem in those terms was to label it such from the very beginning.[3]

These were the people who first conceived the idea of starting a national newsletter for the miniscule movement, and one of them was the first editor. The first issue came out in March 1968 as three mimeographed sheets of paper with no name. Its tag line labeled it "the voice of the women's liberation movement." By the second issue, three months later, it had grown to four sheets offset, and the new editor had elevated the tag line to the name. Under a different editor each issue, the *Voice of the women's liberation movement* served as the main vehicle of communication for the growing movement for the next sixteen months. It represented the national movement to most women receiving it and from it they picked up and used the name. "Women's liberation" became more and more frequent an appellation and "radical women" receded into the background.

Initially, the term "women's liberation" applied only to the younger branch of the movement. Organizations such as NOW considered themselves a part of a women's movement, but not a women's liberation movement. Gradually, however, more and more NOW people and other women associated with one of the small groups adopted the name until today it has a generic meaning. Some feminists still do not like to be thought of as part of women's liberation and some of the latter do not like the term feminist, but for most, the two are synonymous. This dual use of the term women's liberation has created some confusion as most of the small groups have no specific names. It occasionally is difficult to tell whether "women's liberation" refers to the whole movement or just to its younger branch.

The original newsletter ceased publication in June 1969, but during its short life it was one of the most useful organizational tools of the movement. Adopting an expansionist policy, its revolving editors gave most issues away to anyone indicating any interest whatsoever in the women's movement and placed many on bookstore shelves. It was financed by donations, some subscriptions, unpaid labor, and the sale of women's liberation literature at exorbitant prices.[4] Its purpose was to reach any potential sympathizer in order to let her know that there were others who thought as she did and that she was not isolated or crazy. It also functioned to put women in contact with other like-minded women in the same area and thus stimulated the formation of new groups. To do this, all mail had to be answered whether it was simply requests for literature, contacts, or for advice on organizing, as well as news and articles solicited for subsequent issues. This grew to be a herculean task. The

Vwlm grew from 200 copies the first issue to 2,000 the seventh and last; from 6 pages to 25. It was finally killed because the work of keeping it up had grown too big to handle and because the then editors thought no "national newsletter could do justice to the role of 'voice' at the present time."[5]

At the time of its death there were no other major movement publications apart from an occasional local journal. Three months later, the first women's liberation newspaper, *off our backs*, was published in Washington, D.C. The number of feminist papers and journals increased rapidly thereafter. To date there are over 150, and many more were started but did not survive.[6] None of the papers is national in scope though they borrow from one another freely. Magazines range from scholarly to popular to propagandistic, with the majority being literary in nature. Some have a policy of printing literally everything they receive, in the belief that all women have something to say and should be given the opportunity to see their work in print. Some are as exclusive as any professional journal.

MEDIA HOSTILITY

In part this multitude of publications was started out of disillusionment with the commercial press and in the belief that only movement publications would give the movement fair coverage. Young feminists had been hostile to the press from the beginning—significantly more so than other social movements. Some of this fear was traceable to inexperience as even those women with a political background had not done press work before. Much more derived from watching how inaccurately the press had reported the social movements and student protests in which they had previously been active. Unlike blacks, for example, young white women had grown up believing that the press was as objective as it liked to portray itself. When their political experiences made them conscious of the gross discrepancies between what they saw at a particular demonstration and what was reported, they withdrew from any press contact in disgust. Blacks, on the other hand, had never had any illusions about who controlled the press, and saw the media as a tool to be used. Women had wanted to relate to reporters honestly; when the results were not what they expected, they chose not to relate at all.

Most of the media compounded this problem by treating early women's liberation activities with a mixture of humor, ridicule, and disbelief. Some of these early activities did seem funny on the surface. Yippies had utilized zap actions and guerilla theater as a respite from the boring ineffectiveness of mass marches. Women's liberation picked up on this idea as a way of making a political point in an unusual, eye-catching manner. The first major public action, at the 1968 Miss America contest, featured a "freedom trash can" into which bras, girdles, false eyelashes, and other instruments of female oppression were tossed, and a live sheep was crowned Miss America. This impulse was furthered by the spread of WITCH covens (Women's International Terrorist Conspiracy from Hell) to hex objects of local ire after the first incantation on Wall Street in the fall of 1968 was followed by a five-point drop in the stock market.

Some reporters looked at the serious side of these actions, but most only laughed. Whereas reporters had examined the political message underneath the Yippie spoofs, they just glanced at the surface of the women's actions and used them to illustrate how silly women were.[7] The press treated women's liberation much as society treats women—as entertainment not to be taken seriously.

If they thought it would be funnier, newspapers even made up their own actions, of which the "bra-burning" episode is the most notable. There has yet to be a woman in women's liberation to burn a single bra publicly, but this mythical act was widely reported in the press.[8] "Bra" stories and related nonincidents usually got front page coverage, while serious stories on employment discrimination were always on the women's page. Photographers inevitably depicted feminists with unattractive poses or facial expressions. Reporters commented on interviewees' femininity, marital status, or style of dress more than their views. Editors ordered production to "get the Karate up front" and writers to "find an authority who'll say this is all a crock of shit."[9] Underground and New Left papers were often the worst of the lot, frequently running women's liberation stories illustrated by naked women and exaggerated genitalia.[10]

Women's liberation dealt with the conflict between desire for coverage and dislike of misrepresentation by refusing to speak to male reporters. First established at the Miss America contest, this practice soon became an informal rule everywhere, and has only partially broken down. There were two main reasons behind this policy, but it had even more unexpected benefits. The first was to compel the media to hire more women reporters and to give others opportunities to do news reporting usually denied to women. The second was to get better coverage. Young feminists had discovered that even sympathetic men were often incapable of understanding what they were talking about because men simply had not had the same experiences as most women. They did not, for example, understand women's anger at being sex objects. With women reporters feminists could communicate their concerns through discussion of experiences common to women that were incomprehensible to men. And in these early stages anecdotes on such experiences were the main means of articulating women's grievances; the ideas had not yet been refined into specific issues.

Even women reporters covered the early movement only with difficulty. Most young activists would not talk to them at all as they saw no value in distorted coverage in the commercial press. Those who would consent to be interviewed often required anonymity and frequently demanded the right to edit the final copy (which was of course denied). Reporters were tossed out of women's liberation meetings when discovered, hung up on when they phoned; saw their notes grabbed from their hands and destroyed at rallies; had their microphones smashed, their cameras threatened, and their films stolen.[11] They also found some sympathetic feminists who would talk to them at length, give them reams of material to read, arrange interviews and group discussions for their benefit, and direct them to good sources of information.

The immediate results of these policies were seen not so much in the quality of the news stories as in their numbers. There was something intriguing about the very difficulty of covering the new movement. Further, the idea that *men* were being excluded from something, especially male *reporters*, generated much more interest than women normally get. People were *curious* why *men* were excluded; and if the stories ridiculed feminists for discriminating, many women read between the lines and flocked to join. Female reporters joined also. Initially skeptical, they often found themselves much more involved in the ideas of the movement than they intended. What many thought would be an ordinary story turned out to be a revelation.

In the fall of 1969 the major news media simultaneously began to do stories on women's liberation, and they appeared steadily for the next six months. Quickly discovering that only women could cover the movement, they tried to pick reporters known for their objectivity and unfeminist views. It made no difference. Virtually all the initial stories in *Time, Life, Newsweek*, etc., are personal conversion stories. These stories had as much effect on the media as they did on the movement. Women writers, researchers, and even secretaries became conscious of their secondary role on their publications and began protesting for better conditions and forming their own small groups.[12]

MALE EXCLUSION

The exclusion of male reporters was in conformity with the general policy of excluding men from all movement activities. Initially, this was one of the most controversial aspects of the movement to the outside world, but it was and is one of the most uncontroversial within the movement itself. There was virtually no debate on this policy in any city at any time. Originally the idea of exclusiveness was borrowed from the Black Power movement, much in the public consciousness when the women's liberation movement began. It was reinforced by the unremitting hostility of most of the New Left men. Even when this hostility was not present, women in virtually every group in the United States and Canada soon discovered that the traditional sex roles reasserted themselves in groups regardless of the good intentions of the participants. Men inevitably dominated the discussions, and usually would talk only about how women's liberation related to men, or how men were oppressed by the sex roles. In segregated groups women found the discussions to be more open, honest and extensive. They could learn to relate to other women and not just to men.

Women continued the policy of male exclusion because they felt men were largely irrelevant to the development of the movement. They wanted to reach women, and found it both frustrating and a waste of time to talk to men. Of course many did talk to men, usually on an individual basis, and many men eventually formed their own groups around the problem of the male sex role. Initially, women's liberation discovered that there was a tactical value in male exclusion. As with the exclusion of male reporters, their activities were taken much more seriously when they insisted they wanted to speak only with women. The tactic had shock value. A good example, followed many times more, was the organization of a women's discussion group at the August 1968 National Student Association convention at the University of Kansas. To arouse interest in the meeting women stood in the cafeteria lines passing out leaflets to women only. When the man in a couple unthinkingly reached for one, they made a deliberate point of giving it to the woman. When a man took the leaflet from the woman with him, it was taken from him and returned to the woman. The men were indignant, the women curious, and of course everyone wanted to know what the leaflet said. The real purpose of this technique was not to keep men from reading the innocuous leaflet but to catch people's attention and make them think. This it succeeded in doing. It also solved the litter problem; no leaflets were left laying on the floor.

A variation on this theme was used by the sellers of *Notes from the First Year*, a mimeographed magazine of early feminist thought. It sold for $.50 to women and $1.00 to men. One reason for this was that the authors wanted to reach women, thus preferring to keep the price low, but felt men ought to be charged for the privilege of reading the magazine if they insisted on it. They fully realized that a man could get a woman to buy a copy for him at the lower price. That was the second purpose. It was a form of political education to demonstrate to men and women the discomforts of having to go through someone else to fulfill one's desires or needs. It illustrated the true nature of the female role by reverse example.[13]

In her analysis of women's media produced since the beginning of the contemporary women's movement, Martha Leslie Allen pinpointed eight characteristics of women's communication networks:

1. women speaking for themselves, not reporting for others
2. preference for collective rather than hierarchical structure
3. a sharing instead of competitive approach
4. analysis of mass media's role relative to women and women's media
5. a nonattack approach toward different views, avoiding name-calling or discrimination
6. emphasis on an "open forum"
7. provision of information not reported in the mass media
8. an activist orientation[14]

A durable example of these characteristics is *off our backs*, a news journal founded in 1970, less than a year after the *Voice of women's liberation movement* ceased publication. Printed in a tabloid newspaper format, *oob* has published without interruption since its founding, now reaching about 20,000 readers.[15]

Writing in *Media Report to Women* about *oob*'s twentieth anniversary, Donna Allen said *oob*'s "magic" lies in

> the continuing record of women's analyses of events and issues, victories, losses, concerns and controversies that are deepening and enlightening the movement and broadening the involvement of new women ethnically and culturally in the movement. Here one finds the women's movement sophistication that is rarely to be found in mass media newspapers or broadcasts where not only "new" is defined by men, but the issues as well, and even the parameters of debate on women's issues.[16]

In a 1974 survey of feminist editors, *oob* emerged as one of the best-produced publications of the women's movement.[17] Early departments of the newspaper consisted of women's studies, poetry, letters, and "culture vulture"—several pages of feminist criticism of movies, books, and the media.[18] *Oob* avoided celebrity or stardom—the customary features of mainstream media—choosing instead to cover the lives of women and their struggle for liberation from the grassroots level. *Oob* also indulged its sense of humor with crackling commentary.

Off our backs continues to be published by a collective of women. Its twentieth-anniversary issue, which appeared in February 1990, contains commentaries by each of the ten collective members about the process of working in this manner.

Off our backs' statement of purpose from its March 1970 issue is reprinted here.

STATEMENT OF PURPOSE
off our backs
By Nancy Ferro, Coletta Reid Holcomb, and Marilyn Saltzman-Webb

The women's movement can no longer afford to be naive about the nature and function of the mass media in this society. Every major magazine, newspaper and television network has done a story on us and most are clamoring for interviews, permission to do documentaries, and any special coverage they can get. We no longer need to use the mass media to tell people we exist. We now need to develop a practical critique which we can use to guide our future actions and determine how our communication needs can best be met.

Relying on our own experiences, we can see the ways in which the mass media work to serve interests directly opposed to our own. For example, we are attempting to build, within our movement, non-exploitative ways of relating to one another based on trust and concern rather than political expediency. We have serious personal/political intentions in breaking down hierarchical and elitist structures, and for experimenting with leaderless groups and collective decision-making. In dealing with the media these revolutionary principles and practices are destroyed. The media work to create leaders, they know of no way of relating to us on our own terms. Being interviewed and presented as a leader is a real ego trip—the media bring out the most counter-revolutionary traits in people. Elitism, dissension and division are the ultimate results.

Creating leaders also increases the power of the mass media to define our movement for us. What the media-created leader says becomes a standard, usually very restrictive, for the whole movement. Then the press discredits the entire movement by discrediting the leader through attacking her personal life rather than dealing with her politics.

A major misconception is the belief that the media will deal with us seriously and present a truthful picture of who we are. There is no reason to assume that the mass media are free of the sexism pervasive in all other American institutions. The mass media are primarily interested in lining their own pockets and assuring themselves of the continuance of their powerful position in society by kowtowing to the interests of the ruling class. Agnew's attacks are really too high praise.[19] In the end the mass media will capitulate rather than fight for the truth, for to meet the needs of the people and the demands of objective journalism would mean the end of the mass media in their present form.

The mass media serve our society as a reality-definer. By presenting what is news the media define what exists; by interpreting the news the media determine what people should think about what exists. Almost all events and significant communications between individuals and groups of people are mediated by the Establishment press and thus transformed into the reality the media wish to project. Women's liberation does not fit into that reality. Demands for free medical care and public transportation, an end to sexual exploitation and discrimination, the dismantling of an economic system based on profits rather than human needs, make no sense in the nonsensical society in which we live. From the perspective of the mass media *we* are abnormal and absurd. Women who join the movement must be able to see themselves in the liberated woman, she must become "the girl next door." But the media-created liberated woman is not merely unusual and exceptional, but a total weirdo—a bra-burner, man-hater, lesbian, sickie!

In this outrageous society, the mass media have become a prime anesthetizer. They cannot deal with issues in their complexity, but only in a public-relations, simplistic way. Every superficial story threatens overexposure, making it easy for people to ignore the substance of what we are doing.

Building a movement demands confronting people directly in an active process; no one is radicalized by passively watching TV. Using the mass media may look like the easy way to reach many women, but it is ultimately impotent and self-destructive.

Any group of people fighting for liberation must recognize as their enemy an institution whose very survival depends upon the perpetuation of the evils they are struggling against. The mass media are our enemy: no matter how seriously they may approach, no matter how enlightened they may seem, women's liberation threatens the power base of the mass media. Each time we respond to them we legitimatize them and the reality they are defending, and we risk sacrificing all that we are working for.

It is time to call a halt to all dealings with the mass media—no more interviews, no more documentaries, no more special coverage. We don't need them and we don't want them. In the interests of self-defense and honest communication we have begun to create our own papers and our own magazines. Our energies must turn now to the strengthening and expansion of our own media.

Most of the women who were attracted to the women's movement of the late 1960s were well educated and came from a middle-class background. Their relationships with women's liberation varied from sympathy to an activist commitment. What they shared was a desire for change. Some women wanted to change their old style of life; others wanted to be available to women to help them make such changes.

Both types of women combined to form the audience and the editorial board of *Ms.* magazine. Although a number of regional newsletters or magazines and national feminist journals devoted to scholarship and the arts had been developed by 1971, there still was no national feminist publication that could bridge radical and moderate feminist thinking and claim a large share of readers from all over the nation. At this time *Ladies' Home Journal* and *McCall's*, the neck-and-neck leaders of the women's magazine trade, had close to 7 million readers each. It seemed like the time to place a feminist competitor on the corner newsstand. *Ms.* was created.

The founders of *Ms.* originally thought of entering the newsletter market, but felt that they couldn't reach the women they wanted to through that format. So they began to talk about the possibility of starting a magazine. Potential investors were lukewarm, reminding them that some of the giants of the magazine industry—the *Saturday Evening Post* and *Look*—had succumbed to rising costs and postal rate increases. It was nearly impossible to project the size of the market they could anticipate. No one knew how many women would be interested in a magazine about and for feminists, a magazine including articles on women's issues, profiles of women, excerpts from novels, poetry, book reviews—everything the traditional women's magazines had, but from a feminist point of view—and without the emphasis on husband, hearth, and home.

In 1971, *New York* magazine offered the *Ms.* group an opportunity to produce a "preview" issue, with some of the content appearing as a pullout insert in its end-of-the-year "double issue." The group accepted.

The issue set a newsstand sales record for *New York*, and in July 1972 the first regular issue of the new *Ms.* magazine appeared. *Ms.* found its niche quickly, growing to a circulation of about 400,000 within just a few years. *Ms.* published many first-time writers, mixing their contributions with work from more established writers and feminist thinkers.

In 1989 *Ms.* had reached a paid circulation of 543,000. In spite of a core circulation base of loyal readers, profitability eluded the magazine. Costs—of circulation promotion, postage, and production—simply rose faster than revenues. *Ms.*'s feminist philosophy, strong stands on women's issues, and unwillingness to coddle advertisers with favorable copy about their products made difficult the task of bringing advertising revenues in. Several *Ms.* advertisers canceled their advertising with the magazine after an August 1989 cover on a U.S. Supreme Court abortion ruling. The cover carried the headline "IT'S WAR" in large red type.[20] Gloria Steinem recalled that an advertising executive once spat on the magazine when it was presented to him during a sales pitch by a *Ms.* staffer.[21]

The difficulties on the business side persisted through several changes of ownership in the 1980s. *Ms.* found itself with competition that had not existed when it was launched in 1972. New mass-media publications had been launched with a more progressive editorial bent than the traditional women's magazines. The result was that *Ms.* was losing market share.

Amy Farrell noted the irony in this in 1988.

The same competition that forced *Ms.* to be reincorporated is also the strongest indicator that *Ms.* has indeed been successful at forcing the marketplace to expand its hegemonic definitions of meaning. . . . [O]ther, newer magazines, like *Self* and *New Woman* were addressing some of the same issues and attracting some of the same readers as *Ms.* Even older, more traditional magazines began encompassing a more feminist approach. The 50th anniversary issue of *Woman's Day*, for instance, featured decade-by-decade women's history and included only articles and illustrations by women. While this proliferation of magazines with a feminist, or at least pro-woman, stance indicates the power of patriarchal capitalism to turn oppositional strands into a market channel, it also clearly indicates the potential power of readers to make the marketplace answerable to them.[22]

Steinem had noted the broadening acceptability of feminism and the assimilation of aspects of the women's movement in a 1977 address to the American Newspaper Women's Club, five years after *Ms.*'s founding.

I understand . . . by looking at issues then and now that we have become, as the women's movement at large has become, far more radical than we were in 1972. It's interesting because we are perceived as having mellowed. What has happened, I think, is that the acceptance of women's issues has so greatly increased in those five years that our distance from the culture at large has shortened, even though we have become more radical.[23]

That very acceptance helped to dilute, in real terms, the amount of support available to *Ms.*, and the magazine temporarily suspended publication in November 1989. New owner Lang Communications reintroduced the magazine with a June 1990 issue. The new *Ms.* is reader supported; it does not accept advertising. "When *Ms.* stopped publishing, we were flooded with letters and calls," Steinem said. "That's what gave us the courage to try something brand new: a magazine supported and written for its readers, not its advertisers." Steinem serves as a consulting editor to *Ms.*, which is edited by Robin Morgan.

The document that follows, "A Personal Report," appeared in the first regular issue of *Ms.* in July 1972. In light of *Ms.*'s winning battles to continue publishing in the years since, "A Personal Report" has even more meaning now.

A PERSONAL REPORT FROM *MS.*

First, there were some women writers and editors who started asking questions. Why was our work so unconnected to our lives? Why were the media, including women's magazines, so rarely or so superficially interested in the big changes happening to women? Why were we always playing the game by somebody else's (the publisher's, the advertiser's) rules?

Then, there were questions from activists, women who were trying to raise money for an information service and self-help projects, particularly for poor or isolated women, and having very little luck. Mightn't a publication—say, a newsletter—serve to link up women, and to generate income as well?

The two groups met several times early in 1971, and agreed that we all wanted a publication that was owned by and honest about women. Then we did some hard financial figuring. Newsletters that made decent profits seem confined to giving stock-market tips, or servicing big corporations. Some small but valuable ones for women were already struggling along. Besides, newsletters were a fine service for people already interested, but weren't really meant to reach out in a populist way.

So the idea of a full-fledged national magazine came up; a publication created and controlled by women that could be as serious, outrageous, satisfying, sad, funky, intimate, global, compassionate, and full of change as women's lives really are.

Of course, we knew that many national magazines were folding, or doing poorly. Rocketing production and mailing costs, plus competition from television for both advertising and subject matter, had discouraged some of the people who loved magazines most. Even those magazines still flourishing were unresponsive to the silenced majority. Women just weren't getting serious or honest coverage, and we doubted that we were the only people who felt the need for change. Besides, the Women's Movement had raised our hopes; it had given us courage.

So we had many more meetings, and we made big plans: long lists of article ideas, a mock-up of illustration and design, proposed budgets, everything. Then we spent many months making appointments, looking for backing from groups that invest in new ventures—and just as many months getting turned down. Flat.

Why? Well, we usually heard one or several reasons like these from potential investors:

—all around us, magazines are failing; why spend money to buck the tide?

—even though local or "special interest" magazines are making money (curiously, anything directed at the female 53 percent of the population is regarded as "special interest"), they are bad investments compared to, say, apartment buildings, computer hardware, and the like;

—the more we insisted on retaining at least 51 percent of the stock, the more everyone told us that investors don't give money without getting control; who ever heard of a national magazine controlled by its staff?

—setting aside some of the profits (supposing there were any) to go back to the Women's Movement is so unbusinesslike as to be downright crazy—even black magazines or other publications attached to movements haven't managed that;

—and, finally, the investors said, there are probably only ten or twenty thousand women in the country interested in changing women's status anyway; certainly not enough to support a nationwide magazine.

We got discouraged. Some of us thought we would either have to jettison a requirement or two, or give up. But there was support: friendly magazine people who thought we should try to find "public-spirited" money; women in advertising who were themselves trying to create ads that were a service to women; feminist speakers who have been traveling around the country and knew that a mass audience was there.

Most of all, there were the several women writers and editors, one business-woman, and some all-purpose feminist volunteers who were willing to contribute their talents and time in return for very little except hope. "It's very simple," said one of the writers. "We all want to work for a magazine we read."

Then, two concrete things happened to bolster our hopes. First, Katharine Graham, one of the few women publishers in the country, was willing to pretend that a few shares of stock in a nonexistent magazine were worth buying, a fiction that allowed us some money for out-of-the-pocket expenses. (She preferred to be generous in anonymity, but her help—a matter of corporate record anyway—was noted in a newspaper report, so we include her name as an inadequate way of saying thank you for helping women in hard times.) Second and even more unusual was an offer from Clay Felker, editor and publisher of *New York*, a weekly metropolitan magazine. He had thought up an ingenious way of helping *Ms.* produce the thing it needed most: a nationwide test; a sample issue to prove that we could create a new kind of magazine, and that women would buy it.

The plan was this. *New York* needed something special for its year-end double issue, and also wanted practice in producing national "one-shot" magazines (single issues devoted to a particular area or subject). *Ms.* needed the money and editorial freedom to produce a sample issue. Therefore, *New York* offered to bear the full risk of the $125,000 necessary to pay printers, binders, engravers, paper mills, distributors, writers, artists, and all the other elements vital to turning out 300,000 copies of our Preview Issue. (Plus supplying the great asset of *New York*'s staff, without which the expenses would have been much higher.) In return, some of the *Ms.* articles and features would appear first as an insert in that year-end issue of *New York*, half of the newsstand profits (if any) of our own Preview Issue would go to *New York*, and so would all of the advertising proceeds. (We had editorial autonomy but no say about advertising; all but two of the ads were the same as those in *New York*'s issue anyway.)

It was an odd way of introducing a magazine, but a generous and unusual offer—the first time, as far as we know, that one magazine would give birth to another without the *quid pro quo* of editorial control, or some permanent financial interest. Clay Felker made a few gruff noises about how it was strictly a business deal. After all, didn't *New York* stand to make a profit if *Ms.* did very well? (This last was generally said in earshot of his Board of Directors, who might otherwise think he was as crazy as we were.)

Several of us were regular writers for *New York*, however, and we had a different idea. Over the years, we must have convinced him, or at least worn him down. Clay had begun to believe, like us, that something deep, irresistible, and possibly historic, was happening to women.

The Preview Issue

In a small office, with four people working full time and the rest of us helping when we could get away from our jobs, the Spring Preview Issue was put together, start to finish, in two months. There were a lot of close calls and emergencies: cherished article ideas that didn't get finished on time, authors whose other commitments made them drop out at the last minute, indecision about the cover which resulted in doing four of them, and an eleventh-hour discovery that we had one week and eight pages less than we thought.

But the work got done, and the decisions got made. They happened communally. We never had time to sit down and discuss our intellectual aversion to the hierarchy of most offices, where decisions and orders float down from above. We just chose not to do anything with which one of us strongly disagreed. And we didn't expect our more junior members to get coffee, or order lunch, or do all the typing, or hold some subordinate title. We each did as much of our own phone-answering and manuscript typing as deadlines and common sense would allow. On the masthead, we listed ourselves alphabetically, divided only by area of expertise and full- or part-time work.

Feminist philosophies often point out that a hierarchy, military or otherwise, is an imitation of patriarchy, and that there are many other ways of getting work done. We didn't approach the idea so intellectually, but we did arrive at the same conclusion from gut experience. As women, we had been on the bottom of hierarchies for too long. We knew how wasteful they really were.

The crowded *Ms.* office had an atmosphere of camaraderie, of people doing what they cared about. But there was apprehension, too. Could there possibly be even 100,000 women in the country who wanted this unconventional magazine? We had been listening to doomsayers for so long that we ourselves began to doubt it.

When the insert from our Preview Issue appeared as part of *New York* in December, the issue set a newsstand sales record, more than *New York* had ever sold. Of course, said the doomsayers, women in a metropolitan area might be interested. But would we appeal to the women of Ohio or Arizona?

When the full-length Spring Preview Issue of *Ms.* was distributed nationally in January, we packed off all available authors and staff to talk to women's groups around the country, and to appear on any radio or television shows that reached women (thus changing the lives of several of us, who had never spoken in public before).

The Preview Issue was designed to stay on the newsstands for at least two months (which is why it was dated "Spring"), and we wanted to make sure women knew about it. But we got to our various assigned towns only to be met with phone calls: "Where is *Ms.?*" "We can't find a copy." "What newsstands are selling it?"

Worriedly, we called the distributor, and the truth finally dawned on us. The 300,000 copies supposed to last for at least eight weeks had virtually disappeared in eight days. *Ms.* had sold out.

We celebrated. We breathed sighs of relief. And only in that moment did we realize how worried we had been—worried that we would make the Women's Movement seem less far-reaching and strong than it was by creating a feminist magazine that did poorly, worried about *New York Magazine*'s risk, and all the friends who had helped us, worried about letting down ourselves, and other women.

But the most gratifying experience was still to come. Letters came pouring into our crowded office, more than 20,000 long, literate, simple, disparate, funny, tragic and very personal letters from women all over the country, including Ohio and Arizona. They wrote about their experiences and problems. They supported or criticized, told us what they needed, what they thought should be included or excluded, and generally spoke of *Ms.* as "our" magazine. (We've reprinted a few of them in this issue, and we will continue to make more use of readers' letters than most magazines do. After all, using only women who happen to be writers is itself a kind of discrimination, and misrepresents the lives that women lead.)

We were feeling inundated by all the mail, but didn't realize how unusual it was until we asked the editor of another women's magazine—with a circulation of 7 million, compared to our 300,000—how much editorial response each issue got. "About 2,000 letters," she said, "and a lot of them not very worthwhile. Four thousand letters of any kind would be considered quite extraordinary."

Obviously, the need for and interest in a nonestablishment magazine were greater and deeper than even we had thought. More out of instinct than skill, the women of *Ms.* had tapped an emerging and deep cultural change that was happening to us, and happening to our sisters.

When all the returns were in, *New York* breathed a sigh of relief, too. Their share of the newsstand sales was $20,000. And so was ours. We felt very rich indeed, until we figured out that our check wouldn't pay even half the postage for one national mailing of a letter inviting people to subscribe. In fact, if we had paid ourselves salaries, we would have just about broken even. We were learning the terrible truth of how much it costs to start a magazine, even one that readers want.

So we set off again to look for financial backers, but this time we had that magic thing known as a track record. And we also had more than 50,000 subscription orders, each one a potential asset, but each one a promise to keep. . . .

Where We Are Now

After the Preview Issue, we spent another three months looking for investors who believed in the magazine, and who would therefore give us the backing we needed without taking financial and editorial control.

In spite of all the looking, we can't take credit for finding Warner Communications. They found us. We are grateful to them for exploring many kinds of new media. And we are especially impressed that they took the unusual position of becoming a major investor, but minority stockholder in *Ms.* It's a step forward for free women, and free journalism.

We still must reach the break-even point with a third of the money, and in a third of the time, that most magazines required. (The average seems to be $3 million and three years before a national publication begins to show profit.) But thanks to the head start from *New York* and our subscribers, plus the opportunity given us by Warner Communications, we have a fighting chance.

If we do make it, we will own ourselves. We will also be able to give a healthy percentage of our profits back to the Women's Movement; to programs and projects that can help change women's lives.

In addition to financial struggles, the past few months have been spent gathering a staff. Our full-time members now number twenty instead of four, and a few more of us are helping part-time. Soon, there will be more names added to the masthead, mostly in advertising and circulation.

At the moment, we vary in age from 17 to 45, from no college at all to a Ph.D., and from experience as the editor of one of the country's biggest magazines to experience as a taxi driver. We are white Southerners, black Midwesterners, Latin American–born New Yorkers, homesick country-lovers and urbanites who never miss fresh air. One of us, an assistant art director, is male. (Since he was already working for our woman art director, he feels right at home. And so do we.) One of us is a radical Catholic, several are Jewish, and many are garden-variety WASP. We got more or less educated at Malcolm X College, Darien High School, Vassar, Smith, the University of Delhi, Millsaps College, Columbia, Radcliffe, Willamette University, the Sorbonne, the University of Wisconsin, and VISTA. We are married, never-been-married, and divorced. Some of us have children; some don't. Some of us have turned our friends into family, and some have done just the reverse.

All together, we're not a bad composite of the changing American woman.

If you asked us our philosophy for ourselves and for the magazine, each of us would give an individual answer. But we agree on one thing. We want a world in which no one is born into a subordinate role because of visible difference, whether that difference is of race or of sex. That's an assumption we make personally and editorially, with all the social changes it implies. After that, we cherish our differences. We want *Ms.* to be a forum for many views.

Most of all, we are joyfully discovering ourselves, and a world set free from old patterns, old thoughts. We hope *Ms.* will help you—and us—to explore this new world. There are few guidelines in history, or our own past. We must learn from each other.

So keep writing. *Ms.* belongs to us all.[24]

Notes

1. Marilyn Crafton Smith, "Women's Movement Media and Cultural Politics," in Pamela J. Creedon, ed., *Women in Mass Communication: Challenging Gender Values* (Newbury Park, CA: Sage Publications, 1989), p. 285.

2. Anne Mather, "A History of Feminist Periodicals," unpublished thesis, University of Georgia, Athens, 1974, p. 131.

3. Unfortunately, they did not anticipate that "liberation" would be caricatured as "lib," "libbie," and "libbest" and contribute to the women's movement, like women, not being taken seriously.

4. One of the early clashes of women's liberation with the radical movement occurred when the New England Free Press decided to publish women's liberation pamphlets at very low prices. While this made these materials available to a greater public, it undercut the financial base of the newsletter, which was not highly appreciated.

5. *Voice of the women's liberation movement*, or *Vwlm* (June 1969): 25.

6. *New Women's Survival Catalog* (New York: Coward, McCann, and Geohegan, 1973) lists 163 feminist publications.

7. This was not true in all countries. When the *dolleminas* of Holland whistled at men on the streets and held other similar actions, their local press was much more sympathetic; but there was a firmer tradition behind these acts. The *provos* there had developed the idea of *ludik* actions to a fine art. These actions were intended to make people laugh, but always carried a political message. The press became accustomed to looking for the politics and carried this over to reporting *ludik* actions by women.

8. For details of how this myth developed, see Joanna Foley Martin, "Confessions of a Non Bra-burner," *Chicago Journalism Review* 4 (July 1971): 11. It should be remembered that draft-card burning was much in the news those days and many other things were going up in smoke.

9. Sandie North, "Reporting the Movement," *Atlantic Monthly* (March 1970): 105.

10. Sometimes women retaliated. In 1969, Berkeley women held hostage an editor of a new underground newspaper, *Dock of the Bay*, until he agreed to stop publication of a special "sextra" issue designed to raise money for the new paper.

11. North, "Reporting the Movement."

12. *Newsweek* in particular illustrated all these phenomena. The original person assigned to the story was a young writer being "given her chance." Her piece was criticized for unobjectivity, rewritten by a male writer, and

finally dropped. In her place a free-lancer who happened to be the wife of one of *Newsweek*'s senior editors was hired. She was paid in advance, specified no undue editing, and wrote the most personal report of all. Despite the fact that it was quite different from *Newsweek*'s usual style, it was printed. In the meantime, women staffers had watched these developments with great interest and made plans of their own to commemorate the occasion. They chose the day of the special issue's publication to announce their complaint of discrimination filed with the EEOC.

13. Jo Freeman, *The Politics of Women's Liberation* (New York: David McKay, 1976), pp. 110–15.

14. Martha Leslie Allen, "The Development of Communication Networks among Women, 1963–1983," reprinted in Allen, ed., *1989 Directory of Women's Media* (Washington, DC: Women's Institute for Freedom of the Press, 1989). WIFP address: 3306 Ross Place, NW, Washington, DC 20008.

15. Donna Allen, "Comment," *Media Report to Women* (March/April 1990): 12.

16. Allen, "Comment," p. 12.

17. Mather, "History of Feminist Periodicals," p. 80.

18. Mather, "History of Feminist Periodicals," p. 81.

19. Spiro Agnew was vice-president of the United States from 1969 to 1973.

20. Patrick M. Reilly, "*Ms.*, Trying to Survive, Will Drop Ads," *Wall Street Journal*, October 13, 1989, p. B3.

21. Gloria Steinem, address to the American Newspaper Women's Club, Washington, DC, March 12, 1977, p. 14.

22. Amy E. Farrell (of the University of Minnesota), "*Ms.* in Transition: A Change of Skin or Change of Heart?" paper submitted to the Status of Women Committee of the Association for Education in Journalism and Mass Communication, May 1988.

23. Steinem, address to the American Newspaper Women's Club, Washington, DC, p. 8.

24. From *Ms.* 1, no. 1 (June 1972).

19

Women's Magazines

In 1963, Betty Friedan, writing in her ground-breaking work *The Feminine Mystique*, confessed to pangs of guilt over her role in perpetuating the stereotype of the modern American housewife. Friedan wrote for women's magazines. She saw herself and her colleagues as unwitting conspirators in a massive deception of the millions of readers of American women's magazines.[1]

The "deception" to which Friedan refers derives from the very formula that had made this genre of magazines so successful: the pursuit of home, husband, and happiness, the implication being that the third was not achievable without the first two. According to a long-standing formula of mainstream women's magazines, competence in the home and as a guardian of one's family represented the only sure way for a woman to secure self-fulfillment.

A study of fiction appearing in women's magazines in 1957 and 1967 indicated that "the typical heroine in one of these magazine short stories was an attractive, married woman in the 26–35 age group. She lived in a house in a city, had one or two children, and although she had been to college, her main occupation was housekeeping. She was in the middle economic level and her goals were love-oriented."[2]

An analysis of the covers, fiction and non-fiction, and advertisements of women's magazines in 1984 found that the percentage of working women in magazine portrayals was less than the actual percentage of working women in the population. Women's work, in magazines, usually took a secondary position to the man in her life or her family.[3]

Nevertheless, in spite of the chasm between the content's fantasy and reality (and, some would argue, because of it), the longevity and high circulation of women's magazines have enabled their publishers to write one of the most striking success stories of the magazine industry. With the advent of *Godey's Lady's Book* in the nineteenth century, women's magazines became commercial successes. Feminine perfection was a crusade for their editors, according to magazine historian Frank Luther Mott, who wrote that "women were being advised to be perfect ladies so continually that at least some of them must have grown weary of it."[4]

The growth of national advertising after the Civil War brought a new generation of women's magazines, some of which continue publishing to this day: *Ladies' Home Journal, McCall's, Good Housekeeping,* and *Vogue.* These publications emphasized the role of women as consumers and offered advice to their readers on how to dress, what to buy, and how to manage their lives and households. In an era when women's sphere remained chiefly the home, the magazines provided an inexpensive source of guidance.

> The influence of the *Journal* on character was deep and lasting, and the effect on homes and home life was extraordinary. The "services" and the intimacy of the appeal have made the magazine's hold on its readers continuous. Its effect today may be a little more on women's thinking and a little less on their fancywork and rules of etiquette, but in kind it is the same authority and control.[5]

Thirty-five years after Mott published that observation, *Ladies' Home Journal* had adapted even further to the more independent nature of American women; but it, and others in its group, remain loyal to very basic tenets of hearth and home.

Today, women's service books—dubbed the "Seven Sisters" (*Better Homes and Gardens, Family Circle, Good Housekeeping, Ladies' Home Journal, McCall's, Redbook,* and *Woman's Day*)—continue to attract substantial readership. Each month, about 65 percent of American women read at least one of them.[6] The circulation highs of the mid-1970s, when the Sisters had an aggregate circulation of 46 million, had declined to an aggregate of 36 million in 1990. The reason for the decline is twofold: increased competition from newer women's magazines, and publishers' desires to control the costs of adding circulation or sustaining circulation through expensive measures such as deeply discounted subscription offers.

The newer competition is formidable. Since 1978, new titles for women include *New Woman, Working Woman, Working Mother, Self,*

Victoria, *Shape*, *Woman's World*, and *First for Women*. Although their individual circulations are smaller than those of the more established Seven Sisters (some of which are more than 100 years old), their demographics are desirable to advertisers. Other competitors include *Lear's*, *Mirabella*, and *Vogue*. The clout of all these readers—of the newer titles and the old standbys combined—is impressive: Women's magazine categories comprise three of the top six magazine categories in terms of annual revenues (general women's, $2.399 billion; home service and home, $1.114 billion; women's/men's fashions, $516 million).[7]

"The field seems able to accommodate such title expansion because women have become too big and too valuable a target for advertisers from autos to yogurt to ignore," wrote Rebecca Fannin in *Marketing and Media Decisions*.[8]

Additionally, the content of the older women's magazines has become more elastic. Even the most conservative magazines have modified their editorial stance—but only after feeling the shock waves of the 1960s.

Ellen Levine, editor of *Woman's Day*, thinks the magazines became complacent in the 1950s and were unprepared for the upheaval of the 1960s. "They got tired and dowdy," she says. "They were also particularly hard hit by the women's movement. For whatever combination of reality and appearances, the books were perceived as old-fashioned. Now, that's changed."[9]

McCall's, *Ladies' Home Journal*, and *Good Housekeeping* have an entertainment/fashion/service format, although they have made space for emerging social themes and "coping" pieces geared for the woman with a changing lifestyle. *Vogue* and *Harper's Bazaar* cater to readers interested in couture and glittering lifestyles. Helen Woodward, in *The Lady Persuaders*, wrote, "Both magazines were known in the trade as the 'rags,' indicating the cynical attitude toward high-priced clothes within the trade. In their contents they were the acme of snobbishness."[10]

The "shelter" magazines also are popular among women, although their editors say they serve a "dual" readership composed of men as well as women. A top seller is *Better Homes & Gardens*, which provides hints on interior decorating, remodeling, crafts, food, and family projects. *HG* (formerly *House & Garden*) and *House Beautiful* are the *Vogues* of the shelter magazines. They are the "dreamhouse" books, concentrating more on ornamentation than how-to advice.

But at the end of the 1960s, an increasing number of American women were not adequately being served by periodicals edited for "the middle-class American housewife." In 1970 the first "alternative" magazine for mass distribution hit the newsstands: *Essence*, originally a fashion book, directed to the young, urban, black female market. Four years later, *Essence*'s circulation was growing faster than that of any other woman's magazine; it reached 850,000 in 1990.

In the following excerpts from her article, "The Heart, the Mind, the Pickled Okra: Women's Magazines in the Sixties," Nora Magid describes the idyllic landscape painted by traditional women's magazines. There are no feminist collectives or women of color in the painting, because her article antedates *Ms.* and *Essence*. The decade of upheaval that paved the way for more specialized magazines for women—the "Sixties"—was portrayed by traditional magazines in pastel colors with soft edges. Magid's pungent analysis strips away the colors and bares the canvas.

WOMEN'S MAGAZINES IN THE SIXTIES
By Nora Magid

"Jackie Kennedy was like a sister to me, and neither time nor distance can erase the memories of the years we shared together. I wish her happiness and all good things. I cannot express how much she has enriched my life by letting me put one foot in Camelot."

The lady's other foot is parked firmly in her mouth. Jacqueline Kennedy, having refused to perpetuate her own myth—she did, in effect, run off with Eddie Fisher—has become fair game, and Mary Barelli Gallagher, one of an army of former employees with a yen to spill the beans, explodes with secrets: "I'll never forget the first time she wanted me to make an appointment for her with New York hairdresser, Kenneth, for a hair straightening, shampoo and set. The 'hair-straightening' part took me by surprise. Jackie, I had always thought, had a lovely, natural line to her hair. Why would she want to have it straightened? Yet the receptionist at Kenneth's confirmed that Jackie was, indeed, going to have her hair straightened! Beauty was important to Jackie. She had the little dark hairs on her arms bleached. She used Sardo bath oil and a medicinal-type liquid cleanser, Phiso-hex."

Many of the titillating revelations are second-hand, and Provi, the maid, is the unwitting source: (1) "Mees Kennedee like nice, fresh sheets"; (2) "Oh yes, Mees Gallaga, Mees Kennedee likes to find her stockings in nice, neat pile in her closet"; and (3) after the J. F. Kennedy funeral, the punchline, "Oh, Mees Gallaga, that's Onassee, the millionaire."

Mrs. Gallagher says that Jackie's mother said that when Jackie bent over, you could see her garters at the top of her hose. And Jack said that Jackie was extravagant, and Jackie said, "Gosh, I guess Jack was real-ly upset, wasn't he?" to which Mrs. Gallagher said, " 'Well, Jackie, I don't mind so much his being upset. It's just that I'm always in the middle.' She apologized." And when Jackie and Mrs. G. have a squabble, Mrs. G. says, " 'And Jackie, the one thing I'd like to ask now is that you never speak to me that way again. I was never more hurt or humiliated.' She apologized again, asking that we just forget the whole thing." Good old Walter Mitty.

Now the Sixty-Four Dollar Question is who wanted to read such trash? The answer is everybody. We all live two lives, our own and that of the Kennedys, and the above, good for plenty of mileage in every newspaper in the country, was also presumably good for business—for *Ladies' Home Journal* business, that is. Given the insatiable appetite of the public for Kennedy material, the saga had run a predictable course even before calamity befell Teddy. The media created the Kennedys; and up to a point the media collaborate just as cheerfully in their destruction. Over the past ten years, there has hardly been an issue of a woman's magazine without one story and sometimes two on the family; and each periodical has to some extent defined them in its own terms. The *Journal* (mass circulation) capitalizes on that fascination with an animosity toward the rich and powerful that is inherent in Americans. *Vogue*, on the other hand, wealthy and snobbish, once unblushingly captioned a portrait of Mrs. Kennedy, "J.B.K.—the American Woman, a creature possessed of thoughtful responsibility, a healthy predilection for the good and the beautiful and the expensive—". . .

* * *

A columnist bleats, "Recently, I asked a visitor from abroad what were his impressions of America. 'I see a busy, active people,' he replied. 'Busy not merely with earning a living, but with enjoying living. Then he added, 'Your huge volume of advertising has played a tremendous part in bringing all this about.' "

Promotion is then the primary business of the woman's magazines, and like the networks they are first of all self-congratulatory. Every issue carries its built-in praise. They then praise all gadgets, cosmetics, detergents and tires as well as whatever politics occupy the White House. Now many appliances are irrelevant, many mixes are filled with chemicals, many cosmetics and detergents prove harmful, and obviously vary in quality and in effect. Many pharmaceutical developments, inadequately tested, turn out to be premature and/or dangerous. Crackpot diets are regularly endorsed. (Joseph Alsop, for instance, raved about the efficacy of the Air Force Diet; it was four years before *McCall's* mentioned in an article by an expert on nutrition that it was unbalanced and hazardous.) The Pill was widely heralded as "effective and perfectly safe." It is only recently after irresponsible hard-sell tactics that it is intimated that, well, there just might be side effects.

The medical columns, a feature of all women's magazines, are like nothing under the sun. There are usually some straight-forward simple-minded questions, and the answer to these is usually run, do not walk, to the nearest psychiatrist. . . .

Women's worries are ticked off, and they are manifold: How to save your marriage if you are an over-solicitous mother, are cheating your creative talent, have trouble-making neighbors, collect injustices; if your husband is impotent, jealous, rude, stingy, a perfectionist, a gambler, a drunk. What to do if you outgrow one another. How to define femininity, how to define masculinity. "Appreciation of artistic experiences is in no way the sole province of the female. By the same token, enjoyment of sports is not necessarily indicative of a man's masculinity."

There are horoscopes for weight-watching, spring cleaning, job-hunting, budget-keeping. Readers can also learn vicariously what it is like to be a widow, or have cancer or whatever the disease-of-the-month is. And if they persist in telling their troubles at the beauty parlor, *McCall's* psychiatrist-in-residence is permissive. He hopes "that informal care-givers, like hairdressers and bartenders, would read columns like this and increase their understanding of common life predicaments in other ways, so that their counsel would be more consistently sensible." . . .

*   *   *

Anyone who has ever been a literary editor knows that a lot of good fiction is circulated that never gets to see the light of publication. It is right only for women's magazines, and women's magazines do not print it. For fiction, *McCall's* has a large staff. Since all of *McCall's* fiction is by Barbara Robinson, one wonders what the fiction staff does. In the past few years, Miss Robinson has had at least eighteen short stories here, and has also made guest appearances elsewhere. The titles speak for themselves: Three to Make a Marriage, Something Very Much in Common, Someone to Love, Beyond this Moment. . . .

"Almost Any Friday" (*McCall's*, June, 1969), a typical story, is prefaced by a teaser to entice the skimmer: "Rob was in love, his parents supposed, but his plans were suspiciously vague. Did he really want to get married? For that matter does any young man?"

The fiction not written by Barbara Robinson sounds as if it had been written by Barbara Robinson. In *McCall's* for August, 1969, is Evan Hunter's "Wilt Thou Have This Woman?"—"From the big new novel, *Sons*, by one of America's most popular authors: A tender story about a young man back from war, and the home-town girl he had always thought he loved." Same basic situation. Same story. Same ending. Bittersweet happy.[11]

Action for Change: The Sit-in

By 1968 the women's movement was getting some coverage in the mass media. Television, newspapers, and newsmagazines gave space to the movement when the movement, in the opinion of these media, was "news." However, most feminists felt the media had a predilection for sensationalism and did not take the movement seriously enough to get at the reasons behind feminist demonstrations and protests. Women's liberation groups felt that the mass media, because of their own biases, were lumping movement activists into a comic category of "bra-burners" (a form of protest invented by the media, not used by feminists).

But the feminists' dissatisfaction with communication about the movement did not stop with *Time, Newsweek,* the networks, or the metropolitan daily newspapers. Their ire was directed toward the publications whose snub of women's liberation was the most damaging: the women's magazines. These publications had an audience of millions of women that the feminists also wanted to reach. The question was, how could the editors of women's magazines be persuaded to open up their pages to new themes about women?

The answer was, go and talk to them.

Helen Gurley Brown, editor of *Cosmopolitan,* received a visit in 1970 from a group of feminists who hoped to get Brown to reduce the *Cosmo* reader's anxiety about herself by encouraging the reader to develop her own talents and energies rather than overinstructing her on how to be the type of woman she might not be at all. *Cosmopolitan* did run excerpts from Kate Millett's *Sexual Politics* that year.

The more famous of the visits was paid to John Mack Carter, then editor-in-chief of the *Ladies' Home Journal.* On March 19, 1970, about 150 feminists arrived at the Lexington Avenue offices of Downe Communications, then owner of the *Journal,* for a heart-to-heart talk with the *Journal's* managing editors. The group presented Carter and his associates with a dummy of an alternative *Journal,* which included articles on abortion, career versus family, and prostitution. The cover showed a pregnant woman carrying a sign that said "Unpaid Labor." Obviously not receptive to such a sudden departure from his editorial policy, Carter and the feminists sat down for what was to be an 11-hour face-off.

At the end of the negotiations, Carter promised the feminists an eight-page section in the August 1970 issue. Written collectively (everyone critiquing everyone else's contributions, and rewriting them if necessary) by 30 women who did not sign their contributions, the insert appeared on schedule. It presented the authors' frank opinions on education for women, childbirth, homemaking, marriage, love, and sex.

The group of women who invaded Carter's office was composed of members of the National Organization for Women, Media Women (a group of women who worked in media), Redstockings, and New York Radical Feminists. Also in their midst was Vivien Leone, a member of Older Women's Liberation, and she wrote the account that follows below.

It was an active week in New York. Four days before the sit-in at the *Journal*, 46 women at *Newsweek* announced that they had filed a complaint with the Equal Employment Opportunity Commission, charging *Newsweek* with discrimination against women on the editorial staff. Their announcement was timed to coincide with *Newsweek*'s "Women's Liberation" issue. The cover story for that issue had been commissioned to a woman writer who *did not* work for *Newsweek*. (An agreement between *Newsweek* and the women subsequently settled the EEOC complaint.)

And two days after the sit-in, 50 young women marched down Fifth Avenue to protest the passing of the miniskirt. Known as GAMS (Girls Against More Skirt), the marchers won about the same amount of space in the *New York Times* (a 15-inch story with photo) as the women at the *Journal*. The following week *Time* magazine described the *Journal* protesters as "mod- and trouser-clad feminists." After jotting down the demands made, reporters were still careful to note what the protesters were wearing.

Vivien Leone is a writer who collects women's poetry and is involved in the arts. This is her 1970 article, "Occupying the *Ladies' Home Journal*."

OCCUPYING THE *LADIES' HOME JOURNAL:*
MY FIRST HURRAH
By Vivien Leone

I was seven minutes late for the feminist invasion of the *Ladies' Home Journal* on Wednesday morning, March 19, because I couldn't bear to leave the house without eye make-up.

Already full of self-castigation, I compounded it by taking a cab (a cab! Shouldn't the aggrieved inch arduously toward redress?), and passed the ride to 54th and Lexington fighting queasiness.

Could I, a 40-year-old fledgling feminist enroute to my debut demonstration, hope to cope? What a cinch it would be to sour-grape me out on my ear, I thought, as I ticked off my misfitness: overtall, overweight, overage, unmarried, unfamous, unemployed, dreamer, dilettante, divorcee; manless, jobless, childless; physically comfortable, financially fixed, but: aspirationally starved. For what? For choices. For dignity, grace, productiveness and sisterhood. For the vision of an unlimited number of new ways to be a woman.

At 9:07, in front of St. Peter's, the contact point, I picked up a fact sheet and list of demands from a pair of unobtrusive lieutenants and joined the workadailies swarming into 641 Lexington with my eyes peeled.

In case of interrogation, it had been suggested we aim for Avon on the eighth floor and walk down three flights, but I felt hopeless about being able to pass for one of their door-to-doorsters. Since I have seen them only through TV lenses, nobody of my acquaintance ever having been called on (dingaling!) by Avon, it is hard to identify with them in the flesh, which is pretty much the trouble with the women we come to know on glass, paper and celluloid. We spend our lives trying to pass for phantoms of whom nobody has ever actually had any real carnal knowledge.

Luckily, that test did not have to be passed. It was clear that alarm had yet to grip the lobby, and the self-service trip to the fifth floor passed without incident.

Only two of us stepped out. A somber-faced sentinel pointed the way. We went through several doors into what looked like the cheerless corridor of a military hospital ship. Now and then the efficient character of the abandoned cubicles would be broken by some spur of personality—I recall particularly an adoring display of the Many Faces of Paul Newman—but for the most part the atmosphere was colorless, windowless, labyrinthine. Now and then it was necessary to skirt an earnest tri- or quadripartite conversation between Them and Us.

"Why did you pick us?" one of Them asked plaintively. "We're allowed to wear pant suits here." As if liberation were a matter of fashion.

"Not an attractive one in the bunch," sneered an especially doll-like Themer, to which a tiny Us-er with vividly un-madeup Picasso eyes replied,

"That's what flesh-and-blood women look like—if you hadn't been taught from the cradle to hate your own real looks, you'd see how beautiful they are."

At last the overflowing captain's quarters came in view. Experienced headcounters placed their estimates at over 100, but it was still possible to squeeze through. I cleared myself a corner position and decided that we were indeed, beautiful. Every fat, thin, hairy, cropped, tall, short, fancy, plain, young, old, straight, wild one of us. Behind the executive desk we were all facing sat Editor and Publisher John Mack Carter, a cool character if ever there was one.

Despite the context of the occasion, my idiot reflexes, relentlessly moulded by all the Carters of this world, churned out the following: "good looking, might be old enough, but much too short."

Standing behind him was one of his two male managing editors (there are three, and one is female), Dick Kaplan, far from cool, and on the other side, the sole, semi-powerful distaffer, Lenore Hershey, her bewilderment crowned by a Shrafft's-Lady hat. Beside her a faintly beige woman, who was rumored to have been summoned to the foreground as soon as management got wind of our concern over lack of representation for its 1.2 million black readers, stared at us out of scared green eyes. . . .

The least tractable demands—in a short-term sense anyway—were those having to do with the sexic and ethnic composition of the editorial and advertising staffs. Nobody had really expected Carter to turn his chair over to Hershey, although at mid-point she actually did sit in it, and by the finale her point of view had undergone such a startling transformation that many of us would have been glad to see her get it. I remember finding myself moved in the course of this transformation to place my hand on her arm and tell her she was a peach. It happens all the time. The woman thing. Once layers of suspicion and competition crack, we start really digging one another and a new kind of bonding begins.

Draperies were now parted and blinds upped so that a pair of banners announcing the action could be dropped out the windows. And although they blew illegibly in the wind and rain, our sense of reality was somehow enhanced by the dingy light of day. . . .

Throughout this period it kept getting harder to distinguish between the press (print, tape, tube & film), the oppressed (many of us were making our own tapes, films & candids), and the oppressors (one knot of staff-dollies suddenly formed a pyramid outside the door with the top-dolly calling out, "We love you, John!").

Pant suits were no sure indication of allegiances. Pia Lindstrom of Channel 2 was overheard to say she not only did not identify with women's liberation, she didn't even identify with American women! Marlene Sanders of Channel 7, of course, was a filly of another color. She did her job swiftly and feelingly and got out without bumping into anybody.

Not so for the males, the only ones whose high-visibility presence was continually open to challenge. Fellows from such highly unlikely magazines as *Media Marketing* and *Holiday*, insisting they had been invited, were not too hard to expel. Telephone invitations requesting female coverage had been extended shortly after the first wave arrived. WINS and *Women's Wear Daily* were among the many who said they had no woman reporter available, and Dorothy Schiff's *Post* sent a lad who had hardly outgrown his Sigma Chi Blazer.

The reporter from EVO burst in at one point to say she had been manhandled by a staffer who claimed it was her father's fault she'd grown up wrong, that her father should have taught her her place at an early age. Carter's Kentucky-gentleman's code seemed visibly shaken by her tale.

By far the largest segment of time—about three hours—was consumed in setting up the mechanics of negotiation. . . . When it became clear that we would not settle for a future appointment, the emphasis was placed on getting us to adjourn to a second-floor conference room. Orders were even issued to clear the conference room for our hoped-for displacement. "It's four times bigger than this office," Carter explained, "so we can all be seated comfortably and proceed in a democratic manner."

Why we should fail to be lured by the promise of comfort and democracy seemed an utter mystery to him. The lure of coffee and pastry was, however, too strong for us. A collection was taken and $27 worth of nourishment was distributed at about 2 p.m.

Finally, Carter had to be told we might have some cause to suspect that once he got us all onto another floor he could just cut out and retreat to his emptied-out bastion.

The next hurdle was the size of negotiating teams. On this point we made our first concession by agreeing to allow about 14 demonstrators to do the talking. There followed another split between those who wanted to remain—silently—in the room for the talks, and those who agreed to retire to the anteroom. At this juncture I elected to leave with the majority, confident my interests would be superbly represented by Madelon X from my own group.

It's a new group, formed only since the beginning of the year, called Older Women's Liberation (OWL)—and if that isn't laying it on the line, I don't know what is. I believe we were the first group to form on the basis of age, although there is now also a split-off from the Radical Feminists called Over 35, and we each have lists of dozens of candidates clamoring for entry. As products of a much more intensive dose of sexism, we feel we'll be in a position to develop ways of dealing with many of the forces that lie in wait for the activists now in their 20's, forces we have already been shaped and shaken by. We've just been obliged to close ranks at 17 members, and five of us took part in this action. Not bad for a three-month-old group. . . .

Meanwhile, back at the negotiations, the notion of a women's liberation supplement in an upcoming issue was taking shape. The longest stalemate had to do with offensive advertising, until a compromise was worked out whereby the ads could remain intact as long as the liberationists could review them and do a piece explaining which ones were insulting, and why.

Around 4:45, I was acutely thinking about one of our proposed article ideas, "How Psychiatrists Oppress Women," because I had a 5:15 appointment with my Counter-Shrink. I couldn't let him down. He really depends on me to enlighten him about what this woman wants—what, dear God, she really wants. Is this any way to run a healing partnership? You bet it is!

You see, it's the movement that finally is making it possible for me to achieve partnership status. At last I've found the thing I, too, can be an expert on.

Before leaving I copied the number from a convenient phone. That way I could check about coming back if talks were still in progress later on. Neither drizzle nor snow flurries brought me down or stayed me from the swift completion of my appointed 45 minutes of enlightenment-giving on the Upper West Side. The C.S. was so enthusiastic he even suggested I use his office telephone to check out the possibilities of returning to the front.

"Candybars!" my contact gasped, "please come back loaded with candybars."

At 6:30 I carried a large shopping-bag stuffed with dextrose, apples, and grape juice into the lobby, was questioned about my destination by the captain, levelled with him and was turned down. Seems he had explicit orders, etc. As I began to try the elevators, he made a signal to turn the power off. Just for me.

I spent the next half hour moping about trying to look both sad and harmless, which should be a natural for me, since I'm half Russian and half Italian, but it didn't seem to be getting across. I tried to spread out my apples to prove they weren't ticking. Nothing doing. I tried slipping in with an authenticated Milquetoast hireling. I even offered him a candybar, but he kept whispering, "I don't want to get involved." As he disappeared in a special manually-operated car, I called after him, "but you already are involved!"

It finally occurred to me to phone from the lobby, and when managing editor Dick Kaplan himself walked down the stairway to accompany me back up, I knew the tide had turned.

From then on it was Milky Ways (not to mention Lenore Hershey bars), unfermented wine and the original fruit of Eve all the way.

The cast had dwindled to a manageable, totally exhausted 30. The talk was of eight pages as soon as possible, and a probable monthly column, to be created by movement members without bylines. Amazing, when you consider the diminishing demands had been 1) an entire issue (considered virtually unattainable); 2) a column (attainable, but unlikely); and 3) one article on the why of the action (that minimum we were determined to hold out for). The outcome was therefore a partial victory on all three counts—that is, a lot more victory than was strictly needed to get rid of us.

There was little doubt the idea of a takeover issue must have appealed to Carter's business instincts. It's no accident he entered college at 16, was a newsman at 17 and assistant editor of *Better Homes and Gardens* at 21. But the Sulzberger syndrome held back; after all, if you tolerate disrespect for lawful process, what cherished institution will crumble next? Only your postman knows for sure.

There was a spidery first-strand of trust floating shakily in the room. A man who agrees to set up an appointment between someone in his legal department and one of our people who specializes in advising management on the creation of daycare facilities can't be half bad. A man who contemplates setting up an editorial training program so that women will have a chance to advance from clerk-typistry can't be 100 per cent plastic, especially when he makes this startling confession, "You know, I haven't really talked to my staff in about two years."

It was an authentic mind-altering discovery the guy was making, and he was making it out loud. We believed it, as least I did.

After 11 extraordinary hours, nobody wanted to face the long-lingering press. It was one of those moments of such fragile accord that the press can so easily knock out of whack. We pulled ourselves together and casually chose the four most likely representatives. After urging them to report first (Thank you, Carla X and Madelon X and Sally X and Susan X—in alphabetical order), Carter said "See you 2:30 on Monday."

"To work out the details?"

"No, to start working on the issue!"

So. My kind of movement is moving me at last.

I remember how I used to think, in the early 60's, what a great time to be black. It simplifies your life. You can wake up in the morning knowing what's important, and where you fit in, because you're a natural-born expert on the subject.

At long last I'm an Activist.

Right now I really go for the idea of active feminism, but pretty soon I bet I'm going to enjoy some of that newly liberated womanliness.

I think I can work it out now. With a lot of help from my friends.[12]

The years after the 1970 sit-in at *Ladies' Home Journal* were years of rapid change. The Vietnam War ground to a halt; the first U.S. president ever to resign the office did so after the Watergate scandal; *Roe v. Wade* made abortion legal;[13] women streamed into the labor force in numbers unprecedented since World War II. The complacency and idealism of the 1950s had been shattered during the 1960s with the war and the assassinations of national leaders. The 1970s and 1980s were times with harder edges and new realities.

To some extent, women's magazines reflected that tone. "We realized that the whole category of women's service magazines tends to address the mass audience of American women with certain assumptions as to who those women are, but the assertions may not be valid for baby boomers, who tend to see themselves as more fully empowered adults," said *McCall's* publisher Michael Golden in a *New York Times* interview.[14] But the magazines also continued to provide an escape from the cares of a demanding world.

The American Society of Magazine Editors' April 1989 editorial conference featured a panel of editors from mass-market women's magazines. The topic was "What Do Women Want—In A Magazine?" The panel was moderated by Ellen Levine, editor-in-chief of *Woman's Day*, and featured Pat Miller, editor-in-chief of *Woman* (which ceased publication in 1990); Nancy Lindemeyer, editor-in-chief, *Victoria*; and Dena Vane, editor-in-chief, *Woman's World*. Excerpts from their discussion follow.

FROM "WHAT DO WOMEN WANT—IN A MAGAZINE?"

MILLER: Well, the title of the panel is "What Do Women Want?"

There are two lessons here: one, that women want love and the results of love, which is family, which becomes dearer as it grows out and lengthens into different generations; and two, that many women, like me, don't know what they want until they get it given to them—not on a plate, but in a magazine—because whatever it is that you didn't know you wanted has reached out and touched you.

A magazine can do that in a number of ways. It can do it with an idea, and it can do it with a tone of voice. By "tone of voice," I mean using a special language that is almost a private language.

When I was at *Cosmopolitan*, I went around the world for eight years setting up international editions. That's England, France, Australia, Italy, Latin America (there are nine different editions there), Brazil, Greece, Germany, South Africa, Holland, Japan and Hong Kong. I was repackaging the original Helen Gurley Brown concept there in different languages and cultures. . . .

The best thing I learned there was basically that the young *Cosmo* girl wanted the same things, whether she was Japanese or Brazilian: she wanted love, a husband, a better job, more money, more sex—she wanted it all—and, at her age, she thought she could have it all.

At *New Woman*, which was started in 1970 as a ripoff of *Cosmo*, she still wanted love, a husband, a better job, more money, more sex, and so on, but she knew that having it all meant doing it all, and she wasn't about to be Superwoman 24 hours a day.

At *Woman*, which was started in 1980 as a ripoff of *New Woman*, which was a ripoff of *Cosmo*, she still wanted love, a husband, better job, more money, sex, and so on, and she thought she could have it all but not at once. She's old enough now to realize that life is a serial, with a number of different installments. She realizes that love changes. She probably has, or will have, more than one husband, and possibly several careers, as she weaves in and out of families, her own and other people's. The smart buzzword for it is "sequencing."

So there are always new generations of magazines. Essentially they are the same, because essentially, I really do believe that women always want the same things . . . but unquestionably, they want them in different ways because society changes. So we put these ambitions into different context; we give them a different look, and we use a different language. . . .

When Si Newhouse bought *Woman* magazine five months ago, he announced his intention of making it a mass circulation magazine of one million-plus. . . . The current circulation of *Woman* is 550,000, which makes it the smallest of all the [general-circulation women's] magazines. That's O.K. It's the new generation, and we've got a long way to go yet.

LINDEMEYER: I remember when we were at the plant watching the first issue of *Victoria* come off the presses. I was panicked, totally panicked. I thought, "No one is going to buy this. I must pack my bags, I must get going, because no one is going to buy this magazine. It's too much what I love, it's too much what I think is right, and it just won't work.". . .

Starting a magazine isn't easy. Some of you in this room have done it. . . .

It's probably harder to re-make a magazine, because I think it's difficult to throw out the work of good and conscientious people. It's easier to work with a clean slate. . . .

What do women want in a magazine? I think I know—and we always say that the newsstand sales next issue, God knows, will tell us what our readers value in a magazine. Here are some quotes from letters we have received at *Victoria*:

The very first one I don't have to read, because I'll never forget it. It came after the first issue. It was: "Dear Gentle People: How did you know?"— with a woman's signature from Birmingham, Michigan—I try to judge every issue by asking, "Is that person in Birmingham going to like this issue of *Victoria?*"

There are a couple of others: "I come from a family with little passed-on heritage. You touch my soul and being, like the precious heirlooms I will leave for my children and their children. The tradition begins with me." I think there is a yearning out there for women to start their own traditions, regardless of whether they have things that look like the windows of a Ralph Lauren store.

"I'm a successful advertising executive, but most of all, I am a woman, and success is hollow if we lose the graces and dignities of life. *Victoria* illustrates the gentleness of spirit and attention to the details of living. After working eight or more hours a day with corporate men and women who look like robots, it's so refreshing to relax with a cup of herbal tea, play some classical music, and read *Victoria* from cover to cover again. I dress in suits, my home is contemporary and sparsely furnished, but I am *Victoria* at heart."

In terms of our graphics, I think our attention to details is one of the things that women like, that women value, and that they respond to in a magazine. Women are very visual people. . . .

Sometimes our stories work on lots of different levels because we think women's minds also like to function that way—that you're not just talking about fashion, but you may be talking about something literary, something fashionable, some other aspects.

We have a feature we call "Idle Hour" because we think it's very important to remind ourselves all the time that we can take that time off and do something we enjoy, that just takes us out of the fray. I think women need that. We are very busy, we're juggling a lot of things, and a lot of women seem to like the aspect of *Victoria* that says, "Take a moment, take time and relax.". . .

VANE: As editor of a mass-market title, I am actually concerned with the concerns of most women. So, when you're editing, or writing, or indeed, art directing, a mass-market women's weekly, with no subscription sale buffer, in a country where there isn't a long-standing women's weekly buying habit, you've got to be very focused on what readers do and what readers don't want. . . .

I can't afford to ignore the fact that, for the most part, most women would rather be watching television than reading magazines. I very firmly believe that TV is our main competitor, not other magazines. And, of course, most women don't watch on a black-and-white set anymore, they've switched to color; hence, they expect to find—now, this is where the advertising comes in—they expect to find lots and lots and lots—from *Woman's World*, of course—and lots of lovely color in their magazines.

Most women's time-consuming love affair—for that is what I believe it is—with television has actually cut back the amount of time they are prepared to spend reading a magazine. What they want are features that are designed so they can be picked up and put down, features that don't look too time-consuming. And because their boredom and concentration have never been lower, we've got to work that much harder visually at capturing and sustaining their interest. . . .

But in terms of content, what are the big turn-offs? I'll just say this to you. *Woman's World* believes most women in a supermarket, with the kids screaming for candy, actually don't want the sort of magazine which tells them to practice visualization techniques, or pretend they're a candle melting as one with the flame—something I read last week. Zappy pop psychology and such is actually too far removed from their lives—which isn't to say that it's too far removed from everybody's lives, but for most women's lives it most certainly is.

Most women don't want their shortcomings pointed out to them. The sort of women *Woman's World* is aimed at—in other words, most women—doesn't want to be made to feel guilty or lacking. She finds this actually de-motivating. And, incidentally, most women doubt they can have it all, and it's worth remembering that many of them don't even want it. . . .

What most women subconsciously look for in a magazine like *Woman's World* is, I believe, an emotional workout. A good mass-market magazine, like a good love affair, provides all these things. . . .

I think that women are as traditional now in their wants and in their wish list as they have ever been. I really very firmly believe that at core, women today, most women, want precisely the same as their mothers and grandmothers wanted. I really do. They want family, they want love—you know, we're traditionalists at heart. I think if you're operating in the mass market, as I am, you've really got to bear that very, very much in mind.[15]

Notes

1. Betty Friedan, *The Feminine Mystique* (New York: Dell, 1963).

2. Margaret Bailey, "The Woman's Magazine Short-story Heroine in 1957 and 1967," *Journalism Quarterly* (Summer 1969): 365.

3. Sandra E. Bonner, "The Woman at the Checkout Counter: An Analysis

of the Image of Women in Women's Magazines for April 1984," master's thesis (abstract), Northern Illinois University, 1985. See also Sheila J. Silver (Gibbons), "Then and Now: Women's Roles in *McCall's* Magazine, 1964 and 1974," master's thesis, University of Maryland College of Journalism, 1975.

4. Frank Luther Mott, *A History of American Magazines*, vol. 1, *1741–1850* (Cambridge, MA: Harvard University Press, 1957), p. 65.

5. Mott, *History of American Magazines*, vol. 5, *1885–1905*, p. 555.

6. Ed Papazian, "Repositioning the Women's Service Magazine," *Media Industry News*, September 13, 1989, insert.

7. "Top SRDS Magazine Categories by Total 1990 Revenues," Ad Age 300, *Advertising Age* (June 24, 1991): 5–11.

8. Rebecca Fannin, "The Growing Sisterhood," *Marketing & Media Decisions* (October 1989): 40.

9. Elizabeth Kastor, "The Renaissance of Women's Magazines," *Washington Post,* May 7, 1984, p. C5.

10. Helen Woodward, *The Lady Persuaders* (New York: Ivan Obolensky, 1960).

11. Nora Magid, "The Heart, the Mind, the Pickled Okra: Women's Magazines in the Sixties," *North American Review* (Winter 1970).

12. From the *Manhattan Tribune*, March 28, 1970.

13. *Roe v. Wade*, 410 U.S. 113 (1973).

14. Deirdre Carmody, "Identity Crisis for the Seven Sisters," *New York Times*, August 6, 1990, p. D1.

15. Panel discussion at the American Society of Magazine Editors' conference, New York, NY, April 1989.

20

Vietnam Reporters

The late 1960s and early 1970s in the United States were dominated by the Vietnam War. It came to be known as "the living room war" because of the images of combat broadcast night after night on television's evening news. It was the first major U.S. conflict covered in "real time"—not live, as was CNN's coverage of the Persian Gulf conflict in 1991, made possible by satellite technology—but with footage aired in the United States within a day or two of its being shot in Southeast Asia. World War II and Korea had been depicted to Americans through patriotic newsreels and print stories delayed days in transmission. Vietnam was *now*. The speed with which journalists of the 1960s and 1970s were able to move devastating daily images and detailed accounts of battle showed war for what it really is—bloody, painful, ruinous to nations and to individual human beings.

Journalists enjoyed remarkable access to the field of battle in Vietnam. Because it was guerrilla, hit-and-run warfare, there were no distinct front lines. And there were no overarching military restrictions on reporters other than those imposed by individual commanders. "Easy access to the war, rather than changed attitudes toward women, was probably the major reason such a large number of women reported from Vietnam," said Virginia Elwood-Akers in *Women War Correspondents in the Vietnam War, 1961–1975*.[1] No special permission was required to go to South Vietnam during the war. If one possessed a visa and a plane ticket, one could go. Once there, getting accredited as a war correspondent was not difficult, either.

Women have covered every American conflict since the Spanish-American War.[2] In Vietnam, the U.S. military accredited 467 women, 267 of them American, to cover the war. At least 70 of these Americans made major, regular contributions to the journalism about the war.[3]

But they were still a novelty. Edie Lederer, who is based in London for the Associated Press, and is a veteran war correspondent, described the realities of the time:

> In the early '70s, I could actually sit down and count all of the women who worked for the AP—period. There was not one woman foreign correspondent. There were some locally hired women, but not one woman working overseas. So (to be a) war correspondent was unthinkable. . . . When I went to Vietnam (in 1972), it was big deal.[4]

Once there, barriers occasionally presented themselves in the person of the bureau chief or fellow reporters convinced that Vietnam was "no place for a woman."

UPI correspondent Tracy Wood had to fight what she later called "gentlemanly concern" to get to Vietnam in the first place and then to get combat assignments after she arrived. The bureau chief refused to let her cover combat, reminding her of reporter Kate Webb's experience. Webb, then UPI's bureau chief in Phnom Penh, Cambodia, was captured and held for three weeks. While in captivity, she was reported killed. "We can't go through that again," Wood's boss told her.[5] Ultimately, she maneuvered herself into combat assignments and filed stories from the field, but had to "end-run" the bureau chief to do so.[6]

Liz Trotta, the first woman correspondent for television network news to cover Vietnam, recalls,

> When I left New York, the conventional wisdom said I would be mistreated by the American military and the Vietnamese because I was a woman. As it turned out, the best treatment came from these two patriarchal groups and the worst from my "liberal" news confreres, who for the most part felt threatened by a woman competing with them.[7]

A ready excuse to deny woman war correspondents permission to advance to the front lines or accompany a unit on a mission has been the lack of toilet facilities for women. The excuse has been around since the earliest days women have been covering wars, and it was used from time to time in Vietnam to discourage women reporters— without success. "Women reporters who go into the field make professional Army officers nervous, for these men must immediately explain that no, repeat, no toilets exist for us," wrote Gloria Emerson of the *New York Times*.[8]

Women correspondents with previous combat exposure made their way to Vietnam. Reporters Marguerite Higgins and Georgie Anne Geyer and photographer Dickey Chapelle had covered World War II. They knew their way around the chain of command, weapons, red tape, and protocol. Most important, they knew how to improvise to get the story. In covering Vietnam, improvisational skill was important; it was a very different kind of war.

"It was, at best, a wild and crazy war—as opposed to those sober, reasonable wars which one can find anywhere," Trotta recalls.

And if the high command did not understand what was going on much of the time, newspeople were only slightly better off. Each day you carved yourself out a slice of the war pie, nibbling on a battle here, tasting a reconnaissance there, trying to make some sense of it all. Ambiguity was everywhere, as the mistakes of American politicians and commanders aroused, if only by contrast, a certain admiration for the single-minded, cold-blooded dedication of the other side. The Vietcong were world-class low-tech jungle fighters, sweating their noncombat hours in miles of fetid underground tunnels, surviving on a daily fistful of rice and promises from Ho Chi Minh.[9]

Journalist Ethel Payne noted the contrast of Vietnamese tactics with conventional warfare techniques familiar to the American side.

They took me to a place called Ambush Academy, where new persons coming in for combat . . . were instructed in guerrilla warfare. They took me through a simulated obstacle course. The enemy is extraordinarily clever in converting old materials into lethal weapons. For example, C-ration cans could be made into deadly little land mines. . . . They could take bamboo sticks and sharpen them to needlepoint fineness, dip them in human feces, stick these in the ground. . . . [T]hat bamboo stick could penetrate that (boot) heel, get into your foot. You'd have gangrene. All kinds of things like that.[10]

"It was jarring to discover how schizophrenic life could be in Vietnam," Lederer remembers.

You'd be out in the field, covering some awful mess. Then, you'd rush back to Saigon, write a story, jump in the shower, put on a long evening gown and go off to some diplomatic cocktail party that you had to attend to make contacts for your political stories. You'd be risking your life somewhere one minute, and two hours later, you'd be sipping champagne. It was extremely strange. It produced a certain guilt.[11]

Reporters assigned to Cambodia when the war expanded into that region were utterly without any of the perks available in Saigon, the South Vietnamese capital. Sylvana Foa, who arrived in Saigon on her own and lined up a job with *Newsweek*, described her experience in Phnom Penh, Cambodia.

It was very, very dangerous. We didn't have any protection from the Americans which we always had in Vietnam. So we always kind of helped each other a lot.

And every morning at the end of the briefing (by the Cambodian Ministry of Information), we'd each take a road. You'd divide up the roads. I'll take five, you take seven, I'll do two.

At night, you'd come back, and the rule was you always had to be back in the city by three, otherwise we were sure you were dead. . . .

So everybody always had the same story because you know nobody could cover the story from just one road. You need all seven roads. And then we'd file our story and the electricity was turned off promptly at 8:30 and that means no telephone, no telegraph, no nothing. You didn't have to worry about being scooped. . . .

For the last couple of years I was in Cambodia, we didn't have any electricity. And let me tell you it was hard to write without it. I had a towel tied to my typewriter when sweat would be pouring down. We had 110 degrees normal. . . . You'd write by a kerosene lamp and you'd just dry your hands and keep typing. Nobody complained.[12]

No one relished a reporter's participation in the theater of war more than photographer Dickey Chapelle. Born Georgette Louise Meyer in 1918, and nicknamed "Dickey," she grew up infatuated with flying. Her nearsightedness kept her from a pilot's license, so she became a publicist for air shows and two airlines as a way to remain associated with flying.

Through those jobs, Dickey met Tony Chapelle, a photographer who taught her the skills of his profession. They married, and when Tony went to cover the Pacific theater of World War II for *Look* magazine, Dickey landed an overseas assignment with Fawcett Publications. As a writer and photographer, she went ashore with the U.S. Marines in Okinawa, violating an admiral's orders not to do so. Later she covered fighting in Korea and Taiwan.

Her work as a freelance writer-photographer took her to Algeria, Hungary, the Middle East, and Cuba. While in Hungary, she was arrested and imprisoned from late 1956 to early 1957 for illegal crossing of the border. The experience made her a staunch anticommunist. "I intend to spend my life making them sorry they let me go," she said.[13]

When Chapelle arrived in Vietnam in 1961, she was 43. "She was proud of the fact that she asked for no special favors because she was a woman," Elwood-Akers wrote.

She carried her own pack, C-rations from the can, and kept up with the men on the march. In 1961 and 1962, when few Americans were giving any thought to the war in South Vietnam, Dickey Chapelle trudged more than 200 miles, sometimes in 100-degree heat and torrential rain, following South Vietnamese troops and their American advisers on operations which sometimes lasted as long as six days. She did it because she believed that an American outside of the military should have firsthand knowledge of what was going on in South Vietnam.[14]

Chapelle's belief in the importance of being an eyewitness cost her her life. On November 4, 1965, as she moved through low brush with a Marine patrol, someone tripped a concealed wire activating a booby trap. Chapelle was struck in the throat by shrapnel and died in the field. She was the first newswoman and fourth member of the American press corps to be killed covering the war.

Chapelle's sense of pride in the news reporter's role in war and her fierce belief in an independent press are captured in "My Hair Is Down: A Sisterly View of the Second-oldest Profession," a speech dated March 14, 1963. Her comments on government management of military news are eerily relevant to the 1990s. Her speech is excerpted here.

MY HAIR IS DOWN

When I was being raised by an irreverent bunch of elder brothers through a depression and two wars, I had to learn a lot of boys' rules.

Rule One had to do with survival, a matter we took personally. I mean, we figured we had something to say about it, each of us. It wasn't up to Big Government or Big Business or Big Bombs, and at home in Wisconsin I never did hear how nobody could ever do anything much about anything because they were "just one person." (My mother would have snapped, "And how many was Jesus?" But I guess that's not exactly a press-type query.)

My brothers' Rule One was a kind of family thing, now that I think of it, so maybe we never felt like "just one person" anyhow. The rule was that you fought—I was a tomboy and teeth and nails were okay in the local culture—for your own. Whatever your own was. Wherever it was attacked. As hard as you could and as long as you breathed.

Privately I thought *that* was kind of a school-kid notion and pretty silly beside. Girls are born knowing that most of the time there are other ways to meet a threat than by punching it in the nose.

But I learned over a few decades from that depression and those wars and some six revolutions beside that this school-kid notion was roughly what made the world go 'round. In a situation where there was clear and present danger, I never saw any other proposition of human relations applied.

It even worked in peacetime. For example, cops didn't get killed by desperate criminals very often because all criminals knew other cops would get them in the end. Reporters didn't get hurt by those the printed truth hurt because other reporters would reply in kind. This went whether "hurt" to a press person meant a .38 in the back or a cut in take-home pay or an abrasion on our public image in which all reporters were cynical in dialogue, capable in their cups and soft in their hearts of gold.

I can make that point about why nobody ganged up on a newsman more concisely. The newspaper business from the start had a short phrase for it, as if it had invented the principle of looking out for your own. It was "the power of the press."

It was as real as gravity. You walked through war and revolution and pestilence and riot and catastrophe and even free elections feeling shielded by it, sure without thinking that if you get stopped, there were people backing you up who would pick up the pieces (and sometimes you keep on going because if you quit, they'd get the job done anyway).

But lately, I'm not so sure. . . . I guess about the first time I sensed something missing was when Paul Guihard got it.

Paul, you remember, was covering the rioting in Oxford, Mississippi, for the French Press Agency last fall. He was shot dead with a .38—that was the instance to which I was referring a page back—in the middle of the night.

Even half way around the world (I was in South Viet Nam) we heard about it right away. I couldn't learn any details but here was a kind of classic case of an overseas reporter murdered doing his job so the one thing of which I felt sure was the press reaction. We'd use the power of that press to find out what had happened and bird-dog the processes of justice to the end. . . .

I found out pretty quickly I was dreaming. One of the finest organs of Paul's profession, the *Bulletin* of the Overseas Press Club of America, did mention Guihard in the lead story for the week. In the second paragraph.

The first commented that covering Ole Miss was being done under combat conditions. Then the story went on:

"Score at midweek: one newsman dead, several others roughed up—"

In the succeeding eleven paragraphs of the story, three sentences were about Guihard.

Six months have passed and Paul's murder remains unsolved. It took a teenage girl editor at Ole Miss to start a modest memorial fund in his name. But most of us have to check the morgue to spell Guihard right. Yes, I had to, too.

I don't intend to scream and faint about it but I'll be damned if I feel like sticking my neck out to get a story knowing that if I don't make it back, my own colleagues will refer to it as part of "the score." And that will be the end of that. . . .

If he can be murdered on the job and the rest of us can handle that story casually, people who don't like reporters should feel pretty good. "The power of the press" plus a platoon of Marines still will mean something in the matter of keeping us safe from harm at work, just like a medal and fifteen cents means something in getting you on the subway.

Then there was Grant Wolfkill's ordeal. Maybe I wouldn't have felt so personal about that one if (a) I weren't, in foxhole parlance, a broad and (b) I hadn't spent some of the most miserable days of my life—okay, okay, it was only hours at a time—riding on that same helicopter circuit among embattled Laotian villages on which Grant was captured by the communist Pathet Lao in 1961. It's still the only civilian air operation I know where they give the hitch hikers a free course in escape and evasion before every take-off. You know, like the Pan American hostess saying in three languages, "Please fasten your safety belt," the co-pilots of the Air America firm out in Laos used to say in at least two:

"If we crash and you walk away from it, hike into the sunset. *In* to the sun*set*." There were fewer commie troops west than east of our flight path.

Anyhow, Grant never had a chance to find out if he could tell east from west. He and the two pilots made a forced landing and were captured right where they settled. It was about a year and a half before the Reds let them out of the holes in the ground that were their solitary cells and returned the men to the free world. Almost till the last, their captors neglected to notify the next-of-kin of reporter Wolfkill's whereabouts or—ah—welfare.

I didn't know if we'd ever see him again either but at first I almost could bear to think about it because I remembered what happened when the Reds captured an American reporter on the snowy cornfields of Hungary just after the revolution in 1936. They didn't tell anybody where she was either. I wrote *she* meaning me, of course.

'Way before enough time had passed so anybody would be certain I was missing and not just off somewhere living it up without notifying the office, I had colleagues on the other side of the ocean insisting that Deputy Undersecretary of State Robert Murphy demand word of my whereabouts from the Hungarian Foreign Office. Since I was being held in a Budapest secret police cell incommunicado, all Magyar Minister Peter Kos in Washington ever replied was, "Chapelle? How do you spell it, Mr. Murphy?"

The press, I know now, kept right on caring noisily, week in and week out, till I was released. There's even a story from that time to the effect that one news agency man punched a magazine editor in the nose to make his point that the magazine people (technically, I was one of these) weren't doing as much as the news services (to whose corps I was only an adoptee) to spring me, and he—the agency reporter—didn't approve at all.

Anyhow, mine was not exactly prophetic of Grant's experience.

A few months after he'd been captured, there were some rumors that he was going to be released. I was back at the Press Club in New York, and I burbled around happily about the rumor even if it wasn't very convincing.

"Yeah? Who's Wolfkill?" asked a member.

I said everything I thought needed saying and probably some things that did not. Then I got one brain cell working and decided to louse up my perfectly good emotional jag with a fact or two. I phoned the news desk of the people for whom Grant worked.

After I'd identified myself and added that I was just back from South Viet Nam, I asked, "What's the most recent word on your guy in Laos, Grant Wolfkill?"

"How do you spell Wolfkill?" came the answer.

Oh well, it's nice to know that if I'm captured again the circle will be complete with my fellow-reporters instead of some Red stooge saying in a few months, "Yeah? Who's Chapelle?"

For a time there, I thought these straws-in-the-wind didn't prove much except that I've got a low boiling point. So, I told myself, one guy got killed and another one bagged by the commies. They knew what they were getting into, they were over 21, and what's it your business? Reporting still is the best of all possible worlds and the American press, if not so sloppy sentimental as you are, sob-sister, has other virtues like being dependable. You know, if that press says it's raining, you don't have to look out the window to see. It's raining, all right.

Since the issue of news management by government has come up, I'm back off that let's-be-philosophical notion.

There are just too many big stories, too many circumstances of historic decision, not being seen by any reporters at all. Here are four:

1. The Bay of Pigs invasion. (Of course we couldn't have printed what we saw till a long time afterward, till we got ransomed in fact. But at least somebody would know what happened, had a professional observer been there. It's costing Congress quite a lot of tax funds to try to find out now. All the sources are people responsible or who had military missions when the stuff hit the fan. The results in the fact-finding try are about like you'd expect if General Patton had replaced Ernie Pyle.)

2. The armed forces of the United States as they poised to hit Cuba last October. (Again, we couldn't have printed it till after it happened. But I can't find one reporter who was physically aboard a ship or plane in the Caribbean during the bad time—where he'd have had to be to see H hour. The American press never missed a D Day first wave in my lifetime. But we'd have missed this one.)

3. The arms airlift to India. (The government spent taxpayers' money to jetplane a few dozen of us to Calcutta as eyewitnesses. But the Air Force general who commanded the operation told us the only flight we saw, our own naturally, was not part of the airlift. Unfortunately he didn't misspeak—I'm one eyewitness source of that statement. Officially, we never did see a weapon on-loaded in Germany or off-loaded in India. Nor did one of us ever see an American rifle in the hands of an Indian soldier.)

4. The fighting on the India–China border last fall. (A great televised documentary made by a 'way forward photo crew says they heard gunfire. Not one member of the press claims he—or she—saw anything at all of this story. Yes, we all got to the front. But it was days before or weeks after the fighting.)

Common denominator of these four big stories we never eyeballed, of course, is what stopped us. Not lack of enterprise out there. I testify eye- and ear-witness that qualified accredited members of the press repeatedly volunteered to ride, walk, fly, climb, parachute jump or crawl through mud to see all of them. Who said *no?* The governments involved. They even made it stick.

Well, if we looked so good out there, what's dampened my girlish laughter now that we're all back here?

Only that we failed to follow through on our outrage at having been blindfolded. We acted afterward as though such a practice were a rule chiselled in stone on a tablet brought down from the mountain. The end of eyeballing history is being hammered into policy while we stand by. (The American Society of Newspaper Editors last December said it started a long time before this Janie-come-lately said Boo! about it. Their Freedom of Information chairman, John Colburn, wrote: "No real effort or hue-and-cry to gain public support for press coverage were put up by the press when the White House refused to permit coverage of the atmospheric tests in the Pacific. This failure may well have encouraged the Administration in its news manipulation efforts during the Cuban crisis.")

Let's look at what else we reporters have stood still for lately.

There was Arthur Sylvester's pronouncement that "news is a weapon." He of course is the official weaponeer with it, being the Assistant Secretary for Defense.

In February, Mac Kilduff told the Overseas Press Club that the decision had indeed been taken at the White House to ban the press from the Cuban H Hour, should it come, last October. He wasn't defensive about it or talking off-the-record. He was speaking publicly as Pierre Salinger's right-hand man.

Now comes Robert Manning who has just said there would be "chaos" without some "management" of news by the government and the press. He's an ex-newsman and a professional diplomat, an assistant Secretary of State, so you'd kind of expect him to be tactful and mention the press in generalization before a television camera (it was ABC's on March 10th). But what he talked about was how the government proposed to do its share of the managing.

Frankly, there's nothing about which to ricochet off the walls in the fact of these men candidly speaking their pieces.

But when is the press going to reply in kind? When will we candidly speak our piece?

Put it this way:

If, among us, the murder of a working newsman can become three sentences in a story about something else—

If, among us, the capture by the Reds of a working reporter can become a dead story while he still is in a solitary cell—

If, among us, the sight of armed forces in readiness to defend our world can become accepted as properly none of our business (except, afterward if our world still exists, we may question officials about what they want the history books to say happened)—

Then surely I won't finish being raised before the day comes when "it's raining" in print has become the way to tell people that their government thinks it wise to have the world see America as wet. But they'll have to look out the window to find out what the weather's like.

Maybe in a dangerous world, that wouldn't be bad, either.

But it isn't journalism. Not required is the press, meaning a body of people who earn their pay by use of their perceptions to guarantee the integrity of information. We'll be a hair's breadth from an unemployment statistic. And that's a figure from a government source so we could be neatly managed out of mention.

Well, what is the press doing about the kind of news management so matter-of-factly spelled out by government officials?

Something, surely.

The editors—the ASNE I quoted earlier who are the press all right but hardly the majority of us—did make a comprehensive study of news management during the Cuban crisis. It was commented on in editorials and by columnists for a week or so. Reporters had a second chance to learn about it through their professional societies, too. Most of Page 4 of the *Bulletin* was devoted to an extract under the less-than-compelling headline, "ASNE Makes Survey."

Another organized press response led to what I suspect, honest Injun, wasn't the intended outcome. I mean, I'm sure the New York chapter of Sigma Delta Chi, the national fraternity of some 16,000 press professionals, didn't have farce in mind when the thing began. They invited Mr. Sylvester to be their guest and he came. The effect was to give him a new platform. He didn't need it since he has only to snap his fingers and hundreds of accredited reporters including this one zoop over to the Pentagon as if it's all-too-solid concrete were on fire.

Anyhow the fraternity heard him point out that he considered some official sources he'd used during his 37 years on *The Newark Evening News* "jerks" because they had answered his questions.

In their professional role, his listeners were so objective that every major news service carried Mr. Sylvester's piquant defense of his position, the point of view 180 degrees from that of the fraternity's founders. Equal or even any expression for the opposition wasn't involved. . . .

Quoting the ASNE report again to the effect that the White House controls government information, this is a little like trying to save the lettuce crop by letting the rabbits guard the leaves.

If you ask what else is now in the fight against government controls, the silence is deafening.

Maybe we'll all stay tongue-tied. . . .

Maybe we can't boycott lies because they come to us in the voice of a man with an official title. Or because the opposition insists on printing them. (One of my favorite news agency men says he wants a code word for the slugline of the stories he files from overseas solely for this reason. Why a code? Because Press Wireless won't transmit *Bullshit.*) Or because the untruths so well serve a local defense industry or a local politician that we didn't check them and never learned they were untruths.

I know the world won't come to an end just because American press freedom shrinks. Only *our* world. If we're voting by our lethargy for such a reduced world, I guess I can learn to exist in it.

But I'm not going to like it. And I'm going to scream and splutter and hit out and, if I'm lucky enough to have the chance, expand whatever credibility I personally have saved up in the act of somehow holding some outer line some little longer. I don't know a better place to expend it. After all I won't be needing it any more. It's only good among free members of a free press.

But if we American news reporters were to decide to use a school-kid rule like looking out for our own, if we exerted "the power of the press"—wouldn't I seem an awful fool for having put that paragraph down on paper:

I'm willing. I wonder what these older brothers who did all that bringing up of me would say about *that.*[15]

Notes

1. Virginia Elwood-Akers, *Women War Correspondents in the Vietnam War, 1961–1975* (Metuchen, NJ: Scarecrow Press, 1988), p. 8.

2. Christine Martin, "Women Correspondents in Vietnam: Historical Analysis and Oral Histories," master's thesis, University of Maryland College of Journalism, 1988, p. 6.

3. Martin, "Women Correspondents in Vietnam," p. 7.

4. Martin, "Women Correspondents in Vietnam," p. 167.

5. Ron Milligan, "Women War Correspondents Reminisce," *Editor & Publisher*, June 10, 1989, p. 122.

6. Kay Mills, *A Place in the News: From the Women's Pages to the Front Page* (New York: Dodd, Mead, 1988), pp. 204–5.

7. Liz Trotta, *Fighting for Air: In the Trenches with Television News* (New York: Simon and Schuster, 1991), p. 98.

8. Gloria Emerson, "Hey, Lady, What Are You Doing Here?" *McCall's* 98 (August 1971): 108, quoted in Elwood-Akers, *Women War Correspondents*, p. 4.

9. Trotta, *Fighting for Air*, p. 119.

10. Ethel Payne, Interview No. 3 with Kathleen Currie, September 17, 1987, Washington, DC, for the Women in Journalism Oral History Project, Washington Press Club Foundation, in the Oral History Collection of the National Press Club Archives, Washington, DC.

11. Martin, "Women Correspondents in Vietnam," p. 170.

12. Milligan, "Women War Correspondents Reminisce," pp. 135–36.

13. Dickey Chapelle, "I Roam the Edge of Freedom," *Coronet* 52 (February 1961): 136, cited in Elwood-Akers, *Women War Correspondents*, p. 17.

14. Elwood-Akers, *Women War Correspondents*, p. 17.

15. Dickey Chapelle papers, Box 13, Archives Division, State Historical Society of Wisconsin.

21

Challenges to Mass Media

As the 1970s approached, women in journalism still had not reached parity with men either in employment and compensation or as subjects of news coverage. Limitations on their professional development prompted women at a number of news organizations to take advantage of federal legislation and the court system to petition for redress of their grievances and compensation for discrimination in professional assignments and pay. They, and groups of women activists outside news organizations, also developed other strategies to pressure managers in print and broadcast media to reevaluate news and feature coverage—and advertisements—to determine if they offered fair, non-stereotypical treatment of women as opposed to diminishing the contributions of women and their influence on society.

Several landmark efforts are described in this chapter. Presented here are examples of employment challenges mounted by women working in the media and challenges to coverage of women by groups that have monitored media content.

Print Media

Since Title VII of the 1964 Civil Rights Act[1] prohibited discrimination in employment on the basis of sex, the Equal Employment Opportunity Commission has fielded thousands of complaints. Human rights commissions in individual states also have participated in determining culpability. Many grievances have been resolved under threat of an EEOC complaint. The concessions typically made by employers in these cases are pledges to institute affirmative action programs and career training, and integration of job categories where women are present in disproportionately high numbers (such as administrative and clerical posts) and those in which they are represented in disproportionately low numbers (senior management). They also agree to close the pay gap, which often is significant even when men and women in the organization have comparable experience and length of service.

In a frank article in the 1972 volume of *Once a Year*, the Milwaukee Press Club's annual magazine, Dorothy Austin of the *Milwaukee Sentinel* and Jean Otto of the *Milwaukee Journal* observed,

> The woman who was editor of her college paper can never expect to have the same title again, unless she inherits her father's paper or outlives a husband who owns one. Chances are, if she's lucky to be hired at all, the woman journalist will find herself somewhere on the fringe of the action that drew her to the career. While the male journalist covers campaigns, she'll tag along with the candidate's wife and attend luncheons. She'll go to meeting after meeting, reporting the wise words of men who talk to ladies. She'll run into the same women reporters again and again and come to recognize that the haunted looks on their faces reflect the one on her own.
>
> Though she might not trade her job for any other profession, she knows she's been cheated. Like women in practically every other profession, she recognizes that in journalism, a skirt is a hair shirt.[2]

At the Associated Press, a 1983 settlement between AP and the Wire Service Guild concluded a ten-year fight by female reporters and black reporters for equal consideration for assignments and pay with their white male colleagues. The consent decree, in which the AP did not admit any violation of nondiscrimination laws, set a goal of 37 percent women for filling entry-level reporting and editing jobs as well as goals for promotion of women to positions such as correspondent, foreign correspondent, assistant chief of bureau, chief of bureau, and assistant general manager. Women receiving promotions would get bonuses of $1,250. Another $50,000 was set aside to train women for promotions. Black reporters were to share in nearly $500,000, with most of the money earmarked for an affirmative action plan specifically designed to bring black reporters and editors to the AP.

The claim of discrimination was based on statistical analysis of thousands of personnel documents subpoenaed from the AP.[3]

The same year, the *Detroit News* (then owned by the Evening News

Association and now owned by Gannett Co., Inc.) agreed to pay $330,000 to 90 members of a class-action discrimination suit brought against the *News*. The suit dated back to a complaint filed in October 1976 by Mary Lou Butcher. Butcher's request for weekends off after 11 years with the *News* resulted in a punitive transfer to a suburban bureau. Men with less seniority were given weekends off. Butcher's transfer left the *News* with no women reporters in the newsroom during the busy day shift.

At the time, the *News* had no women reporters in the business news department, its Lansing or Washington bureaus, or in sports, editorial writing, or photography. At the time of the settlement in 1983, women were working in all those departments and made up about 30 percent of reporters and editors.[4]

Women at the *Washington Post*, through the Newspaper Guild, filed a sex discrimination complaint against the *Post* with the EEOC, which found in June 1974 that the newspaper needed to improve its record in the hiring and promotion of women. An account of the EEOC's findings follows.

EEOC FINDINGS OF SEX DISCRIMINATION

Charging parties allege, *inter alia*, that females because of their sex are discriminated against with respect to hiring, compensation and other terms and conditions of employment. Specifically, Charging Parties allege that females, because of their sex, receive lower salaries than male employees who benefit from over-scale wage payments; that they are not promoted to higher paying or more responsible positions such as managerial positions; that they occupy the majority of low-salaried positions in many departments; and, that they are neither recruited nor trained by Respondent to reduce the negative impact of the above described discriminatory practices. . . .

Of the 46 females in the higher paying news classifications 39% are paid at rates of $400 per week or more while 67% of the 245 males earn salaries at $400 or more per week. Records further show that of these higher salaried newsroom employees 27 males and one female earn weekly salaries of $500 or more. . . .

Of those 46 females in the news department, over 50% are assigned to the Style or Suburban/City units. The highest concentration of total employees in the news units is in the city unit where among 15 editors and assistant editors there are no females, but where 6 of the 32 reporters are female. The evidence further demonstrates that of 16 news units with 3 or more persons, 3 units employ no females in the higher paying jobs and 4 units, all with an excess of 10 employees, employ only one female. . . .

With respect to terms and conditions of employment, certain Charging

Parties state, and witnesses support, that females assigned to the metropolitan desk, shown on the computer printout as the city and suburban desks, do not receive the same consideration and opportunity for story assignments made by the assigning editors. They specifically cite instances where experienced female reporters have been given assignments typically associated with new and inexperienced reporters, such as night and weekend duty and the writing of obituaries, and denied assignments which would enhance their promotion and career potential. . . .

The Commission has no interest in attempting to regulate Respondent's editorial policies or functions nor in attempting to dictate who should be assigned what stories. Job assignments, however, are clearly a condition of employment and this Commissison is authorized to investigate allegations regarding disparate job assignments based on sex. If the investigation supports a conclusion that females are indeed denied equal terms and conditions of employment with respect to story assignments, we would insist as a remedy that female reporters be given equal consideration for story assignments with male reporters. Such a remedy in no way interferes with Respondent's right to carry out its editorial functions as it sees fit.

With respect to the composition of the editorial staffs or the suburban and city desks, Respondent's records indicate that on the suburban desk, there are two male and no female editors and five male and two female assistant editors. One of the female assistant editors stated during the investigation that she is actually a copy editor and is not involved in assigning stories. The other female assistant editor has left Respondent's employ, according to a witness' statement. On the city desk, Respondent's records indicate that there are 4 male and no female editors and 11 male and no female assistant editors. Thus, the evidence demonstrates that all of the editorial staffs on the city and suburban desks, who presumably are responsible for story assignments, are exclusively male. . . .

With respect to promotions, Respondent's records indicate that in the commercial and news departments the employee initiates the request for consideration for promotion whereas when there are vacancies in managerial positions, the department head/manager recommends those employees believed to be the most qualified for the position. The Respondent provided a listing of all employees promoted between June 1, 1972 and May 1973. This shows the following breakdown by salary ranges of the jobs into which the employees were promoted.

Weekly Salary Ranges	Male	Female
$100–200	27	20
201–300	11	6
301–400	10	2
401–500	10	0
Total	58	28

In addition there were 3 male and 3 female employees promoted but who have hourly wages. There were also 3 males and 1 female promoted but whose salaries were not given.

Thus, of the 58 males promoted, over 50% were promoted into jobs with a weekly salary over $200 while 71% of those females promoted were still in jobs whose salaries were between $100–200 per week. Of all promotions into positions with weekly salaries above $200, 79% are males.

We have previously concluded in Section 1 above that Respondent restricts the opportunities of female employees to occupy its higher paying positions. Respondent's promotion statistics indicate that, while female employees are not denied promotions as such, they do not receive promotions into higher paying positions on a similar basis with male employees. We therefore conclude that female employees are denied equal promotional opportunities with male employees as part of Respondent's pattern of restricting and limiting females from its higher paying positions.

Charging Parties further allege that Respondent discriminates against females by considering the marital or family status of females and not males in hiring, assignments and promotions into higher paying jobs. . . .

Charging Parties contend that married females, especially those with young children, experience greater difficulty in getting hired or promoted into higher paying positions than single females and that such considerations do not affect the opportunities of male employees. One Charging Party specifically stated that she was informed by Respondent that one of the reasons for its denial of a correspondent job for her was that she had a child and the job required travelling. Another Charging Party stated that she was harassed and denied assignments commensurate with her experience and competence after Respondent became aware of her plans to marry another employee. . . .

Statistical evidence presented coupled with witness testimony raises the inference that Respondent prefers single rather than married females for its higher level jobs in the news departments and that it applies no such preference to male employees. To maintain one employment standard for women and another for men is an unlawful employment practice within the meaning of the [Civil Rights] Act, absent a showing by Respondent that the narrow BFOQ* [i.e., bona fide occupational qualification] exception of 703(e) is applicable. We hold that, as a matter of law, the BFOQ exception is not applicable here. Accordingly, we conclude that Respondent's preference for single females, but not males, discriminates against females as a class, in violation of Title VII.[5]

On October 6, 1978, an agreement settling the sex-discrimination suit brought against the *New York Times* by its women employees was filed in the U.S. District Court for the Southern District of New York. The case originated with 90 charges against the *Times* in a complaint to the Equal Employment Opportunity Commission in 1972 and 1973.

When no action followed, on November 7, 1974, the *Times* was sued in federal court by Elizabeth Wade Boylan, then the foreign copy desk head; Louise Carini, benefits administration clerk of the general accounting department; Joan Cook, reporter; Nancy Davis, telephone solicitor in the advertising department; Grace Glueck, art reporter; Eileen Shanahan, domestic correspondent; and Andrea Skinner, news clerk. On April 11, 1977, the district court certified the case as a class action, so that these women were acting on behalf of themselves and 545 other women employees covered by the New York Newspaper Guild contract.

The following excerpts are from the women's October 6 press release statement announcing the settlement of their suit, *Elizabeth Boylan et al., Plaintiffs, v. The* New York Times *Company, Defendant.*

PLAINTIFF'S PRESS RELEASE ON *BOYLAN ET AL. V. NEW YORK TIMES*

The agreement settling the sex-discrimination suit brought against *The New York Times* by its women employees, which was filed today in U.S. District Court, includes an affirmative action program for the placement of women in top jobs on the newspaper that is "unprecedented." Under the settlement, the *Times* pledges to place significant numbers of women at every level in every news and commercial department of the newspaper. . . .

The unprecedented aspect of the affirmative action plan is the *Times*'s commitment to place women in one out of every eight of the top corporate positions during the four-year life of the settlement. I know that there has never been an affirmative action plan in the media, and I believe there has never been one in any other industry, which sets goals for filling the top corporate offices.

The jobs covered by the one-in-eight goal include those of president and publisher, all of the vice presidents, the secretary and assistant secretary, treasurer and assistant treasurer and executives such as the directors of corporate development, industrial relations and manufacturing.

Women will be placed in one in four of the top positions in the news and editorial departments between now and the end of 1982. . . . [These positions include] metropolitan editor, foreign news editor, national news editor, sports editor, financial editor, Washington bureau chief, editors of *The New York Times Magazine*, the *Book Review* and of every major section of the newspaper, plus the posts of executive editor and managing editor.

The 550 women covered by the class action suit will share in a back-pay award of $233,500. The *Times* women will receive their back pay in the form of annuities which mature when the holders reach age 60, but which may be cashed at any time the holder desires.

The *Times* decided to offer the annuities in an effort to camouflage the fact that they were giving back pay.

The fact is, the *Times* will pay, and the amount it will pay per plaintiff is comparable to or better than what has been achieved in other sex-discrimination cases in the media. The cash amounts in the *Reader's Digest* and NBC settlements were widely publicized, but the numbers of women involved in those cases were five to 10 times larger than the number of women covered in the settlement at the *Times*. [6]

EEOC complaints and suits pursued through the courts have succeeded in pushing media employers toward progress for women and minorities. Parity is by no means guaranteed, however; current analyses continue to show disparities in pay for women and men, even though the size of the differences in pay seem to be diminishing. In 1989, the Northern California chapter of the Newspaper Guild filed EEOC complaints against the McClatchy-owned *Sacramento Bee* and the *Fresno Bee*, charging salary discrimination along gender and racial lines. Citing an analysis of payroll data from August 1988, the guild's complaint alleged that the *Fresno Bee* paid its white male employees an average of $710 a week, while paying Hispanic employees an average of $429 per week, Asians $535 and blacks $339 per week. The same analysis showed that women reporters received approximately $39 less per week than male reporters, and that overall, female employees received an average of approximately $613 per week as compared to the $687 the *Bee* paid to its male employees—or the $710 it paid to its white male employees on the average. The complaint also charged that the *Bee*'s use of "subjective factors unrelated to job performance" also had resulted in women, minorities, and employees over 40 getting less desirable assignments and positions.[7]

In terms of women's presence in the news pages—either as writers of articles or as news sources or subjects of news coverage—the profile has improved since women's groups began using content analysis as a tool to quantify the number of female mentions in news coverage. An assessment of the situation in 1989 and 1990 follows.

NEWS COVERAGE OF WOMEN SHOWS GAIN

A month-long study—commissioned by University of Southern California's MediaWatch: Women and Men and the American Society of Newspaper Editors' Human Resources Committee—sought to measure coverage of and by women in photos, bylines and story sources on the front page of 30 U.S. newspapers.

The February 1990 study shows a gain in coverage of females in photos from a similar study conducted in 1989. Little improvement was found, however, in the references to female names quoted as sources in front-page stories or to the number of female bylines on front pages.

The February 1990 study found:
• More women are featured in front-page photos—an average of 32%, compared with 24% in 1989.
• Females quoted as sources in stories averaged 14%, compared with 11% in 1989.
• Female bylines appeared on an average of 28%, compared with 27% in 1989.

The March 1989 study examined 10 major, general-interest newspapers from around the country. The February 1990 study reviewed the same 10, along with 10 more from smaller markets (20,000 to 50,000 circulation).

Major newspapers studied: *Atlanta Journal and Constitution, Chicago Tribune, Houston Chronicle, Los Angeles Times, The Miami Herald, The New York Times, St. Louis Post-Dispatch, The Seattle Times, USA Today* and *The Washington Post.*

Smaller-market newspapers studied: *Albuquerque* (N.M.) *Tribune/Journal, The Beacon-News* (Aurora, Ill.), *The Courier* (Findlay, Ohio), *Daily Camera* (Boulder, Colo.), *Enid* (Okla.) *News and Eagle, The Joplin* (Mo.) *Globe, The News-Times* (Danbury, Conn.), *Pine Bluff* (Ark.) *Commercial, Sun-Journal* (Lewiston, Maine), and *The Tuscaloosa* (Ala.) *News.*

Here is how the newspapers stacked up:

The Albuquerque Tribune averaged the highest number of females quoted as sources, 22% (*USA Today* averaged the highest in 1989 at 21%). The lowest average, 6%, was again found in *The New York Times* (*The New York Times* averaged 5% in 1989).

The Albuquerque Tribune also averaged the highest number of female bylines in this year's study, 51%, beating *USA Today*'s high average last year of 41%. The Findlay, Ohio, *Courier* had no female bylines during the entire study period. Last year's lowest byline average was 16% in *The New York Times.*

The Washington Post had the highest average photo coverage of females, 42%; *USA Today* was highest in 1989 at 41%. The lowest average photo coverage of females was found in the Lewiston, Maine, *Sun-Journal*, 19% (*The New York Times* had last year's low average at 16%).

Both studies were conducted by Junior Bridege, president of Unabridged Communications, a consulting firm in Alexandria, Va.

The 1990 study was conducted for MediaWatch: Women and Men, a program under the auspices of the University of Southern California, and the American Society of Newspaper Editors.

The 1989 study was conducted in conjunction with Women, Men and Media—a conference in April 1989 by Betty Friedan and Nancy Woodhull. The conference was sponsored by the University of Southern California and The Gannett Foundation. Friedan's Media Watch: Women and Men, grew out of that conference.

Following is a guide to conducting a byline study. It was written by Mindi Keirnan, formerly of Gannett News Service, now managing editor/news of the *St. Paul Pioneer Press.*

How to Conduct Your Own Survey of Your Newspaper's Front Page

Here is a step-by-step guide to conducting a survey of your newspaper's front page—or any section front—to determine how often women and men are quoted, photographed and referred to as sources.

• Select a one-month period of papers to analyze and get copies of the final edition for each day.
• Buy two highlighters—one pink, one blue.
• Use blue and pink to mark male and female bylines, photographs and references. (Use proper names only.) Don't highlight pronouns.
• Count the total number of bylines. Count the total number of female bylines. Then determine the percentage of proper names that were female. For example, 5 female proper names divided by 25 total proper names tells you that 20% of the references for the day were female.
• Count the number of times men and women are pictured. Count as one every photograph in which a male or female appears, even if it is a group shot. Divide the number of times females appear by your total for the percentage of times females are represented in the photographs.

Here are a few examples:

One group shot on a page that pictures both men and women counts as two. If that group shot were the only picture on your page, that would mean women were in 50% of the photos for that day.

If there are two pictures, one group including a male and female, and one with only a female, female representation that day would be 66% of the coverage—2 divided by 3.

To compile your monthly results add your daily percentages for each category. Divide the percentage totals by the number of days your paper was monitored. This will give you the average daily percentage of female bylines, female representation in photographic coverage and references to females.[8]

Broadcasting

Broadcasting is the only component of the mass media that is regulated by the federal government. While the First Amendment to the U.S. Constitution guarantees freedom of the press, the finite amount of space on the broadcast spectrum necessitates oversight by an official body to ensure that licensees responsibly occupy the airwaves. If the Federal Communications Commission finds that a licensee has been abusing the public trust its license symbolizes, the FCC can revoke it. However, revocation is rare.

Proving that a radio or television station has failed to serve the public interest is very difficult. Licenses are granted for five-year periods. In the final year of the period, the licensee must apply for renewal. At that time, the renewal application can be challenged by "legitimate representatives" of groups in the licensee's market who can file a petition with the FCC opposing renewal of that broadcaster's license. A group or an individual dissatisfied with a station's performance usually must retain legal counsel to prepare a petition that will pass muster with the FCC.

During the 1970s, women's groups used the "petition to deny" as their means of calling attention to sexist policies, practices, and programming among FCC licensees. Of the 15 TV stations owned and operated by the three major networks during the 1970s, seven had contact with individual women or women's groups seeking to challenge their license renewals.[9] While a petition to deny is complex to prepare and rarely leads to dramatic change, dialogue between petitioning groups and station management can result in meaningful progress. (See the discussion and excerpt later in this chapter on the agreement formed between a coalition of activists and KNBC-TV.)

An alternative to the petition to deny is to submit an "informal objection," which is easier to file and suggests changes in policies or procedures without impugning the qualifications of the licensee to continue operating the station. This is thought to be a more constructive way to open negotiations likely to lead to an agreement between the station and a complainant.[10]

Until 1966, the FCC was inclined to hear complaints only from citizens who had experienced electrical interference or economic injury from a licensee. But that year, in *United Church of Christ v. FCC*, the U.S. Court of Appeals told the commission it must grant "standing" to a citizen group alleging that a station in Jackson, Mississippi, was guilty of racism in its programming. The Court said that "public participation in FCC action was not meant to be limited to writing letters to the Commission, to inspection of records, to the Commission's grace in considering listener claims, or to mere non-participating appearance at hearings." This opened the door to citizens with non-technical complaints about station performance.

So it was with six years of precedent that the National Organization for Women filed a petition to deny the license of WABC-TV in New York City, on May 1, 1972. The NOW petition attacked the station for deficiencies in three key areas: (1) ascertainment of women on their opinions about community issues; (2) news and programming about women's issues; and (3) employment of women at the station. These three points provided the model for petitions that have been drawn up by women's groups in other markets since that time.

Some of the tools used in this petition have become weaker or useless since 1972. "Ascertainment" was a procedure then required by the FCC of broadcast licensees. The licensee had to show that it had formally polled community leaders to determine what constitutes "important community issues" it should cover in its news and public affairs programs. The FCC required only a good-faith attempt on the part of the licensee, not a pure random sample or statistically reliable findings. In its WABC petition, NOW claimed that women were under-represented in the ascertainment process. But in the early 1980s—a decade after the WABC license challenge—licensees were given even broader discretion in ascertainment procedures, so it is more difficult to prove that a station's ascertainment effort is inadequate.

NOW also complained about the way women were depicted in entertainment programs, and said women's issues were ignored or treated with condescension on news and public affairs programs. NOW said the latter was a violation of the Fairness Doctrine, which required a station to show "overall balance" in its programming. The FCC has ceased to enforce the Fairness Doctrine, after becoming convinced by the broadcasting industry in 1984 that the Fairness Doctrine was intruding on licensees' First Amendment rights. Had NOW challenged WABC's license after 1984, then, the Fairness Doctrine would not have been available as a weapon.

In 1989, when a coalition of Philadelphia-based community groups filed a petition to deny the license renewal of six television stations serving metropolitan Philadelphia, there were fewer grounds on which to test station performance, and a more relaxed regulatory environment required stations to generate less documentation about their performance. The petition was filed by the Philadelphia Gay and Lesbian Task Force, the Pennsylvania chapter of the National Organization for Women, the Office of Communication of the United Church of Christ, and Congreso de Latinos Unidos. Their contention was that the stations had failed to address substantive issues of concern to women, African-Americans, lesbians and gays, and Hispanics. The petition to deny licenses was denied by the FCC in 1990; in 1991 the commission reaffirmed its decision on the petitioners' request for reconsideration.

The FCC said that the coalition's study of programming aired by the six stations improperly focused on issues important to the coalition. Said the FCC:

It is clear from a review of the record that the petitioners' study focused on whether the programs aired by the licensees, as set forth in their issues/programs lists, addressed the limited, specific issues petitioners listed as important in their affidavits: comparable worth, barriers to women, gay bashing, rather than the licensees' selection of issues. A challenge to a licensee's issue-responsive programming may not be so limited, but rather must focus on the licensee's overall efforts. Here, for example, the licensee did address issues of concern to women, albeit not necessarily the specific women's issues described by the petitioners.[11]

The outcome in Philadelphia in 1991 was similar to that of the ground-breaking WABC-TV license challenge in 1972. On March 21, 1975, the commission finally handed down a decision, rejecting a petition to deny WABC-TV's license along with the license of WRC-TV, in Washington, D.C., filed by NOW and a host of other women's groups in that area—even though the Equal Employment Opportunity Commission had found "reasonable cause" to believe WRC-TV had discriminated against women in hiring and promotion. In reference to all the points on which NOW built its case, the FCC said that in most cases it would defer to the discretion of the licensee.

Although litigation and regulatory mechanism had "very little formal success," according to Cherie S. Lewis, who has studied the use of these vehicles by women's groups to influence broadcasters,

the filing of television license renewal challenges by women's groups had three major results. One, the process led to improved relations between citizens and local broadcasters. Two, such citizen participation in the broadcast regulatory process directly catalyzed increased programming of interest to women and minorities. . . Three, the challenger had a positive influence on broadcaster employment of women and minorities.[12]

Excerpts from NOW's 1972 petition to the FCC to deny WABC-TV's license renewal follow.

PETITION TO DENY WABC-TV LICENSE RENEWAL

1. *WABC-TV wilfully failed to meet FCC requirements that it ascertain the needs, problems and interests of women in the community to provide suitable programming.*

Letters from individual members of the New York Chapter of NOW (petitioner herein), explaining the nature of their complaints, were first sent to WABC-TV in August 1970. As a result of those letters, a meeting was held in September 1970, between representatives of NOW and WABC-TV. While this meeting, attended by both Mr. Kenneth H. MacQueen, General Manager, and Mr. Al Primo, News Director, evidenced no serious effort on the part of WABC-TV to ascertain or seriously consult with members of the feminist community as to their needs and interests, it did make WABC-TV aware that a segment of the women's community was concerned about its programming service to the community. Petitioner contends that this initial meeting, over a year and a half ago, put WABC-TV *on notice* that a segment of the women's community was ready and available to meet with WABC-TV for the purposes of ascertainment. WABC-TV has not attempted to follow up with NOW for ascertainment purposes.

Subsequent contact between NOW and WABC-TV has only resulted from the dogged, affirmative efforts of NOW alone. Prior to the second "Women's Strike for Equality" in August 1971, Ann Cavallero, Chairwoman of the NOW Image Committee, wrote to Mr. Goldenson, President of WABC-TV, criticizing WABC-TV for failing to give full and fair coverage to the Women's Movement; requesting a camera crew for the Women's March, and offering to serve as a guide for the crew. This letter was never acknowledged. As a result of WABC-TV's failure to respond to this request, members of NOW went to the office of WABC-TV to insist on a meeting with Mr. Goldenson. Frustrated by WABC-TV's total failure to respond, Ms. Cavallero called Mr. McCarthy in November, for the purpose of setting up another meeting with the station and finally arranged for a meeting. This meeting, held on November 23, 1971, was equally unproductive. Members of the station's staff manifested no serious interest in petitioner's grievances and refused to acknowledge its responsibility as a public broadcaster to listen to or respond to such complaints. Again there was no follow-up from this meeting.

On January 23, 1972, Ms. Dorothy Crouch, President of the New York Chapter of NOW, wrote to Mr. Elton H. Rule, President of ABC, Inc., complaining once again of the station's neglect of women's issues in program content as well as in news and public affairs programming. This letter asked specifically that the licensee devote a substantial portion of its programming to the Equal Rights Amendment, including daytime programming, prime time and editorial time, and to present live coverage of the Equal Rights Amendment hearings. On February 1, Ms. Crouch received a response from Mr. K. H. MacQueen, Vice-President and General Manager of WABC-TV, in which he stated that WABC's programming executives would review NOW's request for coverage of a meeting with members of NOW to discuss covering women's rights issues more fully. No further word was heard and no meeting was set up. The Equal Rights Amendment received minimal and demeaning coverage by the station. . . .

When a community group, such as NOW, attempts to inform the licensee of its special needs and interests and to consult with the station on a continuing basis, WABC-TV's failure to consult with the group on a continuing basis constitutes a failure to meet its public obligation and constitutes a fatal defect in the applicant's ascertainment.

Finally, the deliberate omission by WABC-TV of any mention of the meetings already held with NOW and its failure to respond to the individual letters from women who were critical of WABC-TV's programming is in violation of its stated policy of handling complaints and suggestions and can only reflect a deliberate refusal to recognize women as a significant group and meet the needs of this group. This is a violation of FCC requirements for renewal applicants. The withholding of this information from the FCC clearly brings into question the station's entire ascertainment procedure. Unless the FCC has the community ascertainment information, there is no way for the Commission to evaluate whether the station is in fact responding to community needs. Certainly, this factor alone raises substantial issues of fact to warrant a hearing, if not to deny the applicant's license outright.

2. WABC-TV violated the Fairness Doctrine by failing to develop programming which accurately reflects women.

First, the station has wilfully and deliberately excluded issues of concern to women from the list of community needs that they intend to meet. Secondly, WABC-TV's news and public affairs programming is woefully lacking in coverage of issues of particular concern to women. Further, no women host or control any of these programs. Finally, daytime programming, which is almost exclusively directed to a female audience, is totally devoid of any meaningful content. . . .

The most dramatic evidence of the station's blatant refusal to meet the needs of women is demonstrated by the lack of any substantial programming or news coverage dealing with the Equal Rights Amendment (ERA). After fifty years of struggle by women and women's groups, both Houses of Congress have finally passed an amendment to the Constitution which, when ratified by the states, will guarantee equal rights to women.

An amendment to the Constitution is the single most fundamental legal and moral statement this government can make. It is of historic importance. The ERA, because of its long and torturous route, has taken on even greater significance. With the rebirth of the feminist movement in the United States, it has once again become an issue of importance and significance.

Petitioner has made every affirmative effort to communicate its concerns to afford adequate television coverage of the ERA prior to the passage of the Amendment. On January 31, 1972, a letter from Ms. Dorothy Crouch, President of the New York City Chapter of NOW, was sent to Mr. Elton H. Rule, President of WABC-TV, requesting future coverage of the ERA. On February 15, Ms. Crouch received a response from Mr. K. H. MacQueen, Vice President and General Manager of WABC-TV, in which he stated that WABC-TV's programming executives would review NOW's request for coverage and arrange a meeting with members of NOW to discuss fuller coverage of women's rights issues. No meeting was ever arranged, as had been promised, and no further communication was received from the station. . . .

This discriminatory treatment of women's groups is shown by the station's lack of news coverage concerning final passage of the ERA on March 22, 1972. Neither local news show, *Eyewitness News* (6:00 P.M. to 7:00 P.M.) nor the *Eleven P.M. Evening News* (11:00 P.M. to 11:30 P.M.), even reported this momentous event. In a blatant mocking of the seriousness of women's issues, that same night WABC-TV did feature an extensive story about *Cosmopolitan* Magazine's centerfold picture of a male nude.

WABC-TV network *News* at 7:00 P.M. minimally covered the passage of the ERA. The story was not placed on the news board as a major item, and less than ten seconds were devoted to a news flash announcement. Three minutes were given to a mini-documentary on Singapore although there was no "hard" news in that story. . . .

General News.

WABC-TV's minimal news coverage of serious issues affecting women is reflective of the station's deficient ascertainment and indicative of the applicant's belief that these issues are insignificant.

Two monitoring studies were conducted by petitioner in 1971 and 1972. They carefully analyzed and compared the total coverage given to all news stories concerning women and stories about women. The category of "women's topics" is all-inclusive and covers vital issues such as abortion to women's fashions, and coverage of stories of women when treated as sex objects, i.e., the Miss America Contest.

Our studies revealed that, despite the broadness of the category, as delineated above, news concerning or about women accounted for only 14.5% of all news stories reported during the 1971 monitoring period, and dropped to 14.2% during the second monitoring period.

Interestingly, when considered in terms of news time accorded, the time for the above stories diminished to 13.5% and 12.7% of total air time, respectively. But, even more significantly, in 1971, only a mere 1.3% of actual air time was devoted to women's issues of significance, such as abortion, jobs, and equal opportunities. In 1972, this coverage increased to 1.9% of total news time.

A second serious women's issue, women in politics, was also given minimal treatment. The 1971 study revealed that WABC-TV devoted only 2.6% of total air time to this subject. This percentage decreased to 1.2% of news air time in 1972.

In contrast, stories about women in fashion represented 2.1% of news air time in 1971, and dramatically increased to 3.6% of air time in 1972. Coverage of women as "sex object" represented 1.4% and 1.7% of air time in 1971 and 1972, respectively.

WABC-TV's coverage of women's sports stories exemplifies the station's deliberate distortion of news as it relates to women. In the 1972 Winter Olympics, American women won seven of the eight United States medals—four of those being Gold Medals. However, when called upon to report this extraordinary performance of American women, WABC-TV gave only ten seconds in one program, and thirty seconds on the following day. In addition the names of the women were never mentioned. During the same monitoring period, as part of the sports news, two minutes and fifteen seconds were devoted to a women's pancake-eating contest (6:00 P.M. *Eyewitness News,* February 15, 1972), and two minutes and thirty seconds given to women cheerleaders at Notre Dame (11:00 P.M. *Eyewitness News,* February 17, 1972). No doubt, we would have been shocked if, while Jesse Owens was walking away with the 1936 Olympic prizes, the news coverage was devoted to a watermelon eating contest for Blacks. Yet, such lack of coverage of women's achievements is so pervasive that it had previously passed *without review by the FCC.*

Finally, there is only one female reporter on the air out of a total of eleven reporters. During the 1971 period she covered 4.9% of all news. This dropped to 2.3% in 1972.

Public Affairs Programs.

WABC-TV states that it recognizes that public affairs programming is important "to stimulate discussion of and provoke interest in major problems and issues of concern to the public—" Here, too, WABC-TV's stubborn refusal to acknowledge the growing demands for equality made by women is reflected in a lack of programming on significant issues of public concern.

Interestingly, in the area of public affairs, the applicant has exhibited some sensitivity to the real needs of ethnic and racial minorities and has programmed specifically to reflect the needs of a broad segment of the Black and Puerto Rican communities. For example, *Like It Is* is a weekly program devoted entirely to the problems of racial minorities in the United States. Not only does WABC-TV recognize the public significance of programming on these issues, but further recognizes that if the program is to truly reflect community needs, it must be staffed and produced by minority group employees. *Like It Is* makes it clear that when ascertainment is properly conducted, WABC-TV is capable of developing programming to meet the community needs.

In contrast, there is no public affairs program specifically directed by and for women. WABC-TV has not even seen fit to devote any of its infrequent special public affairs programs to women's issues. As illustrative of the station's "policy of presenting (public affairs) programming to meet public needs and interests whether or not commercial sponsorship is available," WABC-TV's renewal application lists 21 programs in addition to specials on space flights and Presidential addresses. Not one of these specials focuses on women's issues. Of forty programs listed illustrating WABC-TV's "application of its policy" of pre-empting regular time to broadcast special public affairs and instructional programs—none dealt with women's issues.

The most prestigious of WABC-TV's public affairs programs, *Issues and Answers*, presented only one woman, the Prime Minister of Israel, Golda Meir, among a list of twenty-five representative guests. None of the guests addressed herself/himself to problems and issues concerning women's status in our society. Further, *Eyewitness News Conference*, the locally produced interview program, is geared specifically to "probe, in greater detail, into issues and problems of concern in the community." Among the twenty-nine representative guests, two were women, Eleanor Holmes Norton and Bella Abzug. But only Ms. Norton directed her attention to women in politics and government. WABC-TV's plans for the future of the *News Conference* follows this pattern— no women's issues are scheduled.

Interestingly, while WABC-TV finds an insufficient community need to warrant public affairs specials on issues such as day care or the Equal Rights Amendment, they do find a need for programs devoted exclusively to the study of American wildlife. On March 19, 1971, *one hour of prime time was pre-empted* for a documentary focused on the American Bald Eagle; five months later, *another hour of prime time was pre-empted* to study the cycle of the American Bald Eagle (November 26, 1971). Prime time was also pre-empted to feature six programs studying underwater life. Only two of the special programs pre-empting the regular schedule featured women at all; one was "A Visit With The First Lady," and the other was "White House Wedding."

Certainly, we do not contend that it is poor programming to expose residents of a metropolitan area such as New York to the study of wildlife that exists totally outside of their normal range of daily experience. However, it is questionable that there existed great clamor by the community for this programming, or any community expression that the extinction of the Bald Eagle was a significant community problem. Such discriminatory weighing of programming raises a substantial question about the nature of WABC-TV's evaluation of community concerns. . . .

The ratings indicate that over 80% of the television viewing audience in the New York metropolitan area, between 9:30 A.M. and 6:00 P.M., is made up of women. Despite this fact, WABC-TV neither offers nor proposes to offer any local programming responding to the community needs of women. Daytime programming begins with a two-hour movie (usually a rerun), and proceeds through another six and one-half hours of network-produced game shows, situation comedies, and culminates in an afternoon of soap opera. Even more insulting, all but the soap operas are programs repeated or reruns originally produced for prime time viewing.

WABC-TV clearly believes that women viewers are a sub-class, lacking the need or interest for decent, informative local programming. During the daytime hours, 9:30 A.M. to 6:00 P.M., there are *no* news programs, *no* editorials, *no* public affairs programs, *no* documentaries. There are not even new and original entertainment shows. . . .

WABC-TV's refusal to present balanced daytime programming, reflecting a wide range of local programming, is clearly violative of FCC policies in two important ways: First, women are equally entitled to information on public issues which affect them as citizens. Second, they, like other viewers, have a right to "balanced" programming—including news and public affairs that licensees are obligated to provide under FCC Rules. The fact that all daytime television, from 9:30 A.M. to 6:00 P.M., is network-produced, is clear evidence that WABC-TV has wilfully determined not to equally service the daytime audience—women. Evidently, when WABC-TV, in its application committed itself to "continue to present a balanced schedule of locally produced and locally oriented programs," they had no intention of applying this standard when the audience was primarily female. . . .

Petitioners would note that media stereotypes about minority groups have largely disappeared. WABC-TV, like other stations, has abandoned the "Amos-'n'Andy" image. It would never call Black leaders "boy" or snicker about the civil rights movement. Nor would it portray Black men exclusively as porters, waiters and song-and-dance men. Women should be accorded similar unbiased treatment.

In sum, the stereotypes described above would be intolerable if WABC-TV presented them about Blacks or any other minority group. They are no less damaging about women. Women are working hard to overcome the barriers against them in employment and other areas. By programming as it does, WABC-TV reinforces those barriers, perpetuates invidious sex-based discrimination, and does a major disservice to its broadcast community as a whole.

ABC News Commentary on the Women's Movement.

Bias against the women's movement is even more overt when WABC-TV discusses the issue directly. Since November 1971, the station has presented no fewer than five full-scale network-produced editorials on "women's liberation" and the role of women, four of them negative, and the fifth one neutral at best.

On November 8, 1971, in "Commentary," *ABC News* correspondent Harry Reasoner argued that putting women into leadership positions won't solve any of the world's problems; we should "deal with people and politics as they are" and "solve the problems of war and peace and strife between nations without calling on women to save us."

On December 9, 1971, Mr. Reasoner reported in another issue of "Commentary" that fashion writer Ann Hencken "reports that the torso is coming back in next spring's fashions. She also says the spring fashions encourage women to be ladylike and to behave themselves." In Mr. Reasoner's view, "that's all to the good."

On December 21, in yet a third issue of "Commentary," Mr. Reasoner attacked *Ms.*, the new women's rights magazine edited by Gloria Steinem. In what must surely be one of the most vicious and irrational series of remarks ever made about the women's movement or its members, Mr. Reasoner compared *Ms.* to *Eros* (whose publisher was convicted for obscenity) and *Fact* (whose publisher was successfully sued for defamation). He noted that the magazine could be successful if it were run by an H. L. Mencken, but that "there is no sign in *Ms.* or indeed in the whole women's movement, of an H. L. Mencken." *Ms.* is "just another in the great but irrelevant tradition of American shock magazines," he concluded, "and its speedy demise is certain."

On December 22, 1971, only a day after the editorial on *Ms., ABC News* commentator Howard K. Smith delivered yet another attack on the women's movement. "Among the multitude of causes in this cause-ridden age," he began, "one that has not—to me, at least—made its case is Women's Lib." Discrimination against women is like "prejudice against every class of human," he said, too inconsequential to "make a federal case out of."

Thus, within a six-week period WABC-TV has presented no fewer than four prime-time editorials opposing the women's movement, its leaders or its views. Even a subsequent editorial, on January 13, 1972, in which Mr. Reasoner professed to agree with women's protests against advertising, said as much about demeaning stereotypes against men as it did about those against women. The editorial was especially ironic since WABC-TV has not exercised its duty to eliminate those commercials which contain such stereotypes. Clearly, the weight of opinion on ABC's "Commentary" is against the women's movement and everything it stands for. By promoting that view without airing the feminist position as well, WABC-TV violates the most elementary requirements of fairness.

General News Coverage.

In other kinds of news coverage, WABC-TV is equally biased. Either the station treats the women's movement as a joke or it ignores women's issues altogether.

On August 26, 1970, thousands of women in New York and throughout the country marched to observe the 50th anniversary of the 19th Amendment. The purpose of this demonstration was to protest sex-based discrimination, yet *Eyewitness News* reporter Roger Grimsby directed his comments to film footage of women in mini-skirts and [made] sneering comments such as, "Women shouldn't complain when they're being supported by men." In addition, Mr. Grimsby interviewed one participant by asking her "How do you and the other girls at the strike office feel about the march today?" When she answered, "I'd like to ask you to refer to me and the other women who worked on the strike as women," Grimsby smirked and said, "Well, is 'female' all right?" By comparison, it is difficult to imagine Roger Grimsby asking a Black male demonstrator at a civil rights march: "How do you *boys* feel about today's march?"

More importantly, the WABC-TV news staff seems determined to ridicule women's efforts to remove sex-based barriers in the job market. In January 1972, the *Eyewitness News* team did a story on the women who, after considerable effort, had won the right to be a baseball umpire. Commenting on this important breakthrough in employment, newscaster Jim Bouton re-marked. "The most important thing about an umpire is eyes; I've seen her eyes; they're beautiful." Similarly, on January 31, 1972, WABC-TV broadcast a story about a new barbershop which trains women to shave male customers. The reporter asked one woman, "If you had a fight with your husband, do you think your hand would slip?" Certainly, other more important aspects of this event could have been discussed. Or coverage might have included an in-depth documentary on women's economic plight in this country and the importance of sex-segregated jobs in maintaining women in an inferior economic position. But WABC-TV saw only a joke.

Besides treating women's achievements as trivial wherever possible, WABC-TV reporters also ignore many important women's news stories altogether. For example, the station provides far less than fair coverage of women's sports. As already noted, although women won seven out of eight U.S. medals in the Winter Olympic Games, only two WABC-TV news programs even mentioned their victories. The women were not mentioned by name, and only forty seconds of air time was given to the issue.

3. *WABC-TV's discriminatory employment practices are violative of FCC rules and regulations.*

Section 73.125(a) of the Commission's Rules and Regulations provides that each licensee shall afford equal opportunity in employment and that no licensee shall discriminate on the basis of sex. Section 73.125(b) of the Rules requires each licensee to establish and carry out a continuing positive program to assure equal opportunity in every phase of employment policy and practice.

The Commission has made it clear that compliance with these Rules is of the highest priority since discrimination on the part of a licensee has a direct and profound bearing on its qualifications to be a Commission licensee. Violation of these regulations reflects on a licensee's attitude toward its community and hampers efforts to serve the public interest since employment discrimination is a violation of federal statutes and policies.

In adopting its employment regulations, the Commission discussed fully the implications of imposing employment standards on its licensees. It is clear from the documents issued by the Commission that its intention was to impose upon the broadcaster a duty in conjunction with its public interest duty to follow federal policy and insure equal employment opportunity. The Commission found numerous reasons to consider these rules to be in the public interest. First, the Commission observed that violation of the equal opportunity rules by a licensee in its internal employment was a clear violation of state and federal laws, particularly Title VII of the Civil Rights Act of 1964. Therefore, violation of these laws by the Commission licensee clearly raises questions as to its qualifications to operate a broadcast license in the public interest.

Second, the Commission pointed to a national policy going beyond specific laws against sex-based discrimination, as embodied in the Presidential Executive Orders, the Civil Rights Act, the Equal Pay Act, the formation of the Equal Employment Opportunity Commission, various Department of Labor pronouncements, as well as numerous other sources. Many commissions have been formed to focus national attention on the problem of employment discrimination, and many federal agencies have directed their attention to this problem.

Third, a broadcaster operates on the basis of a federal license and, by accepting part of the public domain, the broadcaster becomes subject to enforceable public obligations. Given the national policy against discrimination, a broadcaster who acts in violation of this policy by discriminating in its employment on the basis of sex, abuses its federal license and it therefore should be withdrawn.

Lastly, and perhaps most important under the public interest standard, the Commission noted a correlation between programming and employment practices. Discrimination in employment by the station will inhibit the broadcaster in its effort to serve the needs and interests of the community. Each applicant for renewal of license is required to ascertain the community's needs and interests in order to plan programming to meet these needs and interests on an equitable basis. The Commission stated that if a broadcaster pursues a policy of discrimination, serious questions are raised as to whether the broadcaster is serving the *entire* public and whether the applicant is consulting with each significant group to determine its needs and interests.

Nowhere is the correlation between employment discrimination and failure to serve the public interest more evident than in the present case. WABC-TV, as will be shown herein, has failed to comply with the letter and the spirit of the FCC's rules and policies against job discrimination based on sex. Petitioner alleges that the station's failure to employ or promote any significant number of women is reflected in its failure to recognize the needs of women and provide programming to meet them. . . .

The FCC has recognized that the law surrounding sex discrimination, as developed in legislative enactments and case law, has focused on the overall employment practices of an employer that, when taken as a whole, show a total pattern of discriminatory behavior. Since unlawful sex discrimination in employment is generally the result of institutionalized practices rather than isolated acts, the Commission has called for the gathering of statistical information from its licensees to indicate areas of non-compliance with its rules, as well as point out to each licensee its own problem areas. . . .

The [WABC-TV] 1971 Annual Employment Report, Form 395, dated May 26, 1971, shows the following breakdown of men and women in each job category.

Job Category	Men		Women	
Officials and Managers	25	92%	2	8%
Professional	45	88%	6	12%
Technicians	30	100%	None	0%

Sales Workers	13	100%	None	0%
Office and Clerical	14	28%	36	72%
Craftsmen	16	100%	None	0%
Operatives	2	100%	None	0%

Out of a total employment of 189 persons, only 44, or 23.3%, are women. In contrast, the New York State Department of Labor Study shows that women comprise 40.3% of the total work force in metropolitan New York. More importantly, women comprise 66.0% of the total number of employees in the field of communications in the New York SMSA [Standard Metropolitan Statistical Area].[13]

The threat of license challenges and the spreading interest in monitoring news, entertainment, and commercial content in radio and television, brought broadcasters into closer contact with women's groups. Out of conferences between the women and station managers who wished to avoid the expense and length of a license challenge at renewal time, came a new form of commitment: the community women's group/licensee agreement.

The first agreement between a broadcaster and a citizen's group was negotiated in 1969 between KTAL-TV and the Texarkana (Texas) Junior Chamber of Commerce and 12 other associations in that market. The citizen group did not complain about the omission of viewpoints of one sex, but of one race—blacks—and about management's inaccessibility to viewers. After the agreement was signed, the citizen group withdrew its petition to deny renewal of KTAL-TV's license. The station had agreed to hire two black reporters; to implement a toll-free telephone line to service the public information needs of its far-flung subscribers; to make no nonessential reference to the race of a person; to meet monthly with an advisory council to discuss KTAL-TV's programming; and to present a monthly magazine-type program seeking participation from the entire service area.

The Federal Communications Commission gave its blessing to the resolution of differences between KTAL-TV and its audience, but it warned that it would not sanction agreements that deprived the licensee of its discretion in programming.

Since the KTAL-TV and the Texarkana group signed their agreement, other groups have been successful in ironing out their differences with broadcasters. In 1973 KTTV-TV, Los Angeles, signed an agreement with the National Association for Better Broadcasting in which the station agreed to remove certain violent cartoon programs from the air.

Women have negotiated notable agreements in Pennsylvania, Colorado, New York, Tennessee, California, and other states. In California, the Los Angeles Women's Coalition for Better Broadcasting—made up of seven women's organizations in the Los Angeles area—was formed specifically to work toward the goal of obtaining improvements in the broadcast media through negotiated agreements with all licensees in the area. Coalition members monitored radio and television programs, obtained affidavits from women at the stations to document employment conditions, and studied the stations' ascertainment procedures.

In some cases the process involved taking legal action. In 1976 the coalition went to court seeking to obtain an FCC hearing, which the commission had refused to grant them, on their petition to deny the license renewals of KNXT-TV, CBS's Los Angeles station, and KTTV-TV, the Metromedia station.

In other cases, agreements have been reached. In 1974, the Los Angeles Women's Coalition for Better Broadcasting signed agreements, basically similar, with Los Angeles stations KNBC-TV and KABC-TV, the NBC- and ABC-owned stations in that city.

The Los Angeles Coalition for Better Broadcasting consisted of the following groups at the time of the KNBC-TV and KABC-TV negotiations: the Los Angeles Metro Caucus of the National Women's Political Caucus, the Media Group of the Los Angeles Women's Liberation Union, the California Public Interest Research Group, the Women's Equity Action League of Los Angeles, the National Organization for Women, the Comision Feminil de Los Angeles, the California Citizen Research Group, and the Career Planning Center.

The agreement that the coalition negotiated with KNBC-TV was signed by Raymond J. Timothy, vice-president and general manager for KNBC-TV, and stated in a letter of understanding dated October 29, 1974, addressed by him to the coalition members. Excerpts are reprinted here.

LOS ANGELES WOMEN'S COALITION FOR BETTER BROADCASTING AGREEMENT WITH KNBC-TV

After a series of meetings with members of your organization in which we discussed a proposed agreement submitted by your organization to KNBC on September 27, 1974, KNBC is prepared to effectuate the following relating thereto. This letter will be filed with the Federal Communications Commission and will become part of the station's application for renewal of its license. In view of these undertakings, the Coalition affirms its determination to take no action in respect to KNBC's license renewal application. . . .

(1) ASCERTAINMENT OF COMMUNITY NEEDS

(a) KNBC will welcome the establishment of a women's Advisory Council ("WAC") by the Coalition and will meet at least quarterly, at mutually convenient places and hours, with WAC to discuss the problems, needs, and interests of women in the Los Angeles community as well as all other topics encompassed in this letter.

(b) KNBC will establish and maintain a women's resource bank to which the station will refer in seeking qualified female spokespeople to appear on its locally produced programming and news when, in the exercise of KNBC's good faith judgment, such spokespeople are needed.

(c) KNBC will consider for broadcast, in the exercise of its good faith news judgments, information submitted by the Coalition or any women's news sources regarding possible news stories and events. All such information should be directed to the assignment editors of KNBC News. . . .

(2) NEWS REPORTING

In the area of news reporting, KNBC is cognizant of the Coalition's concern with respect to the use of certain prefixes, pronouns, stereotypical language, and other descriptive terms and phrases, and certain interviewing methods, which the Coalition believes are unnecessary, if not demeaning. Accordingly, KNBC is prepared to consider the institution of a series of sensitivity sessions for management level employees and employees with programming and news responsibilities as referred to elsewhere in this letter and will endeavor to continue to avoid the use of such terms and phrases and interviewing methods.

(3) PROGRAMMING

(a) As a matter of policy, KNBC has not and will not accept any program the purpose of which, in the opinion of KNBC, is to ridicule, attack or otherwise misrepresent any individual or group on the basis of race, creed, color, national origin or sex. . . .

KNBC will discuss any Coalition allegation of derisive programming at the above-described meetings with WAC, and KNBC will advise appropriate NBC personnel of any such allegations directed to network programming or programs supplied by outside packagers. KNBC will, as KNBC deems it necessary, endeavor to arrange meetings between the WAC and appropriate network personnel or program packagers.

(b) KNBC has not and will not broadcast any commercial message which, in its good faith opinion, is demeaning to any individual or group. KNBC will discuss any Coalition allegation that a commercial is derogatory or demeaning at the above-described meetings with WAC, and KNBC will advise appropriate advertisers or advertising agencies in the case of local commercials or appropriate NBC personnel with regard to network commercials. In addition, with respect to such allegations, KNBC will, as KNBC deems it necessary, endeavor to arrange meetings between the WAC and advertisers or advertising agencies.

(c) Public Service Announcements. KNBC will consider for broadcast any public service announcements related to the women's movement for equality and woman's role in American society provided such announcements are informational rather than controversial in nature and otherwise comply with KNBC policies and broadcast standards.

(d) Public Affairs Programming. With respect to public affairs programming, KNBC broadcast "The Quiet Revolution of Mrs. Harris," "Working Women and Your Organization," "To Be a Woman," "Momma," "Gloria Steinem," "Women in Law," "August 26 Feminist Celebration" and other programs dealing with aspects of the feminist movement and women's roles in American society.

As a result of input received in response to its ascertainment efforts, KNBC will broadcast during prime time three (3) 30-minute public affairs programs of a similar nature by the end of the 1975–76 broadcast season.

In addition, KNBC will consider in good faith increasing its coverage of issues of concern to women in other programs broadcast during prime time and other periods of the broadcasting spectrum. Furthermore, if the results of its on-going ascertainment efforts conducted during the 1975–76 and 1976–77 broadcast seasons warrant, KNBC will broadcast during the 6:00 P.M. to 11:00 PM prime time period three (3) 30-minute public affairs programs, or an equivalent amount of other such prime time programming, during each of these broadcast seasons.

However, KNBC firmly believes that any additional specific commitment of program hours to such programs would be contrary to the spirit of the ascertainment concept and a deviation from programming flexibility which, according to the Federal Communications Commission, KNBC is required to maintain.

(e) Editorials. KNBC has and will continue to present editorials and replies in opposition thereto in accordance with the dictates of the Fairness Doctrine and the results of its ascertainment efforts.

KNBC welcomes comments on editorial opinions and is willing to broadcast responsible opposing viewpoints. Thus, KNBC circulates copies of each editorial and editorial responses to numerous community leaders and organizations within its coverage area, and will add the Coalition, as well as each of its constituent groups, to its mailing list.

(f) Instructional Programs. KNBC will consider in good faith a wide range of female role models in all instructional programs.

(4) EMPLOYMENT

(a) KNBC has adopted an Affirmative Action Program for the employment of minorities and women at KNBC. KNBC has established three-year objectives, which the station will in good faith endeavor to achieve, for the employment of women, with particular emphasis on the employment of women in the top four categories of Officials and Managers, Professionals, Sales Workers (which includes Account Executives) and Technicians (skilled). As of December 31, 1973, twenty-six (26) women were employed at KNBC in the top four categories. Consistent with the spirit of its Affirmative Action Program, KNBC will increase the number of women in the top four categories combined by at least nine (9) additional women during a period beginning January 1, 1974, and ending December 1, 1977, subject to the following:

1. No decrease in the turnover rate during that period.

2. No adverse change in business conditions. In the event of adverse business conditions the station will be relieved of the specific obligation of adding 9 women by 12/1/77. However, the station will continue to hire and terminate without regard to race, color, creed, age or sex.

3. Availability of applicants who, in the good faith opinion of KNBC, are qualified for the position KNBC is seeking to fill.

(b) KNBC will continue to encourage women to enter all phases of the broadcasting industry . . . providing full opportunities for the hire, transfer, and promotion of women into positions of greater responsibility in this connection:

1. When recruitment takes place at universities or colleges, female students will be affirmatively encouraged to apply for all positions for which applicants are being sought. Further, if recruitment takes place at primarily male institutions, like recruitment efforts will take place at institutions where there is significant female enrollment and affirmative efforts will be made to secure female interviewers.

2. Where advertisements are utilized to solicit applicants for positions at KNBC, such employment advertisements will be placed in media which have significant circulation among women in the Los Angeles area. The Coalition will furnish KNBC with a list of such media.

(c) In its application for employment KNBC will eliminate questions relating to marital status, number of children, height, weight, and number of persons dependent upon the applicant for support, nor will the above factors be considered as criteria for employment. . . .

(d) KNBC does not and will not penalize female employees requiring maternity leave with respect to job status or seniority.

(e) KNBC has urged and will continue to urge unions with which it has agreements to cooperate in the development of programs to assure qualified female persons equal opportunity in employment and such union contracts include a provision designed to eliminate discrimination based upon sex.[14]

With few exceptions, the image of women on entertainment television remains distorted. Despite significant gains and some notable but scattered breakthroughs by women, male characters continue to dominate the TV screen, and male producers, writers, and directors greatly outnumber women in those jobs. That was the major finding of a report released in 1990 by the National Commission on Working Women of Wider Opportunities for Women (NCWW/WOW) and Women in Film (WIF).

The report found a paucity of strong female characters, a dearth of minority characters other than blacks, and a television world that resists portrayal of women over 40.

"TV's universe is at odds with reality," said Sally Steenland, the report's author. "In the real world, women don't disappear at age 40, they don't wear bikinis when they answer the door, and they rarely need to be rescued."[15]

The 80 entertainment prime-time series and 555 characters examined for the report—titled "What's Wrong with This Picture?"—all appeared during the spring 1990 season on ABC, CBS, NBC, and Fox. The report also documented the percentages of women producers, writers, and directors on the 80 shows studied.

"The bias on the TV screen," as Steenland pointed out, "extends not only to gender but to race as well. The emergence of the black sitcom has boosted the numbers of black women on entertainment series, but such shows rarely tackle the real-life issues of prejudice."

The report noted that other minority groups on TV have not noticeably grown during the 1980s: Hispanics, Asians, and Native Americans remained virtually invisible.

"The reason behind TV's distorted picture of women," Steeland added, "is that women continue to be outsiders to the industry. The reality is that the majority of female characters on TV continue to be created and written by men producers and writers. They are women seen through men's eyes. Far too few women create female characters; almost none create male characters."[17]

In Canada, MediaWatch: National Watch on Images of Women in the Media, Incorporated, has headed the monitoring of print and broadcast media in that nation. MediaWatch traces its origins to 1981, when it grew out of a subcommittee of Canada's National Action Committee on the Status of Women. By 1983, MediaWatch had become a national, independent, nonprofit feminist organization. Among the first directors of MediaWatch were four of the public members of the 1979–81 Task Force on Sex-role Stereotyping of the Canadian Radio-Television and Telecommunications Commission (CRTC), the government agency that regulates broadcasting in Canada.

Originally intended as a vehicle for educating Canadian women and girls about issues of sexism in the media, and suggesting ways in which they could communicate their criticisms to the broadcasting and advertising industries, MediaWatch has since expanded its mandate from that of facilitating a complaint process to one that includes the promotion of legislative change, public education, and consumer advocacy, the development of educational and media literacy materials, and research.

Below are excerpts from MediaWatch's brief to the CRTC in June 1991, urging the commission to strengthen its initiatives in holding broadcast licensees responsible for eliminating sex-role stereotyping in the portrayal and employment of women.

1991 MEDIAWATCH RECOMMENDATIONS

Most of the following 24 recommendations have been presented previously to the Canadian Radio-Television and Telecommunications Commission. They represent a position which MediaWatch has developed over the course of the evolution of public policy and legislation concerned with media sexism. This position has been articulated in the numerous presentations, briefs and public-notice response MediaWatch has produced in the last 10 years.

MEDIAWATCH RECOMMENDS THAT THE CRTC

RE: PUBLIC PARTICIPATION

1.1   Conduct hearings across the country that would enable full public participation in discussions and evaluations of public policy in the areas of gender stereotyping and employment equity in the Canadian broadcasting system.

1.2   Create a supervisory body, with public participation to monitor self-regulation and request reports from industry groups. The body will be responsible for issuing rewards and penalties.

1.3   Compensate intervenors in hearings on license renewals. Eligible costs would include those incurred in childcare, travel, accommodation, research and preparation. This compensation should be automatic when an intervention documents non-compliance with guidelines or employment equity by licensees. In other worthy cases, the Commission could exercise its discretion.

1.4   Instruct the Canadian Association of Broadcasters to consult further with representatives and groups informed about the issue of gender stereotyping in the media for revising the Code and Guidelines on gender stereotyping.

RE: SELF-REGULATION

2.1   Conclude on the basis of the evidence that self-regulation has not succeeded in eliminating gender stereotyping in the broadcast media, nor has it even succeeded in improving the image of women in the broadcast media.

2.2 Conclude that a further period of self-regulation will not produce better results and may in fact reflect a decrease in concern on this issue.

2.3 Acknowledge that legislation and regulation are required to improve the participation and portrayal of women in the broadcast media.

2.4 Reaffirm that compliance with the guidelines is a condition of all broadcasting licenses.

RE: REQUIREMENTS OF INDUSTRY

3.1 Require a commitment by all broadcasters to improve the portrayal and representation of women in advertising and in all categories of programming as a condition of license with a goal of achieving equal representation and portrayal for women and men within five years.

3.2 Require that broadcasters achieve equal representation between females and males in news and information programs in on-air roles for anchors/hosts, reporters, interviewees (including experts) within the next license period.

3.3 Develop gender balance indicators for programming and advertising based on those developed by Erin Research, that may include the following:

    i. program staff and persons interviewed in sports by gender;

    ii. apparent age of characters by gender;

    iii. primary roles of performers in television variety by gender;

    iv. on-air radio roles by gender;

    v. roles of major characters by gender;

    vi. characters' dress by gender, etc.;

    vii. voiceovers by gender.

3.4 Require promises of performance submitted on each license or renewal application to contain targets to be achieved on gender balance indicators within the license period.

3.5 Establish apprenticeship programs in television and radio production. The improved portrayal of the four disadvantaged groups (aboriginal peoples, women, persons with disabilities and visible minorities) is contingent upon their increased participation in the broadcasting system. Apprenticeship programs are a way of attaining this.

RE: CRTC RESPONSIBILITIES

4.1 Review the promises of performance of broadcasters at each license or renewal application to determine if the gender balance targets are realistic in light of the overall goal of equal participation and portrayal within five years, and require amendment if necessary.

4.2 Monitor individual stations' broadcast content for compliance with the guidelines at the time of license renewal.

4.3 Monitor broadcast content of overall radio and television programming and advertising again in 1992.

4.4 Apply the principles of employment equity to all broadcasters as required by the Broadcast Act, and require the submission of employment equity reports by broadcasters to the CRTC annually.

4.5 Require from broadcasters in fulfillment of the condition of license that they document the courses provided to their employees, attendance records and plans for future workplace consciousness-raising initiatives.

4.6 Withhold license renewal until compliance has been demonstrated or suspend or revoke license where there is failure to comply with the condition of licensee or to meet gender balance targets.

4.7 Encourage and facilitate the appointment of women to the CRTC with a goal of equal representation among commissioners by the year 2000. One criterion for appointment of Commissioners should be a demonstrated interest in improving the status of women, thereby ensuring that with the benefit of this expertise the Commission can play a leadership role in bringing just representation and portrayal for women and minorities to broadcasting.

4.8 Establish a 1-800 line for registering public comments on broadcast advertising and programming; record and report on all calls received.

RE: GOVERNMENT

5.1 Require that all government organizations employ women for half of their advertising voiceovers.

RE: PUBLICLY-FUNDED MEDIA AGENCIES

6.1 Insist on equal representation for women on the boards of the POR-TRAYAL, Telefilm and all other publicly-funded agencies in the cultural sector, giving special consideration to women from disadvantaged groups.

6.2 Require that the Canadian Broadcasting Corporation set aside specific time and resources for the development of projects from and about the four disadvantaged groups.[18]

Notes

1. Public Laws 88-352 (July 2, 1964), as amended.

2. Dorothy Austin and Jean Otto, "The Media: Where Sex Gets in the Way," *Once A Year*, Milwaukee Press Club (1972): 10.

3. The Wire Service Guild, Local 222 of the Newspaper Guild, news release, June 15, 1983, from Box 3 of the Tad Bartimus Papers, Joint Collection, University of Missouri Western Historical Manuscript Collection–Columbia and State Historical Society of Missouri Manuscripts.

4. M/G and Casey, Incorporated, Detroit, news release, November 23, 1983, from Box 5 of the Donna Allen Papers, Joint Collection, University of

Missouri Western Historical Manuscript Collection–Columbia and State Historical Society of Missouri Manuscripts.

5. Equal Employment Opportunity Commission report of findings, June 1974.

6. Settlement with *The New York Times*: Women Win Numerical Goals and Timetables Providing 1 in 8 Top Corporate Positions and 1 in 4 News and Editorial Positions," *Media Report to Women* (December 31, 1978). This special issue of *Media Report to Women* is entirely devoted to details of the settlement.

7. "Merit Pay at *Fresno Bee* Prompts Bias Complaint," *Guild Reporter* (March 24, 1989) 3.

8. "About and By Women: A Study of Photos, Bylines and Sources on the Front Pages of 20 U.S. Newspapers," a joint project by Media Watch: Women and Men and the American Society of Newspaper Editors' Human Resources Committee, April 1990. Available from the Communications Consortium, 1333 H Street, NW, 7th Floor, Washington, DC 20005. A similar study of 15 Canadian newspapers was released May 6, 1991, by Canada's MediaWatch: National Watch on Images of Women in the Media, Inc., (address in footnote 18).

9. Cherie S. Lewis, "Women Challenge TV Licenses to Get Stations to Listen Up," *Mediafile* (August September 1988): 3.

10. Matilda Butler and William Paisley, *Women and the Mass Media: Sourcebook for Research and Action* (New York: Human Sciences Press, 1980), p. 326.

11. FCC 91-176, *In re License Renewal Application of Certain Commercial Television Stations Serving Philadelphia, Pennsylvania*, Memorandum Opinion and Order, released July 5, 1991, adopted July 7, 1991.

12. Lewis, "Women Challenge TV Licenses."

13. Filed with the Federal Communications Commission (FCC) by the National Organization for Women (NOW), May 1, 1972.

14. In letter of understanding from Raymond J. Timothy to Los Angeles Women's Coalition for Better Broadcasting, October 29, 1974.

15. Sally Steenland, "What's Wrong with This Picture?" report prepared for the National Commission on Working Women of Wider Opportunities for Women (NCWW/WOW) and Women in Film (WIF), 1990. Available for $18 from the National Commission on Working Women of Wider Opportunities for Women, 1325 G Street, NW, Lower Level, Washington, DC 20005.

16. Steenland, "What's Wrong with This Picture?"

17. Steenland, "What's Wrong with This Picture?"

18. MediaWatch brief, in response to Public Notice CRTC 1990–114 (December 28, 1990), "Review of Policy on Sex-role Stereotyping," Vancouver, BC, Canada, June 1991. MediaWatch address: 517 Wellington Street, W, Suite 204, Toronto, Ontario, Canada M5V 1G1.

22

Women in Journalism Today

In the 1990s, women's increased presence in news and news reporting is apparent. The employment challenges of the 1970s, and continued monitoring of employment progress and news content through the 1980s and into the 1990s, have reduced the number of obstacles faced by women as journalists and as objects of news and feature coverage.

Women are now better positioned in the profession to prevent stereotyping, foster new thinking about definitions of newsworthiness, and ensure balance in coverage—in terms of issues covered and points of view included.

"The gatekeepers, to some extent, control what's in the paper," said Katharine Graham, chair of the Washington Post Company. "If more women are in responsible jobs, other topics might get different play. Just to use the example, in the earlier part of this decade [the 1980s], we didn't really follow the abortion legislation through Congress, because men weren't as interested."[1]

The debate over whether women have different values and therefore make different news judgments has not been settled. What has been acknowledged, even by the most traditional of news executives, is that mass media cannot succeed with mass audiences if they are produced only by an elite segment of the audience—white males—and exclude other groups.

At a time when there are more media to choose from than ever before, and as the mass media struggle with reinventing themselves to appeal to more sophisticated, discriminating audiences, diversity of gender, age, and race in news and entertainment employment and portrayal are essential.

Women are important to that process.

"A major shaping force for women both in the news media and in other parts of the culture is that an unparalleled event has occurred in the U.S. paid labor force in the past two decades," said Jean Gaddy Wilson, executive director of New Directions for News (NDN), in 1988. "Since 1960, more than a million women a year have joined the work force, with an increase of 28 million women during the past 26 years. Just within a 10-year period, women changed work patterns substantially. Females were 38% of the work force in 1970 and 42.5% of the paid labor force in 1980. Today they are 44%."[2] Journalism and its allied fields have been powerful magnets for women. The increasing number of working women in general has been mirrored by the media industry. Additionally, more women now aspire to the profession: In journalism schools in the United States, women students outnumber men.

But at this point, the influence of women in journalism has not matched their larger presence in the field. At U.S. newspapers, 35 percent of the work force is female, 65 percent male. About half of new employees are female. Yet women hold only 15 percent of executive positions.[3]

"The overall employment of women as newspaper managers continues to grow in tiny increments," Wilson said. "In 1977, women made up 5.2% of all newsroom managers. In 1987, the level was 13%, just 0.6% over the 1986 level. This snail's pace is typical of the past decade, even though women have made up a majority of journalism school undergraduates since 1977."[4]

Among publishers and general managers, 79 of the 1,454 individual unit heads counted in 1987—5.2 percent—were women. About one-fourth of these were employed by Gannett Company, Incorporated, the largest newspaper publishing group in the United States.[5]

Additionally, newspaper readership by women has declined. There was not much difference in average daily readership between men and women until the late 1970s and early 1980s, according to the Newspaper Advertising Bureau. Since then, women's readership has declined at a slightly faster rate than men's.[6]

In broadcasting, women hold about one-third of the jobs in both TV and radio news—a proportion that has changed little in recent years. Women were news directors at 18 percent of the TV stations and 25 percent of the radio stations surveyed by Vernon Stone for the Radio–Television News Directors Association in 1989—the same as in 1988. Stone found that women and minorities were being hired at rates higher than their existing share of the news work force. While 33 percent of all TV news staff were women, 44 percent of new hires were female. Similarly, in radio, where 32 percent of the work force was female, 44 percent of the new hires were women.

Most supervising was being done by white men, next most frequently by white women, Stone found. Women were supervisors in about the same proportions as their shares of the news work force.[7]

At the networks (including CNN and PBS), in 1990 women correspondents reported only 15 percent of the news stories—a decline of one point since 1989. The number of women newsmakers and experts interviewed on camera increased just 2 percent.[8]

In another survey of 1990 network evening newscasts, only five women appeared in a list of the 50 most prominent network reporters ranked by their number of appearances in newscasts.[9]

Breaking into Broadcasting

Broadcast news remains among the most competitive areas of contemporary journalism, for men as well as women. Evaluation of on-air "talent" goes beyond assessing news-gathering skills and ability to report, articulately, live; also factored in are audience response and the opinion of talent consultants. Appearance and looks matter.

Television reporter/anchor Christine Craft ran smack into a wall of preconceived notions about how a female anchor should look and dress in her tenure at KMBC, a Metromedia station in Kansas City. Craft was axed as a news anchor by the station after management received a consultants' report that said the viewing audience thought she was "too old, too unattractive and not sufficiently deferential to men."

"I know it's silly," Craft recalls her supervisor saying, "but you don't hide your intelligence to make the guys look smarter."[10]

It was 1981. Craft was 37 years old.

Craft sued Metromedia. Her case went through two trials. Both times, juries found in her favor and awarded damages. However, the verdicts were overturned on appeal. Craft appealed to the U.S. Supreme Court, which declined to review the case. Justice Sandra Day O'Connor, the only female on the nation's highest court, was the only justice who favored hearing the case.

Older, experienced women journalists continue to be passed over for anchor positions while their male contemporaries and younger females take those slots. A 1988 study by Victoria M. Fung, conducted while she was a scholar-in-residence at the Gannett Center for Media

Studies (now the Freedom Forum Media Center) at Columbia University, uncovered "a widespread belief in the industry that little had changed, that being young and gorgeous matters more for high-profile, on-air women than professional qualifications and journalistic grounding."[11]

In Fung's survey, nearly two-thirds of the male correspondents were between the ages of 40 and 50; nearly two-thirds of the females were between 30 and 40. Among up-and-coming women, many lack the hard-news reporting experience gained from covering domestic and foreign beats. Much of their track record has focused on anchoring, Fung said.

"The frightening prospect for today's younger women is that they are perhaps being groomed for short-term use, that they'll never get a crack at critical assignments such as anchoring national political conventions and international crises, and that they'll simply be replaced by younger women as they get older," Fung concluded.

Off camera, women's track record is improving, although it is unusual for women to be more than one-fifth of the engineers, editors, and producers.[12] The networks and their local affiliates face increasing competition from cable television and other forms of video entertainment, making for a much tougher competitive climate. This requires cost-cutting, which has included reducing staffs. In turn, this means reduced opportunities.

CBS producer Joan Snyder recounted her odyssey into television news production in a 1988 lecture at the University of California at Berkeley's Graduate School of Journalism. Snyder was one of the first female field producers in network television news. She began working for CBS News in the 1960s. Her lecture, "The Only Girl on the Road," is reprinted here.

THE ONLY GIRL ON THE ROAD

I was a first in many ways, not because I was a Susan B. Anthony of the newsroom. Everything just happened to me by accident. I had not thought of television when I started. I wasn't someone who majored in communications and dreamed of becoming a local anchor woman. It never crossed my mind. I was the first female college correspondent for the *New York Times*. And I was supposed to get a job there after I graduated. Unfortunately, I was missing from campus the day that the story of the year erupted.

That was the end of my print career.

This was a time, in the 1960s, when it was very hard for a woman to get a job in journalism. You were told you could never be anything but a researcher. All the writers were men.

If you did go somewhere where there might be an opening, they would say, "You'll only get married and run off." And you would practically have to take vows of chastity and obedience.

I finally got a job in what was like the coal mines, at United Press International. However, there was no discrimination against women. It was a union shop. Everybody earned $53 a week. And I opened the shop at five in the morning, after taking a bus through the New Jersey meadows at four in the morning. And then, you'd get in and change the paper, and prop up a newspaper in front of you and compose right on the machine. That was the highest order of talent.

After a time doing this, I decided I was going to try to get a job in San Francisco. But while I worked as a temporary secretary, I got a letter from a friend of mine who said, "I've gotten a job with CBS News."

So I went back to New York and I applied. The vice president in charge said, "You have to come in at midnight to Grand Central Station. Girls don't want to do that." And I said, "I've just finished running through Newark at dawn to open the bureau." He said if I did that, I'd do anything. So they gave me a chance as a writer.

You'd think with the millions of dollars of broadcast equipment in that industry, you'd go in and get a little training. Not so. My first night there, it was midnight, and I thought we'd have a little seminar on how to write for television. There was nobody there except a young man in a plum-colored velvet suit. I thought he was the producer. But he was the desk assistant, like a copy boy. He was sitting there writing a biography of P. G. Wodehouse. I said, "Where's the producer?" And he said, "He's over at the Pentagon getting drunk, as usual."

This staggered me. I thought he'd flown to Washington to get drunk with the generals and colonels. It turned out to be the name of the bar across the street. I said, "Well, who's writing the show?" He said, "You are, honey. There's one other writer here. He's been here a week. He knows what he's doing. He'll help you." And there was a guy, lying on the floor, staring at the ceiling for inspiration. He's become a writer of novels since then.

He was lying there, and I said, "Are you going to show me how to write this script?" And he said, "Sh, sh, I've got to think." I stared at him for a while. In walks this beautiful young woman dressed in black leather from head to toe, black glasses, and she says to him in a foreign accent. "You forgot to give me the key." He threw it at her and she vanished.

And I said to myself, this place is a madhouse. So when the producer lurched in, he said, "Use an old script and see if you can figure out how to do it."

Fortunately, in those days, nobody watched the morning news. There were three announcers, one of whom was exactly like Ted Baxter of *The Mary Tyler*

Moore Show, and if the film broke, or if one guy's contact lens popped out in mid-sentence, he went poking around for it, and nobody really cared.

That was good, because one day I was trying to put a script in order, and he went on the air while I still had the script. He didn't know what to say. So I threw it at him, and it was all out of order. He introduced the Secretary of State, and up came an ice skater. And the director said to me with his mouth open, "What's going on?" I said, "The script is all out of order, he doesn't know what he's doing." And he said, "OK, as long as I know."

It was strangely informal. There were no female writers at the time. There had been one during World War II. She'd gotten promoted by the time I got there. But she'd never actually gone out and directed a camera crew, which is what field producing is all about. Working as a writer here was sort of like being an elaborate ventriloquist. You had to master the style of each guy—Walter Cronkite is very different from Mike Wallace, who is very different from Charles Kuralt—and write in their style. By the time I reached Walter Cronkite, I had some experience in producing.

We had a show called *The Morning News* with Mike Wallace. They didn't have enough producers, so they gave us the chance to work all night writing and, for no pay, run around during the day with a camera crew. I did it because I really wanted to be a producer.

The camera crews at that point were essentially drunken, psychotic, woman-hating, talentless creeps. I'm not exaggerating. They would say to me, "I can't take this shot, it's too light, it's too dark, it's too hot, it's too cold." And what did I know? So I'd say, "Try it anyway." It was a desperate situation. The drunken cameraman would disappear. I lost him in the middle of Chinatown, if you can imagine such a thing. I had to go to every bar saying, "Grey-haired man with camera?"

I really wanted to be a permanent producer, but they kept saying, "Wait, your turn will come. It's not the right time for a woman." Finally, it really became necessary to get another job. I was writing about space for Walter Cronkite.

You know how enthusiastic he was about space, and I had to write these animations about the glimace dropping off the framace, while the little parachute hit the lummock and I would get it backwards. And he would say, "No, no, Joan. The parachute hits the glimace and then the lummock."

I could never get it right, and things were really going downhill when a guy named Paul Greenberg who had seen me do those little pieces around town and had a budget for one producer on the weekend news, decided he was going to hire me. And he had to fight with management, who said, "You can't have her with these coarse brutes of cameramen. Girls can't do it, it's too dangerous, too exhausting."

And they fought about it for a while, and I took the old vow: "I will do anything a man would do." What I didn't realize was they were setting up "man," in the image of Ernest Hemingway or Arnold Schwarzenegger. There were plenty of men who wouldn't do all the fearsome things I figured you had to do to be a producer.

In any case, for my first story, I went to Chicago. They said, you've got to shoot this right away, no time for research. I get to Chicago, and the producer had said, "I see an old lady, sitting on a porch, playing the banjo, singing sad songs of home." Well, this was November in Chicago. There are no porches, no old ladies. And every time we tried to get into a building, the Appalachians, who turned out to be very proud, threw us out. Once, looking down the barrel of a gun, and once, chasing us across the lot with dogs.

This story was not going well. Furthermore, the camera crew wouldn't take orders from me. They were very upset about having a female director. And I would very timidly say, "Do you think you could take a picture of these kids looking out the window?" And the cameraman would pretend I wasn't there, and he'd say to the reporter who really didn't know what he was doing, "Let's get a picture of those kids looking out the window."

So, that was the real test. I will say that being a woman in television in those days was horrible when it came to the correspondents and the camera crews. They were extremely resentful, very prone to poke fun in a very hurtful way.

While you would occasionally work with a brilliant, nutty genius like Hughes Rudd, you also worked with a lot of reporters who didn't know what the story was about. It is very much a producer's field in a lot of ways. It's the producer who decides how the story is going to be shot, lines up the day's events, who to talk to, directs the entire shooting.

Then I started doing most of my stories as a producer and reporter. And one of them means a lot to me because of what happened afterwards: that's the story on doctors in rural America.

The Appalachian Regional Commission had been trying to reach President Carter to re-fund it and they decided they weren't going to do it. But after the piece appeared, Jimmy Carter's aides called them, and said we didn't know how bad the situation was, we are going to keep the clinic open. In a world where you see so much misery that you wish you could do something about, sometimes it helps to be reminded that television can have a tremendous impact.

One of the things that happened over the years is that the stories got shorter and shorter. Stories that we would have complained about telling in five minutes if you go over two minutes in hard news, it's considered an extravaganza.

The cutbacks have had profound effects on what we shoot and the way we shoot. When something is not done as well as it could or should be, it's "quick and dirty." Quick and dirty has come to symbolize what they want to do—make a lot of money for the stockholders. There's still some fine work being done, but it's much harder to do it. My career really paralleled the opening, enriching of television. It was when field producing was just being discovered. It was when television got a half hour, with crews all over the world. From the late 1960s to the late '70s was indeed the golden age of television news, when we were free to work long, spend a lot, and do our best work.

The contraction came after that. It's still possible to do long, thorough and good pieces on our documentary units. But there's now the frustration of trying to cram a tremendous amount into a short time.

There's a theory now, that audiences get bored if they see anything longer than two-and-a-half minutes. The fact that *60 Minutes* is the most popular newscast ever just doesn't seem to convince people. People get bored when something goes by so fast they can't get into it or understand it. Not when something is good and holds one's attention.

I have a new job now. I'm on *Sunday Morning* with Charles Kuralt. But I have to tell you that they've laid off about 2,000 people in the past few years. The last was 215 people on what we called Black Thursday last March. I was out on the street shooting a story about the homeless looking for work. While I was out there a guy came over and said, "I used to be a reporter for the *Atlanta Constitution*, and the whole thing drove me to drink, especially after I became an ad man. I'm much happier now. I live in a clean Chinese flophouse and I'm writing a novel." And I said, "We should all get the address probably."

Little did I know. I went back to the office and found out that my best friend at CBS had been laid off after 25 years with the company. I was shocked, even though a lot of good people had been forced to leave. I couldn't believe it. And then somebody tapped me on the shoulder, and it turned out that I was on the list as well. It had nothing to do with work, they assured me, it was just that a certain number of people had to be gotten rid of. So, thanks for everything and good-bye.

It was like *Death of a Salesman* repeated hundreds and hundreds of times. Especially when you consider that we've had so many stories about the cruelty of corporations that throw out good workers after a lifetime with the company, I was more enraged than anything else.

They asked me if I wanted to finish shooting the story I'd begun on finding work for the homeless. And I said, "Thanks just the same, but the next time you'll see me I'll be clearing out my office."

And there I was clearing out my office four days later when the producer came in and said, "Congratulations. You've been re-instated." And it turned out that my old friend Mike Wallace had raised hell about this. And when Mike talks, the president of CBS News listens.

And my first reaction was, "I'll have to think about it." It wasn't the company I had known and had grown up with, and where I had a marvelous and enriching time. But I did stay and joined *Sunday Morning* because there's nobody greater than Charles Kuralt.[13]

Breaking Down Gender-based Assignment Patterns

Twentieth-century editorial tradition has held that women were unsuited for some assignments. News beats dominated by males, or expected to generate reports for predominantly male audiences, usually were closed to women. This narrowed women's chances for varied reporting experience, thus affecting their prospects for advancement and, of course, for higher pay. Among these beats have been business, sports, and foreign/war correspondence.

Women business reporters and editors remain in the minority at the top U.S. business magazines and the top 25 newspapers. Men outnumber women staffers at the top business magazines by 2:1, according to the newsletter the *The Journalist and Financial Reporting*. Of the top 25 newspapers, only three—the *Detroit News, Newsday,* and the *Newark Star-Ledger*—have women heading up their business coverage.[14]

In sports, attitudes of players, coaches, and owners to the presence of women sportswriters in locker rooms for postgame interviews exploded in September 1990. *Boston Herald* sports reporter Lisa Olson went to the New England Patriots' locker room at the request of a player whom she had approached for an interview. Olson had twice requested the interview be conducted in the football stadium's media room, but the player asked her to come to the locker room after practice. It is, in fact, customary for many interviews to be conducted in locker rooms when team members are fresh from practice or a game and can provide an immediate reaction to the team's performance.

On that day, however, a naked Patriots player taunted Olson with lewd comments and suggestive body language. Encouraged by several other players, he accused her of "looking, not writing." The ugly scene was compounded when Patriots owner Victor Kiam later appeared to side with the players. Ultimately, three players were fined, and the team and Kiam apologized to Olson in a letter and full-page newspaper ads.

But for Olson, harassment continued—from the fans. She was jeered at games played in Boston—even when she switched to covering Boston's basketball team, the Celtics. She received threatening phone calls. She was spat upon. In April 1991, Olson filed a suit against Patriots management and the three players, asking for monetary compensation for sexual harassment, civil-right violations, intentional infliction of emotional distress, and damage to her professional reputation. She also left Boston to work in Australia under a newspaper exchange program.

The Olson case is unique only for the viciousness of the incident and the initial reaction of the team's management, which suggested that Olson somehow deserved the treatment she got. Lesser offenses had occurred prior to that incident, ever since women sportswriters began pressuring for the same access to players their male counterparts had. The National Hockey League was the first to allow women reporters into its locker rooms, in 1976. In December 1977, *Sports Illustrated* reporter Melissa Ludtke filed a federal sex discrimination suit to force major league baseball to open its locker rooms to women. (The suit ultimately led to open access for all sports.) At about the same time, sportswriter Betty Cuniberti, then of the *Washington Post*, obtained what is thought to be the first locker-room interview by a woman covering the National Football League (NFL).

In the years since, men's professional teams have grudgingly come to accept the necessity of reporters, including women, in the locker room after a victory or a defeat. But this does not mean that all athletes or team managers will always cooperate. Less than a month after Lisa Olson was harassed in Boston, *USA Today* reporter Denise Tom was barred from the Cincinnati Bengals' locker room. Then–Bengals coach Sam Wyche received a stiff $30,000 fine from the NFL commissioner, Paul Tagliabue, who also levied the penalties against the three Patriots players and the team's management.

Only a few days before Wyche refused to allow Tom entry to the locker room, Tagliabue had sent a directive to NFL teams, urging them to review with coaches the league's media policy, "particularly the section pertaining to equal access and treatment of all accredited members of the media."

Christine Brennan of the *Washington Post* is a former president of the Association for Women in Sports Media. She recounted her experiences covering the NFL's Washington Redskins for the *Washington Post Magazine* in 1988. An excerpt from that article appears here.

MY THREE YEARS COVERING THE REDSKINS

Three years ago, my editors at the *Post* asked me to cover the Redskins. I said yes. I was thrilled. It was not that I was a fan of the team; I'm not. And if I had been a fan, I would have quickly severed my allegiance when I took over the beat. Being a fan and being a reporter don't mix, as I think you'll see.

No, I simply thought it was a great assignment. As a journalist, I would root for the story. This was the best sports beat in town. I was glad to have it.

So in 1985, I enthusiastically walked into the lives—and locker room—of the players, coaches and management of the Washington Redskins. I was then and still am the only woman who has ever covered the Redskins. To do my job, I spent practically every day from July to January with the team: training camp, practices, home and away games.

Some on the team and in the media thought this was a big deal, but, to me, there was no reason to fuss. I had been a sportswriter for nearly four years at the *Miami Herald* before coming to the *Post* in 1984. I covered the University of Miami during its first national championship season. I covered the Dolphins off and on and was one of the first women in their locker room. I covered four consecutive college national championship games. I watched Bernie Kosar, Jim Kelly and Vinny Testaverde practice together. I had been in men's locker rooms about 50 times. Dealing with the unusual demands of being a woman in a man's world was no particular problem for me.

I even had the cocktail-party stories down pat. The two most-asked questions of a woman sportswriter:

1. Do you get into the locker room?
2. What do you see?

Yes.

Not a whole lot.

Now 29, I have been playing or watching sports for as long as I can remember. I grew up with a Tony Cloninger mitt on my left hand, a baseball—not a softball—in my right hand, and a bunch of baseball cards stuffed into the front pocket of my pedal pushers. I was bigger than many of the boys in my neighborhood. (At 5–11, I still am. I'm taller than six Redskins and can see eye-to-eye with nine others.)

I spent hours playing catch in the backyard with my father. I never threw like a girl. I recently tossed a 15-yard spiral toward Redskin assistant coach Dan Henning, who had thrown the ball to me. I must have surprised him. He dropped the pass.

I was a great fan, too. I kept score of all the Toledo Mud Hens games off radio broadcasts in 1968. I was 10. Three years later, for Christmas, my parents gave me a trip to the Tangerine Bowl to watch the University of Toledo Rockets play Richmond. I couldn't think of a greater gift.

I went to Northwestern to become a journalist. I got my bachelor's and master's degrees and soon headed into sports, the so-called toy department of newspapers. I realized I got paid to do what most people pay to do—go to sporting events. This wasn't work. It was a joy.

But I soon found out that sports isn't all fun and games when you're holding a notebook in one hand and a pen in the other. I had to ask players why they were playing poorly. I had to write about controversial injuries. I had to report why someone was about to be traded. I had to ask nasty questions about drugs and financial problems and personality clashes and divorces. I didn't always like doing this, but I did it.

It turns out many of the Redskins didn't like my doing it, either. What I didn't realize as a sports fan, but now know quite well as a sportswriter, is that to simply inform fans about their team can cause all sorts of problems for the person doing the informing. And, sometimes, I never fully understood why.

Perhaps my troubles began because I am a woman. Perhaps they started because I ask a lot of questions. Perhaps it's because I work at the *Post*, a newspaper that is not exactly universally loved by the men and women who work at Redskin Park.

You see, I thought I was just doing my job when I asked the owner of the Redskins if the team was considering trading a key player. I didn't expect such a simple question would cause me to be declared *persona non grata* by one of the world's richest men for three months.

I thought I was well within my rights to write about the contract that the team's general manager was about to sign. I didn't expect him to get angry and refuse to give me a private interview for nearly two years.

And I figured if a former star player on the management staff said something on television, I could report it in the sports pages of my newspaper, right? Wrong. I did that and it ended a fine working relationship I had with that good man—just like that.

Now, three seasons later, I'm leaving the Redskins, moving on to cover the Winter and Summer Olympics. I've come through my stint on the beat in one piece. I enjoyed it—mostly. I'm unscathed. I still think I have the greatest job in the world. But I'll tell you this: The past three years, I ran into the strangest occupational hazards.

For a while, unbeknownst to me, I was the alibi for a player who was cheating on his wife. One of the player's buddies on the team stopped me one day and said that if the player's wife ever asked, I had called their house to interview him.

I didn't get it.

"You see, (Madame X) called one night and (Player X) told his wife it was you."

"Oh, great," I said.

Another time, a player told me word was out in the locker room I was having an affair with a local sportscaster who is married. I wasn't, but that didn't stop players from giggling every time they saw the unsuspecting announcer talking to me. I later told my TV friend. He told his wife. I told a guy I was dating. I think we had the last laugh.

Another player asked me once to stop talking to him as I passed by his locker at Redskin Park.

"The players are gossiping," he said.

This was my first year on the job, so I asked him why this was happening.

"Remember, we're talking about football players," he said. "They have nothing better to talk about."

I probably had a dozen players ask me out. Some were married, some weren't. Maybe I should have expected this. I didn't, at first. Politely, I said no. The tendency was to tell some of them to take a hike. I didn't. What if I had to interview them the next day?

One night, right on deadline, I was typing on my portable computer in my Redskin Park cubicle when I looked up and saw a married member of the Redskin organization (I'm not saying whether it was a player, coach or team official) staring down at me, smiling.

"Do you stay at the same hotel as the team?" he asked.

"Yes."

"Would you like to get together this weekend?"

"No thanks," I said.

He pressed the issue. I politely stood my ground. Within a few seconds, he turned to go.

Then he swung back toward me.

"Would it be okay if I kissed you?"

"No!" I said, startled.

He walked away. I looked back at my computer screen. I'm pretty good at blocking out the strange and bizarre, but this was just too strange and too bizarre. I stared at the screen. I couldn't focus. I had trouble concentrating for a couple of minutes.

The phone rang. It was one of my editors.

"What's taking so long?"

"If you only knew," I told him.

Sometimes, my job got outrageous. Three-hundred-pound defensive tackle Dave Butz laughingly told me if I insisted on interviewing him while he was naked, I should be naked, too. Actually, I avoided naked football players at all costs. I prefer it when the people I interview have their clothes on. A woman in the locker room is a hot topic for some, but consider this: I spent only about four hours out of my 60-hour work week in the Redskins' locker room at practice and after games. (Male reporters had the same time limits.)

In the locker room, I tried to act nonchalant. I maintained eye contact. I made beelines to lockers. I carried large notebooks that conveniently blocked my view of certain areas, should I look down.

But you can't plan for everything. The players knew to expect reporters from noon to 1 p.m. before practice. A few minutes after noon one day, I opened the large, red locker room door and stepped right in.

Whoa!

It was Mark Moseley. Barechested. Pulling on his football pants. Mooning me. (He didn't mean it.)

"Sorry, Mark," I said, turning away.

"We're going to have to put a cowbell around your neck," he said.

It seemed as if we were always dealing with clothes—or the lack thereof. Never had I received so much attention. Some of the players critiqued my outfits, my coat, my silly off-white winter hat, my fur-lined gray winter boots.

"Is it snowing out?" offensive tackle Joe Jacoby wondered when he saw the boots on my feet on a 45-degree day.

He teased me out of wearing them for a few days, until the temperature dropped below freezing.

"The boots are back!" guard R. C. Thielemann exclaimed later. I've got to hand it to R.C. He's observant. Every day I wore the boots, he noticed and said something.

Butz noticed me, too.

"No women in the locker room!" he said 586 times in the three seasons I was in the locker room.

I hated Butz, I loved Butz. He actually had a rule that he wouldn't speak to me in the locker room. He doesn't believe women belong there.

Yet he willingly came to Redskin Park on a day off and spent an hour with me for a feature story I was doing on him. I can't think of another player who would do that.

This season, Butz wanted so badly to play against the New York Jets in the first game after the strike that he checked himself out of the hospital Sunday morning with the flu, but he played very well. Unbelievably well, considering he had lost 20 pounds that week, according to [Joe] Gibbs.

After the game, I wanted to check that figure with Butz, so, despite his rule, I went up to his locker and asked my question.

"Dave, did you lose 20 pounds this week?"

"I don't talk to you in the locker room," he reminded me.

"Well, I'd like to get this right, Dave, with your help."

He shook his head.

I looked around and saw Frank Herzog from Channel 7 approaching Butz.

"Frank, will you do me a favor and ask Dave if he lost 20 pounds this week?"

Herzog: "Dave, did you lose 20 pounds this week?"

Butz: "I lost about 21."

I nodded at Frank, nodded at Butz and walked away. I had my answer.

I never could get too furious with Butz. In my first year, he was concerned that someone was hassling me in the locker room with sexual jokes. Defensive end Dexter Manley had beckoned me over to his locker once, yelling, "Come here, I've got something to show you."

Yeah, right, Dexter.

So, a few days later, after a Redskin victory, Butz called me to his locker for a rare conversation.

"Is anyone bothering you in here?"

"No," I said, stifling an inclination to say, "Yes, you."

"Well, if anyone ever gives you a hard time in here, you just let me know, and I'll take care of them."

I looked up at Butz in disbelief. He was serious. I thanked him and walked away.

More than a year later, over the phone, I finally asked why he did that.

"Because, even if I don't like it that you're in there, you should be treated right when you're there," he said.[15]

Different challenges awaited the women journalists who were assigned to cover the Persian Gulf War. A short but intense conflict that held the world spellbound began in August 1990, when Iraq invaded its neighbor Kuwait. As a group of allies led by the United States began to move troops and weapons to the Saudi Arabia peninsula, journalists began to pour into the region. The military carefully controlled the journalists' movements, restricting most of their attempts to cover the war to shared reports from small pools of escorted reporters. The sophisticated management of news coming out of the Persian Gulf region enraged and frustrated news organizations. Women journalists—about 10 percent of the correspondents registered with military officials there—confronted the additional impediment of working in a society where women are not permitted to operate motor vehicles and are required to keep their bodies completely covered, even in the blistering Gulf heat.

It was a stretch for even the most seasoned reporters. "Add to the inherent challenges [of war] the fact that you're a woman, limited in your movements and behavior, outnumbered and often dependent on men," and you begin to appreciate the complexities of covering the Persian Gulf War, wrote Maria Wilhelm of *People* magazine.[16]

The small number of women journalists in the Gulf reflect traditional gender patterns of overseas assignments. As Wilhelm noted, it also indicates that the view of Nicholas Horrock, Washington bureau chief of the *Chicago Tribune*, is clearly a minority view. Horrock says there is "a tremendous advantage of having a woman (war) correspondent. She's usually less involved in the male bonding, macho thing in the field, and can be more detached about what she covers."[17]

CBS News correspondent Betsy Aaron was a 1991 recipient of a Breakthrough award from the media-monitoring group Women, Men, and Media for her "courage and compassionate coverage of the Persian Gulf War." She has more than 27 years of journalism experience and has reported extensively on the Middle East. Asked if she thought women tend to be more compassionate and antiwar, Aaron said,

I think that's a crazy premise. I think that women have the guts to express their feelings. . . . For example, I was covering the war in Cyprus, and we went to a mass grave. . . . [A]nd all the men were running around taking pictures of the bodies. I looked over and saw all the relatives of these dead people, and that's what brought tears to my eyes, and that's what made me angry, and that's the story I did. Those people were dead. There was nothing I could do about it. But look at what war does to people: look at what it does to families: look what it leaves behind. That's what I saw that the men don't see.[18]

In March 1991, the International Women's Media Foundation and the National Press Club convened a panel called "Women Covering the War." Five women correspondents who had recently returned from the Persian Gulf discussed their experiences. Excerpts from the comments by Linda Pattillo, ABC News, and Christiane Amanpour, Cable News Network (CNN), appear here.

FROM "WOMEN COVERING THE WAR"

CHRISTIANE AMANPOUR:

The Gulf War was my first major story; certainly my first international story. I'd just been made a foreign correspondent about two months before that.

On August 2nd, when Saddam Hussein invaded Kuwait, I didn't know about it until I got into the office [in Paris], and I immediately called up Atlanta, which was our headquarters, and said I want to go. And they said no, no, no, we've got it covered, you know, people are going. And I said well, it's the overnight warriors, and I'm just going to go and make a reservation. So I went into my office, and I booked a ticket for myself and my crew. And I said, look, just in case. And they said, Oh, thank God. We couldn't find the rest—we couldn't get anybody else in, and the connections from everywhere else are terrible, so you've got to go.

So we packed and we were off in about an hour or two, and we were going to Kuwait City. And we didn't know at this time that the airport was closed, so at the airport at Frankfurt we were diverted. We went to Dubai, so we covered, like most of the press, the story from Dubai for the first few days.

Then I went off to Cairo for the Arab League Summit, and then, August 16th, I went to Saudi Arabia, and was there until the first of February. So it was a very long trip.

As for being a woman, at no time did it ever come up, at least with, you know, my editors. They never—it was never an issue. I was just the first person who was available. And I went. And even in Saudi Arabia I would not say that I was treated any—that I was hindered at all by being a woman.

And interestingly for me, I had a female crew, my camera woman and my sound woman. And I think that we were such a curiosity item and such novelties. We sort of turned up on the first day and wanted to do what everybody else was doing. And the Saudis, particularly, were very taken aback; they're not at all used to dealing with women. And I think most often they sort of said yes, because they didn't know how to say no. [Laughter.]

So we got a lot of access, and we were very, very well received by the military, particularly—it's not surprising—particularly by the troops in the field. They were thrilled, usually, to see us as they were to see everybody, because we were their contact with the outside world. They were trying to live in a very inhospitable situation, and we brought them news. They like to talk to us as women, just as they like to talk to everybody else. On that level it wasn't difficult at all.

I was surprised that we in fact got so much access and so much freedom as women in Saudi Arabia, because unlike the Saudis and the other Arabs there we did not have to cover ourselves, we didn't have to veil ourselves, which I had to do when I went to Iran, which is not as conservative as Saudi Arabia. So in that respect it was OK. Oh, we couldn't drive. That was a big pain in the neck.

But on the other hand, I found that I got some quite good access on the social side of Saudi Arabia by being a woman to the women's stories. I did a lot of the women's stories in the beginning. I broke the story of the women's driving protest, purely because I happened to know the women who were involved, some of them, and they called me. So on that level it was OK.

So I had no complaints about being a woman in Saudi Arabia. I enjoyed it.

LINDA PATTILLO:

At 5 a.m. on the morning of January 15th, the phone rang in my Dhahran hotel room and Cathy O'Hearn, the L.A. Bureau chief who was serving as Dhahran bureau chief, said, "Combat pool no. 2 is being called up. I really hate to do this to you, but we think it's a 48-hour trial run for the new people who just joined the pool so that if and when a war starts in a few weeks everyone will know what equipment to bring with them."

Six and a half weeks later I returned to the Dhahran hotel. [Laughter.] I took 40 pounds of gear with me including my chemical suit and my mask, everything that has been issued by the Military JIB (Joint Information Bureau) in Dhahran, and set out with the Second Marine Division to the desert, and was successively moved further north, finally ending up, as a result of the ground war, on the outskirts of Kuwait City.

It was a lot of misery in the desert; I won't try and hide that. We never had a tent. We occasionally had hot food. Showers were extremely infrequent, and towards the end I guess we went about three weeks without access to a shower.

I'd like to say, though, that I don't think that my experience was any different from my male colleagues when it comes to misery. I mean, they didn't have a tent, they slept on the ground, as well as I did. They didn't have latrines.

Certainly in terms of frustrations, though, with the pool system, it was certainly an equal-opportunity war. I don't think there was any difference in being male or female as far as that goes.

In many ways the desert was a welcome escape from being a woman in Dhahran. I had extreme difficulty with the Mutawa—the morals police in Dhahran. About every three days I would go out, and I would be stopped by them and told to cover my hair. One day they said my ankles were showing. [Laughter.] Although I found there are certain analogies between Saudi society and the U.S. military as the war progressed [Laughter.], by virtue of the Marines not putting women in combat roles, even in support roles, really, I ended up being the only woman with the lead regiment of the Second Marine Division. I knew Molly [Molly Moore of the *Washington Post*] was out there somewhere on the battlefield with General [Walter E.] Boomer but not in the same area as I was.

So it was about, I'd say, 5,000 Marines and myself for the four days of the ground war with that division. And I think one of the most memorable experiences of the ground war, aside from being extremely frightened and then shocked at the outcome of what one person called "a fairy tale war," was we had just spent three hours going through the initial breach, through the two obstacle belts. It was frightening, and there was artillery going around on both sides, and the Humvee [armored military vehicle] in front of us had hit a mine. We finally cleared the second minefield, and the combat engineers who had— you know, these very brave units who had gone in first and blown the mines and were standing there kind of directing this, you know, just miles and miles of tanks and Humvees coming through the minefields—and the three guys were standing there, kind of in their bunker, making sure no one broke down, and as we went by I kind of looked over the side of the Humvee, and one guy goes, "It's a *chick*, man!" [Laughter.][19]

Toward Nonstereotypical News Coverage

Has it made a difference? Has the increasing involvement of women in reporting and editing news influenced definitions of news and news-worthiness, and broadened the thinking of the gatekeepers?

The answer must be a cautious maybe, suggest researchers and professionals who scrutinize the American news media. It is also clear that much more work remains to be done before parity and gender-neutral coverage are newsroom standards.

Here are some snapshots of what has been learned since women began agitating for social change in the 1960s:

- In the pioneering study of how newspapers covered women's issues, conducted at George Washington University in 1983, it was determined that ten of the United States' most outstanding newspapers largely ignored or missed opportunities to inform the readers about the impact on them of changing trends in domestic relations, the Equal Rights Amendment, national and international women's conferences, pay equity, and lack of enforcement of laws prohibiting discrimination in education.[20]
- Since by-line studies were first done in the 1960s, reader preference for stories done by males seems to have disappeared. In a 1989 study that tested receptivity to male and female by-lines, Ford Burkhart and Carol Sigelman of the University of Arizona found that audiences

judged articles similarly, regardless of the gender of the by-line. Women were rated no differently than men with regard to bias or the level of information in their stories.[21]

- The Sunday morning "opinion leader" programs have a deplorable record when it comes to the race and sex of their guests. An analysis of program guests on *Meet the Press* since its inception in 1947 through mid-1989 found that 96.3 percent of the guests were male, 93.2 percent were white.[22]

- In an analysis of 15 studies conducted between 1973 and 1988 on the way in which women are portrayed in newspapers, Marilyn Greenwald found "a consistent pattern of unequal treatment of women in the news pages. Interestingly, the treatment of women on the news pages seemed to improve only slightly—or not at all—from the National Organization for Women's 1973 study until recently, despite the entrance of more and more women into the work force since the mid-1970s, and despite the increasing media coverage given to the women's movement and women's rights."[23] Greenwald also noted a study of business section editors that indicated "even when women are equally represented on an editorial staff—or even head one—the editorial representation of women within pages is still not equal to that of men."[24]

- In 1989, the Amateur Athletic Foundation of Los Angeles monitored local and national sports reporting on television, including at the national-level major events such as the National Collegiate Athletic Association (NCAA) "Final Four" basketball tournaments and the U.S. Open tennis tournament. According to their findings, women's sports were underreported and underrepresented in the six weeks of television sports news sampled in the study. Men's sports received 29 percent of air time, women's sports 5 percent, and gender-neutral topics 3 percent. TV sports news did focus regularly on women, but rarely on women athletes. More common were portrayals of women as comical targets of the newscasters' jokes and/or as sexual objects (e.g., women spectators in bikinis). Though the televised sports news was clearly biased against women, in basketball and tennis coverage there was very little of the overtly sexist language, sexualization, and/or devaluation of women athletes that existed in the recent past. In fact, there appeared to be conscious efforts made by some commentators to move toward nonsexist reporting of women's sports.[25]

- A survey of the three major U.S. newsweeklies—*Newsweek, Time,* and *U.S.News and World Report*—released in October 1990 by

Women in Communications Inc. showed a decline in the number of references and photos of women and a slight increase in the number of female by-lines, compared to the results of a similar study in September 1989.[26]

- In February 1991, as the Persian Gulf War dominated the news, a Women, Men, and Media study found that the vast majority—70 percent—of the articles appearing in its sample of newspapers were about men, their jobs, their weaponry, their opinions. Stories about female soldiers were rare; but when they did appear, most often they centered on the women's parental status. Quotes from female soldiers—whether mothers or not—were seldom, if at all, included in these stories. Photos of females during the reporting period were most frequently of women at home showing concern for or grieving over loved ones who were involved in the Middle East. A curious phenomenon was the editorial and news-copy fervor over the impact on families of women going to war. Although most such articles were critical of mothers going to war and expressed extreme concern about the impact on children, there was not one article or editorial on the impact of a father's leaving his children to go to war.[27]

Pulitzer prizewinner Susan Faludi has criticized the news media's pattern of developing "trend stories" about women without making an earnest effort to solicit the views of women the trend is supposed to exemplify. (This same practice was criticized in the George Washington University 1983 analysis of newspapers mentioned above.)

> The trend story is not always labeled as such, but certain characteristics give it away: an absence of factual evidence or hard numbers; a tendency to cite only three or four women, qualifiers like "there is a sense that" or "more and more"; a reliance on the predictive future tense ("Increasingly, mothers will stay home to spend more time with their families"); and the invocation of "authorities" such as consumer researchers and psychologists, who often support their assertions by citing other media trend stories.[28]

Monitoring of news coverage continues, as does the movement of women into and upward in the communications field. But the evidence compiled over the past two decades indicates that the influence of women journalists on coverage decisions lags far behind their presence in the profession.

Notes

1. Katharine Graham, quoted in "Women, Men and Media: Your Guide to the Future," conference program, Washington, DC, April 10, 1989.

2. Jean Gaddy Wilson with Iris Igawa, University of Missouri Graduate School of Journalism, "Women in the United States: Opportunities Today in Employment and Promotion," paper for the International Group for the Study of Women, 1988 Tokyo Symposium on Women, August 25–27, 1988, p. 11. Available in the Joint Collection, University of Missouri Western Historical Manuscript Collection–Columbia/State Historical Society of Missouri Manuscripts.

3. American Society of Newspaper Editors, "The Changing Face of the Newsroom," report, 1989. ASNE address: P.O. Box 17004, Washington, DC 20041.

4. Jean Gaddy Wilson, "Women Make Up 13 Percent of Directing Editors at Dailies," *ASNE Bulletin* (January 1988): 15.

5. Wilson, "Women Make Up 13 Percent of Directing Editors."

6. Albert E. Gollin, "Circulation and Readership Trends and Prospects," address to the American Newspaper Publishers Association Circulation and Readership Committee, Reston, VA, March 15, 1991, p. 7.

7. Vernon A. Stone, "RTNDA Research," Radio–Television News Directors Association *Communicator* (August 1990): 32.

8. "Women, Men and Network News: A Study of Network News Coverage by and about Women" (an annual survey of Women, Men and Media, a project headquartered at New York University), October 1990, p. 2. Additional information on this report is available from the Communications Consortium, 1333 H Street, NW, Washington, DC 20005.

9. Center for Media and Public Affairs study, cited in John Carmody's "The TV Column," *Washington Post*, March 11, 1991, p. B8.

10. Christine Craft, *Too Old, Too Ugly and Not Deferential to Men: An Anchorwoman's Courageous Battle against Sex Discrimination* (Rocklin, CA: Prima Publishing and Communications, 1988), p. 66.

11. *Media Report to Woman* (November/December 1988): 6.

12. Jean Gaddy Wilson, "Women in American Journalism," *Media Report to Women* (March/April 1988): 11.

13. Joan Snyder, "The Only Girl on the Road," lecture, Graduate School of Journalism, University of California at Berkeley, March 7, 1988.

14. *Journalist and Financial Reporting* (June 1988), quoted in *Media Report to Women* (July/August 1988): 6–7.

15. Christine Brennan, "Who Is Christine Brennan and Why Are Jay Schroeder and Joe Theismann and Bobby Beathard and Jack Kent Cooke Always Yelling at Her? Covering the Redskins Is a Great Job, but Still a Job," *Washington Post Magazine*, January 24, 1988, pp. 12–15.

16. Maria Wilhelm, "The Burden of Being Female," *Dateline*, annual magazine of the Overseas Press Club (April 23, 1991): 22–23.

17. Wilhelm, "Burden of Being Female," pp. 22–23.

18. Katherine Turman, "In the Trenches: Reporter Betsy Aaron Discusses the Gulf War and the Battle of Being a Female Journalist," *Village View* (April 12–18, 1991).

19. "Women Covering War: A Panel Discussion," sponsored by the International Women's Media Foundation and the National Press Club, Washington, DC, March 26, 1991.

20. "New Directions for News: A Newspaper Study," sponsored by the Women Studies Program and Policy Center of the George Washington University, Washington, DC, September 1983. The newspapers that participated in the NDN study were the *Arizona Daily Star, Atlanta Journal and Constitution, Cincinnati Enquirer, Dallas Times Herald, Denver Post, Detroit Free Press, Los Angeles Times, Miami Herald, New York Times, St. Louis Post-Dispatch.* The independent think tank, New Directions for News (NDN) at the University of Missouri, is the outgrowth of this landmark research.

21. Ford Burkhart, "When Readers Prefer Women," *Editor & Publisher,* July 22, 1989, pp. 64 and 54.

22. Mark D. Harmon (of Texas Tech University, Lubbock), "Who Will Meet the Press? A Content Analysis of Program Guests," paper presented to the Association for Education in Journalism and Mass Communication, Minneapolis, August 1990, p. 5.

23. Marilyn S. Greenwald (of Ohio University), "The Portrayal of Women in Newspapers: A Meta-analysis," paper presented to the Association for Education in Journalism and Mass Communication, Washington, DC, August 1989, p. 6.

24. Greenwald, "Portrayal of Women in Newspapers,"

25. Amateur Athletic Foundation of Los Angeles, "Gender Stereotyping in Televised Sports," report, August 1990, pp. 2 and 4.

26. Women in Communications Inc., "Second Survey of News Magazines Shows No Improvement in Coverage of Women," news release, October 12, 1990.

27. Women, Men, and Media, University of Southern California (now headquartered at New York University), "As the Gulf War Raged, the Gulf between News Coverage of Women and Men Continued," report, April 8, 1991.

28. Susan Faludi, *Backlash: The Undeclared War against American Women* (New York: Crown Publishers, 1991), p. 81.

23

Language and Image Guidelines

Long a subject of contention in publishing circles has been the use of special language to describe women and girls, or to single them out as being unusual in their achievements because they are women or girls, as if they have overcome a handicap. Language subtly confers acceptance on people; it can empower them or diminish them, depending on how it is used. It can also render them invisible.

The process begins early in life. Textbooks and children's storybooks socialize youngsters to what is customary and expected behavior for boys and girls, men and women. The scenarios used in children's stories and elementary school readers show them the heights boys and girls can reach—or the limits on them.

In her speech accepting the Dodi Robb Award from Canada's MediaWatch in 1990, Doris Anderson, former editor of *Chatelaine* magazine, said,

If a six-year-old child from Patagonia were to sit in front of a TV screen and without knowing anything else about North America, form her impressions from what she saw, she would come to the conclusion:

- that men outnumber women five to one;
- that most women must die before middle age;
- that women must be far more warm-blooded than men because they wear a lot fewer clothes;
- that the most important thing about the North American home is to keep it clean;
- that North American children spend all their time getting dirty and eating;

- that dogs and cats in North America are more intelligent than people.[1]

The socialization of children is deeply influenced by the role models they find in their schoolbooks, the audiovisual resources of their school, and the learning situations their teachers create for them.

Parents—particularly mothers—who have grown concerned about stereotyping in textbooks and teacher's manuals, have banded together in many cities to evaluate the content and language of books being used in their schools. This scrutiny has also been extended to films, filmstrips, and programs on educational television used by the schools as part of their curriculum.

One of the first intensive studies, which evaluated 134 elementary school readers from 14 different publishers, was *Dick and Jane as Victims: Sex Stereotyping in Children's Readers*, compiled by Women on Words and Images, in 1972.[2] Their content analysis exposed a pattern of omission of women in American and world history, and compartmentalization of lifestyles and roles assigned to women. The Women on Words and Images could find almost no mention of single parents or working mothers.

The little girls in the readers studied had low expectations of their ability to achieve. They joined little boys in putting themselves down. Neither girls nor boys expressed a realistic range of emotions, and little boys were further stifled in their need to express sorrow, joy, or compassion. The researchers noted a lack of closeness between husbands and wives. Most interaction, they said, was between parent and child.

Complaints about the sex-role assignments in children's textbooks soon reached the school boards in many cities and counties. Parents and teachers in many locales have organized committees against sex stereotyping, which monitor acquisitions of teaching materials in their school districts and file complaints if the books, filmstrips, or TV programs are found to be sexist. These groups find support in Title IX of the Civil Rights Act, which prohibits discrimination on the basis of sex in any education program or activity receiving federal financial assistance.

The publishing companies began to feel the pressure mounted by coalitions of parents, school board members, and women's groups. They also began to hear from their own employees, both women and men. Several textbook companies, working through committees formed internally, drew up and issued guidelines to prevent sex stereotyping in the educational materials they published. Excerpts from three of these manuals appear here.

GUIDELINES FOR EQUAL TREATMENT OF THE SEXES IN MCGRAW-HILL BOOK COMPANY PUBLICATIONS
McGraw-Hill Book Company

The word *sexism* was coined, by analogy to *racism*, to denote discrimination based on gender. In its original sense, *sexism* referred to prejudice against the female sex. In a broader sense, the term now indicates any arbitrary stereotyping of males and females on the basis of their gender.

We are endeavoring through these guidelines to eliminate sexist assumptions from McGraw-Hill Book Company publications and to encourage a greater freedom for all individuals to pursue their interests and realize their potentials. Specifically, these guidelines are designed to make McGraw-Hill staff members and McGraw-Hill authors aware of the ways in which males and females have been stereotyped in publications; to show the role language has played in reinforcing inequality; and to indicate positive approaches toward providing fair, accurate, and balanced treatment of both sexes in our publications.

One approach is to recruit more women as authors and contributors in all fields. The writings and viewpoints of women should be represented in quotations and references whenever possible. Anthologies should include a larger proportion of selections by and about women in fields where suitable materials are available but women are currently underrepresented.

Women as well as men have been leaders and heroes, explorers and pioneers, and have made notable contributions to science, medicine, law, business, politics, civics, economics, literature, the arts, sports, and other areas of endeavor. Books dealing with subjects like these, as well as general histories, should acknowledge the achievements of women. The fact that women's rights, opportunities, and accomplishments have been limited by the social customs and conditions of their time should be openly discussed whenever relevant to the topic at hand.

We realize that the language of literature cannot be prescribed. The recommendations in these guidelines, thus, are intended primarily for use in teaching materials, reference works, and nonfiction works in general. . . .

PORTRAYALS: HUMAN TERMS
Members of both sexes should be represented as whole human beings with *human* strengths and weaknesses, not masculine or feminine ones. Women and girls should be shown as having the same abilities, interests, and ambitions as men and boys. Characteristics that have been praised in females—such as gentleness, compassion, and sensitivity—should also be praised in males.

Like men and boys, women and girls should be portrayed as independent, active, strong, courageous, competent, decisive, persistent, serious-minded, and successful. They should appear as logical thinkers, problem solvers, and decision makers. They should be shown as interested in their work, pursuing a variety of career goals, and both deserving of and receiving public recognition for their accomplishments.

Sometimes men should be shown as quiet and passive, or fearful and indecisive, or illogical and immature. Similarly, women should sometimes be shown as tough, aggressive, and insensitive. Stereotypes of the logical male and the emotional, subjective female are to be avoided. In descriptions, the smarter, braver, or more successful person should be a woman or girl as often as a man or boy. In illustrations, the taller, heavier, stronger, or more active person should not always be male, especially when children are portrayed. . . .

DESCRIPTIONS OF MEN AND WOMEN

Women and men should be treated with the same respect, dignity, and seriousness. Neither should be trivialized or stereotyped, either in text or in illustrations. Women should not be described by physical attributes when men are being described by mental attributes or professional position. Instead, both sexes should be dealt with in the same terms. References to a man's or a woman's appearance, charm, or intuition should be avoided when irrelevant. . . .

In descriptions of men, especially men in the home, references to general ineptness should be avoided. Men should not be characterized as dependent on women for meals, or clumsy in household maintenance, or as foolish in self-care.

To be avoided: characterizations that stress men's dependence on women for advice on what to wear and what to eat, inability of men to care for themselves in times of illness, and men as objects of fun (the henpecked husband).

Women should be treated as part of the rule, not as the exception. Generic terms, such as doctor and nurse, should be assumed to include both men and women, and modified titles such as "woman doctor" or "male nurse," should be avoided. Work should never be stereotyped as "woman's work" or as "a man-sized job." Writers should avoid showing a "gee-whiz" attitude toward women who perform competently. ("Though a woman, she ran the business as well as any man" or "Though a woman, she ran the business efficiently.")[3]

GUIDELINES FOR CREATING POSITIVE SEXUAL AND RACIAL IMAGES IN EDUCATIONAL MATERIALS
Macmillan Publishing Company

THE 51% MINORITY

More than one-half of the population is female; yet a visitor from another planet, after examining most texts and readers, might assume that males outnumber females by at least ten to one.

GUIDEPOST:

In selecting authors, illustrators, and content of artwork, stories, poetry, non-fiction accounts, and examples, remember that half of the human population is female and should be represented appropriately in our textbooks.

The "Cheerleader" Syndrome

Girls watch boys build a treehouse, reward their big brothers with smiles when they solve a mystery; a mother stands at the kitchen door wiping her hands on an apron while father rescues a treed cat; women urge their husbands on to greater achievements and allow males to take credit for their ideas.

These prevalent images reinforce the notion of woman as passive onlooker, giver-of-support, and non-achiever. Such images act as a straitjacket to females and a painful hairshirt to males who suffer from constant pressure to prove themselves.

GUIDEPOST:

Emphasis should be placed frequently on portrayals of girls and women participating actively and positively in exciting, worthwhile pursuits, while males should be permitted often to observe and lend support. . . .

"The Emotional Sex"

"I'm scared," said Susan, clutching her brother's hand. She began to sob uncontrollably.

"That love stuff is for girls," said Jerry to his friend as they left the movie theater.

Once in a great while, traditional textbooks show little boys on the verge of tears, but they nearly always manage to choke them back bravely. Girls in such books, on the other hand, usually surrender to their fears and dislikes, to the point where they seldom take positive action. In this way, girls are used as a kind of foil to highlight male achievements. Thus girls are programmed to feel that "feminine" emotional weakness is desirable because it helps males build their self-esteem and, in turn, will spur males to solve all of life's problems. This attitude cripples males, too: they are learning contempt for females and an exaggerated image of masculine strength impossible to fulfill. They are being taught to be dishonest about their own feelings and to deny their expression. Boys and girls are further learning to be less than whole human beings when we reinforce the notion that tender emotions, such as love, sympathy, and caring, are acceptable only for one sex.

GUIDEPOST:

Boys as well as girls, women as well as men, should cry or otherwise respond emotionally when appropriate. They may also exhibit self-control and emotional courage in trying circumstances, especially when such restraint enables them to act positively. . . .

Women's Inferior Status—Cultural Perspectives

"The wives were not permitted to vote because the chairman felt they would, in effect, give their husbands a double vote for the same candidate."

"Colonial women were not allowed to own property."

"Cortez received an Indian girl as a present."

Statements such as the above that describe past sexism should be amplified by an explanation of the customs, discriminations, and economics involved. This should include the historical forces that created the inequality, the changes occurring today to ameliorate the situation, and the need for continued efforts to make equal opportunity a reality for women. When discussing male-dominated cultures, try to include specific statements about the suppression of women, and describe the contribution—however submerged—of women within the culture. Sexist statements and events might be included in stories and quotations, but should be cited as examples of attitudes no longer acceptable in our culture.

GUIDEPOST:

Sexist behavior and customs must not be accepted as "givens" but must be explained in the context of the culture and point in history. These explanations should appear in the student's materials, although they might be further amplified in the teacher's editions.[4]

GUIDELINES FOR IMPROVING THE IMAGE
OF WOMEN IN TEXTBOOKS
Scott, Foresman and Company

SEX-ROLE STEREOTYPING

Editors and authors should be cautious when they assign certain activities or roles to people purely on the basis of sex. Many such assumptions misrepresent reality and ignore the actual contributions of both sexes to the activity or role.

EXAMPLES OF SEXIST LANGUAGE:	*POSSIBLE ALTERNATIVES:*
In New England, the typical farm was so small that the owner and his sons could take care of it by themselves. Children had once learned about life by listening to aunts, uncles, grandparents, and the wise men of their town or neighborhood. . . .	In New England, the typical farm was so small that the family members could take care of it by themselves. Children had once learned about life by listening to aunts, uncles, grandparents, and the wise people of their town or neighborhood. . . .

Care must be taken to avoid sexist assumptions and stereotypes in teachers' manuals and other teacher aids.

EXAMPLES OF SEXIST LANGUAGE:	*POSSIBLE ALTERNATIVES:*
Hammers and scissors are good eye–hand coordinators. Hitting the nail instead of the thumb is a triumph for the boys. Cutting out paper dolls and their garments is good for the girls.	Hammers and scissors are good eye–hand coordinators. For a child, hitting the nail instead of the thumb or cutting out a recognizable shape is a triumph.[5]

Action for Children's Television (ACT) has been advocating the eradication of stereotyping since its inception in 1968. In 1971, ACT commissioned the first of an ongoing series of studies of sex roles and racial and ethnic portrayals in children's programs and commercials. Its advocacy work in alerting television executives to stereotyping in programming and advertisers to stereotyping in commercials has helped keep the issue before the public and has forced some adjustments in television images projected to young people.

In 1983, ACT introduced a booklet that offered concrete suggestions to help television fight racism and sexism instead of fostering them. In the handbook, *Fighting TV Stereotypes,* ACT called attention to research showing that racial and ethnic minorities, women, handicapped people, and senior citizens are underrepresented on TV, and that, if they are included at all, they are usually portrayed in a stereotyped manner.

"All television is educational TV to young viewers," said ACT. "By rarely treating women and minorities with respect, television teaches young girls and minority children that they really don't matter. And it teaches children in the white mainstream that people who are 'different' just don't count."[6]

Among ACT's recommendations for improving television's messages are these:

For the industry. Increase diversity in programming of all kinds: Hire and promote minorities and women, especially to decision-making positions; provide access to community groups to ensure a minority voice on cable, low-power, and local broadcast TV.

For the business community. Underwrite children's programs that reflect the interests and showcase the talents of minorities and women; support public television as a valuable TV alternative; fund education and promotion campaigns to develop new audiences and encourage community involvement.

For everyone. Watch TV with children and talk about the role models and stereotypes television provides; call, visit, or write to station managers, producers, writers, and advertisers to applaud, criticize, or suggest new ideas; become involved with cable to make sure children are served and that programming reflects local ethnic flavor and minority-group concerns; support policies at the local, state, and national levels that ensure fair representation for women and other groups—in television and in society at large.[7]

The 1970s were years of vigorous debate over exclusionary and sexist language in news accounts. At the same time ACT was commissioning its analyses of stereotyping on television, communications researchers and journalists began looking at the language used in news accounts of men and women and evaluating the relationship of words to reality.

Studying college students in 1972, sociologists Joseph Schneider and Sally Hacker found that the word *man*, used in the generic sense, meant different things to men and women students. One group of students was asked to look at textbook headings such as "Industrial Man" and "Political Man," while the other group was given corresponding, but nongender-specific, headings such as "Industrial Life" and "Political Behavior." To students of both sexes, use of the word *man* evoked images of males only; the nongender-specific heading evoked images of both males and females.[8]

"Aside from the use of the generic *he*, the use of the suffixes (also known as diminutives) *-ess, -ette,* and *-ix* to differentiate women perpetuates the idea of male-as-norm, female-as-deviant," writes researcher Elizabeth Tarnove.[9] Casey Miller and Kate Swift noted that the addition of such suffixes, even when intended as a courtesy, gives the basic form of the word "a predominately masculine sense with the unavoidable implication that the feminine-gender form represents a substandard variation."[10]

In an effort to make the language of its services inclusive, in 1989 the United Methodist Church published a new hymnal that corrected language considered to exclude women or deemed pejorative to racial minorities or people with handicaps. The hymnal was expanded to included hymns of non-European cultures to reflect all spectrums of the Methodist community.

With regard to language about women, the 1989 hymnal retained the traditional male imagery of God, such as "Father," "Master," and "King." But masculine pronouns such as "him" or "his" were omitted. References to all people as "men" or "brother" or "sons" were changed to gender-neutral substitutes—as in "Good Christian Men, Rejoice" recast as "Good Christian Friends, Rejoice."[11]

This dramatic rewriting of a liturgical work echoed the progressive reworking of language done in the professions during the 1970s. In 1977, the International Association of Business Communicators produced, *Without Bias: A Guidebook for Nondiscriminatory Communication,* a booklet offering guidance on how to encourage gender-neutral language and context in writing, visuals, and interpersonal contact, such as meetings.[12]

In 1975 the National Commission on the Observance of International Women's Year, appointed by President Gerald R. Ford, devoted part of its activities to evaluating the role of women in the media. In addition to compiling "Ten Guidelines for the Treatment of Women in the Media" (which are reprinted below), the commission drew up a "Checklist for the Portrayal of Women in Entertainment Programming and Advertising." It also recommended that the Department of Health, Education, and Welfare (now Health and Human Services) study the impact of television on sex discrimination and sex-role stereotyping, and schedule hearings—to be conducted by the U.S. Commission on Civil Rights—on the impact of mass media on women.

The IWY Commission's "Ten Guidelines" is a roundup of ideas that, by 1975, were showing the first signs of having an impact on the treatment of women in the news and the newsroom. Newspapers, magazines, and the wire services had begun to adjust their stylebooks to eliminate differences in writing about men and women newsmakers. Many newspapers dropped "Mr.," "Miss," and "Mrs." before surnames; and if they retain such titles, often they will follow the woman's preferred usage—including using "Ms." Nonessential references to the appearance of a woman are being discouraged.

The Stanford University Women's News Service recommended an "appropriateness" test to reporters: "When you have completed a story about a woman, go through it and ask yourself whether you would have written about a man in the same style. If not, something may be wrong with the tone or even the conception of your article. Think it through again."[13]

TEN GUIDELINES FOR THE TREATMENT OF
WOMEN IN THE MEDIA
By the IWY Commission

1. The media should establish as an ultimate goal the employment of women in policy making positions in proportion to their participation in the labor force. The media should make special efforts to employ women who are knowledgeable about and sensitive to women's changing roles.

2. Women in media should be employed at all job levels—and, in accordance with the law, should be paid equally for work of equal value and be given equal opportunity for training and promotion.

3. The present definition of news should be expanded to include more coverage of women's activities locally, nationally, and internationally. In addition, general news stories should be reported to show their effect on women. For example, the impact of foreign aid on women in recipient countries is often overlooked, as is the effect of public transportation on women's mobility, safety, and ability to take jobs.

4. The media should make special, sustained efforts to seek out news of

women. Women now figure in less than 10 percent of the stories currently defined as news.

5. Placement of news should be decided by subject matter, not by sex. The practice of segregating material thought to be of interest to women only into certain sections of a newspaper or broadcast implies that news, when no longer segregated, is not covered at all. Wherever news of women is placed, it should be treated with the same dignity, scope, and accuracy as is news of men. Women's activities should not be located in the last 30–60 seconds of a broadcast or used as fillers in certain sections or back pages of a newspaper or magazine.

6. Women's bodies should not be used in an exploitative way to add irrelevant sexual interest in any medium. This includes news and feature coverage by both the press and television, movie and movie promotion, "skin" magazines and advertising messages of all sorts. The public violation of women's physical privacy tends to violate the individual integrity of all women.

7. The presentation of personal details when irrelevant to a story—sex, sexual preference, religious or political orientation—should be eliminated for both women and men.

8. It is to be hoped that one day all titles will be unnecessary. But in the meantime, a person's right to determine her (or his) own title should be respected without slurs or innuendoes. If men are called Doctor or Reverend, the same titles should be used for women. And a woman should be able to choose Ms., Miss, or Mrs.

9. Gender designations are a rapidly changing area of the language, and a decision to use or not to use a specific word should be subject to periodic review. Terms incorporating gender reference should be avoided. Use firefighter instead of fireman, business executive instead of businessman, letter carrier instead of mailman. In addition, women, at least from age 16, should be called women, not girls. And at no time should a female be referred to as "broad," "chick," or the like.

10. Women's activities and organizations should be treated with the same respect accorded men's activities and organizations. The women's movement should be reported as seriously as any other civil rights movement; it should not be made fun of, ridiculed, or belittled. Just as the terms "black libbers" or "Palestine libbers" are not used, the terms "women's libbers" should not be used. Just as jokes at the expense of blacks are no longer made, jokes should not be made at women's expense. The news of women should not be sensationalized. Too often news media have reported conflict among women and ignored unity. Coverage of women's conferences is often limited solely to so-called "splits" or fights. These same disputes at conferences attended by men would be considered serious policy debates.[14]

The mass media have, to a large degree, incorporated these principles into their style manuals for their news staffs. But not all news organizations have caught up completely with the spirit, as well as the letter, of their rules. In her examination of the *Associated Press Stylebook*[15]—the most widely consulted style manual in the news business—Carole Eberly observed that "women are given low status or no status in the *Stylebook*. They are trivialized or just plain disappear."[16]

Eberly says the *Stylebook* states explicitly that "women should receive the same treatment as men in all areas of coverage. Physical descriptions, sexist references, demeaning stereotypes and condescending phrases should not be used." Nevertheless, stereotypes abound in examples the AP uses to instruct *Stylebook* users in the basics of AP style.

Eberly cited these, among numerous others: "To keep complement and compliment separate, the *Stylebook* has these examples: 'The ship has a complement of 200 sailors and 20 officers. The hat complements her dress. The captain complimented the sailors. She was flattered by the compliments on her outfit." And: "He goes to work every day. She wears everyday shoes. . . . The coach told him to hit and run. She was struck by a hit-and-run driver." Women do appear in nonstereotypical examples, Eberly says, but their treatment is inconsistent.[17]

This excerpt from *USA Today*'s Style Guide shows how one news organization specifies treatment of men and women.

SEXISM
From the *USA Today* Style Guide

Always refer to men and women equally and consistently.

Don't use patronizing descriptions of women, such as *the fair sex* or *the distaff side*.

And do not use irrelevant physical attributes to describe an individual: *a buxom blonde, a muscular 6-footer*.

COUPLES

• Do not assume that two people who live together are married. And when two people *are* married, do not assume that the woman prefers to use her husband's last name. Always ask individuals who are to be named in a story what surname they prefer. This applies to children as well. See the entry on LAST NAMES in the main portion of this book.

• In stories about married couples, steer clear of the temptation to identify one individual by his or her relationship to the other: Say *Mary Smith* rather than *his wife, Mary*. Avoid also any constructions suggesting that one partner is the possession of the other.

Wrong: *The pioneers moved West, taking their wives and livestock.*

Right: *Pioneer families moved West . . .*

(Note: The often-used *man and wife* is better phrased *husband and wife*.)

COURTESY TITLES MISS, MR., MRS. AND MS. are not to be used except in direct quotations. When two people share the same last name, most notably a husband and wife, distinguish between them on second reference either by using both first and last name or just the first name, according to the content and tone of the story.

The use of pronouns and other identifiers to avoid repetition of names is fine, but great care must be taken to ensure that it is clear from the context who is being referred to. If in doubt, use the individual's name rather than risk confusing the reader.

HIS, HER. Do not presume maleness in constructing a sentence, but use the pronoun *his* when an indefinite antecedent may be male or female: *A reporter attempts to protect his sources.* (Not *his or her sources*. But note the use of the word *reporter* rather than *newsman*.)

Better yet, when possible, revise the sentence slightly: *Reporters attempt to protect their sources.*

HOUSEWIFE (-HUSBAND). Use only in quoted matter. *Homemaker* is preferred for men and women.

SEX-SPECIFIC WORDS
• Do not use nouns that needlessly specify femininity, such as *authoress, murderess* or *comedienne*. Use *author, murderer* and *comedian* (or *comic*). Two exceptions: actress, waitress.
• Use generic nouns (or do not use sexual modifiers) for those working in fields traditionally dominated by either sex: Use *firefighters*, not *firemen*; *police officers*, not *policemen*; *nurse*, not *male nurse*; *secretary*, not *male secretary*.

SEXUAL STEREOTYPES. Do not express surprise or amusement when a sexual stereotype is broken:
Who would have dreamed that an NFL linebacker would do needlepoint?
She thinks as logically as any man, however.

SPOUSES. Because few groups any more are exclusively male or female, *spouses* should be used instead of *wives* or *husbands*: *The NOW members and their spouses toured the city. Employees and their spouses were invited to the party.*[18]

Writing About Sexual Assault

On July 11, 1989, the *New York Times* published a column by Geneva Overholser, editor of the *Des Moines* (Iowa) *Register* and a former member of the *New York Times* editorial board. In it she wrote,

I understand why newspapers tend not to use rape victims' names. No crime is more horribly invasive, more brutally intimate. In no [other] crime does the victim risk being blamed, and in so insidious a way: *She asked for it. She wanted it.* Perhaps worst of all there's the judgment: *She's damaged goods*—less desirable, less marriageable.

This stigma, this enormously unfair onus, brought most newspaper editors years ago to conclude that they shouldn't worsen the plight of rape victims by printing their names in the newspaper. . . .

Editors do not hesitate to name the victim of a murder attempt. Does not our very delicacy in dealing with rape victims subscribe to the idea that rape is a crime of sex rather than the crime of brutal violence that it really is?[19]

Overholser went on to say that she would continue to honor her newspaper's policy not to disclose the identities of rape victims, but she urged women who have been raped to identify themselves. "I believe we will not break down the stigma until more and more women take public stands," she wrote.[20]

Three weeks later, Nancy Ziegenmeyer of Grinnell, Iowa, walked into Overholser's office in Des Moines. She had read Overholser's column when the *Register* published it. "I want people to know my story," she said. The result, published serially in the *Register* during February 1990, told of Ziegenmeyer's rape, her assailant's trial, and her recovery. The *Register* and reporter Jane Schorer won a Pulitzer prize in 1991 for the series.

Ziegenmeyer's courage, and the *Register*'s commitment to publish the whole unsanitized version of what happened—not to an anonymous statistic, but to a woman who allowed her name to be used and personal details of her life to be included in the series—launched a debate in newsrooms around the continent: Should the media identify rape survivors? Who should decide—the media or the victim?

The majority of editors who spoke for publication on the issue were in favor of concealing the name of a woman who had been raped. At the *Des Moines Register* the policy now is to ask rape survivors if they are willing to be identified and to withhold their names if they are not. Many other papers share that policy, although there are exceptions: "The example I use is the governor's wife," said *Minneapolis Star Tribune* managing editor Tim McGuire. "We would use that name without permission."[21]

The readers of newspapers share the editors' reservations about naming women who have reported being raped. In March 1990, right after the *Register* series on Ziegenmeyer appeared and was picked up nationally, a poll conducted for *USA Today* found that 84 percent of those polled felt the rape survivor should be the one to decide if her name was to be used. Only 5 percent thought the media should decide whether to print or broadcast names.[22]

A year later, the debate was rekindled when NBC News, the *New York Times*, and a handful of other news organizations identified the woman who had brought rape charges against William Kennedy Smith, a member of the well-known political family. Michael Gartner, president of NBC News, wrote in a company memo that NBC News "will consider the naming of rape victims or alleged rape victims on a case-by-case basis." In the Smith case, Gartner made these points:

> We are in the business of disseminating news, not suppressing it. . . . [E]ditorial decisions should not be made in courtrooms, or legislatures or briefing rooms—or by persons involved in the news. . . . By not naming victims we are part of a conspiracy of silence. . . . [A]nd finally, there is an issue of fairness. I heard no debate in our newsrooms and heard of no debate in other newsrooms on whether we should name the suspect.[23]

In the case of the *New York Times*, a similar internal debate was conducted—not only about whether it was proper to identify the woman, but to discuss the nature of the story the *Times* ran about her. The story included details of her romantic history, her lifestyle, and information about her family. Reaction inside the newspaper was strong, much of it angry. More than 100 *Times* staffers signed a petition expressing "outrage" over the naming of the woman and the tone of the story, and the fact that up to that point the *Times* had not done a comparable story on Smith.[24]

In 1986, the Iowa Coalition Against Sexual Abuse produced "A Resource Guide: News Coverage of Sexual Assault," which contained guidelines for covering these kinds of cases. The suggestions below were developed by the Rape Victim Advocacy Program in Iowa City.

SUGGESTIONS FOR REPORTING OF SEXUAL ASSAULT CASES

The following considerations for reporting on sexual abuse are based on the experience of the Iowa Coalition Against Sexual Abuse in dealing with the concerns of sexual abuse survivors and on policies adopted by some news media organizations. The objective is accurate reporting of sexual assault that informs the public about the incidence of the crime. These considerations are intended to help protect survivors from harm and embarrassment and to safeguard their privacy, while at the same time informing and educating the public.

1. Adopt a written policy on sexual assault coverage.
2. Do not report the name of the survivor of a sexual assault or attempted assault or other information that would identify the person unless:
   * The victim is killed, or
   * The survivor consents to being identified.
   As an alternative if the victim is identified, report the reason for the identification so the audience is aware that survivors usually are not identified (if that is the regular policy).
3. Report only the general location of the crime—"in an apartment in the 400 block of Main Street"—unless it occurred in a business, school, institution or similar public place.
4. If a pattern seems to emerge in a series of assaults, report details that may help other potential victims avoid attack. For example, "The assailant has entered unlocked doors on the northeast side of town."
5. In initial reports on assaults and in reports on hearings and trials, summarize details of the assault rather than using elaborate, embarrassing or objectionable descriptions.
6. To be fair, do not report the name of the accused or information that would identify him or her until an arrest is made or, preferably, until a charge is filed.
7. Follow up every sexual assault story that is reported with a story on the disposition of the case.
8. In reporting on the incidence of sexual abuse, use both police statistics and data from a local rape crisis center. Rape crisis center statistics probably will be considerably higher than police statistics because many survivors who use victim services are unwilling to report assaults to police. Rape center statistics are likely to be closer to the actual number of sexual assaults in the community. Even rape center statistics are considered underestimates of the number of sexual assaults that actually have occurred.[25]

Notes

1. MediaWatch (Canada) *Bulletin* (Winter 1990/91): 4. MediaWatch is located at 517 Wellington St. W., Suite 204, Toronto, Ontario, Canada M5V 1G1.
   2. *Dick and Jane as Victims: Sex Stereotyping in Children's Readers* (Princeton, NJ: Women on Words and Images, 1972).

3. "Guidelines for Equal Treatment of the Sexes in McGraw-Hill Book Company Publications," McGraw-Hill Company, New York, 1973.

4. "Guidelines for Creating Positive Sexual and Racial Images in Educational Materials," Macmillan Publishing Company, New York, 1975.

5. "Guidelines for Improving the Image of Women in Textbooks," Scott, Foresman, and Company, Glenview, IL, 1974.

6. News Release, Action for Children's Television, March 14, 1983. In January 1992, ACT announced it was disbanding because government regulations were now in place that would govern all programming for children and the advertising aimed at them.

7. "Fighting TV Stereotypes: An ACT Handbook," Action for Children's Television (address: 46 Austin Street, Newtonville, MA 02160), 1983.

8. See Elizabeth J. Tarnove, "Effects of Sexist Language on the Status and Self-concept of Women," research paper, California State Polytechnic University, Pomona, pp. 4–5.

9. Tarnove, "Effects of Sexist Language," pp. 6–7.

10. Quoted in Tarnove, "Effects of Sexist Language," pp. 6–7.

11. Ari L. Goldman, "New Methodist Hymnal Is Shorn of Stereotypes," the *New York Times*, June 20, 1989, p. B1 and B4.

12. "Without Bias: A Guidebook for Nondiscriminatory Communication," International Association of Business Communicators (address: One Hallidie Plaza, Suite 600, San Francisco, CA 94102), 1977.

13. Stanford University Women's News Service, "Guidelines for Newswriting about Women," in William L. Rivers, *The Mass Media* (New York: Harper & Row, 1975), pp. 593–94.

14. National Commission on the Observance of International Women's Year, "Ten Guidelines for the Treatment of Women in the Media," Leaflet L-1 (Washington, DC: International Women's Year Secretariat, U.S. Department of State, July 1976).

15. Christopher W. French and Norm Goldstein, eds., *The Associated Press Stylebook and Libel Manual* (New York: Associated Press, 1989).

16. Carole Eberly (of Michigan State University), "The Journalist's Bible: Bad News for Women," paper presented to the Association for Education in Journalism and Mass Communication, Minneapolis, August, 1990.

17. Eberly, "Journalist's Bible."

18. "*USA Today* Style Guide," written by news copy desk chief Don Ross, Gannett Company, Arlington, VA, 1990.

19. Geneva Overholser, "Why Hide Rapes?" *New York Times*, July 11, 1989, p. A19.

20. Overholser, "Why Hide Rapes?"

21. Joseph F. Pisani, "Is It Time for Us to Start Naming Rape Victims?" *ASNE (American Society of Newspaper Editors) Bulletin* (July/August 1991): 16.

22. Marjie Lundstrom, "Decisions Shouldn't Be Left to Media," *USA Today*, April 9, 1990, p. 3A.

23. Michael Gartner, "Friday Report #122," NBC News Memo, April 19, 1991.

24. "Naming Names," *Newsweek* (April 29, 1991): 29.

25. From "A Resource Guide: News Coverage of Sexual Assault," Iowa Coalition against Sexual Abuse, Des Moines, Iowa, 1986.

24

Minority Women Journalists

As other chapters in this book show, minority women journalists have been active in the United States since the nineteenth century. They have tenaciously covered social issues that continue to require the attention of us all, and they have provided, through the minority-owned press, an important connection to culture and information for their readers.

Their numbers in mainstream media, while growing, are small. A study released by the American Society of Newspaper Editors in 1991 found that 51 percent of U.S. daily newspapers, mostly in smaller markets, employ no minorities in their newsrooms.[1] But where they are present, minority women in newsrooms at newspapers, magazines, and broadcasting stations are beginning to stretch the thinking of managers who, for the most part, continue to be Caucasian and male.

In 1992, minority women made up 7 percent of the newspaper work force. They were 3 percent of the executives and managers at newspapers. They constituted 6 percent of news–editorial employees—up one percentage point from a 1990 study.[2]

The profile for minority women in broadcast news is similar. The number of women of color filing stories on network news, including CNN and PBS, remains abysmally low, according to a 1990 monitoring study by Women, Men, and Media. Of the total number of stories tracked, only 2 percent were filed by women of color.[3] An annual survey of the "50 most prominent reporters" on network newscasts found only five women on the list, none of them minorities. (One male, of Japanese descent, finished in a three-way tie for forty-eighth place out of 50).[4] Among news directors, minority women are estimated to be 3.2 percent of television news directors, 2.8 percent of radio news directors.[5]

Simple demographic patterns tell us this must change if American journalism is to continue to be in touch with and responsive to all segments of its audience. "In the future, the greatest growth in population will be in black and Hispanic components of society; women will continue to increase in numbers because of their increasing life expectancy," writes Jean Gaddy Wilson of New Directions for News.[6] Minority women will continue to move into the work force in increasing numbers.

Is this being reflected in the mass media?

No, says University of Missouri professor Vernon Stone, who tracks broadcast news employment patterns for the Radio–Television News Directors Association.

Women's share of the work force, both in TV and radio news, has changed little from its roughly one-third level of recent years. Yet, more than half of all journalism graduates are women, and women account for about 40% of the new hires in broadcast news. These figures suggest that the female share of the work force should still be growing more than it is. It probably would be if turnover were not so much higher for women than for men. Previous surveys also show that turnover is somewhat higher for minority than non-minority journalists. Though they have lost positions to minorities and women, white men remain the broadcast journalists who stay in their jobs the longest.[7]

Robert J. Haiman, president and managing director of the Poynter Institute for Media Studies, has said that successes in recruiting minority journalists are all too often undermined by failure to retain them: "It's the problem of broken ladders that keep minority staffers, once they are hired, from rising up; and of revolving doors that all too often dump them back on the street, frustrated, angry and completely disheartened by their experiences on our staffs."[8]

Recruiting of minority journalists by the mainstream media did not begin until some years after the publication of the Kerner Commission Report, written after the United States was stunned by a summer of racial violence in 1967.[9] The report criticized the media for systematically ignoring blacks as part of American society, adding to the sensation that as a group and as individuals they were invisible in their own country. The same "symbolic annihilation" has been experienced by Native Americans, Asian-Americans, Hispanic Americans, and women. Yet still the industry did not immediately respond with strategies to attract more minority journalists and develop more inclusive news coverage.

"The journalism profession tends to be very slow to recognize that there is more than one way to see anything," said Mercedes Lynn de Uriarte of the journalism faculty at the University of Texas at Austin.

The editor defines as objective only his/her own perception in looking at a story. . . . If you look at sociological work done on the media, you find that 85% of sources used in U.S. mainstream journalism represent government or other official sources—white sources. When you turn to other sources, you begin to work with a pool of people who are unknown, suspect. You have to try to credential them to gain a legitimacy that is automatically accorded to white people who are in jobs that carry titles that are familiar— no matter who they are.

Editors need to look at how often they look to people as sources, and for story ideas that they can depend on to be predictable, familiar, reliable—and how often that excludes minorities and the minority community.[10]

Journalist Ethel Payne understood that. She had worked for both the minority-owned press and one of the nation's largest broadcast companies, CBS. In a career that spanned four decades, taking her to the *Chicago Defender* and the Afro-American newspaper group, then to CBS Radio and regional radio and television stations, Payne distinguished herself by her prodigious coverage of civil rights and human rights and her commentary on public affairs.

Ethel Payne died in June 1991 at the age of 79. In 1987, she was interviewed at length for the oral history project of the Washington Press Club Foundation. In those sessions, Payne described the challenges of negotiating her way through official Washington—still a segregated city, still a town where women journalists were a novelty and where black journalists were curiosities. Her story affirms the battle against exclusion so aptly described above by Mercedes Lynn de Uriarte.

In the interview session excerpted below, interviewer Kathleen Currie asks about Payne's comment that she was basically a shy person.

EXCERPT FROM ORAL HISTORY SESSION WITH ETHEL PAYNE
AS INTERVIEWED BY KATHLEEN CURRIE
September 17, 1987

CURRIE: How did you cope with your shyness in order to do your job?

PAYNE: I learned when I came to Washington, in other words, in a very competitive field, and that if I was going to succeed at all, I would have to learn to be as aggressive and tough as the rest of the persons in the pack. Although I was more or less an outsider, yes, I was, and I also was in the position of being on a periphery. When I say periphery, I mean that weekly newspapers weren't regarded too seriously, whether they were white or black. They just weren't supposed to be in the same league as the major media. So the best you could do, most of them could do, was be there as a nuisance value. They were there, but it was sort of like the cat looking with disdain at the mouse, you know. It would not be worthwhile doing anything with. So you had to overcome that. You had to let the people in the press know that you were there for the same reasons that they were there. You were there to do a job, and you were going to do a job, and you had to more or less fight your way in. I had to overcome practically three things: first, as a woman; second, as a Negro; and third is from what they called a minor press—not a minority press, a minor press. So I had those three things to overcome. . . .

One of the things that irritated me at first, but then I overcame that, was that I always felt that blacks who were in key positions in the government or whatever it might be sometimes ignored the black press and gave preferential treatment to the white press. That used to annoy me no end! Oh! I used to get furious about it. And I would protest about it. I would protest vigorously about it. Sometimes they would apologize for it. But I knew that behind it was the need for them to not only get maximum exposure to the larger media, but that it was sort of a recognition factor, the fact that if they could get into the *Washington Post* or the *Daily News* then, or whatever it was, that they had sort of pride. I had to fight for the integrity of the black press as well as my own personal dignity. It took a good while to do that, to earn that kind of respect. Pretty soon, I think, I was able to overcome most of that.

Then when I built up a bank of contacts, that began to come through very well. They would call me. I had one source in the Defense Department; he was just excellent—James Evans. He was wonderful. He would call me and alert me to something that was going on, and tell me about it, and he would give me some other sources. He was one of my best sources.

CURRIE: Who was James Evans?

PAYNE: James C. Evans was the civilian assistant—that was his title—to the Secretary of Defense. He was a black man, but he was there particularly to evaluate and to have a liaison with the blacks in the military as well as blacks in the civilian work force. He was sort of the filter through which news about blacks and their participation in defense [went], so he was an excellent source.

CURRIE: You ended your second interview saying that you had not the money, but the freedom in working for the black press.

PAYNE: Oh, that's one of the joys to this day. I'm going to die poor. [Laughter.] But at the same time, I have never regretted it, because I've enjoyed enormous freedom, much more freedom than I would have, had I been in the majority media. I don't think I could have existed, because of my own character and personality and everything else. I admit that I am biased about anything I see as an injustice; I just get personally very, very indignant about what I see as injustice. I couldn't express myself the way I do in the black press; I couldn't do that, say, if I were on the *Washington Post* or the *New York Times*. I'd have to do the story according to what that particular policy was and what the editor or whoever it was, my superior, would instruct me to do, and it would not be me. This way, I'm expressing myself, and I have been. I think that's the value of being in the type of press where you can write what you feel is right and just, but still, you work within the parameters of good reporting as much as possible. . . .

CURRIE: At one point in the other interview, you were talking about it being difficult for women in the press corps.

PAYNE: Yes. Male chauvinism was alive and well. That was a gender thing, not a race thing. That was a gender thing.

CURRIE: How did that work?

PAYNE: Well, I can remember that aggressive people like Sarah McClendon were almost ostracized and rebuked at times by some of her male peers. I think May Craig stood out because she was a senior member of the White House press corps, and she was highly respected in her own right. But I think Sarah took the heat a lot of times. There was another person—oh, she was from the *Denver Post*, I believe. Oh, she was just regarded as—she was really regarded with great disfavor because she was called a "pushy bitch." But she would push and shove, and she'd go after her stuff. You could feel it. There was always that haughty air about males in the press corps. They had names and reputations. It was almost like they were holier than thou.

Eric Sevareid to me typified that. He was a well known name, and he acted the role. He acted the entire role. At one time, he rebuked Sarah in public, and he was doing pieces for CBS. He was on CBS. I had just been invited to come on board the *CBS Spectrum* program, so I took him to task about his treatment of Sarah. I said, "Let him drown in his own pomposity." I got volumes of letters about that. [Laughter.]

CURRIE: Supportive letters?

PAYNE: No, not all of them. [Laughter.]

CURRIE: I asked this before. Do you think you were ever denied a story because you were a woman?

PAYNE: I think you were ignored to a great extent, as much as possible, and sometimes I used to get so frustrated because I couldn't get to the source of something. I don't think I was that much of a threat to the general press, except on occasions, when they decided that a particular angle was of interest to them. So therefore, when you went after it, you were just given short shrift. They would tell you that either something wasn't available or, "We've already dealt with that." You were just put aside. So that frustrated you, too.

CURRIE: In the last interview, we talked about the Eisenhower press conferences. In the fifties, when you came to Washington, it was a segregated city.

PAYNE: Very much so.

CURRIE: How did that affect your ability to do your job?

PAYNE: It was the first year of the Eisenhower Administration, and one of his campaign promises had been to issue an executive order ending the ban on public accommodations in the city of Washington. So he did sign an executive order to that effect, but you know, it's hard to overcome years of practice, a pattern of practice. So I found it difficult to sometimes get around and to get into places. Hotels, they were still clinging to the old traditions. . . .

CURRIE: We were talking about Washington in the fifties, being segregated, and we were talking about how that might have affected you doing your job. For example, I had heard at one point that the galleries at the House and Senate were segregated, that the bathrooms in the galleries were.

PAYNE: I didn't experience that myself. I never ran into that. They may have been. Like I was telling you before, I know that way back—way back—the story goes around that Thurgood Marshall was speaking about that the other night, that Mrs. Wilson, the wife of Woodrow Wilson, went to the post office, and she saw black men and white women working side by side, and she became incensed at that. So she had her husband order the post office to segregate workers and to make separate bathrooms. And she personally took signs and went and put them on doors—white and colored. That's the first lady of the land did that. So I don't know anything about that.

I do know that Simeon Booker, who was the first black hired at the *Washington Post*—and that's been way back, too—that he was given a separate bathroom, and that's one of the reasons why he left the *Post*.

CURRIE: He had his own bathroom?

PAYNE: Had his own bathroom. That was at the *Washington Post*.

CURRIE: I think you were describing, too, that when you went to apply for credentials at the House and Senate galleries, you got kind of a—

PAYNE: I really got a cold reception, as if, "What do you need this for? Why are you here?" But I had White House press credentials, so there was hardly any reason for them to turn me down, but I don't think they liked it at all.

CURRIE: Why didn't they like it?

PAYNE: Because it was almost—well, it was an all-white preserve, in the first place, and it was almost an all-white male preserve. It was an old boys' network, and they didn't want any stray critters trespassing through there. "What are you here for?" You know. You get that. It's unspoken, but you feel it. I know sometimes I would go up there when there wasn't really any hard news to cover, but I'd just go so it would be a practice that they would see me. Then at one time, one of them came up to me and said, "Well, I don't think there's anything here that you'd be interested in. It's not in your arena."

I said, "What is my arena?"

"Well, uh, ah, I just didn't think it was of any interest." You know, like that.

I said, "Well, who are you to tell me what my arena is? How do you get off with that?" And I just stared him down. I never had any more trouble out of him, but that was gratuitous, and it was nasty, and it was a put-down. So you had to encounter those kinds of things. You had to encounter male chauvinism, you had to encounter the fact that you were black, you were a woman, and you were from a minor press. So you were just like some little flea wandering in. They just didn't like to be annoyed that way.

CURRIE: How did that treatment make you feel?

PAYNE: Well, at first, it makes you feel slightly put down as an inferior thing. Then you get angry, you get real angry. And that's when, like, I got so angry with him, I'd tell him, "Who are you? What is my arena? How do you know what my arena is? How do you know what I want?" Give him a real, real cold stare. You had to go through that. Not pleasant, never was pleasant. I don't go up to the Hill like I used to. I have my credentials, but I don't go up there, because I've just changed my pattern of living. My lifestyle isn't quite the same; I'm not out on the hustings, so to speak, as much as I used to be. But I have the right to go, and if I choose to go, I expect to be treated with respect.

CURRIE: Also, you were talking before about at one point you took the civil service exam for a librarian.

PAYNE: Yes. That was a personal thing that happened to me. That was back in—oh, dear, it was so far back, I can hardly remember. I had not yet really come on board in Washington. I took the exam because it was open, and I just wanted to see how the civil service worked. I passed it; I was in the top category of that particular class. And with it came an announcement of a vacancy in the Justice Department. Well, I thought I would look into it and inquire about it. I was eligible for it. So I happened to be in Washington at the time they were fighting for passage of a Fair Employment Practices bill, so I went over to the Justice Department, and I walked in. There was a woman sitting at the end of the hall, a receptionist, and I told her that I was there. I had called ahead and asked to see the person in charge of personnel for the library. So I handed her this slip that said what my status was. She got up from the desk, and she went down the hall, and she stayed quite a few minutes. Then she came back, and she said in a very sweet southern drawl, "Mr. McPherson will see you now."

I took the elevator up to the fifth floor, and just as the door opened, there was a Mr. McPherson standing there. I guess he identified himself as Mr. McPherson. He said, "I'm glad to see you. You've come about the job. Well, I'm sorry to say that I can't give it to you."

I said, "Why not? Here's my qualifications."

He said, "Yes, you are at the top of the grade here, but I simply just couldn't hire you. Now, if you were Mordecai Johnson's daughter, I might be able to do something."

CURRIE: Mordecai Johnson?

PAYNE: He was then president of Howard University, happened to be a fair skinned man, and his daughter was fair skinned.

So I looked at him just straight, and I said, "Mr. McPherson, am I correct? Is this the United States Department of Justice?"

And he said, "Yes, I know how you feel."

I said, "But I don't understand. What's the rationale for this? I'm fully qualified. How can you dare stand here and tell me that you can't give me the job because I'm a Negro?"

He said, "Well, I'm sorry, but that's just the policy." And then he said to me, "I'm sorry that this is the way it is, but you know, the receptionist had told me that you were downstairs, and she said to me, 'There's this woman down here, this Negro woman down here, who wants to see you, but I'm sure you don't want her, because she's a Negro.' "[11]

Two generations of journalists have followed Payne, each facing different circumstances. *Washington Post* columnist Dorothy Gilliam started her career at 17 at a black-owned newspaper in Louisville, Kentucky, took degrees in journalism at Lincoln University and Columbia, and started at the *Post* in 1961. That was the same year John F. Kennedy, in his inaugural address, asked his fellow Americans—not just the whites, but all of them—to "ask not what your country can do for you; ask what you can do for your country." Dorothy Gilliam still could not eat in many of the restaurants just a few blocks from the White House.

In Kay Mills's book *A Place in the News*, Gilliam recounted some of the frustration. She said she was determined not to be limited solely to stories about blacks and women. "I went to cover somebody's 100th birthday party on Massachusetts Avenue—a high-rent district. First, the doorman really could not believe that I was supposed to come in the front door. This was a black doorman, right? Then when I got upstairs . . . I got, 'You are from the *Post*? Are you sure?' "[12]

As civil rights legislation passed during the 1960s, reporters covering the sweeping changes looked hard at their news organizations to see if they measured up in terms of equal opportunity. Few did. The Federal Communications Commission began to scrutinize more carefully the employment opportunities at stations it licensed and found that most were wanting (see Chapter 21). Some employers sought to improve matters by hiring a "double token"—a woman journalist who was also a minority.

In Judith Gelfman's 1976 book *Women in Television News*, her interviewees commented on the double-edged sword of tokenism. Said Judy Thomas, then of WOR-TV in New York, in a 1973 interview:

> You have to prove that you're qualified to everybody. Most people tend to assume that you're hired because you're black and because you're a woman and because they were desperate. Not because you know what you're doing. . . . Years ago, neither women nor blacks were allowed on television, point blank. Now that we're allowed, it's like they're looking for "qualified" women, "qualified" minorities. And I think the reason I got my job is because they were looking for qualified minorities and women—the combination.[13]

Linda Shen had been hired in 1972 as a summer replacement at WNBC-TV in New York, then dismissed seven months later. "I was hired specifically because I was a Third-World woman," she told Gelfman.

> But I think that had a lot to do with my being let go, as a matter of fact, so it's a double-edged sword. . . . I, as a Chinese woman, was far more expendable than either a black or a Spanish woman. . . . The Asian community is not a large community in New York and it certainly is not a community that plays New York politics. It's a very quiet community. . . . I have been labeled by the news director's office as a radical young upstart, a troublemaker. . . . One of those things has to do with the fact that I have complained about assignments that I thought were either unjust or just set up in an unworkable fashion. . . . As one example, I was assigned to do a story on Thanksgiving Day, on a Chinese Thanksgiving. There's no such thing as a Chinese Thanksgiving. . . . "You're just exploiting my people. I'll do the story as it has to be done." I believe there are different expectations of me, not only because I'm female, but because I'm a minority female.[14]

It is not always easy to communicate the tenor of an era to those who have not lived through it, but this 1974 anecdote about Washington, D.C., television reporter/anchor Renee Poussaint does as good a job as any in capsulizing the strong feelings generated by changes on the race/gender axis during the 1960s and 1970s. It comes from Betsy Covington Smith's *Breakthrough: Women in Television.*

Renee was sent to cover a union meeting of the Chicago Firefighters Association. The only topic on the agenda was how to keep women and blacks out of the union. All night Renee stood in the huge hall surrounded by four hundred firemen and her white, male film crew listening to insults to both women and blacks. Finally, it was over. Emotionally drained, she headed for the exit, trying to keep calm and poker-faced until she could get off by herself and scream. Suddenly, one of the firemen rushed up to her. "Renee," he said, having seen her on television (she was a reporter for WBBM-TV at the time), "we don't want you to leave thinking we're racists and sexists. But, well, it's just that the broads and the niggers are taking over the world!" . . .

[As Poussaint noted,] "Women reporters have been fighting for a long time to prove they're just as capable emotionally of covering any story as men. It's harder if you're a black or a woman because you're going to be exposed to more antagonism and hostility toward you. Professionally, you're supposed to be a neuter, always maintaining an impartial, unemotional attitude. Personally, that's impossible. But you can't afford to restrict yourself only to stories in which you feel no emotional involvement."[15]

After Linda Yu's first appearance as a weekend anchor at WMAQ-TV in Chicago in 1979, viewers bombarded the station with calls asking for Yu's ethnic background. The initial high level of curiosity ebbed; Yu says she has had no difficulty being accepted in a market with a fairly small Asian population. Yet, she says, ten years went by before another Asian appeared on TV news in Chicago: "That says something about the perception that unless you have a huge population of a certain people, you may not necessarily respond in terms of hiring."[16]

The true test of color blindness for news management is not limiting minority hires to communities where the ethnic group to which they belong has a major presence, but also hiring them in markets where there is not such a direct demographic connection.

Another part of the test is spreading them throughout the news organizations so that influence is shared. This has yet to happen. According to a 1991 statistical profile of newsrooms at U.S. daily newspapers, women in the newsrooms—67 percent—are most likely to be reporters or copy editors, "the foot soldiers of the daily press but positions relatively low in prestige, pay and power," compared to 58 percent of all newspapermen, wrote Ted Pease and J. Frazier Smith of Ohio University. "Combining gender and race variables further widens the gap—three-quarters of African-American women, 97% of Latino women and 78% of Asian-American women are reporters or copy editors, compared to 57% of white men."[17]

Pease and Smith illustrate how the nation's shifting demographics are mirrored on news–editorial staffs.

Since minorities tend to be younger than whites, and women younger than men, the age gap between minority women and white men is particularly large. More than 42% of white men are 36 to 40 years old and more than half of Asian-American women are under 30. Taken together, the pattern is of a multicultural and female work force coming up as a white, male work force ages. Overall, the age "peak" among white journalists is five to 15 years older than that of minority respondents. Minority journalists, younger overall, tend to occupy the lower rungs of the newsroom hierarchical ladder, while white journalists—particularly men— are more often entrenched in more senior positions, a sure formula for frustration and resentment.[18]

The disparity shows up in coverage decisions, with minority women journalists being among the most critical of current decision-making practices, according to Pease and Smith. More than 75 percent of Hispanic and African-American women journalists described the coverage of people of color in their newspapers as marginal or poor.[19]

How far down the ladder minority women journalists are influencing newsroom decisions was pointedly underlined by *USA Today* inquiry editor Barbara Reynolds in a 1989 column. Reynolds had just been on the program at the first major conference sponsored by Women, Men, and Media, in Washington. Few women of color had attended. That same month, the American Society of Newspaper Editors (ASNE) had issued a study of newsroom employees that failed to break down the "minority" category into distinguishable groups. Those two events together prompted this column:

FROM THE HEART: MEDIA LEAVE MANY OUT OF THE PICTURE

If the press holds up a mirror to society, as is often said, it is a cracked mirror reflecting distorted images.

That message was communicated by two media groups convening in Washington, D.C., this week. One, co-chaired by Betty Friedan of *Feminine Mystique* fame and Nancy Woodhull, then-president of Gannett News Service [now president of Nancy Woodhull & Associates, a consulting firm specializing in helping corporations better understand women as employees and consumers], was called Women, Men and Media. The other was the annual convention of the American Society of Newspaper Editors [whose members are 10% women and 3.3% minority, according to 1992 data].

Statistics released from the conferences showed:

• Women, 52% of the population, are quoted on the front page 11% of the time. [Best showing of female sources and bylines was by *USA Today*.]

• Only 6% of the top media bosses are female.

• Average female employees earn 64% of male employees' salaries.

• 54% of newspapers hire no minorities. Those that do don't promote them; 95.5% of newsroom managers are white.

These numbers show that white males are having a great time quoting each other, controlling content, cutting women out of fair salaries and promotions, and excluding minorities from the "free press" altogether.

How's that for an industry that canonizes its role as the guardian of fairness and justice for all?

As women rise in the ranks, the new buzzword of many news executives like Woodhull is empowerment—meaning women helping each other up the ladder instead of this Working Girl bitchiness that Hollywood male directors project. Empowerment is no threat to white males, who often fear that fairy tale of reverse discrimination. "All it means is they will no longer have a blatant advantage," said Janet Chusmir, executive editor of *The Miami Herald*. [Chusmir died in 1990.]

But will this empowerment include all women, or just some women?

During the women's conference, a major progress report released had no information about minority women, who are laboring at the bottom rung of the pink and black newsroom ghettos. And the ASNE racial statistics don't give breakdowns by gender.

Thus, if women's media groups overlook race and the male-dominated ASNE overlooks gender, black, Hispanic and Asian women are submerged as the Invisible Presence.

While the women are on the right road to correcting one distortion, there are other images not being seen at all.[20]

Reynolds herself is participating in networking to raise the visibility and clout of those unseen images. Reynolds, Betty Anne Williams, planning editor for the news section of *USA Today*, and Sidmel Estes-

Sumpter, producer at WAGA-TV in Atlanta, chair the Women's Task Force of the National Association of Black Journalists (NABJ), formed in 1990. (In 1991, Estes-Sumpter was elected the first woman president of NABJ, which was founded in 1975.) The goal of the task force is to work on projects related to improving the image of black women in the media, including establishing a speakers' bureau and formalizing a mentoring system.

Other networking groups include the National Association of Hispanic Journalists, formed in 1984 to provide support for Hispanic journalists in English, Spanish, and bilingual media; the Asian American Journalists Association; and the Native American Journalists Association. In 1991, a new organization was formed for minority managers of all ethnic backgrounds and in all newspaper departments: the National Association of Minority Media Executives.

Individual task forces within the American Society of Newspaper Editors, the Society of Professional Journalists, and the Minority Affairs Department of the Newspaper Association of America (formerly the American Newspaper Publishers Association) also are involved in developing research and programs.

A similar effort—not targeting racial or ethnic minorities but gays and lesbians of all racial and ethnic backgrounds—has been undertaken by the National Lesbian and Gay Journalists Association. The group was formed after a 1990 ASNE study of journalists found that homosexuals felt they were barely tolerated by their newsroom colleagues.[21]

The activities of these groups can accelerate change in the newsroom, and ultimately in the newspaper and on the air. This comment from a journalist who has seen news coverage with and without minority staffers on hand puts it well:

We did a series on the Hispanic community in our city, which is growing—it's now up to 12 percent. We did it with no Hispanics on the staff, no Spanish-speaking whites on the staff. We're doing it again, 10 years later. It's a totally different, much more sensitive, much more effective job. We're a better newspaper as a result.[22]

Notes

1. Howard Kurtz, "At Newspapers, A Clash of Perceptions about Push to Recruit Minority Staff," *Washington Post*, April 14, 1991, p. A4.

2. "Summary Report: NAA Survey/Employment of Minorities and Women in U.S. Daily Newspapers, 1992," conducted for the Newspaper Association of America by Belden Associates, Dallas, TX, 1992.

3. Women, Men, and Media, "Women, Men and Network News," released in October 1990, p. 4. The study was conducted for Women, Men, and Media by the Communications Consortium, Washington, DC.

4. Survey by the Center for Media and Public Affairs, Washington, DC, cited in John Carmody, "The TV Column," *Washington Post*, March 11, 1991.

5. Vernon A. Stone, "Minority Share of Work Force Grows for Third Year," *RTNDA Communicator* (May 1991): 21.

6. Jean Gaddy Wilson with Iris Igawa, "Women in the United States Media: Opportunities Today in Employment and Promotion," a paper for the International Group for the Study of Women, '88 Tokyo Symposium on Women, August 25–27, 1988, p. 10.

7. Stone, "Minority Share of Work Force Grows," p. 22.

8. Robert J. Haiman in his preface to *The Next Step: Toward Diversity in the Newspaper Business*, a publication of the American Newspaper Publishers Association Foundation, Reston, VA, and Poynter Institute for Media Studies, St. Petersburg, FL, 1991.

9. Otto Kerner, chairman, National Advisory Commission on Civil Disorders, *U.S. Riot Commission Report* (New York: Bantam Books, 1968), pp. 368–86, cited in Wilson, "Women in the United States Media."

10. Mercedes Lynn de Uriarte, "A Minority Perspective," *Next Step*, p. 19.

11. Kathleen Currie, Interview No. 3 with Ethel Payne, September 17, 1987, Washington, DC, for the Women in Journalism Oral History Project of the Washington Press Club Foundation, in the Oral History Collection of the National Press Club Archives, Washington, DC.

12. Kay Mills, *A Place in the News: From the Women's Pages to the Front Page* (New York: Dodd, Mead, 1988), p. 180.

13. Judith S. Gelfman, *Women in Television News* (New York: Columbia University Press, 1976), p. 119.

14. Gelfman, *Women in Television News*, pp. 127–129.

15. Betsy Covington Smith, *Breakthrough: Women in Television News* (New York: Walker, 1981), pp. 9–10.

16. Quoted in Jon Krampner, "Special Report: Minorities and the Media," *Electronic Media* (July 8, 1991): 29.

17. Ted Pease and J. Frazier Smith, "The Newsroom Barometer: Job Satisfaction and the Impact of Racial Diversity at U.S. Daily Newspapers," Ohio University Monograph Series, No. 1, July 1991, p. 11.

18. Pease and Smith, "Newsroom Barometer," p. 10.

19. Pease and Smith, "Newsroom Barometer," p. 26.

20. Barbara Reynolds, "From the Heart: Media Leave Many Out of the Picture," *USA Today*, April 14, 1989, p. 13A.

21. "Lesbian, Gay Journalists Hold First Professional Meeting," *Media Report to Women* 20, no. 3 (Summer 1992): 6–7.

22. *Next Step*, p. 20.

Additional Resources

1 Overview

To date only three books have given an overview of the experiences of U.S. women in journalism: Ishbel Ross, *Ladies of the Press: The Story of Women in Journalism by an Insider* (New York: Harper & Brothers, 1936); Marion Marzolf, *Up from the Footnote: A History of Women Journalists* (New York: Hastings House, 1977); Kay Mills, *A Place in the News: From the Women's Pages to the Front Pages* (New York: Dodd, Mead, 1988, reprinted New York: Columbia University Press, 1990).

Material from Marzolf's book was printed in *Journalism History* 1 (Winter 1974/75) and 2 (Spring 1975). The winter 1974/75 issue also contained a comprehensive bibliography by Marzolf, Ramona R. Rush, and Darlene Stern titled "The Literature of Women in Journalism." A bibliographic supplement compiled by Marzolf appeared in the Winter 1976/77 issue.

A bibliography prepared by Catherine C. Mitchell, "Scholarship on Women Working in Journalism," ran in *American Journalism* 7 (Winter 1990). The same issue included an article on historical scholarship on women journalists by Mitchell, "The Place of Biography in the History of News Women," and a historiographical essay by Maurine H. Beasley, "Women in Journalism: Contributors to Male Experience or Voices of Feminine Expression?"

Other works focused on individual achievements by journalists. Madelon Golden Schilpp and Sharon M. Murphy, *Great Women of the Press* (Carbondale: Southern Illinois University Press, 1983), sketched the lives of 18 women journalists. Barbara Belford, *Brilliant Bylines: A Biographical Anthology of Notable Newspaperwomen in America*

(New York: Columbia University Press, 1986), provided brief biographies and examples of the work of 24 women journalists. Julia Edwards, *Women of the World: The Great Foreign Correspondents* (Boston: Houghton Mifflin, 1988), detailed the history of overseas correspondents.

Brief biographical material on outstanding journalists appeared in *Notable American Women: 1607–1950* (Cambridge, MA: Belknap Press, 1971), a three-volume biographical dictionary. A fourth volume on the modern period was published in 1980. Edith May Marken, "Women in American Journalism before 1900," unpublished master's thesis, University of Missouri, 1932, listed pioneer women journalists. Volumes 23, 25, 43 and 73 on *American Newspaper Journalists* and *American Magazine Journalists* in the *Dictionary of Literary Biography* series (Detroit: Gale Research, 1983–1985, 1988) included well-researched entries on some women journalists. The first three were edited by Perry T. Ashley and the fourth by Sam G. Riley.

Two books have told the story of women in broadcasting: David H. Hosley and Gayle K. Yamada, *Hard News: Women in Broadcast Journalism* (Westport, CT: Greenwood Press, 1987), and Marlene Sanders and Marcia Rock, *Waiting for Prime Time: The Woman of Television News* (Urbana: University of Illinois Press, 1988).

Other sources are listed at the end of each chapter. Unpublished papers cited in this book can be obtained through ERIC (Education Resources Information Center), 2805 East 10th Street, Bloomington, IN 47408.

2   Colonial Era

Leona Hudak, *Early American Women Printers and Publishers, 1639–1820* (Metuchen, NJ: Scarecrow Press, 1978), and Richard L. Demeter, *Printer, Presses and Composing Sticks: Women Printers of the Colonial Period* (New York: Exposition Press, 1979), gave an overview of the colonial experience for women journalists. Other sources: Ellen M. Oldham, "Early Woman Printers of America," *Boston Public Library Quarterly* 10 (1958):6–26, 78–92, 141–53; and Jessie E. Ringwalt, "Early Female Printers of America," *Printer's Circular* 7 (1872).

Extensive work by Susan Henry included "Notes toward the Liberation of Journalism History: A Study of Five Women Printers in Colonial America," Ph.D. dissertation, Syracuse University, 1976;

"Ann Franklin: Rhode Island's Woman Printer," in Donovan H. Bond and W. Reynolds McLeod, eds., *Colonial Newsletters and Newspapers: Eighteenth-century Journalism* (Morgantown: West Virginia University, 1977); "Margaret Draper: Colonial Printer Who Challenged the Patriots," *Journalism History* 1 (1974/75):145; "Exception to the Female Model: Colonial Printer Mary Crouch," *Journalism Quarterly* 62 (1985):725–33, 749.

Henry focused on the Goddards in "Sarah Goddard, Gentlewoman Printer," *Journalism Quarterly* 57 (1980):23–80. Other work on the Goddard family: Nancy Fisher Chudacoff, "Woman in the News 1762–1770—Sarah Updike Goddard," *Rhode Island History* 32/33 (1973):98–105; Ward L. Miner, *William Goddard: Newspaperman* (Durham, NC: Duke University Press, 1962). The best sources of information are their publications, many of which are preserved in state archives. Files of Mary Katherine Goddard's *Maryland Journal* are in the Maryland Historical Society at Baltimore, which also has photostats of her account book and petitions to retain the post of postmistress. A copy of the Declaration of Independence printed by her is at the National Archives in Washington, D.C. Lists of the imprints from her print shop appeared in Lawrence C. Wroth, *History of Printing in Colonial Maryland* (Baltimore: Typolhetae, 1922).

Background sources on early women printers: Elisabeth A. Dexter, *Colonial Women of Affairs* (Boston: Houghton Mifflin, 1931), and *Career Women of America: 1776–1840* (Francestown, NH: Jones, 1950); Eugenia A. Leonard, *The Dear-bought Heritage* (Philadelphia: University of Pennsylvania, 1965); Alice M. Earle, *Colonial Dames and Good Wives* (New York: Ungar, 1962); Julia C. Spruill, *Women's Life and Work in the Southern Colonies* (Chapel Hill: University of North Carolina, 1938); and Barbara Mayer Wertheimer, *We Were There: The Story of Working Women in America* (New York: Pantheon Books, 1977).

3 Early Political Journalism

The Rare Book and Special Collections Division at the Library of Congress holds a complete file of *Paul Pry*. The *Huntress* is available on microfilm in many libraries. Anne Royall's letters are preserved in the University of Virginia Library, the New York Public Library, the Yale University Library, the Duke University Library, and the Library of Congress, but they pertain more to her career as a bookseller than as a Washington editor.

Her books are in the Library of Congress: *Sketches of History, Life, and Manners in the United States* (1826); a novel, *The Tennessean* (1827); the three-volume *Black Book* (1828/29); the two-volume *Pennsylvania* (1829); and the three-volume *Southern Tour* (1830/31). With the exception of the first two—which were printed in New Haven, Connecticut—all were printed in Washington. *Letters from Alabama*, first published in 1830, was reprinted in 1969 by the University of Alabama Press with a helpful biographical introduction and notes by Lucille Griffith. Information on Anne Royall's pension claim may be found in Claim No. W-8566 in the Department of Veterans' Affairs in Washington. The Columbia Historical Society Library in Washington has miscellaneous Royall scrapbooks and clipping files.

Other biographical data may be gathered from her obituary in the *Washington Evening Star*, October 2, 1854, and in newspaper feature stories (*Washington Post*, February 22, 1891, and October 6, 1901, and *Baltimore Sun*, October 18, 1931). Descriptions of Anne Royall appeared in Allen C. Clark, "Joseph Gales, Junior Editor and Mayor," *Columbia Historical Society Records* 23 (October 1919): 86–146, and in *Life of P. T. Barnum Written by Himself* (New York: Redfield, 1855). Also see Nickieann Fleener, "Anne Royall," in Perry T. Ashley, ed., *American Newspaper Journalists: 1690–1872*, vol. 43 of the *Dictionary of Literary Biography* (Detroit: Gale Research, 1988) pp. 402–8.

Four biographies exist. The most recent—*Virago!* and *Anne Royall's U.S.A.* (both cited in the notes to Chapter 3—contained extensive documentation. Sarah H. Porter, *The Life and Times of Anne Royall* (Cedar Rapids, IA: Torch Press, 1909), argued that Royall had been unjustly treated by history and included original source material. George S. Jackson, *Uncommon Scold* (Boston: Bruce Humphries, 1937), presented a psychological analysis of her activities.

4 Reform Periodicals

Jane G. Swisshelm said that she burned all her papers and wrote her autobiography, *Half a Century* (Chicago: Jansen, McClurg, 1880), strictly from memory. Considerable manuscript material, however, is located at the Minnesota Historical Society in St. Paul. Swisshelm papers are included in collections of the letters of Henry Z. Mitchell, her brother-in-law and a pioneer settler of St. Cloud. Other items are included in material on early life in Minnesota taken from the *Boston Daily Journal* and the *New York Tribune* and in the family papers of Alexander Ramsey and Sylvanus B. Lowry. The society also has complete files of her St. Cloud newspaper.

The Carnegie Library of Pittsburgh holds a file of the *Saturday Visiter* available only on microfilm. Copies of the *New York Tribune* containing her Washington correspondence are available in the Library of Congress, which also has two books by her, *Letters to Country Girls* (New York: J. C. Ricker, 1853) and (written with others) *True Stories about Pets* (Boston: D. Lothrop, 1879).

The best source on her life in Washington is *Crusader and Feminist* (St. Paul: Minnesota Historical Society, 1934), a collection of her correspondence from the capital edited by Arthur J. Larsen. Some material appeared in James Black, *A Brief History of Prohibition* (New York: National Committee of the Prohibition Reform Party, 1880).

Two valuable articles are Lester B. Shippee, "Jane Grey Swisshelm, Agitator," *Mississippi Valley Historical Review* 7 (December 1920): 206–27, and Sterns's "Reform Periodicals and Female Reformers: 1830–1860," cited in the notes to Chapter 4. Chapters in Margaret Farrand Thorp, *Female Persuasion: Six Strong-minded Women* (New Haven, CT: Yale University Press, 1949), are devoted to Swisshelm and Bloomer.

Other material: Kathleen Endres, "Jane Grey Swisshelm: 19th Century Journalist and Feminist," *Journalism History* 2 (Winter 1975/76): 128–32. See also Endres, "Jane Grey Swisshelm," in Perry J. Ashley, ed., *American Newspaper Journalists, 1690–1872, vol. 43 of the Dictionary of Literary Biography* (Detroit: Gale Research, 1985), pp. 430–35.

The best source on Bloomer is Dexter C. Bloomer, cited in the notes to Chapter 4, with lengthy quotations from her speeches, letters, and articles. The *Lily* is on microfilm at Smith College. Manuscript material may be found at the Seneca Falls (New York) Historical Society and the Council Bluffs (Iowa) Free Public Library.

5 Foreign Correspondence

Margaret Fuller has been the subject of numerous biographies, but they tend to treat her as a literary figure and philosopher, not as a journalist. Much of her correspondence for the *New York Tribune* appears in *At Home and Abroad* (1856) and *Life Without and Life*

Within (1859), both edited by her brother, Arthur B. Fuller, and published in Boston, the first by Crosby, Nichols, and the second by Brown, Taggert, and Chase. Joseph Jay Deiss's *The Roman Years of Margaret Fuller* (New York: Thomas Y. Crowell, 1969), gives much detail about her role in the revolution and her marriage.

Standard biographies include Mason Wade, *Margaret Fuller: Whetstone of Genius* (New York: Viking, 1940), Katherine Anthony, *Margaret Fuller: A Psychological Biography* (New York: Harcourt, Brace, 1920), and Madeline B. Stern, *The Life of Margaret Fuller* (New York: Dutton, 1942). Yet, as Arthur W. Brown pointed out in *Margaret Fuller* (New York: Twayne, 1964), some of her biographers take a "Gee whiz!" approach toward her achievements, apparently due to their antifeminist bias.

As noted by Deiss, modern scholarship has established that friends dealt somewhat unfairly with Fuller in *Memoirs of Margaret Fuller Ossoli*, 2 vols. (Boston: Phillips, Samson, 1852), edited by Ralph Waldo Emerson, William H. Channing, and James Freeman Clarke. Other early works on Fuller are biographies by Julia Ward Howe (Boston: Roberts, 1883) and Thomas Wentworth Higginson (Boston: Houghton Mifflin, 1884).

A listing of her contributions to periodicals appears in *The Writings of Margaret Fuller*, edited by Mason Wade (New York: Viking, 1941). Another source is *Margaret Fuller: American Romantic* (New York: Doubleday, 1963), edited by Perry Miller.

Her struggle to become a free individual is depicted in *The Woman and the Myth: Margaret Fuller's Life and Writings*, edited by Bell Gale Chevigny (Old Westbury, NY: Feminist Press, 1977), which aims to correct some of the misconceptions of previous works. Another account: Margaret Vanderharr Allen, *The Achievement of Margaret Fuller* (University Park: Pennsylvania State University Press, 1979).

The most extensive treatment of Fuller as a journalist is Catherine C. Mitchell, "Horace Greeley's Star—Margaret Fuller's *New York Tribune* Journalism, 1844–1846," Ph.D. dissertation, University of Tennessee, 1987. See also Nora Baker, "Sarah Margaret Fuller, Marchesa D'Ossoli," in Sam G. Riley, ed., *American Magazine Journalists: 1741–1850, vol. 73 of the Dictionary of Literary Biography* (Detroit: Gale Research, 1988), pp. 112–23.

6 Ladies' Periodicals

The primary source is *Godey's Lady's Book* available in the Library of Congress, which also has copies of the other books written or edited by Sarah J. Hale—some 50 in all—many of which were compendia of household advice. One of the most ambitious was *Woman's Record, or Sketches of All Distinguished Women from the Beginning to A.D. 1868* (New York: Harper, 1870), an early biographical encyclopedia of notable women.

Biographies of Hale include Isabelle W. Entriken, *Sarah Josepha Hale and* Godey's Lady's Book (Philadelphia: University of Pennsylvania, 1946); Ruth E. Finley, *The Lady of* Godey's: *Sarah Josepha Hale* (Philadelphia: Lippincott, 1931); and Norma R. Fryatt, *Sarah Josepha Hale: The Life and Times of a Nineteenth Century Career Woman* (New York: Hawthorne Books, 1975). William R. Taylor, *Cavalier and Yankee* (New York: Braziller, 1961), contains an evaluation of her writings. Information on *Godey's* appeared in Frank Luther Mott, *A History of American Magazines*, vol. 1 (Cambridge, MA: Harvard University Press, 1938–57), pp. 580–94. See also "The Genesis of *Godey's Lady's Book*," *New England Quarterly* 1 (January 1928): 41–70, and Glenda Gates Riley, "The Subtle Subversion: Changes in the Traditionalist Image of the American Woman," *Historian* 32 (February 1970): 210–27.

For valuable background on the period, see Barbara Welter, "The Cult of True Womanhood: 1820–1860," *American Quarterly* 18 (Summer 1966): 151–74. Also helpful: Fred Lewis Pattee, *The Feminine Fifties* (New York: D. Appleton-Century, 1940); Helen W. Papashvily, *All the Happy Endings* (New York: Harper, 1956); Frank Luther Mott, *Golden Multitudes: The Story of Best Sellers in the United States* (New York: Macmillan, 1947); and James D. Hart, *The Popular Book: A History of America's Literary Taste* (New York: Oxford University Press, 1950).

Other works that discuss the relationship of nineteenth-century culture to women's magazines include Ann Douglas, *The Feminization of American Culture* (New York: Avon, 1977); Karen Hal Hunes, *Confidence Men and Painted Women: A Study of Middle-class Culture in America, 1830–1870* (New Haven, CT: Yale University Press, 1982); and Mary Kelley, *Private Women, Public Stage* (New York: Oxford University Press, 1984).

7 Suffrage Newspapers

Files of both *The Revolution* and the *Woman's Journal* are available at the Library of Congress. Brief excerpts from *The Revolution* are contained in Judith Papachristou, *Women Together: A History in Documents of the Women's Movement in the United States* (New York: Alfred A. Knopf, 1976), p. 57.

The Susan B. Anthony scrapbooks of press comments relating to Elizabeth Cady Stanton are in the Library of Congress. For other material on Stanton, see Elizabeth Cady Stanton, Susan B. Anthony, and Matilda J. Gage, eds., *History of Woman Suffrage*, 3 vols. (Rochester, NY: Susan B. Anthony, 1886); Theodore Stanton and Harriot Stanton Blatch, eds., *Elizabeth Cady Stanton as Revealed in Her Letters, Diary and Reminiscences*, 2 vols. (New York: Harper, 1922).

Alma Lutz wrote biographies of both Elizabeth Cady Stanton and Susan B. Anthony: *Created Equal: A Biography of Elizabeth Cady Stanton, 1815–1902* (New York: John Day, 1940), and *Susan B. Anthony: Rebel, Crusader, Humanitarian* (Boston: Beacon, 1959). Other biographies of Anthony: Ida Husted Harper, *Life and Work of Susan B. Anthony*, 3 vols. (New York: Arno, 1969, a reprint of the 1898–1908 edition); and Katharine Anthony, *Susan B. Anthony: Her Personal History and Her Era* (Garden City, NY: Doubleday, 1954).

Sources on the Blackwells: Elinor Rice Hays, *Morning Star: A Biography of Lucy Stone, 1818–1893* (New York: Harcourt, Brace and World, 1961), and Hays, *Those Extraordinary Blackwells: The Story of a Journey to a Better World* (New York: Harcourt, Brace and World, 1967); Alice Stone Blackwell, *Lucy Stone: Pioneer of Woman's Rights* (Boston: Little, Brown, 1930). See also Laura E. Richards and Maud Howe Elliott, *Julia Ward Howe, 1819–1910* (Boston: Houghton Mifflin, 1916).

For general background, see Robert E. Riegel, *American Feminists* (Lawrence: University of Kansas Press, 1963); Aileen S. Kraditor, *The Ideas of the Woman Suffrage Movement: 1890–1920* (New York: Columbia University Press, 1965); and William L. O'Neill, *Everyone Was Brave: A History of Feminism in America* (Chicago: Quadrangle, 1969).

Bennion's *Equal to the Occasion*, cited in the notes to Chapter 7, contains a chapter on suffrage newspapers. In addition to the *American Journalism* article cited in the notes to Chapter 7, her work includes "Early Western Publications Expose Women's Suffrage Cries," *Matrix* 64 (1979):6–9; "The New Northwest and Woman's Exponent: Early Voices for Suffrage," *Journalism Quarterly* 54 (1977):286–92; "The Pioneer: The First Voice of Women's Suffrage in the West," *Pacific Historian* 25 (1981):15–21; "The Woman's Exponent: Forty-two Years of Speaking for Women," *Utah Historical Quarterly* 44 (1976):222–39.

Other sources: Anne Mather, "A History of Feminist Periodicals," *Journalism History* 1 (1974/75):82–85; 1 (1974/75):108–11; 2 (1975):19–23, 31; and Linda Steiner, "The Woman's Suffrage Press, 1850–1900: A Cultural Analysis," Ph.D. dissertation, University of Illinois, 1979.

8 Newspaper Correspondence

A complete list of the work of Sara Willis Parton can be found in *Ruth Hall and Other Writings*, cited in the notes to Chapter 8. See also Marion Marzolf, "Sara Payson Willis Parton (Fanny Fern)," Perry T. Ashley, ed., *American Newspaper Journalists: 1690–1872*, vol. 43 of the *Dictionary of Literary Biography* (Detroit: Gale Research, 1983), pp. 358–62; and in the same volume, see Donna Born, "Sara Jane Clarke Lippincott," pp. 303–9. See also Maurine H. Beasley, "Mary Clemmer Ames," in Perry T. Ashley, ed., *American Newspaper Journalists: 1873–1900*, vol. 23 of the *Dictionary of Literary Biography* (Detroit: Gale Research, 1983), pp. 3–7.

The careers of nineteenth-century Washington women journalists were described in Beasley, *The First Women Washington Correspondents*, cited in the notes to Chapter 8; "Pens and Petticoats: Early Women Washington Correspondents," *Journalist History* 1 (Winter 1974/75): 112–15, 136; and "Mary Clemmer Ames: A Victorian Woman Journalist," *Hays Historical Journal* (Spring 1978): 57–63.

An interesting manuscript collection in the Rutherford B. Hayes Memorial Library, Fremont, Ohio, includes numerous letters sent to Hayes during and after his presidential term by several Washington women correspondents—chiefly social writers for Cincinnati newspapers. At least one, Austine Snead, complained of sex prejudice. The collection contains a few letters written by Mary Clemmer Ames plus some 50 letters sent to her during the late 1860s and 1870s by readers of the *New York Independent* and personal friends. The library holds a clipping file of Ames's columns in the *New York Independent* from 1876 to 1881 and in the *Cincinnati Commercial* from 1876 to 1879. It also has a file of her obituaries.

For biographical material on Ames, see her novel, *Eirene, or A Woman's Right* (New York: Putnam, 1871), which contains a realistic account of her Civil War experiences; two nonfiction works, *Ten Years in Washington: Life and Scenes in the National Capital as a Woman*

Sees Them (Hartford, CT: Worthington, 1875) and *Outlines of Man, Women, and Things* (New York: Hurd and Houghton, 1873); the sentimental tribute by her husband, Edmund Hudson, *An American Woman's Life and Work: A Memorial of Mary Clemmer* (Boston: Ticknor, 1886); and a sympathetic sketch by Lilian Whiting in *Our Famous Women* (Hartford, CT: Worthington, 1884), pp. 250–75.

Primary sources on Sara J. Lippincott include her columns for the *New York Times* and her Washington correspondence for the *Saturday Evening Post* of Philadelphia from 1850 to 1852, much of which was reprinted in the *National Era*. A complete file of the *National Era* is available at the Library of Congress. Much of the *Post* correspondence was published in the second volume of *Greenwood Leaves: A Collection of Sketches and Letters* (Boston: Ticknor, Reed and Fields, 1852), available at the Library of Congress, which also has *New Life in New Lands* (New York: Ford, 1873), a collection of western correspondence, chiefly from Colorado, for the *New York Times*.

For other background, see lists of correspondents in the annual *U.S. Congressional Directory* from 1870 to 1879 and consult F. B. Marbut, *News from the Capital: The Story of Washington Reporting* (Carbondale: Southern Illinois University Press, 1971).

9   Pioneer African-American Journalists

In addition to the works cited in the notes to Chapter 9, see Nora Hall, "Ida B. Wells-Barnett," in Perry J. Ashley, ed., *American Newspaper Journalists: 1873–1900*, vol. 23 of the *Dictionary of Literary Biography* (Detroit: Gale Research, 1983), pp. 340–46. Wells is included in an excellent comprehensive bibliography on African-American women journalists by Rodger Streitmatter, "African-American Women Journalists: Breaking the Double Barriers of Race and Gender," presented in an unpublished paper at the convention of the Association for Education in Journalism and Mass Communication, Boston, August 7, 1991.

For more information on Ida Wells-Barnett, see her autobiography, *Crusade for Justice* (Chicago: University of Chicago Press, 1970), edited by her daughter, Alfreda M. Duster. Other sources: Mrs. N. F. Mossell, *The Work of the Afro-American Woman* (Freeport, NY: Books for Libraries Press, 1971, a reprint of an 1894 edition), pp. 32–46; August Meier, *Negro Thought in America: 1880–1915* (Ann Arbor: University of Michigan Press, 1968); and Herbert Aptheker, ed., *A*

Documentary History of the Negro People in the United States, 2 vols. (New York: Citadel, 1966).

General material on black women journalists can be found in Alice E. Dunnigan, "Early History of Negro Women in Journalism," *Negro History Bulletin* 28 (Summer 1965): 178–79, 193–97; Frederick G. Detweiler, *The Negro Press in the United States* (Chicago: University of Chicago Press, 1922); and Garland I. Penn, *The Afro-American Press and Its Editors* (New York: Arno Press, 1969, a reprint of an 1891 edition).

Some nineteenth-century religious publications for which black women journalists wrote are preserved in a collection at Drew University, Madison, New Jersey. Nineteenth-century black newspapers, including the *New York Age,* are available on microfilm in many libraries through a project of the American Council of Learned Societies. Nineteenth-century black magazines and pamphlets may be found in the Schomburg Collection of the New York Public Library and the Moorland-Spingarn Collection at Howard University in Washington, D.C.

10 Stunt Reporters and Sob Sisters

Relatively little has been written specifically about Bonfils, usually known as Winifred Black. See Faye B. Zuckerman, "Winifred Black (Annie Laurie)," in Perry J. Ashley, ed., *American Newspaper Journalists: 1901–1925,* vol. 25 of the *Dictionary of Literary Biography* (Detroit: Gale Research, 1984), pp. 12–19. Autobiographical material was contained in "Rambles through My Memories," *Good Housekeeping* (January–May 1936). Her obituaries ran on May 26, 1936, in the *Denver Post, San Francisco Examiner, San Francisco Chronicle,* and the *New York Times.*

Primary sources on Elizabeth Cochrane are her "Nellie Bly" articles in the *New York World* from 1887 to 1895, available on microfilm in many libraries. Elizabeth Cochrane wrote three books: *Nellie Bly's Book: Around the World in 72 Days* (New York: Pictorial Weeklies, 1890); *Six Months in Mexico* (New York: American, 1888); and *Ten Days in a Mad-house* (New York: Monro, 1887). Her biography, *The Amazing Nellie Bly* by Mignon Rittenhouse (New York: Dutton, 1956), is undocumented. Her obituaries appeared in the *New York Times* and the *New York World,* January 28, 1922.

Other biographical sources are Frances E. Willard and Mary A.

Livermore, eds., *A Woman of the Century* (Buffalo: Moulton, 1893), and Ishbel Ross, *Ladies of the Press* (New York: Harper, 1936). Some material on women stunt reporters appeared in Rheta Childe Dorr, *A Woman of Fifty* (New York: Funk and Wagnalls, 1924). "Sob sisters" are described in John K. Winkler, *W. R. Hearst—An American Phenomenon* (New York: Simon and Schuster, 1928). See also John W. Perry, "Women Leaders of the American Press," *Editor & Publisher,* April 23, 1932, pp. 18–19, and Elizabeth Banks, *Autobiography of a Newspaper Girl* (London: Methuen, 1902).

For general background, see Frank Luther Mott, *American Journalism: A History 1690–1969* (New York: Macmillan, 1962), and Michael and Edwin Emery, *The Press and America,* 7th ed. (Englewood Cliffs, NJ: Prentice-Hall, 1992).

11   Investigative Reporting

Biographies include Kathleen Brady, *Ida Tarbell: Portrait of a Muckraker* (New York: Seaview/Putnam, 1988), and Mary E. Tomkins, *Ida Tarbell* (Boston: Twayne, 1974).

In addition to her autobiography, primary sources include these other works, many of which contain articles originally published in *McClure's Magazine* or the *American Magazine:* Tarbell, *History of the Standard Oil Company* (New York: McClure, Phillips, 1904), and a briefer edition edited by David M. Chalmers, New York: Harper & Row, 1966); *The Business of Being a Woman* (New York: Macmillan, 1912); and *The Ways of Woman* (New York: Macmillan, 1915).

For information on her muckraking period, see Louis Filler, *Crusaders for American Liberalism* (New York: Harcourt, Brace, 1939); Frank Luther Mott, *A History of American Magazines,* vols. 3, 4 (Cambridge, MA: Harvard University Press, 1938, 1957); Harold S. Wilson, *McClure's Magazine and the Muckrakers* (Princeton, NJ: Princeton University Press, 1970); David Mark Chalmers, *The Social and Political Ideas of the Muckrakers* (New York: Citadel Press, 1964); and Theodore Peterson, *Magazines in the Twentieth Century* (Urbana: University of Illinois Press, 1956).

Most of Tarbell's papers are at Allegheny College, Meadville, Pennsylvania. Her career is discussed in Margaret Inman Meaders, "Ida Minerva Tarbell, Journalist and Historian, 1857–1944," unpublished master's thesis, University of Wisconsin, 1947.

For general background on the muckraking period, see G. E.

Mowry, *The Era of Theodore Roosevelt, 1900–1912* (New York: Harper, 1958). For a concise sketch, see Nelson M. Blake, *A History of American Life and Thought* (New York: McGraw-Hill, 1963), pp. 409–13. Also useful: Arthur and Lila Weinberg, eds., *The Muckrakers* (New York: Simon & Schuster, 1961).

12 Metropolitan Journalists

For information on Ishbel Ross, see her obituary in the *New York Times,* September 23, 1975, and in *AB Bookman's Weekly,* December 1, 1975. See also Ishbel Ross, "Shall Women Inherit the Fourth Estate?" *Independent Woman* (April 1937): 106–7, 119–20.

Other sources on early twentieth-century women journalists: Florence Finch Kelly, *Flowing Stream* (New York: Dutton, 1939); Catherine Filene, ed., *Careers for Women: New Ideas, New Methods, New Opportunities—To Fit a New World* (Boston: Houghton Mifflin, 1934); Agness Underwood, *Newspaperwoman* (New York: Harper, 1949); Marion K. Sanders, *Dorothy Thompson: A Legend in Her Time* (Boston: Houghton Mifflin, 1973); Edna Ferber, *A Peculiar Treasure* (New York: Appleton-Century, 1939); and Elizabeth Jordan, *Three Rousing Cheers* (New York: Appleton-Century, 1938).

Stanley Walker's views on women reporters also appeared in a chapter titled "A Gallery of Angels" in *City Editor* (New York: Stokes, 1934).

Articles include Catharine Brody, "Newspaper Girls," *American Mercury* (March 1926): 273–77, and Catharine Oglesby, "Women in Journalism," *Ladies' Home Journal* (May 1930): 29, 229.

13 War Correspondents

Primary sources on Rheta C. Dorr are two of her books: *Inside the Russian Revolution* (New York: Macmillan, 1917) and her autobiography, *A Woman of Fifty* (New York: Funk and Wagnalls, 1924). Other biographical information is contained in Ishbel Ross, *Ladies of the Press* (New York: Harper, 1936), and June Sochen, *Movers and Shakers* (New York: Quadrangle, 1973). See also Louis Filler, *Crusaders for American Liberalism* (New York: Harcourt, Brace, 1939), and Door's obituary in the *New York Times,* August 9, 1948.

For general background, see John Hohenberg, *Foreign Correspon-*

dence: The Great Reporters and Their Times (New York: Columbia University Press, 1964); Eugene Lyons, ed., *We Cover the World* (New York: Harcourt, Brace, 1937); and Marguerite E. Harrison, *Marooned in Moscow* (New York: Doran, 1921).

Primary source material on Margaret Bourke-White includes her books—especially *Eyes on Russia* (1931), *Shooting the Russian War* (1942), *Purple Heart Valley* (1944), *Dear Fatherland, Rest Quietly* (1946), *Halfway to Freedom* (1949), and *Portrait of Myself* (1963), all published in New York by Simon and Schuster. See also Margaret Bourke-White with Erskine Caldwell, *You Have Seen Their Faces* (New York: Modern Age, 1937). Her obituary appeared in the *New York Times,* August 28, 1971, and in *Time* (September 6, 1971).

An excellent biography is Vicki Goldberg, *Margaret Bourke-White: A Biography* (New York: Harper & Row, 1986). Her work is evaluated in William Stott, *Documentary Expression and Thirties America* (New York: Oxford, 1973).

Background on World War II women correspondents may be found in Frank Luther Mott, ed., "The Newspaper Woman Joins Up," in *Journalism in Wartime* (Columbia: University of Missouri, 1943). See also Anne O'Hare McCormick, *The World at Home* (New York: Alfred A. Knopf, 1956).

For material on women correspondents in Korea, see Marguerite Higgins, *News Is a Singular Thing* (1955) and *War in Korea* (1961), both published in Garden City, New York, by Doubleday. See also her obituaries in the *New York Times,* January 3, 1966; the *New York Herald Tribune,* January 3, 1966; and *Newsweek* (January 17, 1966).

14   Racial Discrimination

The oral history interviews with Bluford and Cooke are part of a full-scale project by the Washington Press Club Foundation, a successor group to the Women's National Press Club of Washington, to document the achievements of women in journalism. As of 1991, interviews had been conducted with 20 women who started their careers before 1942, and plans were being made to interview those who entered journalism between World War II and the enactment of the Civil Rights Act of 1964. Audiotapes and transcripts are being deposited at the following repositories around the country, in addition to Columbia University and the National Press Club in Washington, D.C.: California State University, Sacramento; the University of Florida, Gainesville; Florida A&M University, Tallahassee; Howard University, Washington, D.C.; Indiana University, Bloomington; Jackson State University, Jackson, Mississippi; Michigan State University, East Lansing; University of Missouri–Columbia; University of North Carolina at Chapel Hill; Poynter Institute for Media Studies, St. Petersburg, Florida; Radcliffe College, Cambridge, Massachusetts; Spelman College, Atlanta, Georgia; and Syracuse University in New York State.

Excellent bibliographic information on Bluford and Cooke, as well as on Alice E. Dunnigan, can be found in Rodger Streitmatter, "African-American Women Journalists: Breaking the Double Barriers of Race and Gender," unpublished paper presented at the Association for Education in Journalism and Mass Communication convention, Boston, August 7, 1991. See also Diane E. Loupe, "Storming and Defending the Color Barrier at the University of Missouri School of Journalism: The Lucile Bluford Case," unpublished paper presented before the same organization, Washington, D.C., August 1989. Material on Cooke can be found in Kay Mills, *A Place in the News* (New York: Columbia University Press, 1990, reprint of 1988 edition), pp. 176–79, 249–51.

15 Newspaper Families

There are two biographies of Cissy Patterson: Paul F. Healy, *Cissy* (Garden City, NY: Doubleday, 1966), and Alice A. Hoge, *Cissy Patterson* (New York: Random House, 1966). See also Ruby Black, " 'Cissie' Patterson Is at It Again," *St. Louis Post-Dispatch Daily Magazine*, April 20, 1938, p. 1.

The Agnes and Eugene Meyer papers at the Library of Congress contain complete files of all the articles that Agnes Meyer wrote for the *Washington Post* and other publications. Also see her autobiography, *Out of These Roots* (Boston: Little, Brown, 1953). Her obituaries appeared in the September 2, 1970, issues of the *Washington Post* and the *New York Times*. Material about the Meyer family can be found in Deborah Davis, *Katharine the Great: Katharine Graham and the Washington Post Company* (Bethesda, MD: National Press, 1987, an expansion of a book originally published by Harcourt, Brace, Jovanovich in 1979 and recalled).

16   Early Days in Broadcasting

Source material on early women in radio and television may be obtained from the Broadcast Pioneers Library, Washington, D.C. Material titled "Our Radio and TV Members," an account of women broadcasters who were members of the Women's National Press Club, compiled by Ruth Crane Schaefer in 1969, is in the Cora Rigby Washington Journalism Archive at the National Press Club, Washington, D.C.

For information on Mary Margaret McBride, see her autobiographies, *A Long Way from Missouri* (New York: Putnam, 1959) and *Out of the Air* (Garden City, NY: Doubleday, 1961), and her obituary in the *New York Times*, April 8, 1975. Other sources on early women in radio: obituaries of Margaret Cuthbert and Martha Dean in the *New York Times*, July 26, 1968, and December 10, 1973, respectively; Beatrice Oppenheim, "Tune in on Radio Jobs," *Independent Woman* (April 1943): 104–6; Rebecca D. Scott, "Women 'On the Air,' " *Independent Woman* (November 1926): 9–11; Paul W. White, *News on the Air* (New York: Harcourt Brace, 1947).

For material on Breckinridge, see Maurine H. Beasley, "Mary Marvin Breckinridge Patterson: Case Study of One of Murrow's Boys," unpublished paper presented at the Association for Education in Journalism and Mass Communication convention, Boston, August 1991. A description of Eleanor Roosevelt's broadcasting is contained in Beasley, *Eleanor Roosevelt and the Media* (Urbana: University of Illinois Press, 1987), pp. 72–74, 113, 131–32.

Pauline Frederick's papers are in the Sophia Smith collection, Smith College.

17   Women's Pages

Timothy M. Kelly, "Yo! You! A research Model Comes to Life as a Weekly Section Aimed at Women," *ASNE Bulletin* (American Society of Newspaper Editors), May/June 1992.

Judith Patterson, "Among the Hats and Gloves: The Double Vision of Women's Pages, 1940–1970," unpublished paper, 1986. College of Journalism, University of Maryland.

Lenora Williamson, "Women's Page 'Relevancy' Stories Should Go to 'Subject' Page, Says Charlotte Curtis," *Editor & Publisher*, April 6, 1974.

18 The Development of Alternative Media

Nancy Cooper, "Feminist Periodicals," *Mass Communication Review* (Summer 1976): 15–22.

Paula Kassell, "Women's Alternative Press," *New Directions for Women* (January 1979): 9.

Deirdre Carmody, "*Ms.* Magazine Prepares for a Life Without Ads," *New York Times*, March 3, 1990.

19 Women's Magazines

Mary Elizabeth McBride, "Women in the Popular Magazines for Women in America: 1830–1956," Ph.D. dissertation, University of Minnesota, 1966.

Roland E. Wolseley, *Understanding Magazines*, 2nd ed. (Ames: Iowa State University Press, 1969).

Virginia Sammon, "Surviving the *Saturday Evening Post*," *Antioch Review* (Spring 1969): 101–8.

"Ladies' Man: John Mack Carter," *Newsweek* (February 17, 1975).

Dorothy D. Prisco, "Women and Social Change as Reflected in a Major Fashion Magazine," *Journalism Quarterly* (Spring 1982): 131–35.

Tamar Lewin, "Women's Magazines: A Fix for Everyone," *New York Times*, August 9, 1982, p. B4.

Cecelia Lentini, "Balancing Act in Women's Magazines," *Advertising Age* (October 19, 1981): S-62.

Sheila J. Gibbons, "Publications for Women Are Changing," *USA Today*, December 7, 1982, p. 1D.

Beverly Loughlin, "The Women's Magazine Short-story Heroine," *Journalism Quarterly* (Spring 1983): 138–42.

Carol Sonenklar, "Women and Their Magazines," *American Demographics* (June 1986).

Eric Schmuckler, "Sob for the Sisters," *Forbes,* April 4, 1988, pp. 112–13.

Linda Robinson Walker, "The '30s Woman: There Were Lessons for a Later Generation," *Washington Post*, July 25, 1988, p. B5.

George Melloan, "A German Publisher Courts American Women," *Wall Street Journal*, March 21, 1989, p. A23.

Nancy K. Humphreys, *American Women's Magazines: An Annotated Historical Guide* (New York: Garland Publishing, 1989).

Deidre Donahue, "The *Essence* Spirit: 20 Years of Saluting Today's Black Woman," *USA Today*, April 2, 1990, pp. 1D–2D.

Nikki Finke, "Birthday Girl: The Times Are Changing, but Not *Cosmo*, Still Hot after 25 years," *Los Angeles Times*, April 20, 1990, p. E1.

Deirdre Carmody, "Mirabella vs. Lear's: Stylish Fight," *New York Times,* November 26, 1990, p. D8.

Veronique Vienne, "Make It Right, Then Toss It Away: An Inside View of Corporate Culture at Condé Nast," *Columbia Journalism Review* (July/August 1991): 28–34.

Roger C. Saathoff and Julie Ann Moellering (of Texas Tech University, Lubbock), "Down the Path of Domesticity: A Content Analysis of Three Women's Service Magazines: 1905–1985," paper presented to the Association for Education in Journalism and Mass Communication, Boston, August 1991.

Ellen McCracken, *Decoding Women's Magazines: From* Mademoiselle *to* Ms. (New York: St. Martin's Press, 1992).

20   Vietnam Reporters

Roberta Ostroff, *Fire in the Wind: The Life of Dickey Chapelle* (New York: Ballantine Books, 1991).

Julia Edwards, *Women of the World: The Great Foreign Correspondents* (New York: Ivy Books/Ballantine Books, 1988).

21   Challenges to Mass Media

Nicholas Johnson, *How to Talk Back to Your Television Set* (New York: Bantam Books, 1970).

Linda J. Busby, "Defining the Sex-role Standard in Network Children's Programs," *Journalism Quarterly* (Winter 1974): 690–96.

Linda J. Busby, "Sex-role Research on the Mass Media," *Journal of Communication* (Autumn 1975): 107–31.

"Sex Role Stereotyping in Prime Time Television," United Methodist Women's Television Monitoring Project (Address: United Methodist Church, 475 Riverside Drive, New York, NY 10027), March 1976.

M. Mark Miller (of Michigan State University), "Factors Affecting Children's Choice of Televised Sex Role Models," paper presented to the Association for Education in Journalism, College Park, MD, August 1976.

Leslie Friedman, *Sex Role Stereotyping in the Mass Media: An Annotated Bibliography* (New York: Garland Publishing, 1977).

Canadian Radio–Television and Telecommunications Commission, "Policy on Sex-role Stereotyping in the Broadcast Media," Public Notice CRTC 1986–351, Ottawa, Ontario, December 22, 1986.

MediaWatch/National Watch on Images of Women in the Media, "Adjusting the Image: Women and Canadian Broadcasting," report of a national conference on Canadian broadcasting policy, Ottawa, Ontario, March 20–22, 1987. (MediaWatch address is given in the notes to Chapter 21.)

Gertrude J. Robinson (of McGill University), "Broadcast Regulation and Sex-role Stereotyping in Canada and the United States," paper presented to the Association for Education in Journalism and Mass Communication, Washington, D.C., August 1989.

Ella Taylor, *Prime-time Families: Television Culture in Post-war America* (Berkeley: University of California Press, 1989).

Marion Goldin, "Father *Times*: Who's on the Op-Ed Page?" *Mother Jones* (January 1990).

Kathryn C. Montgomery, *Advocacy Groups and the Struggle over Entertainment Television* (New York: Oxford University Press, 1990).

Women, Men, and Media, "Age Bias in the Media Industry," 1990.

Lee Jolliffe (of the University of Missouri–Columbia), "Liberal Feminism: The Strategies of an Activist Audience," paper presented to the Association for Education in Journalism and Mass Communication, Minneapolis, August 1990.

David Atkin and Jay Moorman (of Southern Illinois University), "Portrayals of Women on Television in the 1980s," paper presented to the Association for Education in Journalism and Mass Communication, Minneapolis, August 1990.

Mary Ellen Brown, *Television and Women's Culture* (Newbury Park, CA: Sage Publications, 1990).

Paul W. Valentine, "Suit Claims Sex Discrimination against Baltimore Newscaster," *Washington Post*, November 22, 1990, p. D1. Also: Judy Mann, "The Watchdog Needs Watching," *Washington Post*, November 28, 1990.

Amateur Athletic Association of Los Angeles, "Coverage of Women's Sports in Four Daily Newspapers," Los Angeles, 1991.

Judith Michaelson, "Where the Roles Are: As TV Finds That

Women 35 and Over Make Up a Third of Its Prime-time Audience, Older Actresses Are Getting More and Better Parts," *Los Angeles Times/Calendar*, April 14, 1991.

Bill Carter, "Children's TV, Where Boys Are King," *New York Times*, May 1, 1991, pp. C1 and C18.

For general information on media-monitoring guidelines and reports: Office of Communication, United Church of Christ, 700 Prospect Avenue, Cleveland, OH 44115.

22 Women in Journalism Today

Monica B. Morris, "Newspapers and the New Feminist: Blackout as Social Control?" *Journalism Quarterly* (Spring 1973): 37–42.

Gena Corea, "Writer Says Papers Biased in Covering News of Women," *Editor & Publisher*, April 21, 1973, and "How Newspapers Can Conduct Serious Coverage of Women," *Editor & Publisher*, April 28, 1973.

Susan H. Miller, "The Content of News Photos: Women's and Men's Roles," *Journalism Quarterly* (Spring 1975): 70–75.

Jack E. Orwant and Muriel G. Cantor, "How Sex Stereotyping Affects Perceptions of News Preferences," *Journalism Quarterly*, (Spring 1977): 99–108.

Dan G. Drew and Susan H. Miller, "Sex Stereotyping and Reporting," *Journalism Quarterly* (Spring 1977): 142–46.

Judith G. Clabes, *New Guardians of the Press: Selected Profiles of America's Women Newspaper Editors* (Indianapolis, IN: R. J. Berg, Publishers, 1983).

Linda Ellerbee, *And So It Goes: Adventures in Television* (New York: G. P. Putnam's Sons, 1986).

Anthony J. Ferri and Jo E. Keller, "Perceived Career Barriers for Female Television News Anchors," *Journalism Quarterly* (Autumn 1986): 463–67.

Marlene Sanders and Marcia Rock, *Waiting for Prime Time: The Women of Television News* (Urbana and Chicago: University of Illinois Press, 1988).

"Employment of Minorities and Women in U.S. Daily Newspapers," summary report (survey conducted for the American Newspaper Publishers Association by Belden Associates, 2900 Turtle Creek Plaza, Dallas, TX 75219), 1990.

Sherry Ricchiardi and Virginia Young, eds., *Women on Deadline: A*

Collection of America's Best (Ames: Iowa State University Press, 1991).

23   Language and Image Guidelines

Judith Stacey, Susan Bereaud, and Joan Daniels, *And Jill Came Tumbling After: Sexism in American Education* (New York: Dell, 1974).

Lucy Fuchs, "Sexist Language, or What's in a Name?" *Instructor* (November 1975).

Barrie Thorne and Nancy Henley, *Language and Sex: Difference and Dominance* (Rowley, MA: Newbury House, 1975).

Casey Miller and Kate Swift, *Women and Words* (New York: Anchor Books/Doubleday, 1976).

Al Friendly, "Language and the Wopersons' Movement," *Washington Post*, May 2, 1978.

Marie Longyear, ed., "Bias-free Publishing," in *The McGraw-Hill Style Manual: A Concise Guide for Writers and Editors* (New York: McGraw-Hill, 1983).

Rosalie Maggio, *Nonsexist Word Finder: A Dictionary of Gender-free Usage* (Phoenix, AZ: Oryx Press, 1987).

Public Service Commission of Canada, *Update on Stereotyping*, 1987.

Casey Miller and Kate Swift, *The Handbook of Nonsexist Writing: For Writers, Editors and Speakers*, 2nd ed. (New York: Harper & Row, 1988).

Sean Kelly, "BBC to Neuter Sexist Language," *Electronic Media* (December 25, 1989).

Jane Schorer, "It Couldn't Happen to Me: One Woman's Story," *Des Moines Register*, special reprint of the *Register*'s series on the Nancy Ziegenmeyer rape case, 1990.

Geneva Overholser, "My Paper Became Fodder in a Media Feeding Frenzy," *ASNE Bulletin* (May/June 1990), 14–15.

Helen Benedict (of the Graduate School of Journalism, Columbia University), "Victims and Vamps: Sex Crimes in the Press," paper presented to the Association for Education in Journalism and Mass Communication, Minneapolis, August 1990.

Sandra Sanchez, "Rape Poll: No Names, Say 91%," *USA Today*, April 18, 1991, p. 1A.

Also: American Association of University Professors Task Force for

Gender-free Language, c/o Marilyn Schwartz, Managing Editor, The University of California Press, 2120 Berkeley Way, Berkeley, CA 94720.

24 Minority Women Journalists

Claude Reed, Jr., "Black Women Publishers," *National Scene*, magazine supplement to the *Los Angeles Sentinel*, June 1982.

Vanessa J. Gallman, "What to Say When Someone Tells You, 'It Pays to Be a Black Woman,' " *Essence*, March 1983; p. 89.

Mark Fitzgerald, "Recession Undercuts Diversity," *Editor & Publisher*, August 3, 1991, pp. 7–8, 40.

Linda Waller, "Black Women Journalists and the Pulitzer Prize," 1991. Published by the Dow Jones Newspaper Fund, P.O. Box 300, Princeton, NJ 08543-0300.

Asian American Journalists Association, 1765 Sutter Street, Suite 1000, San Francisco, CA 94115.

National Association of Black Journalists, Box 17212, Dulles Airport, Washington, DC 20041.

National Association of Hispanic Journalists, National Press Building, Suite 1193, 529 14th Street, NW, Washington, DC 20045.

Native American Journalists Association, Campus Box 287, Boulder, CO 80309.

National Association of Minority Media Executives, 1401 Concord Point Lane, Reston, VA 22094–1307.

National Lesbian and Gay Journalists Association, P.O. Box 423048, San Francisco, CA 94142-3048.

Index

About the Authors

Maurine H. Beasley is a professor of journalism at the University of Maryland–College Park. She holds bachelor's degrees in history and journalism from the University of Missouri–Columbia, a master's degree in journalism from Columbia University, and a Ph.D. in American civilization from George Washington University. This is the seventh book that she has written, edited, or co-authored/edited pertaining to the history of women in journalism. A past president of the American Journalism Historians Association, she is president-elect of the Association for Education in Journalism and Mass Communication. Beasley is a former staff writer for the *Kansas City Star* and the *Washington Post*.

Sheila J. Gibbons is director of public affairs for the Gannett Company, one of the largest news and information organizations in the United States. She holds a bachelor's degree in political science from the State University of New York at Albany and a master's in journalism from the University of Maryland at College Park. Gibbons formerly edited an internationally circulated special-interest women's magazine and later was a news editor at Gannett New Media, the Gannett Company's research and development unit. A former instructor of journalism at the University of Maryland, Gibbons is editor of *Media Report to Women*, a quarterly newsletter on women and the mass media.